Knowing Women

Studies in Australian History

Series editors:
Alan Gilbert, Patricia Grimshaw and Peter Spearritt

Steven Nicholas (ed.)   *Convict Workers*
Pamela Statham (ed.)   *The Origins of Australia's Capital Cities*
Jeffrey Grey   *A Military History of Australia*
Alastair Davidson   *The Invisible State*
James A. Gillespie   *The Price of Health*
David Neal   *The Rule of Law in a Penal Colony*
Sharon Morgan   *Land Settlement in Early Tasmania*
Audrey Oldfield   *Woman Suffrage in Australia*
Paula J. Byrne   *Criminal Law and Colonial Subject*
Peggy Brock   *Outback Ghettos*
Raelene Frances   *The Politics of Work*
Luke Trainor   *British Imperialism and Australian Nationalism*
Margaret Maynard   *Fashioned from Penury*
Dawn May   *Aboriginal Labour and the Cattle Industry*
Joy Damousi and Marilyn Lake (eds)   *Gender and War*
Michael Roe   *Australia, Britain, and Migration, 1915-1940*
John F. Williams   *The Quarantined Culture*
Nicholas Brown   *Governing Prosperity*
Jan Todd   *Colonial Technology*
Shurlee Swain with Renate Howe   *Single Mothers and Their Children*
Tom Griffiths   *Hunters and Collectors*
Deborah Oxley   *Convict Maids*

Knowing Women

Origins of Women's Education in Nineteenth-century Australia

Marjorie Theobald

Faculty of Education
University of Melbourne

Published by the Press Syndicate of the University of Cambridge
The Pitt Building, Trumpington Street, Cambridge CB2 1RP, UK
40 West 20th Street, New York, NY 10011–4211, USA
10 Stamford Road, Oakleigh, Melbourne 3166, Australia

Printed in Hong Kong by Colorcraft

National Library of Australia cataloguing-in-publication data

Theobald, Marjorie R.
Knowing women: origins of women's education in
nineteenth-century Australia
Bibliography.
Includes index.
1. Women – Education – Australia – History – 19th century.
2. Education and state – Australia – History – 19th
century. I. Title. (Series : Studies in Australian history).
376.994

Library of Congress cataloguing-in-publication data

Theobald, Marjorie R.
Knowing women : origins of women's education in nineteenth-century
Australia / Marjorie Theobald.
    p.   cm. – (Studies in Australian history)
Includes bibliographical references and index.
1. Women – Education – Australia – History – 19th century. 2. Women
teachers – Australia – History – 19th century. I. Title. II. Series.
LC2482.T54 1996
376'.994'09034–dc20   95–39120

A catalogue record for this book is available from the British Library.

ISBN 0 521 42004 0 Hardback

Contents

Illustrations

Tables

Acknowledgements

The research for this book was greatly assisted by grants from the Australian Research Council and the University of Melbourne. The generosity of these bodies meant that I enjoyed the invaluable research assistance of Natasha Dwyer, Carole Hooper (who also read and commented upon drafts of chapters), Tania Jeffries, Fiona Paisley, Shirley Scott and Bruce Theobald.

I also acknowledge the assistance of librarians and archivists at the following institutions: University of Melbourne Archives; Baillieu Library; Janet Clarke Hall Archives; Public Record Office of Victoria; La Trobe Library; State Library of Victoria; Mitchell Library; New South Wales State Archives; University of Sydney Archives; Sydney Women's College (where the Principal, Dr Ann Eyland, offered me the hospitality of the college); Mortlock Library; Public Record Office of South Australia; Barr Smith Library; Queensland State Archives; John Oxley Library; Queensland Department of Education, Educational History Unit; Brisbane Grammar School (where Pam Barnett lost a week of her time attending to my requests); Brisbane Girls' Grammar School; Presbyterian Ladies' College, Melbourne; Melbourne Girls' Grammar School; and Sydney Church of England Girls' Grammar School. I wish to acknowledge especially the generous assistance of Frances Freeman and Catherine Herrick of the Directorate of School Education (Victoria), Education History Research Service.

I thank Cambridge University Press for the assistance given in the preparation of the book, and especially Heather Jamieson, whose talents, which include patience and tact, go far beyond the brief of the copy editor. Many people have contributed to the making of this book through informal discussion of ideas, commenting on drafts of chapters, directing my attention to source material, and giving encouragement in times of need. I wish to acknowledge particularly Geraldine Clifford, Rebecca Coulter, Ian Davey, Donna Dwyer, Bob Gidney, Patricia Grimshaw, Farley Kelly, Lesley Johnson, Noeline Kyle, Gabriele Lakomski, Ros McCarthy, Alison Mackinnon, Rae Massey, Pavla Miller, Wyn Millar, Margaret Pawsey, Alison Prentice, Martin Sullivan, Neil Sutherland, Jan Treweek and Tom Watson. To this list I wish to add my research students and colleagues (academic and administrative) at the Faculty of Education, the University of Melbourne, who can scarcely be unaware that I have been writing a book in recent years. There are three people to whom I owe a special debt: Dick Selleck, who taught me how to write history; my mentor and friend, Ailsa Zainu'ddin, who read the final draft with tact and incision; and my husband, John, who looks after me and shares in the production of my books.

Introduction

In 1885 21-year-old Edith Emily Dornwell became the first woman to graduate from the University of Adelaide.[1] She was also among the first science graduates of either sex in Australia, taking first class honours in physics and physiology. Edith was not from a privileged family, as her immigrant parents made a living buying and selling horses. She was intellectually gifted and determined but her academic success was also a matter of timing. As an elementary state school child in the 1870s she attended the prestigious Central Model School where she was awarded one of six state bursaries to attend the Advanced School for Girls, established in 1879 as the only state high school in South Australia in the nineteenth century. In 1880 she won first prize and £20 for the examination known as the Exhibition for Girls. The University of Adelaide amended its charter to admit women in 1881 in time for Dornwell to continue her brilliant academic career. She began her science degree in 1883, and at her graduation in 1885 Vice-Chancellor Sir Samuel Way greeted her warmly: '[You] have vindicated the right of your sex to compete on equal terms with the other graduates for the honours and distinctions of the University'.[2]

Typical of the first generation of female graduates, Dornwell taught in secondary schools—her own school, the Adelaide Advanced School for Girls, Methodist Ladies' College, Kew, and the privately owned Rivière College in Sydney, where she became headmistress. In 1891 Edith Dornwell applied for the founding principalship of the Sydney Women's College but the committee appointed an overseas candidate. In 1893 she married Lionel Charles Raymond and the young couple sailed for Fiji where he was employed by the Commonwealth Sugar Refineries. Thereafter Dornwell devoted her life to her husband and two sons. Edith Dornwell died in 1943.

In the same year as Edith Dornwell's graduation from the University of Adelaide, 16-year-old Annie Wilkins was attending night school at the Collingwood State School in Melbourne when she found herself pregnant.[3] When the educational state pursued her with a truancy notice (illegally, as she was over the statutory age) she named as the father the headmaster Patrick Kelly O'Hara. The subsequent Departmental inquiry brought Annie Wilkins too into the glare of public notice. O'Hara was

1

exonerated, largely upon evidence that Wilkins was an associate of prostitutes, though her baby was born nine months after her alleged 'seduction'. The night school she attended gathered in the children of outcast
Melbourne, who were not welcome in the state schools alongside the
children of the respectable poor. Annie Wilkins' parents had arrived in
Tasmania as convicts and, by the time Annie's ordeal brought the precarious family to light in Melbourne, they had twelve children. As with
Edith Dornwell, the Wilkins daughters came to the notice of the state,
for they were in and out of reformatories for petty theft and other minor
misdemeanours. In 1882 the Catholic Annie was charged under the
Neglected and Criminal Children's Act and because the charge was of a
sexual nature she was committed for two years to the harsh regime of
the nuns at the Abbotsford Reformatory. Here she received some instruction in the three Rs (mandatory in reformatories subsidised by the state)
and a great deal of instruction in the rougher household arts which, it
was believed, would transform her into a member of the respectable
servant class. By 1886 she could sign her name to the deposition which
launched the inquiry into the seduction affair. Two years later she
married Joseph Roberts and thereafter the circumstances of her life are
known only through the record-keeping of the state. She gave birth to
six more children, two of whom died, and she was three times committed to prison for petty theft or insufficient means of support. Annie
Wilkins' death was duly recorded in 1935.

The education of Edith Dornwell and the schooling of Annie Wilkins
encompass between them the possibilities for the education of women
in the nineteenth century and the relative importance of education in
their lives. Somewhere between these two extremes are to be found the
generality of Australian girls. They went to school in tents erected by the
state as its officers hurried anxiously behind the footloose diggers. They
trekked long distances, some on foot and some on horseback, from crude
selectors' huts to small bush schools. In the cities they travelled many
miles past schools of lesser reputation to attend the prestigious Model
Schools—Grote Street in Adelaide, Fort Street in Sydney and Spring Street
in Melbourne. Incarcerated in the Aboriginal mission schools and in the
infamous industrial schools at Magill, Randwick and Princes Bridge, girls
still learned to read and write. By the end of the century 'going to school'
had become a way of life and the texture of childhood had changed
forever. For female children, going to school had special significance.
Yet we have scarcely begun to think about this extraordinary social
movement in the lives of women.

As Australian children of all social classes began to go to school, a
teaching profession emerged which was itself demarcated by class and
by gender. The least visible members of this emerging profession were

the middle-class women who taught in the seclusion of their own schools and in private homes. It is part of the hidden history of Australian migration that women of learning and culture began to arrive from the beginnings of white settlement, many of them experienced teachers leaving behind the overcrowded market of female employment in Britain to begin again in the colonies. The lady-principal and the governess were the agents of a voluntarist tradition of female education peculiarly suited to a scattered and mobile colonial society in the making. The teaching traditions of the ladies' academy came with the immigrant female household and with impecunious but enterprising spinsters under the auspices of Maria Rye and the Female Middle-Class Emigration Society; with the carefully educated wives, sisters and daughters of the intelligentsia—the university professors, the clergy and the scientific community; and with the Catholic teaching orders from Ireland and France. The ladies' academy tradition was also enriched by the flow of cultured *émigrés* from the political and religious turmoils of mid-century Europe. The educational state also reaped a harvest of well-educated women to staff its elementary schools in the middle decades of the century. Their menfolk did not make fortunes out of gold and, in the manner of migrant families everywhere, they were willing to re-establish the family fortunes in an occupation which they would not have considered at home. When this supply of teachers ran out the educational state began to recruit colonial-born girls as pupil-teachers. The delineation of elementary school teaching as a women's profession had begun.

The lives of Edith Dornwell and Annie Wilkins also bring into focus the problems inherent in writing an 'overview' history of women's education. The ways in which the two women experienced education were shaped as much by social class and religious affiliation as by sex and gender. These experiences were also shaped by the constitutional basis of education which was laid down before World War I and changed little thereafter. Of necessity in the nineteenth century, education was a state responsibility and so it remained after the federation of the Australian colonies in 1901. Though there are clear patterns in the legislation from colony to colony, regional variations could and did make a difference in the lives of individuals. If Edith Dornwell had lived in Victoria, where there were no state high schools until 1905, she would have competed for a state scholarship to one of the new church secondary schools such as Methodist Ladies' College which led the way in the absence of state initiative. Social class, religious affiliation and the nuances of state legislation also shaped the lives of women who were teachers in nineteenth-century Australia. What are the commonalities between Mother Ursula Frayne of the Mercy Sisters who established the Academy of Mary Immaculate in 1857, Louisa Macdonald, M.A., feminist and foundation principal of the Sydney Women's College in 1892, and Abigail Sweeney, briefly an elementary school teacher at the Barker's Creek State School in Central Victoria before her marriage to George Burgdorf in 1878?

Tensions inherent in the writing of a generalist history of women's education are exacerbated by tensions in the writing of women's history itself. Women's history is presently characterised by intense theoretical debates which travel with the speed and ferocity of a bushfire across the treetops. Yet the stuff of women's history remains the rich ethnographic detail of women's lives which must be retrieved with infinite patience from widely scattered sources. While theoretical exchanges take place between protagonists seated at their desks, viable research agendas take longer to implement. In the writing of this book it quickly became apparent that an overview history courts disaster on both counts: on the one hand it cannot do justice to ongoing theoretical debates which underpin issues as diverse as the entry of women to colonial universities and the incarceration of girls in reforming institutions; on the other hand its legitimate concern for breadth and for commonalities bleaches out the personal and the particular which are the life-blood of women's history. The generalist historian runs the risk of pleasing no-one.

The structure of this book evolved in response to these considerations. It is not intended as an encyclopedia of women's education in the past, though the non-specialist reader will emerge with an understanding of Australian education generally. In planning further research for the book I made the decision to deepen my understanding of issues which have engaged my research energies over the last fifteen years rather than to work laterally in a spurious attempt at overview. The only exception is the schooling of 'outcast' girls, an area new to me when I began the research for chapter eight. For many years I have inscribed into my working notebooks the following quotation from Dorothy Dinnerstein:

> I believe in reading unsystematically and taking notes erratically. Any effort to form a rational policy about what to take in, out of the inhuman flood of printed human utterance that pours over us daily, feels to me like a self-deluded exercise in pseudo-mastery.[4]

Dinnerstein's injunction to be less than perfect has saved my sanity and, I hope, helped me to write better history.

Three chapters, one, six and seven, clear a space for theoretical considerations to be developed at some length, though they do not entirely lose sight of women like Edith Dornwell and Annie Wilkins. Chapter one, 'The woman at the piano', explores the links between the 'feminine', culture and education in nineteenth-century society. Here I try to make sense of a bewildering array of discursive practices linking the education of women to the private sphere of home and family. My argument is informed by several conceptual advances in feminist history which have emerged from a dialectic between theory and historical research over the last two decades. Most importantly, feminist historians contend that gender is a central category of historical analysis—that 'political and economic as well as social and cultural history are constituted in gendered terms'.[5] Feminist historians have also challenged the taken-for-granted orthodoxy that the public and the private spheres are substantive, discrete categories of human existence, the former constituting the natural domain of men and the latter constituting the natural domain of women. In the words of Farley Kelly and Marilyn Lake: 'Our aim as historians is to illuminate the relationship between public and private life—between paid work and unpaid work, between developments in the State and in the family, between party politics and sexual politics.'[6] Feminist historians also want to argue that gender itself, in both its masculine and feminine forms, is historically contingent and intimately connected to the dynamic of power between men and women. This perception of gender as historically contingent has been further refined into the notion that the category 'woman' (and therefore the category 'man') is not fixed and is always open to contestation. A feminist reading of history allows for the possibility that women themselves are to be found at the centre of this contestation, though they are usually less powerful and their material circumstances are seldom of their own making.[7]

Chapter six, 'The 'everyday world' of women who taught', returns to these theoretical concerns in a different context. Here the stories of women teaching for the nineteenth-century state are used to engage with the postmodernist challenge to women's history. I ask what happens to the category 'woman' when the women in question are waged workers of the state. I also ask new questions about the relationship of the public and the private spheres when women began to follow their 'traditional' work with children out of the home and into the school.

Chapter seven concerns the least visible players in the history of state education, the girls themselves. Where the historian of middle-class female education thrives upon the sexual politics of exclusion, the historian of state-funded education has no such scaffold on which to build. In the many thousands of documents generated by the state systems of education there is not the slightest suggestion that girls should be excluded from the nineteenth-century dream of a literate society. Indeed there was more official energy expended enticing girls into school than in keeping them out. Scholars in the field have not yet come to terms with this central fact and this silence in the literature is intriguing. Nor is it the only problem in writing about the experiences of girls in Australia's state-funded elementary schools. While historians of all persuasions, feminist and otherwise, have agreed that nineteenth-century state schools were a failure, they have done so on the basis of very little detailed research; there is no substantial body of work concerning the day-to-day life of the classroom, let alone what it might have felt like to be a child at school. Though I set out to write a history of girls in the elementary state schools of Australia, I have written instead a theoretical reflection on the possible directions of a feminist agenda for research. The remaining chapters are also informed by these theoretical considerations, although the narrative and the women themselves are in the foreground rather than the background.

Chapters two, three and four may be read as related contributions to a single debate in the historiography of women's education. This debate concerns the 'reform' of women's education in the last quarter of the nineteenth century, a movement which is customarily associated with the entry of women to the universities and the professions, and the appearance of a new kind of academic secondary school for girls. The first accounts of these events, written before the 1970s, tended to be celebratory in nature; they assembled an orthodoxy that schools like Presbyterian Ladies' College in Melbourne represented a clean break with the past, setting women's education on the path to complete equality with men. These earlier accounts also sought to discredit the older ladies' school tradition, usually without recourse to detailed historical investigation. In the 1970s the second women's movement called into question the efficacy of educational reforms in the past. Women dissatisfied with education in the present demanded to know why apparently radical reforms such as the admission of women to universities had such conservative outcomes for women in the twentieth century. Historians of women's education responded in several ways. They looked again at the politics of women's admission to the universities; at the career paths of the pioneer female graduates; at their political behaviour (usually defined in relation to the suffrage movement); and at their subsequent demographic characteristics. Other historians looked again at schools like the Adelaide Advanced School to consider the possibility that conservative and radical agendas may have co-existed in the new academic girls' schools. Others began revising the history of the traditional ladies' academy and its response to the challenge of the newer schools like Presbyterian Ladies' College. Chapters two, three and four make a contribution to that debate.

Chapters five and eight shift the focus from the education of a middle-class elite to the experiences of the vast majority of Australian women, as pupils and as teachers, in the state elementary schools of nineteenth-century Australia. Where the historian of middle-class education may engage with international debates, the historian of state education must begin by mapping the outlines of what those debates might be. The voluminous documentation on state-funded education in the public record offices of Australia is daunting. It is also a veritable minefield for the historian in search of the grand narrative: marriage bars against women teachers were instituted at different times and in different ways in each state; single-sex elementary schools were legislated out of existence in Victoria in 1872 but survived in other states; women's access to head teacherships varied state by state; teachers became public servants at different times in different states; the creation of state secondary schools followed a different pattern in each state. For these reasons, chapter five began as a study of Australian women teaching for the state but ended as a case study of Victoria's 'lady teachers' in the years 1850 to 1900. Its conclusions will undoubtedly be controversial and, it is to be hoped, stimulate further research among historians whose expertise lies in the other states.

Chapter eight is concerned with the schooling of 'outcast' girls, a term borrowed from Gareth Stedman Jones' study *Outcast London*. The educational state was duplicitous in the extreme in its dealings with children on the edges of respectable society; indeed the state school itself became a sorting device in the demarcation of the respectable from the unrespectable poor. The abduction and remaking of Australia's outcast children was legitimated by a series of Acts and regulations which moved through the 'neglected and criminal' children's Acts of the 1860s, the 'boarding-out' amending legislation of the 1870s, and the establishment of children's courts and the probationary system in the early twentieth century. The inclusion of Aboriginal girls in this study of 'outcast' schooling presents problems at several levels. Aboriginal girls were not 'outcast' from their own people; they were outcast from white society on the grounds of their race. Nor does the trajectory of legislation outlined above explain the chilling experiences of Aboriginal girls at the hands of the nineteenth-century state. To understand the incarceration and remaking of Aboriginal girls it is necessary to examine instead the so-called 'Half-Caste Act' in Victoria in 1886 and the 'Black Act' in Queensland in 1897 and its imitators in the other states. There are also ethical issues involved for the historian of white Australia. In the 1990s the historian of women's education faces a dilemma: on the one hand, there is a sense of guilt at past neglect; on the other hand, many Aboriginal people do not want white historians to write their history. In Canada, the sordid history of the 'native' residential school common to British colonial countries (including Australia) has been forced into public consciousness precisely because First Nation peoples there are reclaiming their own history in their present political struggles. A similar process of reclaiming the past is occurring in Australia.[8]

In 1991 I edited, with my friend and colleague Alison Prentice, a collection of essays on the history of women teachers.[9] In our introduction we affirmed our belief that the agenda for the history of women's education is an exciting one, and we expressed the hope that the book would inspire a new generation of younger feminist historians to embark upon it. This history of women's education in Australia is offered in the same spirit.

CHAPTER ONE

The Woman at the Piano: Women, Education and Culture in the Nineteenth-century Frame of Reference

In the iconography of nineteenth-century female education, a central figure is the woman at the piano. The setting is always the middle-class drawing-room, not the concert hall; the woman is represented as a passive figure, the object of the gaze outside the frame; she is not caught in the act of making music as we see, for example, in the famous portraits of Chopin and Liszt. While such portraits of women and girls are legion, there are few depicting men at the piano, though public performance and musical composition were the prerogatives of men. So powerful was the cultural symbol of the woman at the piano that, for daughters throughout the Western world, learning the instrument became a benchmark of gentility, on a par with the employment of servants and attendance at a private school. In colonial Australia, where religious bigotry was rife, the Protestant ascendancy sent its daughters to Catholic convents to learn the piano if no other teachers were available.

In her novel, *The Getting of Wisdom*, Henry Handel Richardson powerfully invoked the nineteenth-century woman at the piano.[1] On the evening in question, a small group of girls was invited to a soiree in the principal's drawing-room at nineteenth-century Presbyterian Ladies' College. Laura Rambotham, who was new to the school and anxious to be accepted, made herself at home, and at length was called upon to play the piano:

> [She] selected 'Home, Sweet Home', and pranced in. Her audience kept utter silence; but, had she been a little sharper, she would have grasped that it was the silence of amazement. After the prim sonatinas that had gone before, Thalberg's florid ornaments had a shameless sound. Her performance, moreover, was a startling one; the forte pedal was held down throughout; the big chords were crashed and banged with all the strength a pair of twelve-year-old arms could put into them; and wrong notes were freely scattered. Still, rhythm and melody were well marked, and there was no mistaking the

agility of the small fingers. Dead silence, too, greeted the conclusion of the
piece. Several girls were very red, from trying not to laugh. The Principal
tugged at his moustache, in an abstracted fashion.[2]

Music, the author tells us, was as fatal to Laura's equilibrium as wine
would have been. Laura was unaware that she had transgressed until the
next morning when she was summoned into the presence of Mrs Gurley,
the lady-superintendent. A quarter of an hour later, when she emerged
from Mrs Gurley's private sitting-room, her eyes were 'mere swollen slits',
for she had been crushed and humiliated. This study of the woman at
the piano is an exploration of Laura's transgression.

Education and female accomplishments

In May 1872, the Senate of the University of Melbourne passed the
resolution that 'having regard to the general policy of the act of
incorporation, there is no sufficient reason why women should be
excluded from the educational advantages and corporate privileges of
the University'.[3] It is fortunate for the historian of women's education
that Bishop Charles Perry was absent from Melbourne on parish business
in that first week of May 1872. Perry was Church of England Bishop of
Melbourne from 1848 to 1876, a foundation member of the University
of Melbourne Council, and an important figure in the development of
education in the colony of Victoria. By 1872 he had lost the constitutional
battle for the state funding of his denominational elementary schools, but
he had presided over the reconstruction of the English Public school for
boys in the colony, receiving money from the public purse for the
establishment of Melbourne Grammar School and Geelong Grammar
School.[4] His church took no formal part in the education of middle-class
girls until the establishment of Melbourne Church of England Girls'
Grammar School in 1903.

The Senate resolution of 1872 was a pivotal moment in the history of
women's education and Charles Perry knew precisely what was at stake.
Deprived of his right to oppose the motion in the University Senate, he
wrote at length on the matter to the *Argus*. His treatise on the propriety
of female intellect was an eloquent statement of the ideology which
underpinned the education of nineteenth-century women, delivered
precisely at the point of challenge. His views were not those of a crusted
conservative railing against the right of women to be educated; he tapped
into deeply held beliefs about the place of women in society and those
who sought to sponsor women at the University of Melbourne had to

take account of his views. His letter to the *Argus* of 21 June 1872 is therefore worth considering at some length.

Bishop Perry argued that, regard being had to the natural constitution of woman and her relation to man, there were 'very sufficient reasons' why she should not in her youth be 'stimulated to rivalry with man in a contest for university honours'. He acknowledged the high qualities of woman but argued that: 'Her excellency, physical and intellectual is of a different character from that of Man; and for her to imitate him in dress, manners, sports, studies, or professional employments would be to degrade herself.' Perry warned that a manly woman was as offensive as an effeminate man. He appealed to parents to attest a marked distinction between boys and girls from earliest childhood in mental and physical characteristics. Perry argued that woman was distinguished from man by a delicacy of brain in the same manner as she was distinguished from him by the delicacy of other parts of her body. On this distinction Perry based his view that a woman's education should be radically different from that of a man. He rejected the notion that the prevailing system of female education was in need of reform because it tended to 'exaggerate the defects which are natural to women'. This critique, he argued, missed the object of education, which was not to alter man's or woman's nature but to educate and improve their inherent qualities. Perry urged that women should be educated to the highest degree but that their education should be suited to the female character. The intellectual distinction between the sexes he characterised as a matter of difference, not inferiority; the more delicate mind of woman could in its own sphere accomplish much which the stronger mind of man could not.

When Bishop Perry turned to the relationship of woman to man and her function in the 'natural order' of society he was unequivocal; she was to become a wife and mother, and the single woman was to be regarded as 'exceptional and unnatural'. He called upon the authority of nature, commonsense and scriptural revelation: 'The instinct of woman makes her desire the married state, and reason and revelation both teach us that she was designed for it.' Girls should not be educated in expectation of the autonomous single life but on the assumption that they would become matrons 'dependent upon and subject to husbands, and finding happiness in the care of them and their children'. For these purposes only, Perry argued, should the female intellect be educated and 'educated to the highest possible degree'. On these grounds he took his stand against the admission of women to the University of Melbourne.

Charles Perry's careful exposition of his opposition to university education for women is also valuable because he made a clear connection between the ideology, practice and outcome of his preferred system of female education. He believed that 'history, languages, the belles lettres, the phenomena of the universe with popular explanations of them, arithmetic, and perhaps the elements of geography and algebra, together with the arts of music and painting' would supply ample materials for 'disciplining and furnishing' the female mind. Women should not exercise their minds upon 'critical scholarship or philosophical speculation, or on the higher branches of pure or mixed mathematics, or political or professional science'. For these studies they possessed neither the natural inclination nor the capacity. There was indeed a mode of literary and scientific conversation suited to the family and the social gathering, and for this it was necessary to 'store the mind with pleasant memories, refine the taste, and cultivate the imagination'. A university education was inimical to this broad cultural aim. In this manner, Perry articulated the orthodox view of woman's intellect in the nineteenth-century Western world. Though his populist and religious mode of discourse long pre-dated the more sophisticated scientific and medical opposition to the higher education of women, it was similar in intent. His ideas were in direct descent from the conservative English evangelical society of his youth and the Cambridge circle which he entered in the 1820s.

The female accomplishments tradition which Bishop Perry endorsed emerged as the dominant mode of education for middle-class girls in Britain in the late eighteenth and early nineteenth centuries. So complete has been the focus of historians upon the educational reforms later in the century, which Perry opposed, that this earlier transformation of female studies has been overshadowed. Yet it was sufficiently well established as a coherent pedagogical system to be noted by the acerbic cleric, Sydney Smith, in 1810: 'A decided and prevailing taste for one or another mode of education there must be. A century past, it was for housewifery—now it is for accomplishments.'[5] Many British writers of distinction wrote copiously in praise of 'modern' female education, delineating its curriculum, pedagogy, moral dimensions, even architecture and sanitation—many because they were personally involved as teachers, proprietors or sponsors of schools. The scientist Erasmus Darwin's *Plan for the Conduct of Female Education in Boarding Schools* was published in 1797 'at the desire of' the Misses Parker, proprietors of a ladies' school in Ashbourne, Derbyshire.[6] Darwin's pamphlet was both an extensive treatise on the education of girls and a prospectus for the school—the Parker sisters were his illegitimate daughters whom he had carefully educated for their vocation. Darwin testified to the improvement of female education in his own lifetime: 'The parents and guardians of young ladies of the last half century were less solicitous about procuring for them so extensive an education, as modern refinement requires.' Darwin's curriculum was similar to that outlined by Bishop Perry seventy years later, though Darwin's emphasis on science and his concern with the health and physical well-being of the girls reflect his medical background and his involvement with the educational reformers centred around the Birmingham Lunar Society. The Misses Parker's own prospectus, reproduced with a lithograph print of the imposing school and the schedule of fees, sets out a more modest program but the outlines of the accomplishments curriculum are clear. While Darwin's interest was practical rather than polemical, he prefaced his book with an eloquent reminder of the appropriate outcome of female learning. The female character, he wrote, should possess 'the mild and retiring virtues rather than the bold and dazzling ones; great eminence [and] strength of character [are] liable to alarm both her own and the other sex; and to create admiration rather than affection'.

The alacrity with which London publishers like Joseph Johnson issued books about women's education testifies to the ready market among parents and teachers anxious for guidance. The most prestigious women writers of the time—Hester Chapone, Anna Barbauld, Elizabeth Hamilton and Hannah More—published books on the subject which ran into many editions and were used as moral texts for girls in schools and homes.[7] The most widely read and enduring book of the genre was Hannah More's three-volume polemic, *Strictures on the Modern System of Female Education*, reprinted eleven times between 1799 and 1811. Hannah More was one of the most influential evangelical reformers of the time and her rambling, contradictory and heavily moralistic treatise captures the ambivalence of a society struggling to reconcile female learning with female propriety. Hannah More's own life reflects these tensions. Her private girls' school, opened in prosperous middle-class Bristol in 1758 with her four talented and ambitious sisters, became a centre of intellectual life, attracting visitors from all over England, including John Wesley, William Wilberforce and Edmund Burke. Leader of the English bluestockings, Elizabeth Montagu, wrote: 'They are all women of admirable sense and unaffected behaviour and I should prefer their school to any I have seen for girls, whether very young or misses in their teens.'[8] In this manner Hannah More gained access to the literary and theatrical world of London where she became an intimate of Dr Johnson and David Meredith.

Upon her evangelical conversion later in life she gave up such company. *Strictures* is both an evangelical stamp of approval on the female accomplishments and a warning that they must be kept in proper bounds. By the end of the eighteenth century More was no longer the harbinger of a new order of school mistresses; she spoke of an educational revolution which she thought complete. She did not call for change in the role or status of English women whom she saw as enjoying 'the blessings of liberal instruction, of reasonable laws, of a pure religion, [and] all the endearing pleasures of an equal, social, virtuous, and delightful intercourse'. Yet she challenged the 'old standing objection formerly brought forward by the prejudices of the other sex' that intellectual studies necessarily 'absorbed the thoughts and affections, took women off from the necessary attention to domestic duties, and superinduced a contempt or neglect of whatever was useful'. Such prejudices of a bygone age she saw as 'daily receiving the refutation of actual experience'.

Hannah More is important because she articulated in populist form the classical view of women's intellect in the service of her moral goodness. Whatever rectified the judgement, corrected self-conceit, purified the taste and raised the understanding would contribute to moral excellence; to woman 'moral excellence is the grand object of education, and of moral excellence, domestic life is to woman the proper sphere'. Her ambivalence towards the new educational opportunities for women was couched in different terms from those used by reformers later in the century, who saw the accomplishments curriculum as contributing to the disadvantages suffered by women. She feared that the purchase of gentility by the lower middle classes, 'this frenzy of accomplishments . . . [which] rages downwards', would further jeopardise a social order rendered fragile by events across the English Channel. She also feared undue enhancement of the female self-image, which she saw as inimical to the selfless, civilising mission of woman within the home and family. These fears were to sound like a litany through the nineteenth-century debate on female education, both on the vexed matter of accomplishments, and on the admission of women to 'masculine' forms of education later in the century. Woman must be educated for religious and moral purity in her future role as wife and mother; only if intellectual and cultural studies served that end were they the right of the English girl.

The female accomplishments curriculum which Hannah More and Bishop Perry took as their reference point acknowledged no official prescription from church, state or university. Yet it was remarkably uniform—followed informally in the home over a lifetime; systematically with governesses and visiting masters; or in the private female academies which mushroomed to take advantage of the new enthusiasm for women's studies. The accomplishments curriculum comprised two main elements which, in the cryptic language of shared understanding, were referred to as 'a sound English education' and 'the usual accomplishments'. At its best, an 'English education' offered not, as historians have often assumed, basic literacy and numeracy but a comprehensive program in all the elements of the English language —literature, grammar, composition, elocution and calligraphy—with history, geography, arithmetic and the elements of natural science.[9] The terminology 'an English education' was used in contradistinction to the classical education in Latin, Greek and mathematics which was still important in the education of middle-class boys. The 'accomplishments' sometimes referred specifically to the cultural studies of music, art and the modern languages, and sometimes to the totality of women's studies. The female academies also offered dancing, gymnastics, callisthenics, and crafts such as leather work, wax flower modelling and needlework— subjects which historians have sometimes assumed were the main focus of the accomplishments curriculum. As Sydney Smith noted, housewifery had suffered an eclipse.

Although it is inevitably a painstaking task, evidence on early nineteenth-century female education and its institutional settings can be assembled for Britain, the United States, Canada, Australia, New Zealand and South Africa. The phenomenon has received some attention in the United States because the female academies which multiplied at the end of the eighteenth century are perceived as forerunners of the famous ante-bellum academies established by Emma Willard (Troy Seminary, 1821), Catherine Beecher (Hartford Seminary, 1832) and Mary Lyon (Mt Holyoke, 1837). A line of descent can be traced to the women's colleges established by religiously motivated individuals in the decades after the Civil War—Vassar in 1865, Wellesley and Smith in 1875, and Bryn Mawr in 1884, all of which survived to become tertiary institutions of international repute.

There can be no more telling evidence of the popularity of this form of female education than its swift transplantation to the unpromising soil of Australia in the early years of free settlement. Elizabeth Windschuttle first drew attention to the early beginnings and rapid growth of middle-class female education—and to the space opened up for women of the same class as entrepreneur school keepers.[10] Based on detailed research in colonial newspapers, directories and private papers, Windschuttle's study estimates that between 1806 and 1845 there were at least seventy-seven private ladies' academies in New South Wales, most of them in Sydney. Caution is needed in determining which of these schools were of the magnitude of the Misses Parker's school in Derbyshire; many may have been little more than elementary schools for the daughters of families with some claim to gentility in a society sharply divided between convict and free. Windschuttle's work is also valuable because she documents the informal settings in which women set about educating themselves and their daughters.

In the Western nations, thousands of women made a living teaching in the ladies' academies or governessing in private homes; indeed the term 'governess' was interchangeable with 'teacher' throughout the nineteenth century.[11] In London, New York, Toronto and Sydney the men who inhabited the demi-monde of artists and musicians supplemented their uncertain incomes as visiting masters in the ladies' academies or by teaching women as private pupils, though this is rarely mentioned by their biographers. The accomplishments curriculum was common to both Catholic and Protestant female academies, a point overlooked by historians on both sides of the divide. After a decade of revisionist research on this form of education for middle-class girls, it could fairly be claimed that the accomplishments genre developed sooner, was more coherent, more widespread (and more profitable) than secondary education for middle-class boys. Indeed the rise of this gender-differentiated form of the humanities at the beginning of the nineteenth century is one of the most far-reaching, and neglected, phenomena in the history of Western education. Yet as American historian Maxine Schwartz Seller has recently observed, we lack a satisfactory explanation for this cross-national phenomenon. Australian historians, for example, were inclined to see the ladies' academy as evidence of a scramble for respectability by a 'thin' bourgeoisie in a convict society. American historians identified as the genesis of reform the ideology of 'Republican motherhood' which gave women an indirect political role as the first educators of male citizens. Both explanations have validity in their own contexts but they do not explain why the same things were happening in different contexts at the same time.

At the broadest level, this cross-national interest in women's education which worked itself out through the nineteenth century was the culmination of a more general interest in education from the Reformation onwards. The rise of Protestantism, with its emphasis on individual responsibility for salvation through reading of the bible and personal communication with God, fuelled a desire for literacy which long pre-dated the systematic provision of education for any social class. Literacy is a remarkably democratic phenomenon which has its own momentum outside the control of polemicists and policy makers.[12] Interest in female education was also influenced by the Enlightenment, the rationalist, liberal, humanitarian and scientific mode of thought of the eighteenth century. Foreshadowed by the scientific revolution of the seventeenth century, the Enlightenment found philosophical expression in the works of Rousseau in France, Hume in England, Paine in America, Kant in Germany and Beccaria in Italy. It found political expression in the reforms of the 'enlightened despots' such as Catherine the Great and Emperor Joseph II, and in the American and French Revolutions. The Industrial and Agrarian Revolutions, which emerged in England in the last quarter of the eighteenth century, changed attitudes to education in the long run. Understanding of, and exploitation of, the natural world were basic to the new economic order which was emerging, forcing rapid changes in technology and commercial practice which challenged the hegemony of closed knowledge systems based on the classics and theology. Lacking the inherited power and privilege of the aristocracy, the middle classes who rose to dominance with the new order placed far greater importance on education for their heirs.

Yet men and women of the same social class did not experience political, social and educational change in the same way. Carole Pateman's analysis of the political ideology of the Enlightenment reveals that the fraternal social contract which overthrew the rule of the father/king was exactly that—a *fraternal* social contract which overthrew one form of patriarchy only to reinstate the principle in the civil patriarchy of brothers, created separately and in opposition to the family.[13] Women's differential treatment within a political-ideological regime which purported to be universalistic is further explained by the postmodernist critique of the 'individual' as male within Western thought. Women remained excluded from civil society and under the control of fathers and husbands. As civil beings, they were further disadvantaged by the gradual extension of the vote to all men in the nineteenth century. Yet as Mary Wollstonecraft's polemic, *A Vindication of the Rights of Woman* (1792), made clear, the very rhetoric of Enlightenment political thought rendered the exclusion of women problematical. Unadorned claims about the inferiority of one half of the human race became increasingly untenable and a new language of exclusion began to emerge.

Intellect, education and sexual difference

Bishop Perry's blueprint for the containment of women's intellect drew its authority from the notion of symmetry or complementarity between the sexes. This was, in essence, an attempt to establish the psychological validity of the ancient dominance-by-right of men over women. In this view, women were not inferior; men and women brought to the common stock of humanity different, but complementary, characteristics. The notion of complementary sex differences was a metaphor derived from complementary male/female functions in biological reproduction and from anatomical differences between the sexes. The metaphor from biology was extended to establish complementary differences in the nature, role and status of men and women. Man's nature was held to be particularly marked by strength of

will, energy, courage, enterprise and aggression, attributes which defined
his role as outward-turning to the world—to provide, to struggle, to
achieve and to rule in the public domain. His status was, therefore, held
to be superior to that of woman. The 'moral physiognomy' of woman
was held to be essentially nurturant and selfless, passive and dependent,
morally pure and chaste, attributes which defined her role as inward-
turning to the closed world of home and family. Within the family, her
dependent, submissive nature fitted her for her secondary role as 'help-
meet' of her husband; her nurturant qualities and her moral purity fitted
her to be the first socialiser of children and the moral guardian of the
family. While the aggregate goodness of British matrons was held to
constitute the moral conscience of the nation, it was the lot of men to
transact the rough business of the world. This delineation of the female
make-up is the genesis of the ideal Victorian woman and the cult of
domesticity which have been a key focus of women's history in the last
decade. Effusive elaborations of the ideal woman were commonplace in
nineteenth-century polemical writing, effusions which would now be
amusing had they not been encoded in British political and legal codes
for much of the nineteenth century.

The notion of ethereal, domestic woman was shaped within the
culture of middle-class England in order to resolve tensions in the new
society which was emerging. These tensions have been conceptualised
by some writers as a crisis in patriarchy which affected different levels
of society differently.[14] The point to note here is that, as the capitalist
mode of production separated the workplace (the public sphere) from
the family (the private sphere), men and women of the newly powerful
middle classes were set in differing life trajectories. Separated from the
means of production, middle-class women became identified exclusively
with home and family in the same decades in which middle-class men
became politically, economically and intellectually empowered to
prosecute the industrial capitalist enterprise.

The historical reality of these transitions in everyday life is delineated
in Leonore Davidoff and Catherine Hall's study, *Family Fortunes: men
and women of the English middle class*.[15] Using fine-grained studies of
three generations of families such as the Cadburys of Birmingham, they
track the delineation of gender differences and the gradual separation of
the public and the private spheres in a time of rapid economic, political
and social change. They argue that 'gender and class always operate
together [and] that consciousness of class always takes a gendered form'.
Men who sought to be 'someone' on account of their wealth and
influence constructed a gendered public culture which would in turn
reflect back their status and their worth: civic and municipal office;
evangelical religious affiliation; the superintendence of Sunday schools;

the anti-slavery and temperance movements; philanthropic organisations such as hospitals and asylums; quasi-scientific and learned societies. Though they sought to define themselves as morally superior to the 'decadent' aristocracy above and the 'perishing' classes below, the men of the new middle-classes also defined themselves as existing in complementary otherness to their own women. The unique contribution of Davidoff and Hall is to argue from empirical evidence for the centrality of the separate spheres in the development of the capitalist mode of production.

As Davidoff and Hall's study implies, the ideal of domesticated woman evolved in response to complex aspirations and imperatives: she was a symbol of wealth and status, conspicuously idle and opulent in dress; she was the embodiment of a private morality which atoned for otherwise intolerable moral contradictions in the public world of capitalist man; and she was the high priestess of the cult of childhood which also emerged as the family and home lost their economic importance. Idealised Victorian woman was a complex creature: innocent and pure, for the perfect wife and mother was in ignorance of her own body; full of bustling commonsense in the management of the home; quasi-professional in her role as the first teacher of her children; a worthy intellectual, cultural and social help-meet to her husband; and elevated in her moral influence over the private sphere. The ideal Victorian woman was not the simple yeoman's wife; her exacting dimensions called for an education of a different kind. Yet woman's intellect presented a problem in that her existence as a sentient moral and rational being had to be reconciled with her secondary and subservient role. These tensions were also resolved with reference to complementary sex differences.

The metaphor of sexual difference was extended to encompass the intellect by Bishop Charles Perry's analogy between the constitutional delicacy of woman and her less robust mental powers. The nineteenth-century notion of the mind as a muscle to be exercised led easily to the conclusion that the female mind would be less robust, but the delineation of gendered intellectual and moral functioning was more complex. Consequent upon her delicacy of brain, woman's mode of knowing was characterised as intuitive and therefore not amenable to the rigorous, rational thought of the male mode. Untrammelled by rational thought processes, a woman had quicker perceptions, readier sympathies, livelier imagination, greater dependence upon her emotions and a natural affinity with moral truths. Woman's intuitive faculty was the basis of her selfless devotion to the needs of husband and children. Even on the mundane level of everyday routine, her intellect was peculiarly well adapted to her natural domestic milieu in that she excelled in the orchestration of a mass of small details. She could not, however, readily grasp the relationship of the parts to the whole, an essential constituent in the creative process of original thought. Writers on the education of girls, from Hannah More to the Taunton commissioners, endorsed the notion of intuitive woman. Hannah More likened the female intuitive faculty to the 'sensitive and tender organs of some timid animals, as a kind of natural guard to warn of the approach of danger'.[16] Over sixty years later the reforming Taunton commissioners warned that:

> It is only on the whole, and balancing one quality against another, that we can speak of the equal intellectual capacity of the sexes. Many differences, such as the tendency to abstract principles in boys contrasted with the greater readiness to lay hold of facts in girls—the greater quickness to acquire in the latter with the greater retentiveness in the former—the greater eagerness of girls to learn—their acuter susceptibility to praise and blame—their lesser inductive faculty—and others, are dwelt on by our witnesses.[17]

These complementary differences in male and female intellectual modes echoed the dominant philosophical and moral concerns of the day. This philosophical debate concerned the relative worth of the intuitionist and the utilitarian moral positions and their respective theoretical cognitive underpinnings. The emergence of the utilitarian moral position, which asserted that moral notions, and knowledge itself, can only be based on experience inductively examined, was influenced by underlying economic and structural changes in British society. These changes derived from the evolution from an aristocratic world of inherited position and privilege to the new society of the Industrial Revolution and the capitalist mode of production. The utilitarian philosophy under-pinned the middle-class challenge to the old social order and asserted the primacy of the individual will as the driving mechanism of society.

The paradigm moral dilemma for the utilitarian is one in which he must reason inductively before he knows what to do. Utilitarianism thus presents a morality which is impersonal and individualistic, appropriate to survival in the larger world—a prerequisite for the scientific frame of mind and for the operation of capitalist man in the society created by the Industrial Revolution. The paradigm moral dilemma for the intuitionist is one in which he knows immediately what he should do by reference to *a priori* moral truths, but must discipline his will to make himself do it. Intuitionism presents a morality which is appropriate to the medieval world view, the aristocratic society, the known relationship within the small group—the prescribed world of nineteenth-century woman. In the world (a term which had pejorative overtones in the nineteenth century) her intuitive mind was poorly equipped to think inductively to reach a moral decision based on reason. She was quickly exposed as morally fragile and subject to involuntary corruption as her intuitive reflex became progressively weakened by exposure to evil. She must learn from the maxims of reflection and wisdom and not from the rough discipline of the world.

Nineteenth-century polemicists of both sexes strove to articulate the notion that learning must 'adorn' the female mind, not shape it in the ways of autonomous thought necessary for survival in the public world. The much-admired author of *The Women of England*, Sarah Ellis, wrote: 'There is a voice in women's hearts too strong for education—a principle which the march of intellect is unable to overthrow.'[18] In this way, the patriarchal structures of nineteenth-century society, which concentrated political, legal and economic power in the hands of men, were underpinned by notions of woman's characteristic mode of knowing and her fragile moral nature. It is salutary to discover that 'women's ways of knowing' have a very murky history.[19]

The profound unease which attended the encounter between knowledge and the female mind threw up two powerful stereotypes in the nineteenth century. The term 'bluestocking' was coined in the eighteenth century to encompass an informal sisterhood of intellectual women which included Elizabeth Montagu, Elizabeth Carter and the youthful Hannah More, who, as already noted, recanted after her evangelical conversion in later life. The word hardened into a term of mocking abuse in the nineteenth century, as female learning spread beyond a small group of 'exceptional' women. It carried powerful psychological sanctions against the wrong use of woman's intellect. The ridiculous figure of the bluestocking was pressed into service to carry a shared understanding that forms of knowledge, and the manner of their acquisition, are gender-specific and intimately connected to moral propriety. The stereotype of the bluestocking comes to life most vividly in nineteenth-century cartoons which typically depict the learned woman as plain, boyish in physique (she is usually angular, flat-chested and hirsute) and poorly groomed. If the bluestocking is married she assumes the proportions of a Valkyrie, her unkempt and undernourished children clinging to a small, ineffectual husband. The incongruity of masculine knowledge with the female character and the private sphere is depicted in Elizabeth Sandford's famous portrait of the bluestocking:

The *bas bleu* pants for notoriety . . . she accumulates around her the materials of learning, and her very boudoir breathes an academic air. Its decorations are sufficient to proclaim her character: its shelves are filled with books of every tongue; its tables are strewed with the apparatus of science; the casket of jewels is displaced for the cabinet of stones; and the alembic occupy the stand allotted for the work box . . . Here she sits enshrined; her dress arranged with studied negligence; her head a Babel; her speech a jargon of hard terms, and words of Johnsonian length.[20]

The bluestocking was the woman who appropriated knowledge in a manner which went beyond the proper bounds of woman's sphere and offended the canons of a patriarchal society.

While the bluestocking represented the unacceptable outcome of female learning, the accomplished woman personified its preferred outcome. While she was seldom the subject of cartoons, she was often the heroine of didactic novels. Matilda Howard, the heroine of Catherine Sinclair's best-selling *Modern Accomplishments* (1836), is an accomplished woman.

> It was rare indeed, to meet with one so lovely, who was unconscious of her own charms . . . graceful without affectation, and pleasing without an attempt at display . . . her accomplishments always ready for the service of others . . . her conversation abounding in good sense and information, but flowing on without the smallest effort, untainted by pedantry, unsullied by satire; a heart expanding to every benevolent feeling, and a countenance beaming with intelligence. Such was Matilda Howard.[21]

In contrast to the bluestocking, the accomplished woman's learning was deployed in the private sphere, enhancing her own womanly excellence and serving others. 'Accomplishment' signified more than an area of study, a method of study, an attitude to study, or a standard of achievement, although it owed something to each; it symbolised the appropriate use of woman's intellect in man's society. The accomplished woman did not appropriate knowledge in order to enhance self-esteem, moral authority or economic independence. Knowledge-as-accomplishment did not confer autonomy and hence did not affront patriarchal notions of woman's place.

Implicit in these two powerful normalising categories of woman is the notion that the propriety of intellect can transform the female body itself. These dual stereotypes signal an obsession with the aesthetics of female intellectual activity. The injunction that learning should 'adorn' the female body ran like a litany through sermons, prescriptive literature and cartoons alike. Nineteenth-century discourse concerning the aesthetics of female education is given fresh meaning by recent feminist theory which is attempting to rethink the meanings of the female body. In Elizabeth Grosz's terms, this is an attempt to conceptualise a 'corporeal feminism' which rejects a misogynist biological essentialism but accepts the specificity of the female body as a starting point for new forms of female identity. Grosz argues that the body is 'a political object *par excellence*', that its form, capacities, behaviour, movements and potential are 'primary objects of political contestation'. She argues that, if the body is a social as well as a biological object, the meanings which we attach to it can be contested and its place in culture transformed.[22] With Foucault and others, Grosz articulates a notion of the body as an interface between 'privatised' experience and signifying culture. In this view, the external inscription of the body and the internal structure of subjectivity, the acquisition of 'appropriate cultural attitudes', are inextricably linked—what one 'is' becomes embodied. An intuitive grasp of this two-way process between mind and body produced the caricatures of the bluestocking and her alter-ego, the accomplished woman.

Elizabeth Grosz builds on the work of earlier theorists such as Sherry Ortner and Michelle Zimbalist Rosaldo who located a primary source of women's oppression in the binary opposition culture-male/nature-female.[23] This in turn, Grosz suggests, is derived from the enduring binary opposition of mind/body within Western philosophy. Yet the mind/body opposition cannot adequately explain the nineteenth-century obsession with the woman at the piano. She belongs unequivocally to the realm of culture, a nineteenth-century reincarnation of woman as the ancient civiliser of man. In the words of Sylvana Tomaselli, 'the view that woman civilises, that she cultivates, refines, perhaps even adulterates and corrupts, is as recurrent as the view that she is nature's most dutiful and untouched daughter . . . lower than man in the Great Chain of Beings'.[24]

In the nineteenth-century debate over women's education, woman, body, mind and culture remained inextricably interwoven. The point was further underscored when the medical profession entered the debate when women demanded entry to universities and medical faculties. Henry Maudsley's article, 'Sex in mind and body', appeared in the English journal, *Fortnightly Review*, in 1874, the first explicit discussion of female reproductive physiology to appear outside the medical literature. His ideas owed a great deal to Edward H. Clarke's *Sex in Education*, published in the United States in the previous year. Both were university medical men—Maudsley at University College, London, and Clarke at Harvard—and both published their work in the year in which their respective universities agreed to allow women to sit for examinations under their auspices.[25] The essential point for the present discussion is that both Maudsley and Clarke purported to prove that, while women might succeed at men's studies, their reproductive physiology would suffer, their secondary sex characteristics would be impaired and they would risk sterility. This was not a radical departure from popular belief (it is implicit in the mannish body type of the bluestocking caricature) but it bestowed the imprimatur of science

Charming and Astute Professor. — I ASSURE YOU, MRS. LUKYDYGAR, YOUR DELIGHTFUL LITTLE DAUGHTER IS A PERFECT PRODIGY.

Mrs. Lukydygar.—I DUNNO WHAT YOU MEAN BY A "PRODIGY," MR, GAMUT. THE ONLY ONE AS EVER I SEE, WAS KEP IN A BOTTLE O' SPERRITS AT A SHOW. BUT SHE DO PLAY BEAUTIFUL TO BE SURE.

Melbourne Punch lampoons the woman at the piano.
(*Melbourne Punch*, vol. 1, no. 1, 1856)

upon folk wisdom that the female mind and body were mutually implicated for good or evil. There was no corresponding concern about the effects of intellectual activity upon the male reproductive system. Yet the repositioning of woman within the nature/culture debate does not necessarily rearrange the relationship between knowledge, power and female subjectivity. It is fundamental to an understanding of nineteenth-century female education that it attempted an historic uncoupling of the nexus between power and knowledge, between learner and subjectivity. In this debate, the female mind *itself* was different and woman was therefore differently positioned in relation to culture.

Women and culture

The link between woman, culture and power inherent in the notion of the accomplished woman is important in understanding the accomplishments curriculum and its emergence at the very time when the cult of domesticity seemed to call for a renewed emphasis on the more mundane arts of housewifery. Housewifery in its eighteenth-century connotation symbolised woman's culture of a different kind—the ancient sisterhood of women and their knowledge about childbirth, the treatment of the sick and vital household skills. Carl Degler, Carroll Smith-Rosenberg, Nancy Cott and other historians have explored this earlier form of women's culture, which was diminished by the evolution of the nuclear, privatised family under the capitalist mode of production and by the rise of male-dominated professions.

Subliminal understandings of nineteenth-century woman's relationship to culture should not be separated from a more general evolution in Western consciousness, which threw up the idea of culture and the word itself in its modern usage, as a response to the industrial civilisation which was emerging. In *Culture and Society*, Raymond Williams argues that the idea of culture came into English thinking with the Industrial Revolution and the rise of democratic institutions. The notion of culture is, he suggests, intimately related to responses in thought and feeling to changes in English society since the late eighteenth century. Williams traces from Coleridge to Ruskin the construction of culture in terms of the arts, the association of the general perfection of humanity with the practice and study of the arts. The arts became endowed with a superior reality, constituting 'the opposition on general human grounds to the kind of civilisation that was being inaugurated'. The construction of culture in these terms facilitated a critique of the new industrial civilisation and provided a bulwark against the disintegrating tendencies of the age. Williams points to the emergence of artists and intellectuals as specialists endowed with moral authority, symbolising the 'practical separation of certain moral and intellectual activities from the driven impetus of a new kind of society'.[26]

The rise of the accomplishments curriculum in the education of middle-class women in the same period cannot be coincidental. The relationship of women to culture, defined in this narrower sense, is complex. The emergence of the notion of culture as, in Raymond Williams' words, 'a saving clause in a bad treaty', parallels the emergence of the cult of domesticity which romanticised women as another saving clause in the same bad treaty. There are also striking similarities in the delineation of the female mind and that of the romantic, creative genius of the period. The intuitive and imaginative modes of thought, and the validity of personal and private experience in the revelation of eternal truth, were elements attributed in common to women and to the creative genius. Indeed they permeated the entire romantic movement, although it was never envisaged that women would be admitted to Coleridge's clerisy or to the ranks of Carlyle's men of letters. The moral and intellectual physiognomy of woman was inimical to the creative force of genius, the transforming process of human consciousness at its highest level. In the patriarchal frame of reference, woman's role was one of moral influence rather than one of moral authority. Thus the accomplished woman retained within herself an integration between art and life more characteristic of the eighteenth century. She was herself an artefact of culture, an imitator and reflector of a culture created and arbitrated by men and, as such, a passive civilising influence within the private sphere of home and family. Thus the accomplishments curriculum was bolstered by an elaborate ideology linking cultural studies to the private sphere.

It is over two hundred years since Mary Wollstonecraft delivered her perspicacious judgement on the notion of female accomplishment as 'the received wisdom of female excellence separated by specious reasoners from human excellence'.[27] With the benefit of hindsight we are in a position to note that, with the rise of the accomplishments curriculum in the nineteenth century, we are witnessing the translation into mass educational practice of the enduring and oppressive myth that there is a natural affinity between the humanities and the female mind—with its equally enduring and oppressive implication that there is a natural affinity between science and the male mind. Patriarchal social formations have proved remarkably resilient in periods of rapid economic and social change such as that set in motion by the rise of industrial capitalism. In the nineteenth century, men's knowledge was undergoing a historic swing from the closed, largely symbolic knowledge/power systems of the classics, theology and the liberal arts to the open, utilitarian knowledge/power systems of science and technology, based on the understanding and exploitation of the natural world. The rational, scientific frame of mind of necessity underpinned the activities of capitalist man in the industrial and agrarian exploitation of the natural world. The middle-class beneficiaries of the new order challenged aristocratic power on the grounds of moral superiority; they felt an urgent need to educate their daughters but to educate them for life within the private world of home and family. The scientific frame of mind and the new knowledge about the physical world had to be gendered and ancient taboos on women's learning had to be reworked. The icon of the woman at the piano was enthroned many decades before the scientific frame of mind had a serious impact upon the institutional education of elite Western men. Almost a century later, in the Edwardian era, the swelling discourse on the efficacy of 'domestic science' for women was certainly connected to contemporary campaigns to force upon Australian universities and secondary schools a serious commitment to science. Feminist historians have rightly exposed the pseudo-science of domesticity as an assault upon the intellectual subjectivity of women. Yet they have failed to note that women's exclusion from the great intellectual adventure of the twentieth century was already a *fait accompli*.

We have now returned full circle to the transgression of Laura Rambotham in the drawing-room of nineteenth-century Presbyterian Ladies' College. Laura, the woman at the piano, transgressed her womanly role as artefact of culture and claimed instead the masculine prerogative as shaper of culture. Absorbed by her own passionate performance she was transported beyond the micro politics of the drawing-room which constrict the mind and body of the female child. Music was indeed as fatal to her feminine subjectivity as wine would have been. That the incident is set in one of Australia's first academic secondary schools for girls and not in a female academy should give us pause for thought. The author of the novel, Henry Handel Richardson, was Ethel Richardson (1870–1946), who attended the Presbyterian Ladies' College in the 1880s. The novel is, to an extent which is debated by scholars of literature and history, autobiographical. Of one thing we can be sure; Ethel Richardson was indeed the woman at the piano. While at the school she won a music scholarship to the Royal Conservatorium in Leipzig, Germany. There she met her future husband, John Robertson, later a distinguished professor of literature at the University of London.

She turned from music to writing and established an international reputation as a novelist. It is this possibility of subversion which is the well-spring of feminist history, and the following study of the ladies' schools of colonial Australia is written in that spirit.

CHAPTER TWO

The Lost Ladies' Schools of Colonial Australia

When the novelist Joan Lindsay sent the girls from Mrs Appleyard's College for Young Ladies on their fateful picnic to Hanging Rock she also wrote an epitaph for the education of middle-class women in the accomplishments tradition.[1] Set down like an 'exotic fungus' in the Australian countryside, Appleyard College stood for all that was wrong with the education of women. Mrs Appleyard's credentials were veiled in obscurity; 'with her high-piled greying pompadour and ample bosom, as rigidly controlled and disciplined as her ambitions, . . . the stately stranger looked precisely what the parents expected of an English Headmistress'.[2] Raw colonial parents with ambitions to gentility were duped and the college turned a handsome profit. Stereotypes abound: the beautiful and soon-to-be-married Mademoiselle Poitiers taught dancing and French conversation, and attended to the boarders' wardrobes; the raw-boned spinster, Miss Greta McCraw, taught mathematics. Learning itself was incidental to the defence of social boundaries, the acquisition of 'polish' and the business of finding a husband. With this harsh judgement historians have agreed.[3] On the basis of very little research, they have concluded that educational provision for middle-class women until the last quarter of the nineteenth century was meretricious and misguided. Parents cared little about the education of their daughters. The governess in the private home, the lady-principal in her female academy and the ubiquitous music master presided over a nether-world of education which was costly, pretentious and haphazard, teaching a smattering of the 'ladylike' accomplishments to groom daughters for the marriage market. In this view, girls were educated by default or not at all.

The Misses Thompson and the education of Catherine Deakin

The briefest acquaintance with the lives of many women throws doubt upon this orthodoxy. Catherine Deakin was one such woman. In nineteenth-century terms, she was an accomplished woman; indeed she was among the most highly educated people in Australia. She would have lived and died in obscurity had it not been that she was the sister of Alfred Deakin, six years her junior and three times prime minister of Australia. Catherine was not from a privileged family. She was born in Adelaide in 1850, the daughter of William and Sarah Deakin. The family joined the exodus to Victoria with the news of gold and there William Deakin and his brother-in-law set up a coach service between Melbourne and the goldfields. As an adult, Catherine was fluent in the modern languages and played the piano to concert pianist standard. She was extremely well-read in literature and politics; as one of her biographers comments: 'At 84 [she] could well have contributed invaluable comment and criticism at any newspaper's editorial conference on the international scene'.[4] She taught briefly at the Presbyterian Ladies' College, at the Corea Ladies' College and in private practice as a music teacher; but for the greater part of her life she used her education in the private sphere and in the service of others.

Catherine Deakin had several suitors but did not marry. She centred her emotional and intellectual life around her brother; their correspondence reveals that they were passionately devoted to each other. Deakin the public man was supported by adoring female relatives all his life—his mother, his sister, his wife Pattie (née Browne) and his three daughters Ivy, Stella and Vera.[5] Catherine's role as his intellectual and emotional amanuensis continued after his marriage in 1882, eventually causing a rift between sister and wife. During his years in the Victorian Parliament and when Federal Parliament met in Spring Street, he walked through the Botanical Gardens to Catherine's home in Adams Street where he could discuss with her his immediate reactions to ideas, colleagues and events. Though Catherine's role in his burgeoning career was little known, Deakin himself was in no doubt about his debt to the beloved 'K' of his diaries. On her birthday in 1899 he wrote: 'Ever dearest sister . . . To have you always just at my elbow at all events within call has been so lifelong an experience with me that it seems out of the order of nature to find myself driven to the stiff pen, the bald paper and the cold ink.' Catherine Deakin played a large part in the education of his daughters until they went to Melbourne Girls' Grammar School in the Edwardian era. Deakin's slide into insanity, concealed from general knowledge, was searing for Catherine; he died in 1919 and she lived on until 1937.

How did Catherine Deakin come to be so highly educated in an era when women were shut out from the institutions to which their brothers had access—the grammar schools, the universities and the learned societies? Catherine Deakin was an only child for six years and her father encouraged her development, a common theme in the lives of intellectual women. He was a well-read and thoughtful man who read poetry and classical prose to Catherine and Alfred. He introduced them to the great writers of the eighteenth and nineteenth centuries, and these works they read avidly. Their home had many visitors of a similar intellectual bent. In an affectionate memoir of his great-aunt, journalist Rohan Rivett wrote: 'Catherine was privately educated and did not have a chance of formal schooling until Professor Charles Pearson, a distinguished Oxford and London scholar, helped to establish the first major secondary school for young ladies—the Presbyterian Ladies' College—in 1875.'[6] Perhaps because Catherine kept a photograph of Pearson on her mantelpiece, Rivett concludes that her ex-headmaster had 'more influence on Catherine's development and thinking than anyone outside her father and brother'. Certainly the Deakin and Pearson political fortunes became entwined, and Catherine remained an acquaintance and a devotee of Pearson's speeches and writing. Presbyterian Ladies' College, Melbourne, has cultivated its reputation as the 'first major secondary school for young ladies' in Australia, and it has been happy to claim Catherine as a distinguished past student—as the sister of the 'great man' and as its first student to pass the matriculation examination of the University of Melbourne.[7] In 1876 she became the first of many past students to return as a teacher. As the school's historian notes, the college could hardly take full credit for her achievements as she was twenty-five years old when she enrolled and she stayed only one year; nor did she remain for long on the staff. No reference was made to her former place of education.

It is salutary then to discover that in her autobiographical note, published in *Records of the Pioneer Women* towards the end of her life, Catherine herself records that she was for ten years a pupil at a school run by the Misses Thompson. She attended the school initially in the central Victorian town of Kyneton, and later when it moved to the Melbourne suburb of South Yarra in 1863.[8] The Thompsons and their school appear briefly in J.A. La Nauze's biography of Alfred Deakin, although the references are scattered and the reader needs to know about the sisters beforehand to make the connections. La Nauze is intrigued by the fact that the future prime minister also attended their Kyneton school as a small boarder in the care of his sister, surely the foundation of the lifelong bond between them, although he gives no explanation for this remarkable family decision. La Nauze provides evidence that the Deakins held the Thompson sisters in high esteem, although he rarely mentions them by name. We are told that the Deakins moved from Fitzroy to South Yarra in 1863 to be near Catherine's school rather than to be near Alfred's school, Melbourne Grammar. He mentions

The building in which the Misses Thompson conducted their Kyneton Ladies'
Academy in the 1850s.

that Catherine had 'a good grounding at her school . . . and in music
which was her forte'. La Nauze gives more attention to John Henning
Thompson, a head prefect and young teacher at Melbourne Grammar,
who was hero-worshipped by the young Alfred Deakin. If he knew, La
Nauze does not make explicit that John Henning Thompson and the
proprietors of the South Yarra Ladies' College were brother and sisters,
though this proved a vital link in the search for the Misses Thompson.
There is a family tradition that Catherine Deakin was in love with John
Thompson and that Alfred opposed the marriage, an intervention into
his sister's life which preyed upon his mind in his last years.

Who then were the Misses Thompson and what is it possible to add
to this fragile Deakin connection? Even by the standards of women's
history the search is hard-going. Through their relationship to John
Henning Thompson it can be established that they were the daughters
of John Thompson, a London banker, and his wife, Margaret (née
Henning), and that the family arrived in Victoria in 1856. Consistent with
Catherine Deakin's evidence, the sisters were advertising a school in the

Kyneton Observer by September 1857. Here is the nineteenth-century ladies' academy at the point of cultural transplantation to the colonies: 'The general course of instruction [is] to comprehend all the branches of a sound English Education, viz., Reading, Writing, Arithmetic (practical and mental), Grammar, Geography, ancient and Modern History, Composition, Chronology, Use of the Globes, with Plain and Ornamental Needlework.' The 'usual accomplishments' were pianoforte, vocal music, drawing, French and dancing.[9] Miss L. Thompson, who gave her credentials as 'pupil of a professor of the Royal Academy', was in charge of music. At a time when the Deakins' yearly income was £300, fees for boarders were forty-five guineas a year without the accomplishments for which extra fees were charged. The advertisement included the usual list of referees—clergymen, local dignitaries and parents. In the following month the Thompson sisters advertised their '*extremely* low terms . . . considerably under any other first-class establishment in the colony', perhaps a reference to the other girls' schools in the town—Miss Bennett's Kyneton Academy and Mrs Fleck's Campaspe Villa. The Misses Thompson aimed to make study entertaining, to promote the health and happiness of the girls and to make the change on leaving home 'as little felt as possible'.[10] They noted the 'well known salubrity' of Kyneton and the health-giving properties of their leased bluestone residence, Lauriston House, which still stands in Piper Street, on the main route through Kyneton to the goldfields. Further advertisements add little except the fact of their survival until, in January 1863, Catherine Deakin's memory is again corroborated by the announcement of their move to Melbourne.[11]

The Thompson sisters renamed their school the 'Ladies' College, South Yarra', describing its location as 'near the punt', opposite the main gates to the Botanical Gardens. This places the school in Anderson Street, almost certainly on the site of the present Melbourne Girls' Grammar School. Here they had rented the home of Colonel Anderson, possibly the imported Indian bungalow, 'Old Fairlie', demolished by Melbourne Girls' Grammar in the Edwardian era. Their list of referees now included the Dean of Melbourne, Hussey Burgh MacCartney. Throughout the 1860s, their advertisements advised that 'Professors from [the] Church of England Grammar School . . . attend this establishment daily'.[12] J.C. Hearle of the Training Institution for teachers taught English literature; Aristides Dellas, who was later on the staff of the Presbyterian Ladies' College, taught French; and George Tolhurst, organist at Christ Church, South Yarra, and music teacher with the Board of Education, taught music. Again, there is little to add from their regular advertisements until, in August 1870, the Thompsons sold the goodwill of their school to Mrs Alexander, a member of the Deakin circle, who renamed it Lawn House.[13]

Catherine Deakin's diary is among the Deakin papers in Canberra. Although it begins in January 1866, the year after she left the South Yarra Ladies' College, it is clear that Catherine maintained close links with the Thompsons and the school, probably teaching music there, as she spends a good deal of time copying music.[14] Her diary also yields the names of two sisters—Edith and Louisa—the latter presumably the musical Miss L. of the earlier advertisements, whom Catherine records as departing for England in 1866. Mrs Thompson, who is mentioned frequently, may have been matron-housekeeper at the college. Catherine often visited the school, sometimes staying overnight. She attended their annual concert at the end of 1866 and noted approvingly in her diary the performance of the Italian tenor, Signor Cesare Cutolo, who taught in many Melbourne ladies' schools at that time. The diary continues to 1875, Catherine's year at the Presbyterian Ladies' College, but she notes only briefly her first day at the 'College' and later the fact that she has passed matriculation. There are no further traces of the Misses Thompson. It is tempting to speculate that they moved with their brother to Kew High School, a private school which he purchased in 1875, but there is an awkward five-year gap in the timing, and they do not appear in the small collection on John Henning Thompson in the archives of the present school on the site, Trinity Grammar School.

The search for the Misses Thompson illustrates in microcosm the problems and possibilities of retrieving the lost ladies' schools of colonial Australia. Nearly 700 women advertised what they claimed to be 'select' female schools in the Melbourne *Argus* between 1850 and 1875; some advertised for one day only and others for the entire period. A similar list could be drawn up for any capital city or provincial centre. Yet as the schools and their proprietors acknowledged no prescription from church or state, sources are scarce and widely scattered. A large amount of time is required to retrieve fragments which yield their information obliquely: newspaper advertisements, directories, rate books, prospectuses, private papers, memoirs, and the usual repositories of biographical data such as wills, obituaries, shipping records, and certificates of births, deaths and marriages. The 'Deakin factor', that extra windfall which enables us to put flesh upon the bones of names, dates and places, is in itself a lesson in the politics of historical survival.

Ellinthorp Hall, Tasmania

Ellinthorp Hall has maintained its precarious toehold in the history of early Van Diemen's Land because its location in the interior at Ross made it a convenient and convivial staging post for important people like

Lieutenant-Governor Sir George Arthur, who mentioned it in dispatches. It is also remembered because it was attacked by bushrangers and subsequently fortified as a military outpost. Legend has it that the girls were filed past the body of a slain bushranger and that one of the governesses with an interest in phrenology read the contours of his skull. Historians have settled comfortably into the assumption that Ellinthorp Hall was the only ladies' school worth mentioning in the early years of Tasmanian settlement. The school's history properly begins when Hannah Maria Davice, Elinor Binfield and a young apprentice teacher, Susannah Darke Purbrick, a relative of Davice, arrived in Hobart from England aboard the *Berwick* in June 1823. According to their advertisements they had been running a school in England. It is apparent that they came with the intention of establishing a school, as they brought with them their tools of trade to the value of £465: musical instruments, printed music, drawing materials, a school library, and a set of globes and charts.[15] Davice and Binfield also brought capital—in Davice's case, over £3,000, sufficient to have kept her in respectable idleness at home and sufficient to entitle to her to a grant of 2,000 acres in Van Diemen's Land. One month after their arrival they advertised in the *Hobart Town Gazette* the opening of their school in Buckinghamshire House, a large, two-storey building on the corner of Macquarie and Harrington Streets, which they rented for £125 per annum. They advertised their system of education as:

> already followed with great success . . . in England [combining] all the essentially useful and solid acquirements with the more feminine and ornamental accomplishments, so as to ensure to those entrusted to their care an opportunity of acquiring all that is necessary to form and adorn the female character.[16]

Both women married within two years, Binfield in March 1824 and Davice the following December. Elinor Binfield married Joseph Archer who prospered as a landowner and was elected to the first Legislative Council. She retired from teaching and became part of the colonial aristocracy, entertaining lavishly and travelling abroad frequently. Hannah Davice was possibly engaged to George Carr Clark when she arrived, as she selected her 2,000 acres adjacent to his grant in preference to another block which the Lieutenant Governor had advised her to take. Unlike Binfield, she did not give up the school upon her marriage. Instead, her advertisement in the *Hobart Town Gazette* in mid-1825 announced that the school was moving to Carr Field House, built by her husband at a cost of £1,235 opposite the Post Office in Murray Street.[17] In November she gave birth to a still-born daughter at Carr Field House, returning to teaching almost immediately. A year later the Clarks took the risk of moving the school to their property at Ross where they renamed it Ellinthorp Hall, after the Clark family home in Yorkshire. As a married woman Hannah Clark no longer had the right to own property or income which she earned. Ellinthorp Hall gained a reputation as an excellent school, although it was dismissed as inconsequential by Lady Jane Franklin when she was honing her own plans for a high-class ladies' school under vice-regal patronage.[18] Ellinthorp Hall was visited by the Quaker clergymen travellers, James Backhouse and George Walker, who wrote of it in glowing terms:

> We had much interesting discourse with the wife of G.C. Clark, and were gratified to find so conscientious and intelligent a person at the head of such an establishment. Her husband is quite independent; but she continues the school from a sense of duty, and to gratify the wishes of her benevolent heart, by rearing and educating a number of children who have been deprived of the means of a liberal education, but whose birth might have seemed to entitle them to it. Several are orphans or motherless, and at present, one-fourth of the school are educated at a very reduced expense, or altogether gratuitously.[19]

Despite its reputation as the leading girls' school in Tasmania, among the girls in residence were the two illegitimate daughters of Margaret Eddington, one by Lieutenant-Governor David Collins and another by George Watts, an illiterate convict bushranger. Backhouse and Walker did not canvass the possibility that Hannah Clark followed her profession as a school teacher for its own sake, nor did they mention that her husband also taught in the school. During her seventeen years as owner-principal of Ellinthorp Hall Hannah Clark gave birth to six children, ironically, closing the school in 1840 when she took them back to England to be educated. She died there in 1847. A prospectus and several accounts for fees survive in the papers of George Robinson, Protector of Aborigines, who sent his daughter to Ellinthorp Hall. The school in a sense lived on, as the devoted Susannah Purbrick eventually established her own school, Carr Villa, near Launceston in 1848. She was apparently well paid for her services as English mistress at Ellinthorp Hall over the years as she accumulated sufficient capital to bring out her orphaned brother and sister. She also applied, unsuccessfully, for a grant of land. She married while at Ellinthorp Hall and her husband, John Knight, obligingly took up residence there to enable her to continue teaching. Purbrick always advertised her Launceston school as modelled on Ellinthorp Hall and it is a measure of her reputation that Carr Villa lasted until 1866, forty-three years after the three women arrived in Van Diemen's Land.

The Tripp family and East Leigh

Mrs Elizabeth Tripp (née Leigh) was owner-proprietor of one of Melbourne's leading ladies' schools, East Leigh, from 1859 to 1881 when she leased it to the Bromby family.[20] Elizabeth was born in Devonshire, England, in 1809, the daughter of William Leigh, solicitor, and his wife Frances. In 1831 she married her cousin, lawyer William Upton Tripp, son of a Church of England clergyman. Their first child, Mary, was born in 1834 and when the Tripps arrived in Victoria in 1850 they had five daughters and one son. Two other sons died in the colony. The marriage ended in an estrangement, though William was brought back to East Leigh to be nursed through his final illness in 1873. With five daughters to support and educate, Elizabeth Tripp turned to school teaching. By mid-1859 she was advertising her ladies' school in Prahran Street, South Yarra, as 'conducted by Mrs Tripp and her daughters, assisted by the best masters'.[21] The school moved to new premises on the corner of Commercial and Williams Roads, Prahran, in October 1861 and took the name East Leigh.[22] Five years later the Tripps were again on the move, over the road to a two-storey Georgian house set in three acres of garden which Mrs Tripp purchased with money from her marriage settlement. Perhaps because she possessed a measure of independence by virtue of the settlement, Tripp was a business woman of considerable acumen; she speculated successfully on the share market in the notoriously treacherous area of goldmining, and her investments in land and property withstood the collapse of the 1890s.

The Mackinnon family papers in the La Trobe Library contain twenty-three letters from Mrs Tripp to pastoralist, John Hastie, concerning the education of his orphaned niece, Jane, who was at East Leigh as a boarder in 1863 and 1864.[23] John Hastie apparently had decided views about the education of his niece, for in January 1863 Mrs Tripp wrote to him:

> I feel very much obliged by your having stated so frankly the particular object you have in view in sending your niece to school—I shall do all I can to form her mind and judgement, as well as to advance her studies, and I trust she may derive all the benefit for which you hope—you may rest assured that no effort on my part shall be wanting.

Jane Hastie was escorted to East Leigh by a friend of the family, the Rev. Alexander Campbell who, as a founder of Geelong College, also had decided views about education. 'I saw your niece safely consigned to Mrs Tripp's house last Monday', he wrote to Hastie, '[and] I was very much pleased with the look of the lady and her Establishment. The house is airy—situated in a healthy locality with three acres of garden surrounding it—order and good sense seemed to characterize the Establishment. I think your niece is likely to derive much benefit from her stay there.' He also discussed Jane's education with Mrs Tripp—'I asked Mrs Tripp to ascertain what she was most deficient in and also what she was fitted to excel in and to judge accordingly'—but asked that she be thoroughly grounded in English grammar, history and spelling. He cautioned against going beyond French, music and drawing as extras for the time being.

Elizabeth Tripp wrote to John Hastie in February: 'I feel it will be satisfactory both to you, and to myself that you should hear from me from time to time.' She had already purchased clothes for Jane, 'so that she may be attired as are the rest of our pupils'. In April, Jane's first report followed, although it is missing from the Mackinnon papers. Jane 'required of course correction at times'—music practice seemed to be the problem—but was giving satisfaction. One of the Tripp daughters had escorted her to the Geelong train where she was to spend the Easter holidays with an aunt. In the fine print of the quarterly accounts for Jane's education we find evidence of other excursions from the school: cab fares for trips to the dressmaker, for shopping trips to town, to see the fireworks, to the Exhibition of Fine Arts (where the Tripp sisters exhibited), to a missionary meeting, to St Paul's Cathedral. Mrs Tripp recommends dancing lessons for next quarter—'I think it good for girls to learn dancing, it improves their carriage and general bearing'—at a fee of two guineas. There was discussion as to when Jane should begin German lessons (at three guineas per quarter): 'We have a lady now residing with us who is a first rate German scholar'. In July Mrs Tripp wrote, full of solicitude about John Hastie's ill health, urging him to visit East Leigh when he was in Melbourne. Jane had returned from holidays looking well and in good spirits. The blend of the personal and the professional which characterises the letters is captured in Elizabeth Tripp's request to John Hastie: 'If you have any opportunity to do so, I shall be very much obliged by you mentioning my school, as I prefer to be known by private recommendation than by advertisement'.

In April 1864, John Hastie wrote to Elizabeth Tripp informing her that Jane would be leaving East Leigh in June. Her disapproval is palpable. She enclosed a typical quarterly account for £29.18.6 and added:

> [Jane] is a kind hearted girl and with careful training will be a sensible and useful woman. I hope she will not go much into Society just yet. She is too young to do so, and being an attractive girl may be led away by the attention

that would be paid to her, whereas over a year or two, her character will have matured, and then she will better estimate the value of such notice. I have endeavoured to give her right notions, and to make her value what is good and estimable; I shall continue to take an interest in her and it will give me the greatest pleasure to learn that she is growing up a really sterling character.

Mary, Margaret, Frances and Florence Tripp all taught at East Leigh at some time in their lives. Surviving family letters leave little doubt that there was a price to pay for this apprenticeship; nor can there be any doubt as to who was in control of the school. The teaching labour of several highly educated and conscientious daughters contributed to the profits which were used to speculate in shares and property. Margaret Tripp did not marry and was financially dependent upon her mother until well into middle age. She was thirty-three when she sailed for England alone in 1872. Her letters home are those of a deeply intellectual, professionally committed woman, yet her style is confessional, submissive, even pleading: 'Tell me about everything and everybody and criticize me freely. I do so hope you will approve of all I do . . . I can truly say I think of you all day and night.' There are glimpses of life going on without her at East Leigh: her mother is building yet again ('selfishly I am very glad to be out of it'); an unspecified alliance is under negotiation with Eliza Bromby ('I think we should do well to be associated with her . . . if we could make an arrangement satisfactory on both sides'); she is 'thankful to hear of the welldoing of the school' and feels that 'we must do our best to profit by this tide of prosperity which may not last always'; there are comings and goings of staff, both academic and domestic. Only once did Margaret Tripp initiate discussion on a professional matter. In Cambridge in 1873 she wished to enrol at Anne Clough's two-year-old Newnham College. She wrote to her mother: 'What an advantage it would be . . . for the school. When I see . . . the . . . increased demand for qualified and certificated teachers I feel convinced that this feeling, a most natural and justifiable one, will shortly extend to the colonies.' She evidently received no encouragement for she wrote again as the time for enrolment was running out:

But mind, dearest Mother, I cannot *ask* you to let me remain a day longer in England after all your great goodness to me, especially not being on the spot and able to judge, as you are, whether I could possibly be spared, and whether the advantage of passing the exam would counterbalance the inconvenience and expense my stay in England would entail . . . I wish you to decide quite as to the general good of the school and family, and quite irrespective of my wishes.[24]

Margaret Tripp did not go to Newnham College, where she would have been the first Australian woman to study at Cambridge, but money was apparently not the issue for she went instead to Paris in 1873 to study the more conventional fare of singing, French and German at Madame Bouten's School. She wrote to her mother that she felt 'rather old for the systematic study of French, and especially to learn to speak it'. Margaret Tripp made one other request from the safety of England: that when she returned to East Leigh she might be excused from sleeping in the dormitories with the girls. She returned to Australia in time to witness the misery of her father's death in September 1873.

Margaret Tripp's long apprenticeship to her mother ended when the Tripps withdrew from East Leigh in 1881, though it was some years before she established her professional independence. In 1888 she applied for the principalship of Trinity Women's Hostel at the University of Melbourne (later Janet Clarke Hall) and, although unsuccessful, she was invited to join the Ladies' Council appointed to raise funds for the permanent premises. She was at the centre of the very public brawl between the Warden of Trinity College, Dr Alexander Leeper, and Emily Hensley, principal of the hostel and one of the original five students at Newnham College, Cambridge.[25] If Margaret Tripp visited Newnham in 1873 they may well have met, as the college was then a handful of young women in a cottage. With Melbourne sinking into the economic depression of the 1890s, Margaret Tripp founded Rewe, a private school in Washington Street, Toorak. Her advertisements used the Tripp and East Leigh names to the full and the 'experienced governess' listed in her first advertisement was her sister, Florence. They were soon to be joined by the widowed Frances. Three years later they moved to the nearby premises of Toorak College, a private boys' school 'lately occupied by J.T. Craig'. When their mother died in 1899, leaving them financially secure, the Tripp sisters sold Toorak College to Ellen Pye who was also assisted in the school by her unmarried sisters, Rachel and Ann. This school was the ancestor of the present Toorak College at Mt Eliza.

Jane Hamilton's Young Ladies' School on the Victorian goldfields

Jane Hamilton's school on the goldfields of central Victoria survives in the historical record because her letters home to Scotland are included in the Brown family papers.[26] The letters detail the rise and fall of a ladies' school from a more intimate perspective. As Jane Brown, she migrated reluctantly from Cumnock in Scotland in 1859 to join other members of the interrelated Brown, Hoey and Hamilton families on the goldfields at Sandhurst (later Bendigo). In hindsight it is apparent that tuberculosis was endemic in the three families and that their Australian venture was doomed from the beginning. Her sister, Maggie Hoey, was dying of the disease when Jane came to Australia to nurse her and to look after her two children, Maggie and Robert, whom she subsequently brought up as her own. One year later in Sandhurst, 33-year-old Jane Brown married Andrew Hamilton, also from Cumnock, whose wife Janet Hoey had died in 1840.[27] Jane and Andrew had three children, two of whom survived. On the marriage certificate Andrew Hamilton is described as a Melbourne merchant but, by 1867, the date of the first surviving letter, he was engaged in deep lead mining in Sandhurst. His ventures were apparently unproductive—'that weary mining!', Jane wrote to her mother—and by the mid-1860s it was clear that he too had contracted tuberculosis. The establishment of Jane Hamilton's Young Ladies' School in California Gully in 1867, against her husband's will, was indeed the last throw of a desperate woman—an enduring stereotype of the lady school-keeper— but that is not the impression left by the letters which she wrote home to her family in Scotland.

With her letter in April 1867 she enclosed her printed prospectus, headed 'Young Ladies' School, California Gully, Dunedin Cottage, opposite east side of Windmill Hill'. The prospectus introduced her as 'Mrs Hamilton, who has experience as a Teacher both in Glasgow and in North Germany', and she was still corresponding on professional matters with German friends during her years in Australia. Her letter continues:

> I have been meditating this step for months past, but as I knew it would be a great struggle for Mr H. to let me take it, I kept my thoughts to myself, besides I always hoped something would turn up for us in some other quarter. But at last Providence seemed to indicate this step and I do trust in Him to bless my efforts. Andrew has been quite borne down with care in consequence of that unsuccessful prospecting, so in order to help to meet daily wants . . . I made up my mind to try a school. A. did not oppose me, altho' it vexed me to see the deep depression he was in for a few days after I made up my mind . . . During the cold days we had, about three weeks ago, he got as bad, if not worse, than he was last winter, which all the more confirmed my purpose.[28]

She had been busy canvassing for pupils, with the help of the local Presbyterian minister and his wife, placing advertisements in the newspaper, arranging for her prospectus to be printed, buying school furniture and chasing up suitable text books through a bookseller in Melbourne. She was very conscious that a school without a piano was at a disadvantage and, though she was short of space and capital, the search for a suitable instrument became a hardy perennial of her letters home. 'I am sorry to think', wrote her brother James, 'that you are so hard wrought and that you have competition to such an extent in your school. But I have no fear of your success. When you get the piano it will enable you to bid for a higher class of pupils.' Her preliminary inquiries found a number of potential students for French, but not for German, her preferred language, and she began immediately to bring her French up to standard. The school was to be held in her front parlour, which had necessitated the building of a chimney to provide another sitting-room for the family. The letter to Scotland setting out her plans was written two days before the school was due to commence: 'Of course I feel nervous after making all those professions and yet I believe I shall manage. I trust in help from above and I am glad to say I already know of as many pupils to make a beginning with, as to keep me from despairing'. Jane's letter elicited a flurry of correspondence from Scotland. Her sister-in-law, Kate Brown, wrote warmly: 'I only wish that "Mrs Hamilton's Seminary" were in dear old Scotland . . . I envy you the ability Jane, and the possession of an education fitted for such a sphere of usefulness—I fear were I left alone . . . I would make a poor fend of it.' Several members of the family sent Jane money, ostensibly to help with the upkeep of the orphaned Hoey children, but actually to help with the establishment of the school.

In her next letter Jane Hamilton reported 'a nice manageable number' and was in hopes that this would increase when the days grew longer and the weather finer. In July 1867 she was approached by several families in nearby Eaglehawk to move her school there and, afraid that her pupils might be lured away, she reluctantly agreed to do so. The move involved her in the expense of renting a cottage in Eaglehawk and trudging back and forth daily with her own children. She lamented that in the depressed state of the goldfields they could not sell their house and move to Eaglehawk. Though there were 'several other Ladies' Schools in the locality', by September she had twenty pupils, thirteen of whom were paying 10/6 extra per quarter for French and German, among them a banker's wife. An urgent subtext in the letters was the plight of another female relative on the goldfields, Nena Hoey, whose husband Tom had apparently disappeared, leaving his wife and children destitute.

The establishment of the school in April 1867 coincided with Jane's third pregnancy, unwelcome news which she confided in a letter to her cousin, Jane Frew, but not immediately to her mother. She continued to walk daily to Eaglehawk until the beginning of December when the hot weather and her advanced stage of pregnancy made the journey impossible. She was obliged to give her pupils six weeks holiday to await the birth of her child. Jane Elisabeth was born the following January. Jane Hamilton wrote again to Jane Frew describing the ease of the birth and the consequent late arrival of the midwife; the child was born with only a female neighbour and young Maggie Hoey present. Thereafter, Maggie is referred to as a willing nursemaid. Jane was exuberant about the ease of the birth and the blooming health of the child who bore a strong resemblance to the baby girl, Jessie, who had died the year before. The same letter contained the ominous news that ten days after the birth, her husband, Andrew Hamilton, had haemorrhaged badly. Jane had nursed him day and night until he slowly began to improve. She was now obliged to move the school back to her home in California Gully but in the meantime many of the pupils had disappeared. 'I feel more anxious now than ever to have a school', she wrote in January 1868, and she began to give lessons three afternoons a week 'to accommodate those young Ladies who have been put about by my unexpected giving up'. She took up the school again full-time at Easter 1868. It was still apparently in existence in March 1869 when Kate Brown wrote: 'Concerning your school affairs, we often wish you were at Brighton near Melbourne for the sake of a better and higher class of Scholars, but I suppose you are tied to your present neighbourhood in the meantime.' Andrew Hamilton died in 1870 and Jane returned to Scotland.

The Brown family papers include copies of testimonials which establish that she subsequently became 'Lady Principal' of the co-educational Dowanhill Institution in Glasgow. In April 1873, the Principal, W.M. Begbie, wrote of her: 'Mrs Hamilton takes much pleasure in teaching, and has been very successful with her classes. She is a good English, French, and German Scholar, and well read in the literature of these languages.' This testimonial she reproduced in a prospectus for her next venture, the Young Ladies' School, Sea-View House, Largs, which, according to the surviving documents, ran successfully for many years. She continued to advertise her Continental teaching credentials but she did not mention Dunedin Cottage on the Australian goldfields.

Vieusseux Ladies' College, Melbourne

Only in the case of the Vieusseux Ladies' College, Melbourne, has the elusive tin trunk of records so far come to light, handed down in a family which remained in education until the 1920s and understood the school's historical significance.[29] The register of pupils has survived, with details on the 886 girls who attended in the twenty-six years of the school's existence—a who's who of Melbourne in the 1860s and 70s. There are three prospectuses—for the years 1863, 1873 and 1878—containing annual addresses, prize lists, lists of staff, the curriculum, methods of

Detail of the wedding portrait of Julie and Lewis Vieusseux, proprietors of the Ladies' College, East Melbourne from 1857–1882.
(Courtesy of Mrs Phyllis Gray)

school organisation and examination papers. There is a generous collection of photographs and newspaper clippings. Subsumed within the Vieusseux papers is a smaller collection concerning the progress of Edith Luke through the school: these documents, which include her diary after she left the college and several of her work books, survived because Edith Luke became the second Mrs Vieusseux. The Vieusseux collection also contains fine pieces of antique furniture, including a piano with candelabras still intact, which give a sense of the opulence of the prosperous ladies' college. The Vieusseuxs' handsome wedding portrait by Chauvin has survived, along with some of Madame Julie's own paintings.

This unusually intact collection invites the conclusion that the Vieusseux Ladies' College was the high point of the private girls' school in nineteenth-century Australia. Certainly it is the most accessible. Julie and Lewis Vieusseux were among the many cultured and cosmopolitan European immigrants who brought their own version of the ladies' school tradition to Australia. She was born Julie Matthieu in 1820 in Holland, the daughter of Catherine (née Van de Winkle) and Louis Emile Matthieu, a captain in the Belgian army. She regarded herself as a native of French Flanders. In 1849, in Salford, England, Julie Matthieu married Lewis Vieusseux. Lewis was born in England of Swiss parents, educated at the Enfield Grammar School near London, and trained as a civil engineer, architect and surveyor in Europe. He was fluent in English, French and German, and a scholar in the literature of all three languages. Their first two children, Lewis and Stephen, were born in London. The family arrived in Victoria aboard the *Fortitude* in early 1852, among the first wave of migrants drawn by the news of Australia's new-found wealth in gold. They were accompanied by Julie's twenty-year-old sister, Marie Matthieu, who also became the owner-proprietor of a ladies' school, Esplanade House, in St Kilda. In November 1852, their second son, Stephen, died at the age of fifteen months and a third boy, Edward, was born in April 1854. Julie Vieusseux had been educated in Paris and was an artist and linguist of distinction. She established herself first as a portrait painter in the Kyte's Buildings, Fitzroy:

> Mrs Vieusseux has the honour to announce that she follows her profession as PORTRAIT PAINTER and in soliciting the patronage of all lovers of the Fine Arts, she respectfully invites them to visit her studio, where several beautiful Oil Paintings, also specimens of her Likenesses may be viewed daily. Portraits taken in Oils, Chalks and Pencils, after the most approved styles.[30]

Among her few surviving works is a portrait of fellow artist and friend, Eugen von Guérard. She entered her work in the Victorian Society of Fine Arts' exhibition in 1857 with two other women, Georgiana McCrae and Ellen Davitt of the National Model School. Although Julie Vieusseux enjoyed some success as a portrait painter—Hugh Childers, politician and founding vice-chancellor of the University of Melbourne, was among her clientele—the direction of her professional life is discernible as early as November 1853 when her advertisements began to offer: 'Drawing and Painting Classes for Young Ladies, who can enjoy the advantage of French conversation.'[31]

The Ladies' College, as it was known for over twenty years, began its formal existence in July 1857 on part of the site now occupied by St Vincent's Hospital. The 'objects of the institution' were: 'To impart a solid and superior education . . . comprehending . . . the development of the Intellectual Faculties and high Moral and Religious Training [and] those graceful accomplishments proper to ladies.'[32] Among the referees were the Rev. Henry Handfield, Judge Robert Pohlman, Dr Godfrey Howitt, Sir Archibald Michie and the a'Beckett family. There were also daughters from the Hawdon, McCrae, Sargood and Liardet families, all in their own ways to be reckoned with in Melbourne society. There was a strong contingent from the von Guérard circle of artists and musicians, most of whom taught at the college at some time: Victoria von Guérard, Bessie Strutt, Fanny, Isabella and Lizzie Carandini, and the daughters of George Leavis Allan. Senior boarders paid twenty guineas per quarter and day girls four guineas per quarter, without the fee-for-service extras of music, art and languages.

Julie and Lewis Vieusseux struggled to impose order upon a school population with varied previous educational experiences, a reality which they shared with grammar schools and elementary schools alike. The register of pupils indicates that groups of sisters arrived and departed together; the Vieusseuxs themselves calculated that the average stay of the first 200 school leavers was only five quarters. To cope with the varying attainments of their pupils they evolved a system of ability grouping in different subjects which would still revolutionise many schools today. As they noted in their prospectus, this necessitated a larger staff and separate classrooms, but was 'decidedly more advantageous to the pupils'.[33] The college had an elaborate system of daily class marks and twice-yearly examinations which allowed the ranking of each girl in her class, and this ranking Lewis wrote beside the names in the register of pupils. The Vieusseuxs set high academic standards. Both taught full-time in the school, taking the language and literature classes in English, French and German; Julie also taught drawing, painting and craft classes. Discipline was strict, even severe. One of her pupils remembered Julie Vieusseux as 'the most elegant, dignified and graceful woman I have ever known. To see her enter and walk across a room was a lesson in deportment . . . Madame's word was law, her graceful dignity, in and out of school, holding us all in deep reverence and awe.'[34]

The Vieusseux Ladies' College fared well in the decades of prosperity following the discovery of gold in the 1850s. Within three years the college had outgrown its Victoria Parade home and in May 1860 it moved to new premises overlooking the Fitzroy Gardens on the corner of Clarendon and Albert Streets, East Melbourne. Its new home was a Georgian terrace, indistinguishable from the surrounding homes of its clientele. The capital investment in the enterprise was considerable. The only year for which the enrolment can be established accurately is 1863 when there were 103 girls, but with an average of fifty-four new enrolments in each of the next three years, this may have gone much higher. The school was large by the standards of the day, and the Vieusseuxs were obliged to erect two new classrooms and a lecture-hall (which was also used as a gymnasium) in the grounds. The entire school moved to Brighton in order to facilitate a complete overhaul of the premises, returning a year later in 1872. This prosperity, at a time when Geelong Grammar School and St Patrick's College had both collapsed financially amidst public scandal, prompted the Rev. Dr John Edward Bromby of Melbourne Grammar School to note in his diary:

Mr Vieusseux notwithstanding his French name is a Yorkshireman, and looks it. His profession properly is that of an engineer; but having married a lady of French Flanders has turned his name to profitable account, by producing the idea that the ladies educated at [their] Ladies' College would have the same advantages as if they had been sent to Paris. They have realized a goodly fortune.[35]

Despite the documentation on the Vieusseux Ladies' College, Julie herself remains elusive. None of her personal papers survive but the private woman is evoked by three documents among the family papers. In the summer of 1858, her eight-year-old son Lewis and his pony wandered away from the family on a picnic in the Dandenong Ranges. The first document is a letter from the chief commissioner of police describing the search and regretting his failure to find the child. The second is a semi-literate ransom note which attempts to extort money from the parents in return for the child. The third is a coroner's certificate permitting the burial of the bones of a child found in a hollow log in the vicinity two years later. When Julie gave up hope of finding the child alive she painted his portrait using his brother Edward as a model. She wrote on the flyleaf of the family bible: 'Lewis Stephen Arthur Vieusseux . . . lost 2nd January 1858.' Julie Vieusseux died in March 1878 at the age of fifty-eight while still principal of the Ladies' College. The school did not long outlive her, for in 1875 the Presbyterian Ladies' College opened half a block away in Albert Street. The drop in enrolments was immediate and catastrophic, and the Vieusseux Ladies' College closed in 1882.

The ladies' school and women's work

One of the few studies of the many nineteenth-century Sydney ladies' schools is Noeline Kyle's account of Mary Ann Flower's Sydney Ladies' College which existed from 1854 until 1888 when she sold it to Anne and Mary Hales, daughters of the Archdeacon of Tasmania. Canvassing the familiar problems of evidence and interpretation, Kyle posed the question: What do we do with 'herstory' when we find it?[36] It is apparent from the work of Elizabeth Windschuttle and Noeline Kyle in New South Wales, Gerald Noble in Tasmania, Helen Jones in South Australia, and Noreen Riordan in Western Australia that there existed in the nineteenth century long-forgotten private schools which did in their own way for middle-class daughters what Scotch College, St Peter's and Shore did for middle-class sons.[37] Though the ladies' schools were not part of a formal system, they were systematic in their provision of the traditional accomplishments education. They were not exclusively primary, secondary or tertiary in orientation but took in pupils, either as boarders or as day girls, and made appropriate arrangements to educate them, hiring the best teachers available on a fee-for-service basis. Proprietors lived on their wits, rising and falling with their reputations and connections. They cultivated close links with the churches; indeed the Church of England entered the field of secondary education in Victoria at the end of the century by taking over existing ladies' schools. As state administrations provided only aggregate numbers of children in the private sector in the nineteenth century, a statistical profile of these schools is now beyond our reach, but they rivalled the Catholic sector in popularity with parents.[38]

The ladies' school phenomenon brings into focus a diaspora of highly educated and independent British women on the move across international boundaries at a time when migration for unaccompanied women was considered ill-advised or downright dangerous. The activities of the London-based Female Middle-Class Emigration Society, which assisted over three hundred women to migrate to Australia in the nineteenth century, focused attention upon the issue, and much of the debate was far from encouraging.[39] There was a general consensus that Australia needed servants, not educated women who declined to soil their hands. Colonial newspapers were eagle-eyed for stories of new-chum governesses who fell into the hands of shanty brothel keepers, became lost in the bush, or languished in Sydney and Melbourne awaiting replies to their advertisements. Despite these lugubrious predictions, it is clear that many middle-class women—female-headed households, women alone, and women with their husbands and children—used the female school as a means to migrate and make a new beginning in the colonies. The ladies' school is part of the hidden history of women's work. Women are often to be found, within weeks of their arrival, renting the best premises available, investing capital in the purchase and renovation of premises, importing or buying equipment, furniture and pianos, printing prospectuses, placing advertisements in the newspapers, and canvassing for patronage and pupils. This purposeful deployment of resources is also reflected in the division of family labour: typically, one sister was academically oriented, obtaining a university degree when that became a possibility; one sister specialised in music; another fulfilled the role of matron-housekeeper; while mothers were to be found in any of these roles. Younger brothers and sisters, nieces and nephews, elderly parents, even alcoholic husbands were accommodated in the female family school. Marriage was clearly no barrier to the successful lady-principal. Yet the ladies' school also provided the means to live an independent life outside the common estate of marriage. It is a measure of the subjective gains for these women that their personal histories reveal the same demographic characteristics to be found in the first generations of women graduates later in the century: they married less often; they married later; and they had fewer children than other women of their generation.[40] These intimate connections between family, school and work reveal a striking pattern of matrilineal descent, with mothers bequeathing to their daughters capital, expertise and that intangible sense of inevitability usually associated with the patrilineal reproduction of farmers, lawyers, merchants and tradesmen.

Despite these unmistakable signposts, it has gone largely unremarked that the ladies' school tradition nurtured its own form of teacher training in the nineteenth century. Victoria was the only state which legislated for registration of non-government schools and teachers in the period under discussion.[41] Over 7,000 private school teachers, of whom the majority were women, sought registration under the Teachers and Schools Registration Act 1905. It was an article of faith among the promoters of the Act that the unqualified female teacher represented the nadir of professional skill in the private schools which, in the interests of national efficiency and prosperity, the Act sought to regulate. As Ailsa Zainu'ddin has argued, the 'poor widow', who allegedly destroyed the minds of children in her desperate search for a livelihood, underpinned the government's case for the regulation of middle-class education.[42] Yet the paper work generated by the Act has left ample evidence that the women who were obliged to seek registration, sometimes after a lifetime of teaching, did not regard themselves as unqualified. As women were unlikely to be formally qualified (there were only 213 women graduates of the University of Melbourne in 1906), responses ranged from very brief to detailed resumes of professional experience over several decades, including details of informal teacher training, school prospectuses, copies of references, and, for those who went in and out of governessing, names of families and pupils.

Adamsdown Ladies' College in Alma Road, Caulfield, run by Elizabeth, Effie and Martha Bruford, emerges as one acknowledged centre of teacher training.[43] Elizabeth Bruford's life is typical of the three sisters. At the time of registration in 1906 she had twenty-six years teaching experience. In the years 1879 to 1881 she trained with her mother and older sister in their family school in England. She spent part of that time in Paris studying languages and music, and sent with her application for registration a reference which said in part: 'Lizzie Bruford écrit le Français comme une Française'. To extend the family's teaching repertoire her sister Martha went instead to Germany and names of referees from both countries remained on the Adamsdown prospectus three decades later. Elizabeth taught privately from 1882 to 1884, then began her own school. In 1889 the three sisters came to Australia, establishing Adamsdown in the following year; when it gained registration in 1906 it was one of the leading private girls' schools in Melbourne with an enrolment of over one hundred girls. Annie Westmoreland, whose own school gained registration as a kindergarten training college, was on the staff of Adamsdown from 1888 to 1902 as 'trainer of teachers and Director of the Kindergarten and Sub-primary department'.

The sisters Amy and Elizabeth Rudd, by 1906 co-principals of Strathclyde Ladies' College in Toorak, gave their place of education and teacher training as the Geelong Ladies' College.[44] Amy Rudd's application states that, in the years 1871 to 1881, she progressed from pupil-teacher to head assistant teacher, passing the matriculation examination in 1875. She included a reference from owner-principal, Mrs Jenny Fischer, which read:

> Like her sister, she is fond of her profession, and her inclination aided by thorough fitness makes her highly valuable as a teacher. She is familiar with the routine and management of a large school and has proved herself a teacher in the best sense—by making her pupils like their work and by her skill in adapting her instruction to the varying tastes of her pupils.

Amy Rudd continued to teach at the Geelong Ladies' College under its next owners, the musical McBurney family, until in 1882 she became private governess to the Millears, a pastoralist family in the Western District of Victoria. She alternated between private governessing and school teaching until the establishment of Strathclyde in 1893. Several women gave Richard Hale Budd's Educational Institute for Young Ladies as their place of teacher training. The septuagenarian principals of Ormiston Ladies' College, Anna and Elizabeth Singleton, replied tersely, 'thirty-three years' experience, privately trained'.[45]

Some proprietors of ladies' schools were explicit about their intentions to train and accredit women as governesses and teachers. Mrs Louisa Andrew of Holstein House in South Yarra ran evening classes 'for young ladies of more advanced age, [and] for those desirous of improving themselves for the purposes of tuition'.[46] Her Methodist constituency and the presence of state school scholarship holders suggests that she was catering for girls who were more open about their intentions to work for a living. Her son, Professor Henry Martyn Andrew of the University of Melbourne, acted as examiner at Holstein House. Susan Wigmore of Leigh House in Richmond, pilloried in the memoirs of her most famous pupil Dame Nellie Melba, advertised her school as a centre of teaching training and offered to prepare young women for the examinations of the Education Department.[47] While schools like Holstein House and Leigh

House were explicit about their courses for intending teachers, it is probable that the classes for external students which were held in most ladies' schools were used in that spirit by women preparing themselves as teachers and governesses. Indeed it is a central paradox in the history of female education that mastery of the accomplishments curriculum constituted professional preparation for those who sought to enter teaching, the one respectable profession open to middle-class women.

The success of the ladies' school in nineteenth-century Australia was not simply an artefact of women's ingenuity in turning to account their combined family talents and the family home. It is also part of 'herstory' that the lady-principal was implicated in the struggle over female subjectivity in ways which do not sit easily with feminist agendas in the present. Nineteenth-century polemicists, educators and parents understood that the 'externals' of learning, its geography, architecture and rituals, were important in the shaping of gender in ways which we are only just beginning to understand. The ladies' school was obliged to take as its institutional and psychological paradigm the mother and her daughters in the private sphere. The shaping of the female persona necessitated constant surveillance of all transactions within the school, and between the school and the outside world. The ultimate sin of sexual transgression was nowhere mentioned, yet, as Foucault reminds us, it was everywhere alluded to: in the timetables which accounted for every minute of the day and night; in the rules and regulations which hedged about the acts of sleeping, dressing and bathing; in the close monitoring of conversations, reading material and letter writing; in the strict segregation of day girls and boarders; in the chaperonage of males within the precincts of the school; and in the presentation of body, hair, facial expression and voice. Indisputably, many stories of life in the ladies' schools have been crafted over the generations to speak obliquely of female bodies as sexual objects: the bushranger attack at Ellinthorp Hall; Nellie Melba's cold showers taken under an umbrella; the parachutist *en déshabillé* on the roof of Ormiston Ladies' College.[48]

In the makeshift and footloose society of nineteenth-century Australia, it may be that the lady-principal was the guardian of an ordered family life which had been put on hold—or even that she was the precursor, not the imitator, of a form of total mothering which was still emerging. In either case, she was an anomalous figure, enjoying a special dispensation in a society which frowned upon women in paid employment yet insisted that women must be the educators of women. Her school must be seen to be her home; within the familial boundaries of space and authority she was still the accomplished woman presiding over the private sphere. Unlike the professional spinster headmistress who succeeded her, she was lady-teacher, mother, daughter, wife or widow. She stood as a symbol of moral certainty in a patriarchal order, a reassuring intermediary in the encounter between knowledge and the female mind.

The shaping of female subjectivity demanded a congruence between ideology and architecture. While the owner-proprietor might lease, purchase or build handsome premises, the school must be indistinguishable from the domestic architecture of its clientele, surrounded by acres of garden and high walls. There are many surviving examples of purpose-built female schools. Mrs Elizabeth Fleck's bluestone Campaspe Villa, built by her architect husband in the 1850s, still stands in Wedge Street, Kyneton.[49] As late as 1889 Eliza Bromby re-housed Ruyton in purpose-built premises on the corner of a'Beckett and Barry Streets, Kew. The timing of events suggests that her father financed the initial stages of the ambitious two-storey mansion and that Eliza finished the house with her inheritance after he died in that year. One purpose-built ladies' school which did not survive was Miss Bennett's Kyneton Academy. Miss Bennett herself has defied the most determined efforts to establish her identity, but the school was described in some detail by the *Kyneton Observer* when it fell victim to an incendiary at the end of 1862. The midnight spectacle of the girls and the governesses, 'some of them half-dressed and others escaping in their bare feet', made good copy. 'It was', the report concluded, 'a splendid pile of buildings, which was an architectural ornament to an isolated corner of the town, and in which flourished one of the best of those local institutions of which Kyneton is so justly proud':

> The Kyneton Seminary was a large, two-storey wooden building of elegant construction, and fitted up in first class style for lady boarders. Miss Bennett also had recently, at considerable expense, got baths erected, and otherwise improved the premises ... Miss Bennett is herself a heavy loser, as her property was only covered by insurance to the extent of £600, though it was worth far more than that.[50]

Though four pianos and a large quantity of valuable furniture were saved from the downstairs rooms, many of the governesses were left virtually destitute, and their selflessness in rescuing the younger girls from the burning building prompted the people of Kyneton to raise money on their behalf.

Congruence with the private sphere also shaped the ways in which the lady-principal solicited her clientele, obliging her to speak the language of a social peer who was 'at home' to the daughters of her friends. Newspaper advertisements displayed considerable ingenuity in reconciling the sanctity of the private sphere with the intent to turn a profit. A typical school advertisement read:

A lady, who has received a highly-finished English and Continental education, accustomed to tuition, will receive a limited number of young ladies as Resident Pupils. She will be assisted by her only daughter, who is a superior musician and thoroughly educated, a German governess, and visiting masters. The education is strictly private, and terms moderate. The residence, having a shower and plunge bath, is surrounded by a garden, and pleasantly situated.[51]

On St Valentine's Day 1900 Mrs Appleyard of Appleyard College did what no lady-principal could afford to do: she lost two of her girls and one of her governesses on a picnic at the spectacular volcanic outcrop known as Hanging Rock. Miss Greta McCraw, Marion Quade and Miranda, the 'Botticelli angel', were never found. The college mystery was front page news, 'embellished with the wildest flights of imagination, public and private'. Girls were withdrawn *en masse*; Mrs Appleyard began to drink heavily. Drawn by some mysterious force she too was compelled to climb the Hanging Rock where she threw herself over the precipice, bouncing and rolling from rock to rock, 'until at last the head in the brown hat was impaled upon a jutting crag'. Appleyard College was consumed by bushfires in the following summer.

It was perhaps a reasonable assumption that the fictional Appleyard College was modelled upon Clyde Girls' School at Macedon near the Hanging Rock, especially as Joan Lindsay herself attended the school from 1911 to 1914.[52] It is then a short step to the conclusion that the ritual slaying of Mrs Appleyard in the novel was the revenge of the schoolgirl Joan upon her own headmistress, Isabella Thomson Henderson, of Clyde. As Sarah Frith has argued, fact and fiction in *Picnic at Hanging Rock* are hard to disentangle.[53] Clyde Girls' School was still in St Kilda when Joan Lindsay attended it and did not move to Macedon until 1919; her intimate knowledge of the Macedon area came from holidays spent there with her family who make their appearance in the novel as the Fitzhuberts. She did not despise her own headmistress; on the contrary, in 1964, she agreed to write the preface to Olga Hay's history of Clyde, acknowledging Henderson's part in her own development as a writer.[54] Clyde Girls' School did not rise and fall with some real-life incarnation of Mrs Appleyard: its links go back through Oberwyl and Faireleight to Elizabeth Macarthur's school in 1838, and forward to the present co-educational Geelong Grammar School at Corio. Isabella Henderson did not self-destruct by throwing herself from the Hanging Rock. On the contrary, her career marks the emergence of women into the arena of public policy in the Edwardian era.[55] She was appointed to the Registration Board which in 1906 oversaw the registration of non-government teachers and schools, including her own. She was a founding member of the Incorporated Association of

Registered Teachers of Victoria, the University of Melbourne Schools Board, the Free Kindergarten Union of Victoria, and the Headmistresses' Association which welded the heads of the Edwardian ladies' schools into a powerful and cohesive group. Miss Henderson and her school were survivors. Any account of the reform of women's education in the latter part of the nineteenth century must encompass that remarkable fact.

CHAPTER THREE

The Keystone of the Arch? Women and the Universities in Colonial Australia

In December 1883 Bella Guerin received the 255th degree of Bachelor of Arts awarded by the University of Melbourne and became the first woman to receive a degree from an Australian university.[1] She was twenty-five years old, Catholic and the daughter of the Chief Warder of the Ballarat Gaol. Guerin lived out the worst fears of the opponents of higher education for women. Though she earned only a meagre living by teaching, she was an independent woman. She married twice, briefly and unconventionally, and bore only one child. In the thick of the women's suffrage movement, she was an orator on the Yarra bank, an outspoken anti-conscriptionist during World War I and, by the end of her life, a socialist. Needless to say, she did not become an icon of Catholic womanhood.

Bella Guerin was followed in 1885 by Edith Emily Dornwell of the University of Adelaide, whom we have already met. Later in the same year Guerin and Dornwell were joined by two female graduates in arts from the University of Sydney, Isola Florence Thompson, daughter of a public school teacher, and Mary Elizabeth Brown, whose father was a Methodist clergyman.[2] Isola Thompson, who did not marry, made her career in teaching at the Sydney Girls' High School where her progression to the headship was blocked by the remarkable Mrs Lucy Garvin. Mary Brown was appointed to the Brisbane Girls' Grammar School after her graduation. There had been a friendly inter-colonial rivalry to produce Australia's first female graduate and all four women were briefly the toast of their capital cities, the novelty of women in mortar boards deflecting attention away from their symbolic significance in the emancipation of women. Their admission to this bastion of male intellectual supremacy preceded the far more acrimonious battle for women's political rights which emerged in Australia in the mid-1880s.

The admission of women to colonial universities

Local circumstances ensured that Australian women had an easier path into the universities than women in Britain. Colonial universities were state-funded and therefore vulnerable to the demands of classical liberalism for equity and fair play; they were secular, leaving them free of the clerical influence which kept women out of the Oxbridge colleges; and they were unencumbered by the traditions of centuries. This was the view of Cambridge-educated Emily Hensley of the Trinity Women's Hostel when she spoke at the opening of her new premises in 1891:

> As regards actual university privileges . . . the women of Australia are far more highly favoured than were the women of England when their colleges were established. Here the battle has been fought and won already. Women are treated most liberally and are admitted to all the same corporate privileges as the men in the Melbourne University, except that they have not seats and votes in the senate.

This favoured treatment she saw as a happy consequence of 'what is not always a subject for congratulations, viz., the absence of traditions and their binding influence'.[3]

If there were women in the audience who had entertained ambitions to university education in the 1870s, Emily Hensley's retrospect would have been tinged with irony. The University of Melbourne precipitated the only sustained campaign for the admission of women to Australian universities when in 1871 it borrowed from recent English practice to open its matriculation examination to women.[4] The decision was by no means a radical reappraisal of women's right to higher education. It was based upon the conservative view that the private ladies' schools of Melbourne should have some standard by which they could demonstrate the worth of the education they offered. Many girls' schools took up the challenge and by 1875, the year in which the Presbyterian Ladies' College opened its doors, over one hundred females had passed the matriculation examination.[5] Even the conservative *Argus* applauded the decision to admit women, unsettled by the rumour that the University of Sydney planned to admit women to its public examinations.[6]

To the people of Melbourne at the beginning of the 1870s the idea of a young woman attending the university would have seemed outlandish. The struggling institution in Parkville was cut off geographically and spiritually from the mainstream of life in the brash, bustling city one mile to the south. Transport was difficult, even for the male undergraduates, most of whom made the journey on foot or in horse-drawn vehicles. Bicycles became popular only from the 1880s onwards. From its inception the university had been shaped by the classical vision of its founding chancellor, Irish lawyer and judge of the Supreme Court Redmond (later Sir Redmond) Barry. One biographer suggests that, from his arrival in the colony, Barry had 'pitted all his strength' against the values of the get-rich-quick democracy which provided his university with its annual grant of £9,000.[7] Though he was a generous, hardworking and public-spirited man who was not above rolling up his sleeves to dig in the garden at the university, Barry came along somewhat behind the intellectual ferment of his time. As the new university was secular and non-collegiate, it could not replicate his *alma mater*, Trinity College, Dublin, on colonial soil. But it must be dedicated to creating a ruling class of the intellect and it must be 'founded on the rock of the classics'. Though the classics were leavened by natural science, history, literature and political science, 80 per cent of the 620 undergraduates who had enrolled by the mid-1870s had not completed degrees and the average number of graduates in the years 1867–74 was eleven. Redmond Barry's determination to keep women out of his imposing quadrangle, his lecture rooms and his well-tended gardens was exceeded only by the indifference of Melburnians to the university itself.

The stage was set for a ten year wrangle over the admission of women when in 1871 25-year-old Mary Creed passed the matriculation examination and attempted to matriculate, that is, to enrol at the university itself. In October 1871 the University Council responded with the motion that:

1. In the opinion of this Council the Act incorporating the University, and the Statutes do not authorize the matriculation of females.
2. In the opinion of this Council females may be admitted to the matriculation examinations, although such females are precluded from Matriculation.[8]

Only the Vice-Chancellor, Sir Anthony Brownless, opposed the motion and his sixteen-year-old daughter Maria entered for the examination from Mrs Philippa James' Grantown House Ladies' School the following July. Under the sway of the conservatives Redmond Barry, George Rusden and Bishop Charles Perry, this remained the position of the Council until 1881.

Throughout the 1870s the issue was kept alive by a small band of men inside and outside the university, most of whom had daughters or sisters who eventually entered higher education.[9] The campaign began in October 1871 when the Rev. Dr John Edward Bromby noted in his diary his intention to support Mary Creed when she applied to sign the matriculation roll in order to proceed to an arts degree.[10] Bromby had personally coached Creed for her matriculation examinations and three

A WOMAN'S REASON.

Ladies (who have passed matriculation examination).—"PRAY, SIR REDMOND, *WHY* ARE WE NOT TO BE ADMITTED?"

Sir Redmond.—"ASK ME NOT WHY, LADIES. WE HAVE NO REASON. WE WON'T ADMIT YOU BECAUSE——BECAUSE——WE WON'T——THERE."

Melbourne Punch, 14 December 1871 on the (non) admission of women to the University of Melbourne.

of his daughters, Eliza, Constance and Jenny, sat successfully in the next two years. As they were all adults and already established teachers, their conspicuous presence at the examinations in the Melbourne Town Hall has about it the air of a planned campaign. Women's right to a university education was not the only issue upon which he was prepared to defy his bishop, Charles Perry, for he had spoken from the public platform expressing his belief that Darwin's theory of the origin of species could be reconciled with religious belief. He later lent his name to the cause of women's suffrage. With his liberal views, limited income and five daughters he was in many ways typical of the men who underwrote the right of women to a university education. Throughout the 1870s he made strategic use of the University Senate or, more specifically, reports of its doings in the public press, to embarrass the Council on the issue of women's admission to degrees. Indeed the women's cause fell victim to the adversarial tripartite system of university government—council, senate and professorial board—as much as to outright misogyny on the part of the majority of the players.

In 1875 an attempt was made to break the stalemate by shifting the campaign to the Victorian Parliament. In that year John Gavan Duffy, son of Charles Gavan Duffy and a recent law graduate, moved a private member's bill in the Assembly to remove any legal impediment to the admission of women. His sister Harriet passed the matriculation examination in the same year. The bill lapsed in the grotesquely undemocratic Legislative Council, a fate which awaited many women's suffrage bills in the coming decades.

In the same year a new platform was erected from which to prosecute the cause of women's higher education. In 1875 the Presbyterians established their 'Ladies' College in connection with the Presbyterian Church of Victoria' and appointed Charles Pearson as its founding headmaster. This appointment transformed Pearson into a powerful and eloquent advocate for the women at a time when the campaign was running into the sands of disillusionment. Pearson was one of the most distinguished academics ever to be appointed head of an Australian secondary school. He had narrowly missed appointment as professor of modern history at Oxford and he had taught at King's College, London, and at Cambridge. The year 1874 found him teaching at the University of Melbourne where the low salary, uncertain tenure and lack of academic freedom contributed to his decision to accept the headmastership of the Ladies' College.

Pearson, more than anyone else in Australia, understood the nature of the movement for the higher education of women in England. He was at King's College when Christian socialist F. D. Maurice and his colleagues established Queen's College for women, an event which is seen as a catalyst for the movement for the higher education of women. He had lectured in the university-affiliated 'lectures to ladies' which were sweeping England in the 1860s and, as a colleague of Henry and Eleanor Sidgwick in Cambridge, he had witnessed the birth of Newnham College, which grew out of the Cambridge lectures to ladies program. He could scarcely have overlooked the ideological feud which developed from the beginning between Emily Davies of Girton and Anne Clough of Newnham over the 'same or different' issue in women's higher education. In June 1874 he wrote to the *Age* describing the reform of women's education in England, his own contribution to it and his faith in the ability of women to profit by university education.[11] In the same year that Pearson became headmaster of Presbyterian Ladies' College he was elected to the University Council. There he joined a growing band of reform-minded members who were dubbed by the old guard the 'school master element'.

In 1877 Pearson was dismissed from Presbyterian Ladies' College, after squatters withdrew their daughters in protest at his public espousal of a progressive land tax on their estates. He did not abandon the women's cause, for his next attempt to achieve their admission to the university came as chairman of a royal commission into public education, an appointment widely viewed as a pay-off for his support of the Berry government on the land tax issue. He produced his report in 1877. Pearson was typical of the university reformers of his day, both in Britain and Australia, in that he coupled the admission of women with the modernisation of the curriculum (recommending in his report the creation of a 'faculty of engineering and practical science') and the democratisation of the student body (in this case, the abolition of fees for lectures).[12] Yet the terms under which he proposed that women should be admitted are ambiguous. In the draft bill appended to the report he stipulated that only when twenty women presented themselves for any course should the university be obliged to 'provide means for the delivery of such lectures to such female students therein'. Given Pearson's sympathies, the clause is open to the interpretation that women could present themselves for examination without attending lectures.[13] How the unrepentant University Council would have responded is academic, for Pearson's wide ranging and ambitious report was not acted upon.

In 1879 Charles Pearson's successor at Presbyterian Ladies' College, Andrew Harper, kept alive the hopes of women to enter the University of Melbourne by the simple expedient of presenting successful matriculation candidates to sign the roll. The final skirmishes took place in the Council between October 1879 and April 1880.[14] Even so, the women had to await the passing of the University Constitution

Amendment Act in April 1881, and this withheld from them the right to sit in the University Senate (and therefore to vote in council elections) and the right to study medicine.

Though the University of Sydney also kept women out for a further ten years after it admitted them to the junior and senior public examinations in 1871, there was little public conflict over the issue in the 1870s.[15] In 1871 42-year-old Anne Jane Bolton won the Fairfax Prize of the University of Sydney for the best female candidate in the Senior Public examination. Unlike Mary Creed, Bolton did not force the issue by attempting to matriculate, although the fact that she later went to New Zealand to do a Bachelor of Arts at Canterbury University suggests that she may have been privately warned off. One of the more controversial of the early Australian graduates, Bolton eventually returned to Melbourne where she studied art with Louis Buvelot and became a painter. Anne Bolton brings into focus a network of powerful people who eventually sponsored women at the University of Sydney. She was the sister of Lady Mary Windeyer, an indefatigable worker for women's rights and later president of the Womanhood Suffrage League of New South Wales. Mary was the wife of Sir William Charles Windeyer, liberal minded politician and judge whose labours on behalf of women included the Married Women's Property Act of 1879, advocacy of state high schools for girls, a compassionate administration of the divorce laws, the founding chairmanship of Sydney Women's College and the legal defence of Annie Besant's publication on contraception, *The Law of Population*.[16] It was not until 1877 that Mary Kemmis of Bathurst made an unsuccessful attempt to enrol at the University of Sydney and it can hardly be coincidental that her mentor was William Windeyer. He became chancellor of the University of Sydney in 1895.

Sir William Manning, chancellor of the university and judge of the Supreme Court, was also well disposed towards the admission of women by 1878, for he canvassed the idea in his Commemoration address in that year. He was rebuked by the *Sydney Morning Herald* for his suggestion that the university would consider the proposition only when there was sufficient demand.[17] By March 1881, and with the University of Melbourne on the brink of admitting women, Manning had firmed up his commitment, which he expressed in terms of classical liberalism:

> I came, with others, to the final conclusion that the right course was to settle and declare the principle of women's rights to equality within the University, and that it would be better to open its portals at once, so that the sex might plainly see their way to enter whenever they should be disposed to climb up to it by the necessary paths of preparation,—rather than that the Senate should wait till they come to our gates knocking for admission.[18]

The recommendation admitting women was passed by the Senate in May 1881 and confirmed when the University Extension Bill received royal assent in May 1884.[19] Like its Melbourne rival, the University of Sydney had stagnated since its establishment in 1851. When women were admitted it was still poorly attended, seriously under-funded (there were no well-kept gardens), overly concerned with the classics and socially exclusive. If there was a Redmond Barry figure at the University of Sydney it was the Professor of Classics, Rev. Charles Badham. Though he ultimately supported the admission of women, Badham believed that 'the more steadily the University adheres to the traditional functions of a University, by making classical study the instrument of culture, the more fully will it answer the purpose for which the people instituted and endowed it'.[20] His daughter Edith was still cleaving to these views when she became founding headmistress of Sydney Church of England Girls' Grammar School in 1895.

When women entered the University of Sydney the Faculty of Arts was the only one in existence and, although the university was legally empowered to grant degrees in arts, law and medicine, women preceded medical degrees on to the campus. The practical outcome of Badham's policies was an enrolment of fewer than seventy students in the mid-seventies. Only after Badham's death in 1884 was Sir William Manning able to expand the curriculum and in this he was greatly assisted by the Challis and Fisher bequests. A separate faculty of science was established in 1882, the complete medical course in 1883, a chair of law in 1890 and, throughout the decade, the offerings in arts were steadily expanded. By 1893 the *Sydney Mail* could claim with some truth that:

> The [university] is one of the most progressive and expansive institutions of which the colony can boast. It has extended the range of its operations; it has widened the field of its teaching, instead of holding itself high and dry upon the heights of classics and mathematics; it has established chairs of modern literature, philosophy, and history and called into existence schools of medicine, engineering, and mining; it has brought itself into touch with the people by means of its evening and university extension classes, and has opened new careers for the young women of the colony.[21]

The circumstances surrounding the admission of women to the University of Adelaide are different again.[22] The Act of Incorporation in 1874 included the words 'open to all classes and denominations of Her Majesty's subjects', a generic form of language which women often found was not intended to include them. In this case, however, and without any public debate, the founders did intend the words to include women.

This is all the more remarkable as there were at that time no British or Australian precedents. The problem encountered lay not with the men who established the University of Adelaide—John Hartley, Allan Campbell, Samuel Way and George Hawker all believed in the right of women to higher education—but with those charged with steering its charter through to royal assent in England. The Adelaide men were rebuked not only because they intended to admit women but because they were determined to grant degrees in science. In February 1875 the Governor of South Australia received a dispatch in which Her Majesty's Principal Private Secretary for the Colonies warned of the fate likely to befall any petition for science degrees or degrees for women. Although the London *Times* ignored the proposal to admit women, it was inclined to make merry with the notion of science degrees:

> A bachelor . . . of science would [in its opinion] be like one of those insignificant dignitaries in the Society of Odd fellows or Foresters. How far his titled and jewelled badges were genuine or fictitious must be a puzzle which none but a South Australian would put himself to the pain of guessing.[23]

The proposal to include science degrees gives some insight into the character of the university which the Adelaide founders hoped to establish, for they looked to the radical newcomer, the University of London, rather than to Oxford and Cambridge. In order to gain the Royal Charter to its Act of Incorporation, the University of Adelaide had to remove the offending clauses concerning science and women. Despite this heavy disapproval from Westminster, women were present as unofficial students from the first day of lectures in 1876, when the university began in temporary premises in the Teachers Training College. Among the fifty-two students were thirty-three women, though they were non-matriculated and therefore not eligible to proceed to degrees. Chancellor Bishop Short welcomed them in his annual report of 1876:

> It is a gratifying sign of the times that so large a number [of women] . . . attended some of the university classes during the first year of its operation, for it is certain that high mental culture on their part *must react on the other sex*, and give a powerful impetus to self-education, and the acquirement of literacy as well as social knowledge. It is hoped that ladies will become matriculated students, and compete for degrees and scholarships.[24]

As in Melbourne and Sydney it may be that the founders were not entirely altruistic for, as late as 1882, the *Advertiser* noted that the great want of the university was more students. Whatever the motivation, the University of Adelaide honourably returned to the attack in 1878 when the Registrar was instructed to raise the matter again with Westminster, pointing out that in the meantime the University of London had provided a precedent for the admission of women to degrees. In 1880 the Colonial Secretary relented, writing that 'having regard to the strong feeling entertained in the Colony' her Majesty would be advised to assent. The Letters Patent were granted on 22 March 1881 admitting women to degrees at the University of Adelaide and four years later Edith Dornwell graduated as the first woman and the first science graduate. In 1894 South Australia became the first Australian colony to grant women the vote.

The first generation of university women: sex and politics

The politics of women's admission to the three colonial universities are notable for two closely related phenomena: the widespread support from men—the Melbourne renegades were a laughing stock by the late 1870s—and the reticence of women to prosecute their own case as they did in England. The historiography of women's higher education in England is still grounded in the celebration of female militancy.[25] Emily Davies orchestrated the admission of girls to the Oxford and Cambridge local examinations in the 1860s, a reform appropriated by the University of Melbourne for its own more conservative purposes in 1871. Thereafter Davies' restless ambition for women centred on her more controversial scheme to establish Girton College in Cambridge. Dorothea Beale of Cheltenham Ladies' College and Frances Buss of the North London Collegiate School are credited with inventing a new form of academic high school for girls. The sisters Emily Shirreff and Maria Grey founded the Girls' Public Day School Trust which rapidly established academic high schools on the corporate model throughout England. Women like Elizabeth Garrett Anderson and Sophia Jex-Blake fought bitter and protracted campaigns for the right to medical training and practice. Yet institutional barriers to women's higher education were dismantled in Australia virtually without the organised intervention of women.

In 1979 Joyce Senders Pedersen warned that a preoccupation with the feminist vanguard can obscure understanding of the wider context in which the reforms which they sponsored took place.[26] The English women, she suggested, would have had little chance of success had they not had the backing of powerful men who looked to a different form of education for their daughters in the changed circumstances of mid and later Victorian England. Certainly, the robust strain of colonial liberalism which Stuart Macintyre has explored in the Australian context had no difficulty encompassing the right of women to higher education. His protagonists, Charles Pearson, George Higinbotham and David Syme, all

Edith Dornwell, first woman graduate of the University of Adelaide, 1885.
(Barr Smith Library, University of Adelaide)

supported the entry of women to the University of Melbourne and they had their counterparts in New South Wales and South Australia.[27] The striking feature of the movement is the omnipresence of men from the 'new classes', that substratum of the middle classes inhabited by the intelligentsia—professionals, university men, clergymen, the upper echelons of the public service and, increasingly, school teachers—who rose to power without benefit of capital in the generally accepted sense of the word. They accumulated what Pierre Bourdieu called 'cultural capital' within social arrangements which were increasingly disengaged from inherited power and privilege, coalescing instead around impersonal, meritocratic institutional structures. Lacking traditional forms of wealth they were anxious to hand on this new form of capital to their daughters as well as their sons. Of the seven women who petitioned for entry to the Melbourne medical course in 1886, Lilian Alexander was the daughter of the proprietor of Lawn House ladies' school; Anna Higgins was the sister of politician and judge Henry Bournes Higgins; Margaret Whyte was the daughter of Paddy and Ellen Whyte, Melbourne's 'first family' of state school teachers; Annie and Elizabeth O'Hara were the daughters of school teachers; and Grace Vale was the daughter of a politician. Alison Mackinnon's demographic study of the first 200 female graduates of the University of Adelaide also found 'intellectual workers' to be disproportionately represented among the fathers of the students.[28] By the 1880s the right of women to a dignified independence before marriage was no longer contested; indeed the swelling discourse on marriage, triggered by the Married Women's Property Acts in England and Australia, had produced some agreement that women should marry only if they chose. That the same class of men who facilitated the entry of women to university could not carry the day as easily with female suffrage underlines the reality that votes for all women constituted a challenge to men's control of the public sphere whereas arts degrees for a few women did not.

Historians have been ingenious in their search for the meanings of education for these first generations of university women. Studies of their subsequent demographic characteristics began early, as women's colleges in particular had an urgent need to counter the belief that university education was unnatural for women and would render them unmarriageable, even sterile. Eleanor Sidgwick published *Health Statistics of Women Students of Cambridge and Oxford and Their Sisters* in 1890.[29] Barbara Solomon draws on several of these early studies in her study of college-educated women in the United States.[30] According to Farley Kelly, there was a medical investigation of children born to Melbourne's first female graduates but it was never published and she was unable to track it down.[31] The myth concerning the sterility of university-educated women was easy to debunk but there was no getting round the fact that, when compared with their cohort, the first generation in Britain, North America and Australia married less often, married later and had fewer children when they did marry.[32] These early studies did not mention the prevalence of long-term same-sex relationships between university-educated women.

Alison Mackinnon's study of the first 200 Adelaide female graduates comes to the same demographic conclusions, although her study bears the stamp of a different age. She argues that historians who castigate the early graduates for their timidity have been looking in the wrong places and that these demographic characteristics should be interpreted as radical outcomes of university education for women. Mackinnon's work mounts a challenge to historians like Jill Kerr Conway who in the 1970s shattered the cosy consensus that the experience of co-educational universities had been beneficial for women. Conway argued that, in these institutions, women's sense of themselves as intellectual beings was distorted to the extent that they failed to mount a critique of women's place in society.[33] She castigates the pioneer women graduates for developing what she terms the pseudo-professions based on women's traditional work in philanthropy and domestic economy. This argument has more cogency in the context of North America where, unlike Britain and Australia, faculties of domestic economy were established, both nurturing and confining generations of female science graduates in the twentieth century. To the extent that American women were radicalised, Conway argues, they were radicalised by the great social movements such as the anti-slavery movement in the nineteenth century and the civil rights movement in the twentieth century. Since the early 1970s, Conway's thesis of intellectual sabotage has been elaborated by feminist theorists like Dorothy Smith, Carol Gilligan, Mary Field Belenky and others.[34] They argue in different ways that women's access to dominant modes of discourse such as those practised in academia has placed male heads on female shoulders, an ironic twist to the position espoused by conservative opponents of women's admission to the universities in the first place.

As Conway's concern indicates, another focus of historiography in the area has been the career choices of the early graduates. Farley Kelly writes that, in 1906 when the University of Melbourne celebrated its golden Jubilee, 213 women had graduated: 160 in arts, thirty-nine in medicine, eleven in science, two in law and one in music, a tally which far outstripped both Sydney and Adelaide. In the following year, Bessie Wingrove, by then teaching at her old school Ruyton, and Kate Flynn, a teacher in the state service, took out the Diploma in Education, and Fannie Gray became the first female Bachelor of Dental Science. As to the destination of the arts and science graduates Kelly has no doubt, for she writes that 'the history of women's higher education is educational history in a double sense'.[35] Nearly 70 per cent of these women became secondary teachers, an immeasurable advantage to the girls at school, but hardly a radical outcome of the new educational opportunities for the women themselves. Even at the turn of the century, science was still a shy newcomer in Australian universities and it did not yet offer rich pickings as a career for men or women.[36] The graduates in arts and science reshaped a traditional female profession, pushing their less qualified sisters down the ladder, especially in Victoria after the Teachers and Schools Registration Act of 1905 mandated a degree and diploma of education for secondary teaching. Many Melbourne women—among them Emily Edeson, Helen White, Frances Stretch, Sarah Eyres, Isobel Macdonald, Nancy Jobson and Minnie Hunt—became headmistresses of prestigious girls' schools interstate. A surprising number of graduates went back into small, privately owned girls' schools, at least thirty of them as owner-principals. Constance Tisdall's family-owned school, Rosbercon, remained true to its charter as a 'progressive' institution for three decades; Mary Morris and her family bought Merton Hall from Emily Hensley in 1898; Katie Tait and Mary Brady bought Hohenlohe College in Warrnambool; Elizabeth and Ellen Whyte followed a long family tradition of teaching when they purchased Sydenham Ladies' College in Moonee Ponds. A small number of hardy souls obtained their degrees part-time while working as elementary school teachers in the state service. Christina Montgomery rose through the system from pupil-teacher to become head of MacRobertson Girls' High School in 1922, although she resigned before the school moved to the present premises and took on the name of its benefactor, Sir Macpherson Robertson.[37] The sisters Kate and Julia Flynn came via the same punishing regime, Kate to become founding headmistress of Canterbury Girls' High School and Julia, more controversially, chief inspector of secondary schools.[38] Unlike the Sydney women, graduate women in Victoria were slow to enter the service of the state, even when the new state secondary system began to expand in the Edwardian era. Though there have been no systematic studies of the career destinations of the Adelaide and Sydney graduates there is convincing anecdotal evidence that the preference for secondary teaching was just as marked.

Too old to take advantage of the new educational opportunities, nineteenth-century South Australian writer and feminist, Catherine Helen Spence, recorded her disappointment in the contribution of the first generations of university-educated women. She made one exception to what she termed 'the aloofness of people with degrees and professions from the preventible evils of the world'. The women doctors, she believed, had 'a keen sense of their responsibility to the less fortunate'.[39] Whatever the shortcomings of the teaching women as radical innovators, the same charge cannot be laid against the medical women. As Farley Kelly observes, there could be no pretence that they were preparing themselves to be better wives and mothers, or filling in the time between school and marriage by teaching.[40] They broke new ground against fierce opposition from a misogynist profession which lagged behind growing community concern that women would not seek medical treatment unless they could be treated by women. While in Adelaide and Sydney women were admitted to medical degrees from the outset, in Melbourne the last ditch attempt to keep them out prompted the only documented case of a campaign for admission led by women. The horror with which diehard opponents regarded the suggestion that women enter the medical profession is encapsulated in the speech of Solicitor-General Townsend McDermott when he opposed the amendment to the University Act before parliament in 1875:

> The admission of women to University degrees implies their subsequent admission into the learned professions and in particular to the medical profession. I ask honourable members with sisters to picture to themselves a modest woman . . . having, in an open dissecting room to dissect the body of a dead man. Fancy the degradation the sex must be exposed to in passing through so abominable a scene . . . I believe only the lowest and most degraded of the other sex would ever expose themselves to it.[41]

Yet there were such women to be found, for in January 1887 Helen Sexton and Lilian Alexander, the latter already a graduate in Arts and teaching at Ruyton, wrote to the *Age* asking other women interested in pursuing a career in medicine to contact them. Six women replied and, remarkably, all but one stayed the gruelling course to become Victoria's first female doctors, Clara Stone and Margaret Whyte graduating first in 1891. The women and their families proved to be astute lobbyists, for a compromise was reached in time for them to enrol in the general first year of medicine in 1887. Ahead loomed the infinitely more controversial matters of specialist lectures, dissection and hospital practice. The University of Melbourne itself came down on the side of medical co-education on the grounds of cost and practicality, though the Dean of Medicine, H.B. Allen, agreed that this would not be 'to the complete satisfaction of conventional notions of decency'.[42] Lecturer in surgery, T.M. Girdlestone, protested that it was not practicable to teach certain sections of the surgical course to mixed classes—by this he meant venereal diseases, diseases of the bladder, and diseases of the male and female genitalia—and that 'ladies would require separate instruction in the surgical operations on the dead body, as well as . . . in the wards of the hospital'.[43] Surprisingly, given their willingness to defy convention, the women students agreed with Dr Girdlestone and from 1887 until 1895 an uneasy compromise existed while the women attended the same lectures but dissected in a separate room adjoining the pathology laboratory. In 1895 Professor Allen put his foot down and required the women to dissect in a corner of the laboratory.[44] Initially, Council had resolved that the women should also have a separate hospital but the Alfred Hospital refused to comply and hospital practice remained a source of bitter conflict between the medical women and the authorities until well into the twentieth century. The prestigious Melbourne Hospital was particularly resistant to admitting the women as residents even when their consistently good results entitled them to that privilege. The establishment of the Queen Victoria Hospital, by women for women, was a direct consequence of this discrimination, though in one sense it was a pyrrhic victory, for it allayed the fear of male doctors that women would seek to compete with them equally in all fields of medicine. The idea for the 'Queen Vic.' grew out of an outpatients' clinic established by ten women doctors in 1896 in La Trobe Street, one of the poorest parts of Melbourne. The response was overwhelming as working-class women, often with no money to pay for the service, flooded into the clinic. The movement gained momentum with the hugely supported 'shilling appeal' on the occasion of Queen Victoria's Jubilee in 1897 and the Queen Victoria Hospital opened for in-patients in 1899.

In 1884 Dagmar Berne became the first woman to enrol for medicine at the University of Sydney. When Dean of Medicine, Professor Anderson Stuart, was consulted by the Melbourne men he commented: 'I have had a lady in my classes for over two years, as gentle and modest a lady as I have ever seen, as such she came to us and as such she had remained'.[45] Yet in her history of women at the University of Sydney Ursula Bygott claims that Berne's time at the Sydney Medical School was far from happy and that for this reason she went to England to finish her training. Berne returned to Sydney to practise but died of tuberculosis at the age of thirty-four. It was not until 1893 that Iza Coghlan and Grace Fairley Robinson graduated in medicine. The Sydney medical women suffered the same hostility and discrimination in the practising hospitals as their Melbourne sisters. As late as 1905 Susie O'Reilly was refused residency by the Royal Prince Alfred Hospital, the North Shore Hospital and the Sydney Hospital. In the same year Jessie Aspinal was offered a residency by the Medical Board of the Royal Prince Alfred Hospital but the Conjoint Board decided otherwise. Both cases caused considerable public disquiet and Aspinal gained admission after intervention by the premier, while Susie O'Reilly was accepted at the Adelaide General Hospital. By that time a handful of women had graduated in medicine from the University of Adelaide, including Laura Fowler (Hope), Helen Mayo, Rosamond Benham (Taylor) and Phyllis McGlew (Cilento).[46] Only the legal profession proved to be more misogynist than the medical profession, excluding women so effectively that the history of women lawyers belongs to the twentieth century.

The political behaviour of the first generations of female graduates continues to absorb historians of women's higher education today. Yet, as Alison Mackinnon argues, their behaviour needs to be understood in the context of their times. The small band of pioneer university women made a daily journey into territory which was marked with the masculine gender. Its signposts and its contours were alien to women, who must account for their movements through public space or pay for their temerity with loss of good name. The ritual larrikinism of the undergraduates—on average, three years younger than the women—the heroic theatre of the lecture-hall and the laboratory, and the social relationships of strangers were productive of the public man, not the private woman. The humiliating chaperonage which lingered on at Oxford and Cambridge was nowhere in evidence, a measure of more relaxed colonial mores, but the women confined themselves. Only at the University of Sydney was this separation officially endorsed by the appointment of a 'tutor to the women students', but the position did not develop into the prestigious 'dean of women' as it did on North American campuses.[47] University women were aware that they carried a double burden: on the one hand to prove that they could succeed in the male intellectual domain; and on the other hand to convince even their mentors that they could remain 'true women'. Whether we interpret this as an onerous burden of 'double conformity', a phrase coined by historian Sara Delamont to account for the apparent timidity of the first generations, or as productive of new and resilient ways of being a woman is, as we have seen, still a matter of debate.[48]

On the photographic evidence the early female students veiled their sexuality beneath modest attire, usually long dark skirts and white blouses, although more elaborate dresses can be glimpsed under robes in graduation photos. They sat together in the front row of the lecture theatre and they withdrew in the interstices of time to spaces which had been designated female. Towards the end of her life Constance Tisdall could still recall vividly her first day at the University of Melbourne in 1898. Educated in her parents' state schools, she scrambled through 'matric' with the aid of her family and tutors, arriving at the university ill-prepared to cope with the compulsory subjects of mathematics, Latin and Greek. Anxious to arrive on time for her first lecture she set out on her five mile bicycle ride too early and arrived at the university at eight o'clock. Further embarrassment followed. As nine o'clock approached she was unable to find her lecture room and arrived late. The tall and dignified professor of classics, T.G. Tucker, was about to begin his lecture, and motioned her to join the handful of young women seated in the front row. Above them rose tier after tier of male undergraduates. 'The tramp, tramp, tramp, of heavy boots' kept time to her timid footsteps as she made her way across the room where she sat down and hid her flaming face in a notebook. 'The rest of that hour has faded [she recalled] but the emotional experience will remain with me till I die.'[49] At lunch time she was rescued by another female student while trying to find somewhere to eat and taken upstairs from the quadrangle to the women's clubrooms above the lecture rooms of law professor, Harrison Moore. Here she 'put in her time as best [she] could' until five o'clock when she found her way to Trinity College which had awarded her a scholarship to attend lectures.

From 1888 until 1915 the Princess Ida Club which recruited Tisdall on her first day was the centre of female undergraduate life at the University of Melbourne. In Farley Kelly's words it provided undergraduates and graduates alike with a 'protected enclave, a source of enduring friendships and a sense of collective identity for the women students of the University during their first quarter century'. As Tennyson's fictional Ida had established a women's university which was off limits to men, the joke was apparent 'even to the most obtuse male undergraduates'.[50] In 1885 women at the University of Sydney were given accommodation in a temporary building originally erected as a laboratory in the south-eastern corner of the quadrangle. There is a photograph of the Women's Common Room, as it was known, sitting modestly behind the newly completed Fisher Library in 1910.[51] In 1917, with 559 female students enrolled, a new women's centre, Manning House, was built to replace the inadequate weatherboard Common Room. Adelaide's female undergraduates had only a cold and uncomfortable common room until 1917 when they were accommodated in a small cottage on the western boundary. This was replaced by the Lady Symon building in 1929.[52]

Was this separate women's culture, rejected so decisively by later generations of university women, productive of a feminist consciousness as it was at Newnham and Girton where a generation of young women were consumed by the cause of women's suffrage? Kelly concludes that the Princess Ida Club chose not to identify itself too closely with the suffrage movement, though individually the women were known to be sympathetic to the cause.[53] A suffrage petition from individual female graduates was presented to the Legislative Council in 1899 but it has disappeared without a trace. The minute books of the Princess Ida Club disappoint those in search of an emerging feminist consciousness. A few

'Princesses at Play: Professor Harrison Moore objects to the noise made by the members of the Princess Ida Club whilst he gives his lectures to the students. What sort of a man has the heart to disturb the charming Princesses in their innocent enjoyment?' *Melbourne Punch*, 1897 on the Princess Ida Club at the University of Melbourne

Princess Ida members were active in the suffrage movement outside the university; Violet Chomley and Helen Sexton were co-founders of the Women's Social and Political Reform League in 1894 and others served on various suffrage committees, among them two proprietors of girls' schools, Annie Laing and Mary Morris. As the suffrage campaign in Victoria lasted from the mid-1880s to 1909, this does not amount to organised militancy on the part of the university women. In South Australia the issue of female suffrage had been settled by 1894. Helen Jones has demolished the myth that women in general played no part in the campaign, but university-educated women scarcely had time to influence the course of events had they been inclined to do so.[54] At the University of Sydney a different pattern emerges and this brings into focus another locus of women's culture on campus, the university women's colleges.

While down-at-heel common rooms could be designated women's space in the day-to-day routine of administration, the establishment of female colleges within the university precincts involved 'due process' laid down before the question of admitting women arose. In Sydney the establishment of colleges was governed by the Colleges Endowment Act of 1854. A government grant of up to £20,000 was payable to any religious denomination which subscribed half that amount as well as £500 per annum towards the salary of the principal. Under these generous terms men's colleges were not long in appearing: St Paul's College (Church of England) in 1854; St John's College (Catholic) in 1857; and St Andrew's College (Presbyterian, and delayed by dissension within the ranks) in 1870. Wesley College (Methodist) was incorporated in 1860 but did not open until 1917.

In Melbourne the incorporation of colleges was subsumed within the original legislation of 1853 and, beyond the allocation of sites, no money was forthcoming from the public purse. Understandably, men's colleges at the University of Melbourne were longer in appearing. An order-in-council in 1866 clarified that they were indeed to be denominational colleges when it granted ten acres each around College Crescent to the Anglican, Presbyterian, Methodist and Catholic Churches. In the same order, Trinity College was established in 1872, Ormond College in 1880 (aided by a donation of £20,000 from Francis Ormond), Queen's College in 1888 and Newman College during World War I, by which time the university was considering taking back the Catholic site. Under these ground rules the possibility of an autonomous women's college was remote as, in both universities, female undergraduates were obliged to present themselves as adherents of particular denominations rather than as women. In the nineteenth century the churches could barely sustain their colleges for men let alone set aside scarce resources to accommodate their small number of female adherents in separate institutions.

In the 1880s, the three Melbourne colleges all had a small number of female students affiliated in ways which stopped short of full rights to membership and residence.[55] The obvious course of action, to combine in the provision of one interdenominational college, was aired from time to time but fell victim to the rivalries of three men increasingly powerful in university affairs: Dr Alexander Leeper of Trinity, the Rev. Edward Sugden of Queen's and John (later Sir John) MacFarland of Ormond. St Hilda's College was finally established by the Presbyterian and Methodist Churches on Queen's College land in 1964.[56]

Trinity Women's Hostel, University of Melbourne

It was the Warden of Trinity College, Alexander Leeper, who made the decision to push ahead with a college for women and the troubled beginnings of Trinity Women's Hostel (later Janet Clarke Hall) cannot be understood without some understanding of the man himself. Irish-born, Leeper was an accomplished classicist from Trinity College, Dublin, taking out his LL.D. in 1884, by which time he had been warden of the Melbourne Trinity for eight years. He was immensely talented but also dictatorial, mercurial and opinionated, characteristics which led to the 'Trinity rebellion' at the men's college in 1890, which he survived by a whisker. As the historian of Janet Clarke Hall remarks, Leeper was encumbered by 'many of the prejudices of his class, place and period'.[57] To these we cannot unequivocally add the prejudices of his sex, for he believed in the right of women to higher education and in their right to physical space within the university to pursue their studies. What he did not believe was that women could manage these matters for themselves.

In 1883, against considerable opposition, Leeper accepted Lilian Alexander as an informal student at the men's college. Fourteen more women were to follow before Leeper coaxed from his reluctant council an agreement to establish the Trinity Hostel for women in rented accommodation in Sydney Road in 1886. Leeper himself took financial responsibility for the hostel and, indeed, for many of its inmates, for he recruited students with scholarships paid from his own pocket. Yet the hostel did not flourish. Early appointments to the principalship were undistinguished and there were four in as many years. In March 1889 Leeper signed with the Trinity College Council an agreement that henceforth he had complete control over the hostel and that the principal would be his deputy.

There is little doubt that the Trinity Hostel would have failed had not Leeper, in 1888, persuaded Janet Lady Clarke, millionaire benefactor whose menfolk were already generous donors to Trinity College, to give £5,000 for the building of a permanent home for the hostel. The donation, generous as it was, should not be allowed to float free of context. It followed closely upon a scheme presented to Leeper in July 1888 by his *protégée* Lilian Alexander for an autonomous, undenominational and state-funded women's college affiliated with the University of Melbourne.[58] The absent presence in the correspondence between Lilian Alexander and Leeper was the Sydney Women's College, by then well into the planning stages along precisely the lines which Alexander now proposed. Leeper demolished the scheme with all the sophistry of an outraged father, calling upon the discourses of religion, propriety and commonsense to bolster his case. Janet Lady Clarke's benefaction, tagged securely to a Church of England hostel, followed soon after. The question of a suitable site became a matter of urgency. Leeper favoured an off-campus site on the grounds of propriety but, when the Trinity Council agreed to make available the present site in the Trinity grounds facing Royal Parade, he changed his mind.

In the white heat of battle with Lilian Alexander, Leeper had undertaken to establish a 'council of women' to govern the Trinity Hostel, with little interference 'except on very rare occasions'. In September of 1888 the Trinity Council did indeed appoint a Trinity Hostel Ladies' Council, with the more modest brief to raise funds and to 'assist in the management of the Hostel'. Its members were drawn from the powerful Church of England establishment families, clerical and lay. They included Janet Lady Clarke herself; Eliza Bromby, who in that year purchased Ruyton Ladies' School; Jessie Grimwade and Isabella a'Beckett; Charlotte MacCartney, daughter of Dean Hussey Burgh MacCartney; and Lady Mary Stawell, whose daughter Melian was resident in the hostel. In this manner Alexander Leeper captured the agenda for a women's college at the University of Melbourne. It should be noted that the status of the Ladies' Council was anomalous for, alongside its womanly duties of fundraising and housekeeping, was the power to appoint the principal of the Trinity Hostel, subject to the approval of the Warden of Trinity and the bishop. For a brief moment women had entered the closely guarded precincts of university governance by the back door.

In 1889 the Ladies' Council appointed Emily Marianne Hensley as the hostel's fourth principal. Under the terms of her bequest Janet Lady Clarke had stipulated an Oxford or Cambridge woman, and Emily Hensley was among the original five students at Newnham College,

Cambridge. That she did not take the tripos is no reflection upon her abilities, for she belonged to the period when Newnham College was still cleaving to the 'equal but different' philosophy which set it at odds with Emily Davies and Girton. Hensley was born in England in 1853 and little is known of her education until she arrived at Newnham College. She left there in 1874 and in the intervening years had accumulated 'long and valuable experience' as a governess, a teacher and a headmistress.[59] She was recruited in England by Alexander Leeper himself towards the end of 1889, though he was at pains to point out that it was the prerogative of the Ladies' Council to offer her the position. She came highly recommended by Anne Clough of Newnham College, several Cambridge dons and her clerical Church of England kinfolk. Back in Melbourne and struggling to keep the new building on schedule, Leeper corresponded cordially with Hensley, sending her plans of the hostel, newspaper clippings reporting the laying of the foundation stone (on which occasion he had announced her appointment) and copies of the *Australasian*.[60]

For her part Hensley set about visiting the women's colleges at Oxford and Cambridge to bring herself up to date. In London she met two members of the Ladies' Council—Lady Stawell and Lady Davies—for further discussions. Her questions to Leeper about the hostel and its prospects were perspicacious. She established that she was to be paid £200 per annum; she was to 'farm' the hostel; rooms were to be allotted free of charge to her and her companion Alice Taylor; and her passage from England was to be paid. Leeper wrote in February 1890: 'If the Hostel succeeds as I hope, you ought, after the first year at any rate, to make a considerable profit'. The correspondence ends with Leeper's letter of welcome in September 1890 and the news that the hostel building was not yet fit for habitation; Emily Hensley and Alice Taylor spent their first weeks in Melbourne sharing a tiny bedroom in the warden's lodge. Nevertheless, we can scarcely blame Emily Hensley if she arrived in Australia in 1890 confident that she was to establish an Oxbridge college for women in the southern hemisphere.

By the time Emily Hensley placed this ambition on the public record in her speech at the opening of the new buildings in April 1891, relationships between her and Leeper had already soured.[61] From the beginning, two forceful and ambitious people did battle over the leadership of an institution where only one was required. Hensley insisted that Leeper had never informed her of his position in authority over her at the hostel and that she had been brought to Australia under false pretences. She bitterly resented her quasi-domestic and subservient role, and indeed there are no documents surviving that acknowledge her as one of Australia's first female university academics. The situation was exacerbated by the reluctance of the female undergraduates to enrol; at the opening ceremony there were four students and throughout 1891 Hensley's professional and economic prospects did not improve.

The timing of Emily Hensley's principalship was also unfortunate for, in 1891, Melbourne was sliding into the economic depression which engulfed many families who in better times might have sent their daughters to the Trinity Hostel. The capital which provided Hensley's salary disappeared with the English and Australian Mortgage Bank. To make matters worse there was no Church of England girls' school similar to the Presbyterian, Methodist and Catholic secondary schools which could have sent women on to the Trinity Hostel. The tardiness of the Church of England in the matter of girls' secondary education raises again the denominational issue in the fortunes of the Trinity Hostel. Issues which bedevilled the negotiations between Leeper, Sugden of Queen's College and MacFarland of Ormond College over the matter of female students remained unresolved. Was the hostel to be an institution for Church of England women or for all denominations? Was Anglican religious observance to be insisted upon? Could women enrolled at Queen's and Ormond live at the Trinity Hostel but maintain their allegiance to their own denominational college? Could they live at the Trinity Hostel but attend lectures at the other colleges? As the young women of the University of Melbourne steadfastly refused to enrol at the Trinity Hostel, Emily Hensley and the Ladies' Council inclined more and more to the ecumenical solution to these problems, while Alexander Leeper remained committed to his vision of a distinctively Church of England institution.

By June of 1891 the Ladies' Council and Emily Hensley had joined forces to demand that the hostel be transformed into an autonomous women's college for all denominations, subject only to the authority of the Trinity College Council. The nub of the women's case was this: they too had been kept in ignorance of the warden's pre-eminence over the lady-principal; they had financial responsibility for the Hostel but no say in its governance beyond mundane domestic matters; unlike Trinity College they had received 'not one farthing' of church money; and their hostel, to which over £10,000 of public money had been subscribed, was still being run under a private agreement between the warden and the council more suited to the original boarding house in Sydney Road.

Negotiations between the Ladies' Council and the Trinity College Council were acrimonious and futile. In July 1892 vice-presidents Jessie Grimwade and Isabella a'Beckett wrote to Bishop Goe, chairman of the Trustees of Trinity College: 'Are the Trustees and Council of Trinity College going to comply with the wishes of the Ladies' Council, or with the wishes of the Warden? In the latter case the present Ladies' Council will be compelled to resign.'[62] They did more. When the Trinity College Council backed Leeper, the women published their resignations and the full text of their correspondence with the council in the *Argus* of 3 September 1892:

> We publish the correspondence [they wrote] with deep regret, but we feel that it is right that the public, whose money we have spent, should know why more than half our beautifully furnished rooms are unoccupied, why the efforts of our admirable principal are confined to only five students, why we have been thus unsuccessful, and why we now resign our position in connection with a work in which we feel the deepest interest.

Alexander Leeper's tactics in appointing a committee of conservative women as a bulwark against the rising tide of feminist consciousness are by now familiar. Janet Lady Clarke is typical of the group. In her philanthropic work she was deeply concerned with the plight of women but she was not committed to a radical change in relationships between men and women. She declared her hand in the suffrage movement late in the day by accepting the presidency of the Women's National League, formed when the enfranchisement of women was inevitable, to educate them to vote for conservative candidates. What is remarkable in the Trinity Hostel affair is that the women themselves saw nothing untoward in extending their traditional philanthropic role to the governance of a university college. This rendered them vulnerable to Leeper's charge that they were not qualified to manage the academic affairs of the hostel and it was this argument which won the day with the Trinity College Council.

Emily Hensley also resigned at the end of 1892 and with Alice Taylor prepared to return to England. At the last moment they were persuaded to stay in Melbourne to open a 'high-class Church of England boarding and day school' with financial backing from the Clarke and Grimwade families. Merton Hall began in February 1893 in South Yarra and became Melbourne Church of England Girls' Grammar School in 1903, some years after Taylor had married and Hensley had returned to England. Alexander Leeper was a key figure in its acquisition by the church and he remained on its governing body until his death in 1934.[63] Its success under the talented Morris family in the Edwardian era was to be crucial to the recovery of the Trinity Hostel. Although Janet Lady Clarke resisted the blandishments of Alexander Leeper and remained aloof for many years, in 1921 the hostel was renamed Janet Clarke Hall. There was no autonomous women's college at the University of Melbourne until the establishment of Women's College (now the co-educational University College) in 1937. Janet Clarke Hall itself became an autonomous institution only in 1961.

Students and staff of Merton Hall in Domain Road, South Yarra, c.1894. Alice
Taylor and Emily Hensley are seated in the second row, third and fourth from
the left.
(Melbourne Girls' Grammar School Archives)

Women's College, University of Sydney

On St Patrick's Day 1892, a few months after Emily Hensley's arrival,
Louisa Macdonald arrived in Australia to open the 'Women's College
within the University of Sydney'.[64] The Australian careers of the two
women could hardly be more different. Louisa Macdonald is still
celebrated as pre-eminent in a distinguished succession of principals at
the Sydney college. She wore her authority with easy grace in the Sydney
society which descended upon her with alacrity, in the college where
she was greatly admired by the students and in the university itself,
though she failed in her attempt to be the first woman elected to the
University Senate. The college achieved an effortless Newnhamite
succession from Louisa Macdonald to Susie Williams in 1919 and the Hon.
Camilla Wedgwood in 1935. When Macdonald prepared to return to

The Women's College, University of Sydney, c.1900.
(The Women's College Archives)

England in 1919, the making of a legend was already under way. It is salutary then to read in the diary which Beatrice and Sidney Webb kept of their Australian tour in 1898:

> Dined at the women's College. A refined and intelligent Scotch woman (graduate of London University) Miss Macdonell [sic] is the Principal, and has gathered from all parts of New South Wales and Queensland, 14 students. Like the rest of the University the Women's College is depressed; is, in fact, struggling into life in spite of the steady indifference, if not hostility, of Australian Society.[65]

While in this respect Sydney Women's College fared no better than Janet Clarke Hall in its first decade of existence, the creation of women's space at the University of Sydney was different from the Melbourne experience. The legislative basis for the creation of the new college, the public money which underwrote it and the support of the powerful secular university community made Louisa Macdonald's situation very different from that of Emily Hensley in Melbourne. The establishment of the Sydney college appears to have followed without controversy from the admission of women to the university itself in the early 1880s. In 1887 an establishing committee was formed which included the chancellor, the vice-chancellor and all of the professors; most were to be generous donors to the building fund. The committee carried the matter forward with some panache for, in May of that year, it called a public meeting chaired by the Governor of New South Wales, Lord Carrington. The meeting passed several resolutions, all of which were important, although one was of particular importance given the Melbourne experience. It was decided that the women's college at the University of Sydney should be undenominational. In 1889 the focus of the campaign turned to the New South Wales legislature where a bill to establish the college was debated during Henry Parkes' fifth ministry. As he was on record as an advocate of higher education for women, the Act to Establish and Endow a College for Women was assented to on 21 September 1889 without incident. The governance of the college was thus a matter of public record, the principal was to be a woman and her salary of £500 per annum, to be financed from the public purse, would place her among the highest paid women in Australia. On one matter only does the legislature appear to have lost its nerve, for it declined to grant more than £5,000 towards the building fund, a quarter of the sum paid to the men's colleges. No Janet Lady Clarke emerged to finance the college and a committee of women was obliged to establish a network of collectors throughout New South Wales to solicit small donations from hundreds of subscribers. The manuscript evidence of their Herculean labours survives in the college archives. It was not until the Women's College Endowment Act of 1916 that the women's college was placed on the same financial footing as the men's colleges.

When the Sydney Women's College committee turned its attention to the appointment of the principal in 1891 it followed Australian tradition and appointed a search committee based in England which included three principals of the Oxbridge women's colleges—Anne Clough of Newnham, Elizabeth Welsh of Girton and Agnes Maitland of Somerville.[66] These colleges were less than twenty years old and still regarded as illegitimate by Oxford and Cambridge but they were well known and much admired by Australian women. A two-way traffic was quickly established, with Oxford and Cambridge women such as Emily Hensley taking the plum educational positions in Australia and young Australian women setting off to study at what they considered to be the centre of a female intellectual renaissance.

The Sydney men were unaware that Anne Clough had little academic standing at Newnham where the Sidgwicks ruled on academic matters, nor did they know that Elizabeth Welsh of Girton played second fiddle to her *de facto* head, Emily Davies, who detested living at the college she had created and ran its affairs in dictatorial fashion from London. Fifty-seven women applied from Britain, many of them with qualifications from Oxford and Cambridge, and only eight women applied from Australia, among them Edith Dornwell of the University of Adelaide. Though Anne Clough was literally on her death bed and did not attend the meetings in London, she preferred Louisa Macdonald over several of her Newnham *protégées* on the grounds of Macdonald's scholarship and the broadening influence of her travel.

Louisa Macdonald was born in 1858 in Arbroath on the east coast of Scotland.[67] She had experienced at first hand the ferment over women's education in Britain. With her older sister Bella, one of the first female doctors to qualify in England, Louisa studied secretly for the Edinburgh matriculation examinations in 1878, a subterfuge which was presumably exposed when she was placed first on the lists. As the University of Edinburgh had not then opened its doors to women, the two sisters again qualified to matriculate, this time at the University of London which admitted women in 1878. Louisa graduated B.A. with first class honours in classics in 1884 from its affiliated University College and M.A. in 1886. Remarkably, she was appointed a fellow at University College and embarked on a promising research career in classical antiquities at the British Museum. She left behind in London her professional and personal lives with considerable misgiving, writing in her memoirs fifty years later that she could not enjoy the scent of lily of the valley because her close friends farewelled her with bunches of the flower.

Macdonald established the Sydney Women's College in a rented house near the University of Sydney with one student, Dorothy Emma Harris, educated at Abbotsleigh and the daughter of the headmaster of King's School, Parramatta. When the college moved to its present Italianate premises in the university precinct in May 1894 there was still only a handful of students. The university and the city were still sufficiently intimate to contemplate inviting the entire staff and the leading citizens to the opening ceremony. The occasion went off well, though Louisa noted with her usual sardonic humour that the official photographs failed to show any of the main benefactors of the college. The creation of Louisa Macdonald as Australia's first female university academic was a public affair, extending far beyond the official jurisdiction of the university men. Sydney's closely interwoven intellectual and political elites were agreed that Macdonald was a scholar and this fiction was maintained as her research career slipped inexorably away. In fact, she was at the beginning of a promising career with one or two publications to her credit when she accepted the Sydney appointment, a decision which she herself realised was incompatible with her scholarly interests. Macdonald was an able college principal, quickly establishing its reputation for academic excellence but, in her Sydney years, she was not a scholar. Though they promoted her as an academic of distinction, Macdonald's admirers were in agreement that she was not a bluestocking; unionist and politician Arthur Rae recycled the opinion of the *Sydney Morning Herald* when he wrote to Rose Scott:

> [Macdonald] is no bluestocking but likes a fair share of the fashions and pleasures of her sex. I like that because it shows that women can be clever without ceasing to be as purely human as ever. I never doubted it but many do. I am glad that one who will wield much influence will probably show their fears to be quite groundless.[68]

Macdonald was urbane and charming in company; she did not alarm men and she was always fashionably dressed, a style adopted after she parted company with her student friends in London. As the college struggled through the economic depression of the 1890s she felt obliged to go about in the society which might support her with its daughters and its money. Her letters home reveal that she was frequently out and about two or three times a day.[69] For the sake of the students she replicated this social round at the college itself, holding monthly 'at homes' to ensure a constant flow of cultivated and well-to-do visitors.

Yet Macdonald's personal correspondence reveals that she was profoundly ambivalent about the Sydney society which did so much to create and sustain the triumphant Louisa of the college years. To her London friends she was casually arrogant about things Australian; she assiduously cultivated herself as an outcast, her identity in constant danger of dissolving in this alien place. She borrowed from the racist imagery of Empire to cast Sydney as the white man's nemesis—enervating, amoral, materialistic, childlike and uncivilised:

> It is not possible for you to realise [she wrote in 1895] the emptiness of life out here! I do not mean it unpleasantly . . . It has its counterbalancing advantages that the experiences and sensations one has should be so few as each to stand out distinguished from a clear vacant background; but we perceive them differently from you at home to whom everything is in proportion . . . we have no standard to judge by . . . our opinions are like those of children, often singularly clear and true, equally often barbarously false and ignorant.[70]

She was both attracted and repelled by her Australian students, writing to a London friend in April 1894: 'You see what I want altered in them is really their whole world, standards, ideals, conduct, manners, everything'. Despite her feminist hospitality to new forms of womanhood, developed in the robust female student culture of London,

Macdonald never seemed to contemplate that what she termed the 'larrikinism' of her Australian girls might be a form of liberation to be encouraged rather than despised.

Louisa Macdonald's feminism also became part of her agreed-upon public persona. Turn of the century feminism was orthodoxy among the university wives and daughters—Maybanke Anderson, wife of Professor Francis Anderson; Lady Caroline David, who, as Caroline Mallett, had been principal of the Hurlstone Training College; Lady May Manning, wife of the chancellor; and Margaret Windeyer, daughter of Sydney Women's College chairman, William Windeyer. Macdonald was free to identify herself and the college publicly with the upsurge in women's political consciousness which engulfed the 1890s. She joined the Women's Literary Society and its successor the Womanhood Suffrage League soon after her arrival and here she met Rose Scott, the most influential of the Sydney feminists. Scott's biographer Judith Allen suggests that the friendship was 'a crucial and enduring one' and that Macdonald had a profound influence upon the less formally educated Scott. They were later to clash over Scott's endorsement of compulsory domestic education for girls which Macdonald characterised as 'one of the most serious blows to women's freedom' and a ploy on the part of middle-class women to obtain servants.[71]

Macdonald's feminism long pre-dated her arrival in Sydney. For many years Louisa Macdonald wrote regularly to her close friend 'Pixie' Grove, principal of Louisa's own student residence in London, College Hall. They exchanged feminist journals, which Louisa left strategically in the students' common room. Mrs Millicent Fawcett, the English suffragist who had been among Louisa's referees for the Sydney job, addressed Pixie's students back in London:

> I wish we could have Mrs Fawcett out here [wrote Louisa in August 1896]. To have anyone like that speak to my students would be just the kind of education I long to give them. If ever she feels inclined to make a world tour and study the question of the suffrage out in these parts tell her—please, I shall be delighted to offer her the College hospitality.[72]

She did not go as far as that when theosophist and birth control advocate, Annie Besant, made her controversial visit to Australia in 1894. Louisa encouraged the students to attend Besant's lectures, although she was amused by the reaction of Sydney society which polarised over Besant's ideas. Pixie and Louisa discussed the huge women's suffrage petition to Westminster in 1896: 'I should like to be with you, Pixie, when you registered your vote for Parliament for the first time—after the effort of so many years.' One of the college scrap books contains a letter which

Louisa Macdonald (on right), principal of the Women's College, University of Sydney, with an unidentified woman, possibly Hortense Montefiore, a student at the college from 1893 to 1895.

Louisa Macdonald wrote to the London *Times*; it is undated, but sometime after Australian women were granted the vote at Federation:

> The women with whom I am most intimately acquainted, the students and the maids of legal age in the Sydney Women's College . . . vote with keen and intelligent interest. There has never been rioting or disturbance at the polling stations, and each member of the household has gone to register her vote either in company or alone without anxiety or trouble . . . [surely] that should be a calming reflection to those who fear a revolution as a consequence of granting women the vote in Britain.

Thus while Sydney Women's College was not the creation of the women's movement, in the person of Louisa Macdonald the two causes came together as the women's suffrage movement grew in the 1890s. That her views were shared by the students is apparent in a telegram to the premier 'from the Principal tutor and fifteen students' in support of the suffrage bill before the New South Wales parliament in 1900.[73]

Louisa Macdonald's espousal of the suffrage cause was a public avowal of her private commitment to what she termed 'the cause of happy single women'.[74] Her letters to Pixie reveal that she was not only feminist but woman centred. In October 1893 she wrote:

> Sometimes my heart faints at the prospect of this College . . . at the aloneness of the principle it represents. There is nothing to answer to it in the whole of Australian Society . . . The idea of the mutual interdependence of women is quite foreign to Australian modes of thought. The unit of their society is a pair—male and female—as it was in the beginning, only with a touching humility [the women] combine to believe that it is very good for men to be alone.[75]

It is difficult to find the appropriate words for the relationship between Louisa Macdonald and Pixie Grove. To say that Macdonald was 'in love' with the older woman is to deliver them back into the language of the heterosexual relationships which they sought to escape; 'infatuated' sounds demeaning; that they were close friends misses the mark just as surely. Certainly, the relationship began in a situation of unequal power between student and college principal in London and was disrupted in the geographical sense before Louisa could transcend her dependence upon the older woman. Though Grove's letters have not survived, it is apparent that she cultivated her emotional hold over Louisa and the anxious, almost childlike Louisa of the letters is in the strongest possible contrast to the public Louisa of the Sydney years.

Louisa Macdonald's painful separation from Pixie Grove did not preclude her from forming other significant relationships with women.

She was joined from England by the woman who was to become her lifelong companion, Evelyn Dickinson, whom she paid out of her own salary to assist in running the college. It was Dickinson rather than Macdonald who was the flamboyant face of the 'new woman' in Sydney. She qualified as a doctor while in Australia, she wrote 'advanced' novels, she cycled, wore 'rational' dress and set up a gymnasium in the college tower. The summer of 1897 found a reluctant Louisa, by now grown somewhat stout, cycling with Evelyn through Tasmania, pursued by the smoke of bushfires.

Women like Evelyn Dickinson are marginal to traditional historiography of women's higher education but central to a new generation of historians like Martha Vicinus, Patricia Palmieri and Elizabeth Edwards who have reconceptualised the women's college as a site of new possibilities for the feminine.[76] Dickinson and Macdonald were an unselfconscious public twosome, in Sheila Jeffreys' terms, enjoying an Indian summer of public tolerance before the enemies of the spinster began to assemble the psychology of deviance in the Edwardian era.[77] Though their relationship remains enigmatic, they were in private agreement that relationships between women were superior to those between women and men. They were not anti-men, as was Rose Scott in her darker moments; they were against the institution of marriage as it was presently constituted. They were among the first generation of educated women who were free to mount such a critique for they were not obliged to marry in order to support themselves. With palpable glee Macdonald quoted in a letter to Pixie an epitaph from a Sydney paper: 'Martha Brown, wife of Timothy Brown, she lived with her husband for fifty years, and died in the confident hope of a better life'.[78] In Martha Vicinus' frame of reference, homosocial relationships for these economically independent women were not complementary to heterosexual relations but in opposition to them.[79]

Louisa Macdonald was in full flight from domesticity, yet repelled by the public life which ambushed her from the minute she left her private rooms within the college. Time and again she broached with Pixie the new constellations of gender and power possible for the female head of a public institution. Privately she described herself as 'a strange mixture of ineffectual presence with a capacity . . . of getting my own way with all the outside public'.[80] She returned often to the theme of her public and private selves:

> Judging from my own experience I think that a life that is lived much in public leads first to a habit of trying to look at yourself as other people see you, then to posing, and lastly to deceitfulness and more or less conscious hypocrisy. That may be perhaps specially the case with me—though I think and hope

there are other things which might prevent the worst evils in my case, besides I am not public enough . . . I think just now I am a bundle of confused ideas, with a large capacity for being bored, all moved by a strong force of habit.[81]

She had no wish to recreate within the college the hothouse relationships of the Victorian mother and her daughters which Elizabeth Edwards has documented at Homerton College in Cambridge. These claustrophobic relationships of dominance and submission Macdonald regarded as antithetical to the scholarly life and several times she paid the fees of students out of her own pocket to save them from having to return home. Nor is there any suggestion that Macdonald and Dickinson played husband and wife to the girls in the college. Macdonald refused to play the mother/guardian figure, though occasionally she caricatured the role with sudden enthusiasms like learning to make pastry. In her letters she reflected at length upon her relationship to the students, wary of intimacy but resentful of the few who kept her at a distance. She was taken aback when two of her students came to see her in confessional mode, to report that the youthful Professor of History had invited them to tea at his 'bachelor establishment' in Glebe. Reporting the incident to Pixie, Louisa had some difficulty in deciding that she was 'touched' by their confidence but we are left with the impression that she would rather not have known about the incident. Yet she was obliged by the financial situation of the college to share with Dickinson the role of housekeeper and the minutiae of domesticity provide a peevish subtext in the letters to Pixie. Just as surely she despised the loutish masculine culture of the men's colleges which intruded itself uninvited upon the women's college from its inception. To Louisa Macdonald and her generation, the Sydney Women's College was women's space in more than its official charter; but it was fluid space, waiting for the imprint of the feminine in ways which were not yet clear to them. In despair at the financial situation of the college she wrote to Pixie:

> There is one great comfort I have. It seems to me that . . . the College . . . has a tendency to create a feeling of solidarity amongst the women of the country, those who have worked for it, those who live in it or merely visit it; and I think if it accomplished that all the labour of collecting for it and planning it have not been empty.[82]

In the 1960s, before women began to write their own history, Australian historian Ailsa Thomson Zainu'ddin was outraged to discover that women had not been present at the University of Melbourne from the beginning. Indeed it was this discovery which led her to write the history of women's entry to the university.[83] The collective failure by earlier generations of Australian university women to nurture their own traditions is all the more remarkable in her case because she herself graduated from the University of Melbourne in 1948 as a resident of Janet Clarke Hall; her mother, Thelma Thomson (Roberts), graduated from the University of Melbourne in 1918; and there is a family tradition that her grandmother, Emily Pearce, had hoped to do so until the early death of her father made it impossible. If a university education was indeed the 'keystone of the arch', without which women's education could have neither stability nor permanence, Australian women had long since learned to pass beneath it, secure in its presence but oblivious to its significance.[84] The first generation of university women bore their double burden with distinction; they proved that women were indeed the intellectual equals of men and they remained, by and large, 'true women', confining themselves respectfully to the cracks and crevices of university life. All but a tiny minority retired from professional life when they married. The keystone of the arch supported an edifice erected by men; when women again began to enter the university as a conscious act of sexual politics in the 1970s they were no longer content to inhabit the cracks and crevices of university life.

CHAPTER FOUR

Inventing the Secondary School for Girls: Brisbane Girls' Grammar School and Sydney Girls' High School, 1875-1910

In May 1875 the feminist English periodical *Journal of the Women's Education Union* reprinted from the Melbourne *Argus* the announcement of a new school for girls:

> The higher education of women [in Australia] has received a new impulse from the establishment of a ladies' college in connexion with the Presbyterian Church. This religious body deserves the thanks of the community for being the first to move in this direction, and with praiseworthy liberality the college has been established on such principles that it can be taken advantage of by all classes.

Though it was Presbyterian in its affiliation the college aimed to be free from sectarianism, it had appointed staff 'in whom the public have the utmost confidence' and, although the college building was not yet complete, enrolled a large number of pupils.[1] The new Australian ladies' college was in good company. We also learn that Girton College, six years old and removed from Hitchin to Cambridge, was in search of a new principal; that the Girls' Public Day School Trust (formed three years earlier by the sisters Maria Grey and Emily Shirreff) had opened another school at Clapham Common; that Dorothea Beale's Cheltenham Ladies' College had presented its twenty-first report to its shareholders and governing body; and that there were women studying at the Universities of Zurich and Geneva, among them an English woman. Within months of its establishment the new colonial ladies' school had been claimed for the 'movement for the higher education of women'. This unlikely consensus between the feminist English journal and the conservative Australian *Argus* over the significance of Presbyterian Ladies' College soon became orthodoxy, and this view underpins Kathleen Fitzpatrick's centenary history of the school.[2]

It would be idle to deny schools like the Presbyterian Ladies' College pioneer status as a new kind of female secondary school. The same middle-class imperatives which opened the colonial universities to women had an influence upon the secondary education of girls. By 1873 the quixotic Sir Charles Lilley, liberal politician, judge and man of advanced views on education, was insisting before the Queensland parliament that girls had an equal right to all forms of education funded by the state, whether primary, secondary or tertiary.[3] In 1880 Sir Henry Parkes, whose widowed daughter Menie ran a ladies' school, rejected the charge that his proposed high schools would 'draw women from their proper sphere of life'[4]. With the most advanced thinkers of his age he did not question the traditional role of women, but he had become convinced that a secondary education similar to that available to their brothers would not unfit them for this role. To the good intentions of the Presbyterians of Melbourne, men like Lilley and Parkes added the suggestion that the state should interest itself in the provision of high schools for girls. In 1875 the Brisbane Girls' Grammar School was established as a department of the state-funded boys' grammar school, a milestone not recorded in the *Journal of the Women's Education Union*; four years later in 1879 the South Australian Education Act was invoked to create the Advanced School for Girls, Adelaide, though there was no state high school for boys in the nineteenth century. Under the provisions of Henry Parkes' New South Wales Public Instruction Act of 1880, the Sydney Girls' High School was established in 1883.[5]

From these events institutional historians intent on celebration have fashioned a 'watershed' thesis of change in female education. In this view, education for middle-class women before the 1870s was deplorable. After that time, we are told, women's education was set on a steady course towards equality with men, unfolding from an English and feminist inspired blueprint for a new kind of academic secondary school. Of the first generation at Sydney Girls' High School Lilith Norman wrote: 'They had seen the door open. And their daughters and grand-daughters would never again feel that there were barriers of education that women could not cross.'[6]

This orthodoxy has something to recommend it, but it does conflate the process of reform with the process of masculinisation. The hallmarks of reform are pinpointed with remarkable accuracy: the admission of women to public examinations (the Oxford and Cambridge 'locals' in England; the university matriculation examinations in Melbourne); consequent upon that privilege, the appearance of classics and mathematics in the female curriculum; the appearance of a new type of 'masculine' public school for girls (Cheltenham Ladies' College and North London Collegiate in England; Presbyterian Ladies' College, Melbourne, and the Advanced School for Girls, Adelaide); the admission of women to the universities and, in due course, to the professions.

Yet there are awkward intrusions into this pilgrim's progress of female education. The Catholic Sisters in Australia had already developed a model of systemic female education which had proved itself capable of orderly multiplication and adaptation to the needs of its clientele. In 1870 there were fifteen Catholic female secondary schools; by 1910 there were 212.[7] The comparable figures for boys were four and thirty-three. The major establishing orders were the Mercy, Charity, Sacred Heart, Benedictine, Dominican, Good Samaritan, Ursuline, Presentation and Loreto Sisters. The achievements of women like Mother Ursula Frayne and Mother Mary Vincent Whitty of the Mercy Sisters were all the more remarkable as they received little financial help from their Australian bishops.[8] In the establishment of their secondary schools the sisters looked back to ancient traditions of female learning and forward to the renewal of their orders. Nevertheless, their female convent schools in Australia were in part a pragmatic response to local imperatives. As with the Mercy Sisters' Academy of Mary Immaculate, opened in Melbourne in 1857, they typically established fee-paying female secondary schools in order to finance elementary schools, orphanages and female refuges for the Irish poor of their constituency, a pattern which was set even before the cessation of state aid to Catholic schools in the 1870s and 1880s. Though anti-Catholicism was an art form in nineteenth-century Australia, many non-Catholic families enrolled their daughters in convent secondary schools, a practice which obliged the Church of England to make its belated entry into the field at the end of the nineteenth century.

Nor were the ladies' schools which were the focus of chapter two discouraged when Presbyterian Ladies' College opened its doors in 1875; on the contrary, there is ample evidence that they flourished anew in the 1880s. The so-called 'free, secular and compulsory' education Acts passed in all states between 1872 and 1893 caused a hardening of middle-class attitudes against the publicly funded schools which were now expected to gather in the children at the other end of the social scale. In the prosperous 1880s daughters could be sent to private schools where they would be safe from the contaminating influence of the state school child. In New South Wales, several important girls' schools—among them Normanhurst, Redlands, Abbotsleigh and Ascham—were established in the 1880s.[9] In Victoria Ruyton, Tintern, Oberwyl (which later became Clyde) and Lauriston were established or renewed under new ownership in the last quarter of the nineteenth century.[10] And in South Australia Unley Park, Tormore House, Hardwicke College and Dryburgh House all grew in size and prestige during the 1880s.[11] The ladies' schools adapted, chameleon-like, to the new demands of their clientele, establishing small matriculation classes and competing successfully for the services of early women graduates. Women like Eliza Bromby of Ruyton, and Louisa Gurney of Kambala (where Louisa Macdonald of Sydney Women's College was a frequent visitor) practised a discreet coterie feminism which enclosed within their private circle the intellectually ambitious girls, usually from professional families. This coterie feminism co-existed with the agendas of the traditional clientele who continued to require the demarcation of a female elite until the 1970s when the survivors among the ladies' schools—those who had made alliances with churches or formed themselves into corporate schools—were obliged to accommodate a new generation of parents demanding prestigious careers for their daughters. With their first cousins, the Catholic convent schools, the private ladies' schools remained numerically and ideologically dominant in female secondary education until the expansion of the state systems in the twentieth century.

The new secondary schools themselves present theoretical and methodological problems for the historian who ventures beyond the brief of the institutional historian. It quickly becomes apparent that there was no blueprint for reform; in the last quarter of the nineteenth century, the academic secondary school for girls had yet to be assembled. Though each school laid claim to new pedagogical space for women, they stood in different relationships to the interested parties of church, state, and clientele. Newly fashionable ideas on the education of middle-class daughters encountered local imperatives which were different in each case. 'The establishment of a good public school for girls [wrote the *Brisbane Courier* in 1875] has been looked upon as more or less of an experiment.'[12] This sense of venturing into unknown territory was exacerbated by uncertainty of purpose in secondary education more generally. As Tyack and Hansot observe of the American high school, Australian secondary schools in the nineteenth century were 'diverse, controversial, and ambiguously connected with the larger society'.[13] The same forces which had precipitated a battle between the traditionalists and the modernists for possession of the curriculum in the colonial universities were at work reshaping the curriculum of the boys' schools in the very years when the new schools for girls made their appearance.[14] E.L. French has argued that although Charles Badham at Sydney and Redmond Barry at Melbourne ensured that the classics enjoyed an Indian summer in the colonies, new middle-class elites with a new relationship to knowledge demanded that the curriculum of the boys' secondary schools diversify to include utilitarian subjects such as English, modern languages, commerce, drawing—and eventually science.[15] This challenge to the ancient humanist tradition had occurred first in Scotland and the presence of numerous Scots in Australia hastened this change in purpose and in practice. Understandings of a secondary school for boys were further clouded by events in England in the middle decades of the nineteenth century. In those years, the English Public school, exemplified by Eton, Winchester and Harrow, underwent a transformation in morals and in organisation which came to be identified with Thomas Arnold of Rugby. If this uncertainty of purpose and institutional form characterised the secondary education of boys, where the links between masculinity and breadwinning were clear, it did so even more in the case of girls where no such links were apparent.

Brisbane Girls' Grammar School

The Brisbane Girls' Grammar School was established in 1875 under the rubric of the 'movement for the higher education of women'. The framers of the Queensland Grammar Schools Act of 1860, passed within a year of the colony's proclamation, did not need to expressly exclude girls from its provisions; at mid-century, the 'advantages of a regular and liberal course of education', set out in the preamble to the Act, referred self-evidently to men.[16] Nor did the emerging discourse of the 'modern', which had begun to challenge the traditional grammar school, have any resonance for female education. In 1860 the legislators made their decisions about the secondary education of Queensland youth amid the din and strife of denominationalism and for this reason there was no mention of 'religion and morality'. This marked the Queensland Act out from its predecessor, the Sydney Grammar Schools Act of 1854. It was not until the mid-1890s that a headmistress at the Brisbane Girls' Grammar School asked permission to open the day with prayers. The Education Act, also passed in 1860, established elementary education under a Board of General Education and there was no provision that the two systems of state-supported education should be governed in common.[17] Though the Queensland Education Act of 1875 placed state elementary education under a minister of the crown and a department, the grammar schools remained autonomous; no rival state secondary schools were established until the twentieth century, nor were the grammar schools subject to official inspection until 1901.[18] The machinery for the creation of a grammar school virtually delivered the institution into local hands. Generous government endowments were triggered by locally raised funds, and each school was governed by a board of seven trustees, four appointed by the government and three elected by the subscribers. Power was vested in the trustees to make regulations, subject only to the approval of the governor in council.

When the new ideas on the education of women entered the discourse of Queenslanders in the 1870s, it was to the grammar school model that they turned to put those ideas into practice. Of the ten grammar schools established under the Act in the nineteenth century, four were for girls— Brisbane (1875), Maryborough (1883), Rockhampton (1892), and Ipswich (1892).[19] The new grammar schools for girls exemplified those structural properties which Joyce Pedersen suggests marked the new secondary schools out from the traditional ladies' schools.[20] They were the creation of the new middle classes who looked to meritocratic achievement and institutional affiliation in increasingly complex urban settings. They were corporate in the sense that they were created, owned and governed by an alliance between the state and local interests. Their tripartite system of governance—by parliament, trustees and principal— shifted the locus of power in favour of the school and weakened the control which individual parents had wielded over the proprietor of the private ladies' academy. Though the hefty fees excluded many families, the exclusion of pupils could not be seen to be arbitrary as it had been in the ladies' academy.

Yet the Queensland Grammar Schools Act proved to be an effective device for the creation of an exclusive secondary school for girls. Under its provisions politicians and the leading citizens of Brisbane (or any other locality) could further their interests in common; indeed politicians, parents, and trustees of the Brisbane Girls' Grammar School were in many cases the same people. Sir Charles Lilley, whose views on the education of girls have already been noted, was pre-eminent among the founding trustees in 1875 and he remained in office until 1887.[21] His daughters attended the school, and his grand-daughter, Kathleen Lilley, was later principal. There were four other politicians among the trustees, three of whom had daughters at the school. The trustees were all men, though there were women among the subscribers. The leading citizens of the town provided their capital, their imprimatur and their daughters, while the state ensured the financial security of the institution. It was not incumbent upon the trustees to articulate the school with the public elementary schools, an arrangement which would have driven the leading families out and resulted in a very different school. Until the end of the century the boarding house, a site of intense anxieties about female sexuality, was a private venture of the headmistress, an arrangement which ensured that exclusionary practices could go on unremarked even within the ranks of the grammar school clientele. The outcome was the creation of a new kind of quasi-public space for women's education in which the proprieties of class and gender remained inviolate. It may have been premature for the *Brisbane Courier* to report in November 1875 that the private ladies' schools had already been run out of business, but its instincts were sure as to who would attend the Brisbane Girls' Grammar School.[22]

The Brisbane Girls' Grammar School, which began as a branch school with about fifty girls in a rented house in George Street in March 1875, was not the product of local and government initiative in the manner prescribed, but of administrative fiat on the part of the Brisbane (Boys') Grammar School trustees. There was no money raised by interested citizens and there was no election of trustees. The contrast with the opening of the boys' school by Governor Samuel Blackall in 1869 was marked. It is difficult from the surviving evidence to be certain whether the trustees of the boys' school contemplated an autonomous school for girls at some time in the future, or whether an attempt at co-education, urged upon them by influential parents against considerable opposition, became unworkable in practice. The initial regulations, adopted at a meeting of the trustees in December 1874, referred to the proposed provision for girls as 'a branch of the Grammar School'.[23] The plan became general knowledge when Thomas Harlin M.A., headmaster of the Brisbane Grammar School, announced the establishment of the girls' branch in his annual address in February 1875. He apologised to the parents of the promised pupils, explaining that difficulties in finding a suitable house and in selecting a lady-principal had delayed the opening. In the event, his own rented house in George Street was selected, and Mrs Janet O'Connor of Ballarat was appointed 'from the large field of candidates'.

The appointment of Janet O'Connor as founding head of the Brisbane Girls' Grammar School signals the survival of older traditions in the new secondary schools for girls. She was born Janet Dods in 1827 in Truro, Cornwall, and according to one source, educated at 'Military College, Bath'.[24] In 1851 she married Daniel O'Connor and the couple arrived in Victoria in 1854. By the late 1860s Janet O'Connor was running a ladies' school in Eureka Street, Ballarat.[25] In the next few years she published two slim volumes of poetry.[26] O'Connor did not apply for the Brisbane position from Ballarat, but from Mrs Wigmore's ladies' school, Leigh House, in Richmond where she was presumably on the staff.[27] The advertisement for the Brisbane school appeared in the Melbourne *Age* in mid-January 1875 and by late February Janet O'Connor, her husband Daniel and her four children were on board a steamer headed for Brisbane.

Though the trustees had experienced some difficulty in appointing the new head, they did not publicly canvass the more fundamental issues of leadership in a new kind of girls' school. If they were in search of a model the only one available to them was Presbyterian Ladies' College,

Melbourne; by late 1874 the dual male headship of the Rev. George Tait and Charles Pearson was public knowledge. This model was adopted by Methodist Ladies' College, Melbourne in 1882. Though there were no female graduates of universities in Australia or Britain at the time, this dispossession of women was not a foregone conclusion. The new girls' secondary schools in England had female heads and the Taunton Commission, which inquired into middle-class education in England in the 1860s, agreed that this was desirable. In the event, the men in Brisbane contrived a system of dual control which was unworkable and by November 1875 Janet O'Connor had resigned.

The O'Connor affair is the first of the public reckonings which give the history of the Brisbane Girls' Grammar School its distinctive cast. Local control ensured that its day-to-day administration was in-house; the documents which might shed some light on its daily life are scarce. Yet as a quasi-public institution it was vulnerable to sudden demands for accountability; the record is skewed by conflicts which, despite the best efforts of the trustees, escaped from time to time into the press and parliament. Much of the correspondence between the main players in the O'Connor affair was published in the *Brisbane Courier* in November and December of 1875. The events which were ultimately to cast O'Connor as a disorderly woman are difficult to retrieve from the intricacies of charge and counter, but they do give some insight into the differing agendas surrounding the establishment of Queensland's first 'public' secondary school for girls.

The original draft of the regulations governing the girls' school placed the headmaster of the boys' school, Thomas Harlin, in authority over Janet O'Connor—with the rider 'for the time being'—and the trustees in authority over both.[28] When the regulations were gazetted this clause had been dropped. Thomas Harlin was a difficult man and when Janet O'Connor arrived in Brisbane his principalship at the boys' school was widely regarded as a failure. To complicate matters further, as secretary to the trustees he was also the medium of communication between the lady-principal and her employers, a situation which in the words of one irate parent, 'gave full play to [his] well known exceeding skill in raising differences between persons whose interests are the same'.[29] Harlin chose to interpret his overlordship of the girls' school in the light of the original version of the regulations (which he had drafted) and he maintained throughout the affair that O'Connor had accepted the headship under those terms.

The problems of staffing a new academic high school for girls were experienced alike by the Melbourne Presbyterian Ladies' College, Brisbane Girls' Grammar School and Sydney Girls' High School. In the early years, many of these problems arose from the unpalatable fact that in the absence of qualified women, men had to be employed to teach nubile young women, especially in those subjects which marked the schools out as a new departure in the education of girls—mathematics and classics. The visiting master was not new, but his transformation into a permanent member of staff was a different matter.

After the first of many acrimonious exchanges with O'Connor, Harlin agreed to send his masters for twelve hours a week to teach Latin, German, French, mathematics and drawing in the girls' school. It was also his responsibility to carry out the biennial examination of the school required by the regulations. O'Connor had only two female teachers, Mrs Elthea Elcock and Miss Sarah Cargill, who had also applied for the principalship. Relationships between O'Connor, Harlin and the visiting masters quickly soured. In her account (disputed by the men) times of lessons were often changed, or masters could not be spared at all; she did not approve of the masters giving daily marks, as many of the girls were 'imperfectly educated and . . . needed all the encouragement [she] could give them'; her girls were accused of misbehaving, though she was rebuked when she interceded; one of the masters was 'far too young a man to teach in a ladies' school'.[30] There was one particularly damaging exchange between O'Connor and the second master, William Crompton, over what she considered to be an inappropriate examination paper. On that occasion, O'Connor lost her temper and, in front of the girls, accused him of attempting to discredit her school. Both O'Connor and Crompton were called before the trustees and censured 'for want of judgement'. Ironically, Crompton had been appointed to the boys' school shortly before Harlin received a warning from A.B. Weigall of Sydney Grammar School that he was unsuitable.[31]

Matters came to a head over the issue of chaperonage. In ladies' schools, O'Connor insisted, a governess was always present when masters taught; it was a 'recognised custom akin to that of sending a girl to a party or public place under the care of a chaperonage'.[32] Several of the masters took offence and refused to come at all; it was in their view 'an indignity which should only be offered to the class of men that usually taught in ladies' schools'. It was unfortunate that O'Connor chose to invoke this familiar discourse of sexual danger against the male teachers at the school, for it deflected attention away from the real issues at stake. When O'Connor offered her resignation in November 1875, the dispute ostensibly arose over the matter of an additional woman teacher to make good the disappearance of the men, but it was fundamentally over the issue of control; she was endeavouring, she said, to be 'made mistress in [her] own school'. To those who did not know the situation she appeared quixotic and demanding: 'Her sudden resignation [remarked the *Brisbane Courier*] seems to indicate some lack either of temper or of judgment'.[33]

Though Janet O'Connor had been in office for only nine months she had garnered considerable support among the mothers. They wrote letters to the editor of the *Brisbane Courier*, affirming their confidence in the lady-principal and calling on the trustees to effect a reconciliation; there was a meeting of mothers at the Brisbane Town Hall which sent a deputation to wait upon the trustees. The girls themselves drew up a petition to the trustees, 'Praying that the resignation of the Lady Principal, Mrs O'Connor should not be accepted'.[34] They also used the occasion of the school's first speech day to affirm their confidence in their principal, presenting her with a testimonial on vellum and an expensive silver inkstand.

Janet O'Connor's own interventions in the public debate were provocative to say the least, for in November 1875 she made a full disclosure of her version of events to the *Brisbane Courier*. If the statements of the trustees reported in the paper were allowed to go unchallenged, she warned, 'no other public school committee will employ me, [and] my children and myself must starve':

> On all sides I have been asked to open a private school; I shall never do so. My whole heart is with the cause of education, no private school can do . . . what a Government school can do, for the public is rich and never dies. If I were to open a private school I would close the Girls' Grammar School. I should stifle the germ that I hope may grow up to be a grand and noble tree.[35]

The trustees regretted the tone of her public disclosures and accepted her resignation. Though on that occasion the trustees allowed her to withdraw her resignation, twelve months later a similar dispute between O'Connor, the new headmaster, R.H. Roe, and the male teachers flared, this time over the matter of the examinations. This time O'Connor was dismissed. In January 1877 she placed an advertisement in the *Brisbane Courier* seeking 'an engagement either in a school or private family', but this was quickly followed by an advertisement for her own school, to open in February in temporary accommodation in the Synod Hall.[36] The school's historian estimates that half the enrolment, about thirty girls, went with Mrs O'Connor to her new school. It moved through various addresses until she built extensive new premises at Oxley, eight miles south of Brisbane, which she named 'Duporth'. When Janet O'Connor died in 1895, her daughters Kate, Alice and Janet took charge of the school. It was sold to the Ursuline Sisters and opened as the Ursuline Convent in January 1925.[37]

As O'Connor herself predicted, things did change as a result of the affair. In December 1875 Thomas Harlin received a letter from the trustees informing him that he was no longer in charge of the girls' section.[38] The trustees gazetted new regulations in December 1876, softening the hierarchical relationship with the boys' school which O'Connor had found unworkable. Thereafter there were to be 'two Divisions of the School, styled respectively the Boys' Division and the Girls' Division'.[39] Harlin's own troubled career at the Brisbane Grammar School ended tragically with his bitter speech of self-justification delivered before the governor, trustees and parents in March 1876.[40]

The new headmaster, Oxford-educated Reginald Heber Roe, put the Brisbane Grammar School back on its feet between 1876 and 1909. Selected for the position by the Dean of Westminster in London, he went on to become inspector-general of Queensland schools and founding vice-chancellor of Queensland University. In November 1877 he wrote an impressive report on the future of the girls' department.[41] The existing relationship between the two departments he characterised as too indefinite and too dependent upon the idiosyncrasies of individuals. He did not make a bid for complete control of the girls' department, on the grounds that no one person could do justice to both schools. Nor did he advocate thoroughgoing co-education, on the grounds that the management of mixed classes was too difficult, and the public was not yet ready to accept it. The present arrangements he regarded as tolerable only while the 'want of lady-mistresses in the colony' made them necessary. Such women would, he believed, ultimately be procured from 'home' and from among the women trained in Australia. When that was possible, the girls' school must become entirely separate, though not until the people of Brisbane had shown 'a sufficient appreciation of the education offered to them to justify the outlay'. The Brisbane Girls' Grammar School became an autonomous school with its own endowment in 1882, though not without some skirmishing in parliament and in the press, and moved to its imposing premises in Gregory Terrace in 1884.

Problems of leadership continued to beset the school. In it first twenty-five years, Brisbane Girls' Grammar School was to have six principals, at least three of whom departed after disputes with the trustees. O'Connor's assistant mistress Sarah Cargill was appointed head in January 1877, possibly a temporary arrangement, as she left in May 1878, apparently without rancour, and later established a boys' preparatory school as a feeder school for the Brisbane Grammar School.[42] Presumably acting upon the advice of Reginald Roe, Charles Lilley wrote 'home' to find her replacement, in this case to the principal of Girton College, Cambridge, Marianne Bernard. It was, he wrote, 'a difficult matter in the

Brisbane Girls' Grammar School.
(Queensland State Archives)

colonies to obtain the services of a lady of high-class attainments and with due educational experience'.[43] He was at pains to delineate the present relationship between the two departments, a relationship which he characterised as temporary, until such times as there was sufficient support for an autonomous girls' school. In a significant departure from the requirements when Janet O'Connor was appointed, he stipulated that the new principal should be capable of teaching the higher work of the school, especially in Latin, Euclid and algebra, with French or German as additional subjects. She should have some experience of teaching and she should not be too young—by this he meant not under twenty-seven. The result of this search was the appointment of Englishwoman Mary McKinlay.[44] She resigned in December 1881 to marry Sir James Dickson, former premier of Queensland and already the father of thirteen children. Her successor, Sophia Beanland, arrived in early 1882 in time to work with the architect, Richard Gailey, on the design of the new premises. In her appointment Lilley again sought assistance from Bernard of Girton.

Though she did not go public on the matter, Beanland resigned abruptly in mid-1888 when the trustees refused to back her in a dispute with an assistant teacher. She had also been very ill with typhoid fever, and her elderly mother found the Brisbane climate very trying.[45] Charlotte Pells of Newnham College, Cambridge, was recruited from the Presbyterian Ladies' College, Melbourne, where she had held the position of lady-superintendent. The historian of Presbyterian Ladies' College implies that the 'very severe' Miss Pells was not greatly missed by the girls in the boarding house.[46] Pells had to cope with the economic recession of the early 1890s and, as was the case with Sophia Beanland, her health broke down. The circumstances of her departure are ambiguous, but her relationships with the senior girls were so poor as to warrant a mention in her final speech day address. Despite this unhappy record of leadership, Beanland, McKinlay, and a later principal, Milisent Wilkinson, all left part of their estates to the school.

In 1899 Brisbane Girls' Grammar School was again engulfed in acrimonious public debate. The 'Fewings affair' so caught the imagination of the Brisbane public that its coverage in the *Brisbane Courier* eclipsed the impending referendum on federation and the sensational Dreyfus case in France.[47] Indeed in the white heat of battle the martyrdom of Eliza Fewings, sixth headmistress of the Brisbane Girls' Grammar School, was publicly compared with that of Captain Alfred Dreyfus.

English-born Eliza Ann Fewings was thirty-nine years old when she was recruited from the principalship of the Dr Williams' Endowed High School for Girls in Dolgelly, North Wales.[48] The Dolgelly school had been established in 1878 under the auspices of the Charity Commissioners who stipulated that funds from ancient endowments must be used to establish schools for girls. Fewings belonged to that enigmatic generation of women epitomised by women like the founder of Girton College, Emily Davies, who give the lie to their own insistence that women had been denied education, and whose task it was to lead the movement for the higher education of women until the new elite of university graduates made them redundant. Fewings was trained as a teacher by her brother, head of King Edward VI Grammar School, Southhampton, and at the Friend's School, Bristol, then worked as an assistant mistress at the Roan School, a secondary school of 350 girls in Greenwich. Welsh historian W. Gareth Evans acknowledges her as an influential and respected figure in the education of Welsh women, counting among her victories the admission of women to University College, Aberystwyth, Wales.[49] Indisputably she saw herself in the company of pioneer heads like Dorothea Beale and Frances Buss, and she had applied unsuccessfully for the position of founding principal of Sydney Women's College in 1891.[50] Her appointment to Brisbane was something of a coup, and it turned largely on the recommendation of her friend Helen Downs, outstanding educationist and highly respected headmistress of the Rockhampton Girls' Grammar School.[51] It came to light later that, at the time of appointment, the trustees had no clear information about Fewings' literary qualifications, but had 'hoped that any defect in this regard would be counter-balanced by advantages to be derived from her excellence in other qualities required in a headmistress'.[52]

By 1899, a quarter of a century after the establishment of the Brisbane Girls' Grammar School, the board of trustees which appointed Fewings had taken on the characteristics of a cabal; they were to all intents and purposes self-appointed, the original subscribers having died, left the colony, or lost interest; most were of long standing and their biographies reveal a network of powerful men, many of them owing their present eminence to a grammar school education. The chairman was ex-premier Sir Samuel Griffith, now out of politics and Chief Justice of Queensland; there were three other lawyers, among them John Woolcock, private secretary to Griffith and by 1899 parliamentary counsel, and Edwyn Lilley, son of Sir Charles Lilley who had died in 1897. Lewis Bernays, a trustee since 1875, was now Clerk of the Queensland Parliament.[53] The trustees seldom visited the school, and their meetings, which often failed to raise a quorum, were held in town.

In the first three years of Fewings' headship there was nothing in the annual reports to forewarn of the troubles she would encounter in 1899. For the first intimations of discontent it is again necessary to refer to the *Brisbane Courier*, for in December 1897 a series of letters appeared, deploring the intentions of the new headmistress to modify the curriculum with domestic and recreational subjects such as music, dancing, cookery, millinery and sport.[54] Miss Fewings' belief in the efficacy of domestic education was on the public record both in her annual speech day addresses and in an interview she had given to the *Queenslander* soon after her arrival.[55] Yet to conclude, as some historians have done, that Fewings was an anachronism, reaching back to the ladies' academy tradition for inspiration, is mistaken. Her previous career in Wales is a matter of public record. In the mid-1890s domestic education for secondary school girls presented itself under the banner of reform, and Fewings was among the first educationists in Australia to take up the cause. The letters of December 1897 are written with inside knowledge of the school; they also deplore the recent departure of classics and mathematics mistresses, Amy Barrington and Mary Raymond, and their impending replacement by a history specialist; they point out that Elinor Bourne, the most brilliant girl yet to attend the school, had been obliged to study almost exclusively at the boys' school; and that the coveted Fairfax Prize of the University of Sydney had eluded the girls for the previous three years. Neither the trustees nor Eliza Fewings made any public comment on the issues raised in the letters at the time.

In hindsight the 'Fewings affair' began with the appointment in January 1898 of Maud Sellers of Newnham College, Cambridge, the history specialist referred to in the letters of 1897. By her own testimony, Fewings had met Sellers in England on several occasions and was enthusiastic about her Brisbane appointment. Indeed as the letters implied, she was prepared to overlook the fact that Sellers' specialist teaching subjects were not what was required. Sellers had taken the historical tripos at Cambridge in 1892 and served for five years as second mistress (a position equivalent to vice-principal) of the prestigious Baker Street High School for Girls, London.[56]

To put in perspective Maud Sellers and her influence at the Brisbane Girls' Grammar School it is necessary to understand the missionary spirit in which the Cambridge of her time sent forth young women to be secondary school teachers. The early Cambridge women perceived their world as fragile; unlike the first generations of university women in Australia they set out to nurture the next generation. A network of Cambridge-educated heads—among them Sara Burstall of Manchester High School, Edith Creak of Birmingham High School, and Jane Dove of Wycombe Abbey—kept close links with Eleanor Sidgwick of Newnham and Emily Davies of Girton, sending back their most academically able girls, many of them on scholarships, to renew the cycle of educated young women.[57] The alumni volumes of Newnham and Girton reveal the extent of this traffic.

In this atmosphere of missionary endeavour it was but a short step to Empire, and succeeding heads of both colleges exhorted their young women to go as teachers to India, Australia, South Africa and Canada. By the 1880s Australian girls' schools had become part of the network of the Cambridge women, networks sustained through their alumni and professional associations and through personal correspondence with their heads of college. In their first decades the Queensland girls' grammar schools recruited many Cambridge women: Hannah Lister of Girton, whose articles of agreement with Brisbane Girls' Grammar School survive in the archives; Charlotte Pells of Newnham whom we have already met; Caroline Darling of Newnham, headmistress of Maryborough Girls' Grammar School and close friend of Beatrice Webb; Amy Barrington of Girton who published articles on the education of Australian girls in the *Girton Review*;[58] and Mary Sybil Raymond, also of Girton, who followed Barrington as second mistress at Brisbane. The appointment of Maud Sellers was by no means unique. The Australian diary of Sidney and Beatrice Webb described Sellers as 'a somewhat unpleasant example of the pioneer woman intent on dominating her new home' and on this occasion the supercilious Webbs may have been right.[59]

The mutual dislike between Maud Sellers and Eliza Fewings is palpable in the surviving documentation. Sellers disagreed fundamentally with the organisation of the school under Fewings, and her self-published exposé of the inner workings of the school is a unique practitioner's view of the English high school for girls at the end of the century.[60] By May 1899 she was writing to the trustees asking to be relieved of her position as resident second mistress on the grounds that she could no longer tolerate the responsibility without the authority to put things right.[61] Sellers maintained throughout that the crucial issue was one of school organisation; whereas the most advanced secondary schools in England were organised around the specialist teacher who taught her own subject vertically through the school, Eliza Fewings had reorganised the Brisbane school around the generalist teacher who took the same class for a wide range of subjects on the model of the elementary school. Sellers also alleged that Fewings was not qualified to be headmistress and was not capable of exercising the necessary supervision over the work of the school. Griffith and Woolcock were appointed as a subcommittee to inquire into her charges and their report was presented to their fellow trustees in July. They concluded that Fewings had indeed radically altered the organisation of the school which had been based on specialist teaching by specialist staff geared more directly to examinations. In their view, in order to 'command the intellectual respect and deference of the rest of the staff' the headmistress of a public school should be qualified to supervise the senior work and to teach at that level herself. They now alleged that Fewings was not so qualified, that it was a matter of 'notoriety' that she exercised no such supervision, and that she taught only the junior classes. Fewings, who had been interviewed in the course of the inquiry, was invited to reply in writing to this damning indictment and she refused to shift from her position that, as a leading figure in girls' education for twenty-five years, she was better able to judge how the school should be run than Sellers or the trustees.[62] She asked repeatedly for an impartial inspection of the school but none was ever held. In hindsight it is clear that the chairman of the trustees, Samuel Griffith, expected her to go quietly but this she refused to do.

On the morning of 18 September 1899 the Brisbane Girls' Grammar School descended into farce. Trustees Edwyn Lilley and John Woolcock were deputed to attend the school at 9 a.m. to see Miss Fewings off the premises and to install Miss Sellers in her place as temporary headmistress. Fewings was waiting in her office with a prepared statement, attended by two representatives of the press who took down verbatim the ensuing exchange. It was, she insisted, a matter of public interest. She obtained a stay of execution on a technicality but Lilley and Woolcock returned two hours later with further instructions from Griffith, after which Fewings left the school and did not return. Next day the *Brisbane Courier* was in fine form.

For the second time in its history, Brisbane Girls' Grammar School became public territory, as conflicting notions of a secondary school for girls were debated as a matter of public interest. There were disclosures in the press by Fewings, Sellers and the trustees; there were crowded public meetings, deputations, editorials, and letters to the editor; once again the spectre of central control was raised in parliament; even the English *Journal of Education* intervened in the debate.[63] The *Brisbane Courier* constructed a sense of overwhelming support for the headmistress but even without its intervention the spectacle of the diminutive and ladylike Eliza Fewings 'daring to meet in open battle so distinguished . . . a general as the Chief Justice' was bound to arouse the chivalrous instincts of middle-class Brisbane. The *Brisbane Courier* fuelled the flames with its editorial position that, whatever Miss Fewings' failings were, fair play had been denied her 'by a body of men presided over by the Chief Justice himself'.[64]

As the actions of Janet O'Connor and Eliza Fewings reveal, the creation of a state-funded school for girls gave women themselves access to public discourse. In their response to the sacking of Eliza Fewings we can see the traces of women where they are usually to be found; in localised and personal struggles over the possession of structures which are seldom of their own making. They too constructed their own Eliza Fewings, and the transformation of the Fewings affair into a women's issue was swift. Leontine Cooper wrote to the *Brisbane Courier* in 1899:

> I think it is a woman's quarrel, though in a difference sense to that intended by you. It is . . . a woman's question, when a woman who for three years . . . had held the responsible position of training the future women of the colony has her professional reputation wrecked and is summarily dismissed . . . the women of Brisbane are highly indignant at the injustice done to one of their number, who during her residence among them has won general respect.[65]

'Elizabeth', a grammar school mother and a member of the committee which organised the 'influential protest' of behalf of Fewings, called for a board of management composed of 'persons of both sexes'. The female members, she suggested, 'should be women of social standing and education, allied to a capacity for business and domestic management.'[66] 'What can two barristers, however talented, know about the internal economy of a girls' school?', 'Junius' demanded to know.[67] Several letters from women warned that they would remove their daughters from the

Eliza Fewings
(John Oxley Library, Brisbane)

school if Fewings were not reinstated, and women's political groups such as the Women's Equal Franchise Association and the Women's Christian Temperance Union passed resolutions of support.[68]

In their eagerness to testify to Fewings' achievements as headmistress, some of her supporters fell into denigration of the school before her time. May McConnel, whose detailed knowledge of Fewings' career in England invites the suspicion of collaboration, claimed that the 'public mind' had never been satisfied with the grammar school:

> The elementary work had been bad, the moral tone by no means high, the physical well-being of the girls a thing of little consideration, the home refinement within its walls nil, and there has been a general understanding that the honours taken by some of the scholars were taken by dint of hard cram, at the expense . . . of more ordinary scholars.[69]

In McConnel's view, within weeks of Fewings' arrival, the moral tone of the school had changed; girls no longer loitered about the gates of the boys' school, or paraded the streets after school hours. The home life of the school was refined: 'a well-appointed table and decent cooking, well-trained servants, and the general attributes of a lady's home' replaced the gauntness of the previous regime. In girls' education, McConnel concluded, these are the things which 'make a refined woman of her, and give her an influence peculiarly her own in home and nation'. Testimony such as this drew an angry response from former students protesting at this calumny which 'brand[ed] as ill-bred hundreds of gentlewomen, now scattered through the colony'.[70]

These sentiments made good copy but they did not save the headmistress. Taken at face value, they were unlikely to throw light upon the everyday reality, the unpredictable trajectory of pedagogy in practice, which had led Eliza Fewings to reorganise the school. A new reading of the Fewings affair, divorced from personalities, raises important theoretical and methodological issues in the history of women's education.

In common with all the new secondary schools for girls, the founding mission of the Brisbane Girls' Grammar School was to prove that women were the intellectual equals of men. In the circumstances of the times, this could only be achieved through success at the public examinations conducted by the University of Sydney. The regulations also mandated a twice-yearly internal examination of the school, 'conducted by such examiners as the Trustees may appoint'; into the twentieth century the published report ranked the girls in order of their performance. The same reports listed an abundance of honours, prizes and medals, presented before 'a large and fashionable audience' at the annual speech day. Pre-eminent among these awards was the Lady Lilley Gold Medal and in the exacting requirements for its bestowal (first class honours in the traditional academic subjects) we may read Sir Charles Lilley's vision of a secondary school for girls. The words 'not awarded' occur regularly on the school's honour board. Yet this elaborate technology of assessment was not enough. In January 1877, as the dust from the O'Connor affair settled, the *Brisbane Courier* devoted an editorial to the success of the boys' school at the public examinations of the University of Sydney, concluding: 'Our Girls' Grammar School will no doubt send some representatives to the next of these interesting competitions, for it is by such means that the efficiency of the teaching power of a school . . . can be tested'.[71] The daily and reluctant procession of masters to the girls' school was to achieve precisely that end. One of the charges against O'Connor was that she had 'evaded' the public examinations, though this she vigorously denied.[72] The first public examination successes came during Sarah Cargill's short tenure and in 1878 Bertha Marie Burdoff won the Senior Fairfax Prize for the top female candidate in the University of Sydney Senior Public Examination.[73] Thereafter the school quickly established its reputation as the premier academic school for girls in Queensland. The pinnacle of achievement was the Fairfax Prize, junior and senior, and the arrival of a telegram from Sydney, rushed on to the stage at speech day, was a not uncommon event at the girls' school. By 1900 the Brisbane girls had won the junior award five times and the senior award ten times.

Examination results were at the centre of the Fewings affair. Griffith charged that under her headship the school had slipped from first to last among the girls' grammar schools of Queensland and that the academic reputation of the school had suffered as a result. Both sides to the dispute fell eagerly upon the results of October 1899, in search of ammunition. Fewings herself published a detailed examination of the results in her term of office, in which she argued that no such decline had occurred, and that in any case 'results' were an artefact of many things.[74] Several grammar school headmistresses over the years had publicly expressed concern over the examination fetish and its early and enduring grip on the life of the girls' schools.[75] This 'evil' also blighted the life of the boys' schools but it fell with particular force upon the nineteenth-century girls' schools.

The modern schoolgirl did not spring, fully fledged, into existence. Like the female secondary school itself she had to be agreed upon; at the end of the century she was still an ambiguous figure, poised between childhood and womanhood, and between home and school. Her sexual self and her scholarly self had yet to part company. Prefects, houses, uniforms, and 'games'—Thomas Arnold's technologies of the masculine self—were still suspect in the production of the female elite. The invention of the schoolgirl required a shift in the locus of power away from the home, yet the nineteenth-century state was loath to require the middle-class child to attend school. Girls at the new secondary schools were a disorderly lot. They continued to behave as the girls at the ladies' schools had always done: they enrolled at any time throughout the year; they came and went at all ages; they came and went as groups of sisters; they came late; their attendance was sporadic, dependent upon the weather, their menstrual cycles, the demands of their mothers, and the ever-present threat of childhood epidemics. In times of economic recession they were abruptly withdrawn. In Amy Barrington's view, Queensland parents were malleable in the hands of their daughters:

> If a girl likes a school she continues to attend it, [Barrington wrote home to Girton in 1894] if she dislikes it, or takes offence at her teacher's conduct, in most cases her removal is only a question of time. If she imagines her school education has lasted long enough, the parents appear to be easily persuaded to adopt the same opinion. With regard to the subjects they learn, the only real check on girls giving up subjects they dislike is the determination of the Head Mistress, for the parents seem quite ready to support any request of the child.[76]

In her report of 1897 Eliza Fewings estimated that the average age of admission was 14.4 years, and the average length of stay two years. The term 'grammar school polish' had entered the vocabulary of middle-class Brisbane by the time of the Fewings affair.

Fee-paying girls were not obliged to demonstrate upon entrance their special fitness for a grammar school education beyond a simple test in reading, writing and arithmetic; indeed the exclusion of daughters from the powerful families of Brisbane would have been impossible. Nor were the new secondary schools for girls articulated with a system of preparatory education. New arrivals were variously educated at home, at private girls' schools, and by the state; nothing could be assumed about their standards of attainment. No matter how outstanding the staff, much time had to be spent on foundation and remedial work. The monolithic vision of academic purpose which the new schools publicly projected was also put at risk by a perverse desire on the part of parents and girls to cling to the older accomplishments curriculum which they carved out of the new offerings with remarkable ingenuity. Even at the most academic of the new schools like Presbyterian Ladies' College in Melbourne, music, painting and modern languages retained their popularity, as individual parents put pressure on the school to modify the prescribed program.[77] These factors rendered problematical the aspirations of the new girls' schools to 'modern' pedagogical practice; the classification of students by age; simultaneous instruction by the classroom method; the recruitment of the specialist teacher; and an orderly progression through prescribed courses of study towards public examinations.

These daily realities in Australia's new secondary schools for girls forced into existence the controversial figure of the scholarship girl. At once central and marginal to the school community, she was the alter-ego of the disorderly schoolgirl. The scholarship girl was governable, her continuing presence subject to quarterly reports to her mentor, the educational state; 'It is hoped that you will continue to persevere in those habits of attention and industry which have enabled you to carry off this prize', ran the standard letter from the under-secretary of the Queensland Department of Public Instruction.[78] Upon the shoulders of the scholarship girl rested the academic reputation of the grammar school; she was expected to get 'results'. The scholarship girl walked a carefully guarded bridge between the grammar school and the state school. She was selected by competitive examination, encoding both the democratic impulses of the state, and its arrogant assumption that only the occasional working-class child could profit by a secondary education. The percentage of scholarship girls at the Brisbane Girls' Grammar School in the nineteenth century ranged from 11 per cent in 1890 to 36 per cent in 1898. In absolute numbers, the high point was reached in 1897 with forty-three scholarship girls out of an enrolment of 134.[79] The scholarship girls, many of them from families who may have patronised the school in any case, were financially and academically crucial to the Brisbane Girls' Grammar School.

This then was the texture of everyday life for Eliza Fewings at the Brisbane Girls' Grammar School. Whereas their descendants in the twentieth century juxtaposed the evil of 'cram' with the education of the whole child, the headmistresses of Fewings' generation juxtaposed the cramming of the few with the orderly progress of the many through the academic program to the achievement of examination honours. This was one of the many issues upon which they sought to distinguish themselves from the traditional ladies' schools. Eliza Fewings was one of the first headmistresses to sense that this monolithic vision of academic purpose was illusory.

Even as the battle raged around her, Eliza Fewings rented premises and hired staff; on 5 October 1899, barely two weeks after her dismissal, her new school began. Like Janet O'Connor before her, she took many of the girls with her, and her own school grew quickly into the largest girls' school in Queensland. As Somerville House, it is still in existence today.[80]

Maud Sellers was not appointed headmistress as she had hoped; the trustees appointed instead Milisent Wilkinson, headmistress of the Maryborough Girls' Grammar School. In 1900 Sellers herself was dismissed by Wilkinson, again in the full glare of public disclosure, eventually returning to England to doctoral studies and a distinguished career as a historian and archivist to the Merchant Adventurers of York.[81]

Sydney Girls' High School

Unlike the Queensland grammar schools, the state high schools of New South Wales were created contiguously with the state system of elementary schools and the Department of Public Instruction. The Public Instruction Act of 1880 legislated for the establishment of high schools, and provision for girls' schools was separately mentioned.[82] The initiative for the establishment of the schools was taken by George Reid, Minister of Public Instruction in 1883, who wrote in January of that year: 'I am determined to establish these temporary schools without delay. The architect will lose no time in carrying out the necessary alterations, for which plans should be submitted without delay ... Urgent.'[83] An avuncular figure who later became premier and prime minister, he was still to be found at speech days three decades later impressing upon the girls his chivalrous intent in the establishment of their school.[84] Reid pressed ahead and at the end of June 1883 the *Sydney Morning Herald* carried advertisements for the headships of the two Sydney high schools, offering a salary of £600 for the male head and £400 for the female head.[85] Two weeks later advertisements appeared for the headships of girls' and boys' high schools at Maitland, Goulburn and Bathurst. Though they did not all survive, this was to be the extent of the state's incursion into secondary education in the nineteenth century. The regulations were gazetted in July, and their substance—the content and standard of the entrance examination, the fees, and the scholarships to be awarded— were published in the press in August.[86] The Sydney advertisements carried the additional information that Joseph Coates, M.A., presently headmaster of the Methodist Newington College, had been appointed as head of the boys' school, and Lucy Wheatley Walker (no other details given) head of the girls' school.

The *Sydney Morning Herald* pre-empted the opening of the Sydney Girls' High School with an editorial intimating that the new schools had run into trouble: Sydney Boys' High School had opened the week before with only a modest enrolment; the response in Bathurst and Goulburn had been dismal; Maitland was not scheduled to open until the new year. This was in spite of the fact that at two guineas per quarter the fees were half those of existing secondary schools. Cheapness, the editorial continued, should be the chief attraction of the state high schools. Nevertheless, it warned that:

> by a large number of parents the new High schools will be regarded as nothing more than experiments. Schools like any other things have to work their way into public favour, and in the matter of schools, and of middle-class schools especially, parental taste is occasionally capricious.[87]

At the opening ceremony for the Sydney schools in October 1883, George Reid made light of these inauspicious beginnings. The choice of Professor Charles Badham to deliver the inaugural address was a timely reminder that, although the parents of New South Wales were in no hurry to enrol their daughters and sons in the new schools, the University of Sydney, always on the look-out for students, had a close interest in their success. As if to underscore the point Badham adapted for the occasion a speech he had delivered to the university students some years before, though on this occasion he did not give it in Latin.[88] In the event, the Sydney high schools began with 54 boys and 43 girls.

The hasty conversion of the former St James' Denominational School as temporary accommodation may have cut through the red tape at head office, but it also condemned the new Sydney high schools to cramped and unsuitable conditions for many years. The boys moved to new premises at Ultimo in 1892, and the girls to the present Moore Park premises in 1921, where they were subsequently joined by the boys. Like many of the denominational schools which came into the hands of the new Departments, the interior of St James' betrayed its origins as a monitorial school built by Governor Macquarie in the 1820s. The huge downstairs room still had its tiers of desks, and for some years three classes were taught side by side. Joseph Coates was on many occasions outspoken about the primitive conditions in which he was obliged to establish the premier high school of New South Wales. Enrolment had risen quickly to 145 boys and 100 girls by the end of the first year, and when the boys departed in 1892, leaving the girls in sole occupation, the combined enrolment was over seven hundred. Annual reports of the minister soon began to draw attention to the deplorable condition of the Sydney premises.[89]

The situation was exacerbated by the fact that until 1892 two autonomous schools existed in the same building. The proprieties of gender and geography required that the girls enter from Elizabeth Street and proceed up a flight of stairs to the second floor, while the boys entered from Castlereagh Street and used the ground floor. Even on the most stifling of Sydney days the boys were forbidden to open the ground

Sydney Girls' High School
(Mitchell Library, Sydney)

floor windows on the Elizabeth Street side. Though the existence of two
schools may have escaped the notice of the casual passer-by, for Lucy
Wheatley Walker, her staff and the girls, this administrative separation
created a space which would be denied to women in the co-educational
secondary schools of the twentieth century.

English-born Lucy Wheatley Walker was thirty-two years old when she
was appointed founding headmistress of the Sydney Girls' High School
in 1883, and she was to remain in the position for thirty-five years. Her
various biographers cannot agree on the circumstances of her arrival in
Australia, although they do agree that she trained as a governess in her
youth. The most likely version is that she came to Australia as governess
to the children of Charles Badham.[90] With Janet O'Connor and Eliza
Fewings she belonged to the pre-university generation of female leaders
in education, though she lacked their experience as a headmistress.
George Reid placed on the public record that it was Badham who chose
her for the position from a field of twenty-two candidates, and she
remained close to the Badham family, attempting unsuccessfully to
appoint Julia Badham to the staff by the back door.[91] In June 1891 she

unexpectedly married William Charles Garvin, a draughtsman ten years her junior. The marriage has caused more consternation among historians than it did at the time, as in 1891 there was no regulation excluding women from the service upon marriage, and many chose to continue teaching.[92] Lucy Garvin gave birth to three children between 1892 and 1897, on each occasion applying for three weeks' leave.[93] Garvin's husband William died suddenly in February 1898.

When Sydney Girls' High School opened at the end of 1883 Isola Thompson and Mary Brown were well into their Arts degrees at the University of Sydney. The curriculum of the school reflected from the outset the new orthodoxy that women had a right to an academic education leading to public examinations, the university, and the professions. Nevertheless, the framers of the girls' school curriculum still hankered after the reassuring markers of sexual difference.[94] The girls did not study Greek, and Latin was optional, whereas the boys studied Latin, and Greek was optional; the boys studied mathematics while the girls studied 'elementary mathematics'; for girls, the study of French and German was compulsory, while for boys French was compulsory but German was not; boys were offered geometrical and perspective drawing while the girls were offered freehand and perspective; girls were offered music, cookery and needlework while the boys were not. Only English language and literature, elocution, history, and physical science appeared alike in the girls' and boys' prospectus, though elocution meant very different things for boys and girls, and laboratories appeared in the boys' school long before they appeared in the girls' school. Cookery was ephemeral, reflecting the scepticism of the headmistress and the parents, though speech day orators were inclined to impress upon the girls their duties in that regard.

Like the Brisbane Girls' Grammar School, Sydney Girls' High School quickly developed a reputation for academic excellence; indeed speech day reports and ministerial reports spoke of little else. At speech day in 1889 Lucy Garvin reported that the girls had already won the Fairfax Prize three times, and by the time she coaxed from Under-Secretary John Maynard permission to install honour boards in 1895, the girls had accumulated an impressive array of matriculation honours and prizes.[95] The names of past pupils distinguishing themselves at the University of Sydney soon began to appear in annual reports; in 1889 Minister Joseph Carruthers noted the progress of Ella Sutherland, who became the first girl from the school to graduate from Sydney, and Fanny (Iza) Coghlan, one of the original thirty-nine students, and one of the first two women to graduate in medicine.[96] In 1907 Garvin claimed that of the 206 female graduates of the University of Sydney, one hundred had matriculated from Sydney Girls' High School.[97]

As it was from the beginning administered centrally by the Department of Public Instruction, Sydney Girls' is more transparent than its counterpart in Brisbane; its daily and acrimonious transactions with head office are voluminously preserved in the Archives of New South Wales. For many years, Garvin too had male teachers for mathematics, classics, modern languages and drawing, many of them shared with the brother school downstairs. Dr Etienne Thibault, member of the French Academy, and reputedly a friend of Victor Hugo, was modern languages teacher to both Sydney high schools. He clashed fiercely and often with Mrs Garvin. In 1885 he wrote to the Department demanding that 'this Headmistress be distinctly called . . . to a sense of her duties and attributions, and severely ordered to cease all her persecutions and underhand work'.[98] On this occasion he had been accused of striking one of the girls a 'violent blow on the head with a book', a charge which he claimed was orchestrated by Garvin in her campaign against him. The Department continued to back the authority of its headmistress but the skirmishing continued. Edward Blackmore, visiting teacher of Latin and mathematics in 1884, had the virtues of decrepitude and respectability, but as he could neither teach nor discipline the girls, his services were dispensed with.[99] William Crompton had made the transition from Brisbane to Sydney Boys' High and he fared no better with Lucy Garvin than he had done with Janet O'Connor. In Garvin's view his manner was over-familiar, wanting in 'delicacy and refinement' and ill-suited to a girls' school.[100] A series of unsatisfactory visiting teachers of classics and mathematics came and went, though Walter Holmes, an M.A. from Cambridge, was an inspirational teacher of classics at the school for over thirty years.[101]

Lucy Garvin began in 1883 with two female teachers, Marion O'Brien, who held the position of first assistant until her marriage in 1889, and Lucy Higgs, who left in 1884 to become the second headmistress of the short-lived Goulburn Girls' High School. Higgs was the first of many of Garvin's staff to be appointed headmistress in the state high schools. The first female graduate to be appointed to Sydney Girls' was 23-year-old Isola Florence Thompson, and she was to spend her whole teaching career at the school, succeeding Marion O'Brien as first assistant in 1890. Thompson would almost certainly have become headmistress had not Garvin outlasted her, and she applied unsuccessfully for the principalship of the residential Hurlstone Training School for women teachers in 1903.[102] She had come through the state system and qualified as a pupil-teacher, listing on her original application her experience in assisting her father in his various public elementary schools. Deputy Chief Inspector Frederick Bridges was impressed, and recommended her as a 'decided acquisition' to the staff of the high school. The first past student to return as a teacher was Ruth Bowmaker. According to her referee she was from a 'respectable family . . . in straitened circumstances', and had attended Paddington Superior Public School, gaining a scholarship at the high schools' entrance examination. She was a brilliant student, a Fairfax Prize winner matriculating at the age of fourteen, and dux of the school in 1888. Her Arts degree was equally distinguished (she graduated B.A. in 1892 and M.A. in 1895) and by the age of nineteen she was marking time as governess to the children of the Countess of Jersey.

> I should much prefer a position in a school to being a governess [she wrote to the under-secretary in 1892]: in the High School especially I have always taken the greatest interest, and as I spent so many years there, I am familiar with the routine of the school . . . I trust that the fact of my having received the bulk of my education under the Government will be some recommendation to the department to consider my application.[103]

Lucy Garvin welcomed her *protégée* back to the school as a probationary teacher in 1893.

Though the insularity of the Department of Public Instruction ensured that insiders like Thompson and Bowmaker became the preferred recruits to the new girls' high schools, initial recruitment was of necessity more eclectic. Annie Fraser Watson, twenty-three years old, was newly arrived from Scotland and teaching at Miss Thomas' Ladies' College in Bathurst when she applied for a position at the Sydney school in 1885. She had attended the West End Public School, Elgin, and taught there as a pupil-teacher before entering the Moray House Training College in Edinburgh. She taught at the Merchant Companies High School in Edinburgh, passed the University locals, went to Germany to study for a year, and then taught in London and Paris.[104] Annie Watson was appointed to the Sydney Girls' High School in 1885 but stayed only two years before her appointment as head of Maitland Girls' High School in 1887. Jeanette Grossman was teaching at Methodist Ladies' College, Melbourne, when she applied for a position in 1889.[105] She had graduated B.A. in 1882 and M.A. in 1883 from the University of Auckland, obtained a Teacher Training Certificate from the Board of Education in North Canterbury, and taught in schools in New Zealand before coming to Australia. In 1890 she followed Annie Watson as headmistress of Maitland Girls' High School, where she stayed until 1914 when she became headmistress at North Sydney Girls' High School.[106] Several women had attended private girls' schools or taught there before applying for positions at the state high school. Caroline Whitfeld, daughter of Edwin Whitfeld, classics master at Sydney Grammar School, was not a graduate but her senior Fairfax Prize and her six years' teaching experience in a private school were sufficient to gain a position at Sydney Girls' in

1886.[107] She applied unsuccessfully for the principalship of Brisbane Girls' Grammar in 1888 when Charlotte Pells was appointed.[108] Her younger sister Eleanor (Madeline) Whitfeld, did attend Sydney Girls' High School, where she was dux in 1890. She went on to the University of Sydney where she entered Sydney Women's College on the Grace Frazer Scholarship in 1892, graduating B.A. with first class honours in 1895. She applied for a position at Sydney Girls' in 1896, but appears to have taught instead at Ascham until her marriage to historian G.A. Wood in 1898.[109] Ettie Artlett, B.A., was educated at Emily Baxter's Argyle School. Pearl Ella Barnes, M.A., had 'training in the . . . art of teaching, under Miss Hodge of Shirley', and had taught at Abbotsleigh.[110] The Cambridge women who staffed the Queensland grammar schools in the early decades were conspicuous by their absence, except for Hannah Lister who, as Mrs Binns, taught mathematics at various Sydney high schools until she was over seventy.[111]

Though they were aristocratic among women workers and idolised by the girls, the youthful mistresses worked long hours under difficult conditions for modest salaries. In 1885 second mistress Isola Thompson received £150 per annum, Annie Watson £120, and Caroline Whitfeld £100. As a percentage of the salaries paid to teachers of the same rank in the boys' school, female salaries ranged from 75 per cent for the first assistant to 45 per cent for the fourth assistant.[112] Salary increases were granted or denied on the whim of head office, only sometimes in consultation with Lucy Garvin. In 1887 Isola Thompson applied to the chief inspector for a salary increase on the grounds that she now had two years' teaching experience and had gained her M.A. Lucy Garvin reported to the chief inspector that she was 'unable to speak very highly of Miss Thompson's success as a Teacher', and the request was denied.[113] In 1901 Ruth Bowmaker wrote protesting that after nine years of service her salary was still only £120, while another teacher, very much her junior, had just been appointed on a higher salary. Bowmaker's salary increase was also denied.[114] On these modest salaries, the women were often supporting relatives. Lucy Garvin, whose salary rose a paltry £27 in the first decade, had three children to support after her husband died in 1898. Jeanette Grossman took with her to Maitland her mother, two adult sisters, one of whom became a pupil-teacher, and a sixteen-year-old brother.[115] Isola Thompson lived with her widowed mother and was presumably partly financially responsible for her. Many of the women were continuing with their university education while teaching at the school. Poor health and 'nervous debility' were commonplace. Caroline Whitfeld wrote in 1905: 'During the last three months I have felt tired out mentally and physically. This has resulted sometimes in sudden loss of memory with regard to everyday matters: or in attacks of sleeplessness.

The unexpected death of my father . . . has been a great shock'.[116] Garvin appealed often, but usually in vain, for more staff.

The problems of staffing Sydney Girls' High School were symptomatic of a larger reality which shaped the everyday life of the school. While the Brisbane Girls' Grammar School eventually commanded respect as new kind of school, the Sydney school was engulfed in the egregious mentality of the nineteenth-century public elementary school. Sydney Girls' High School was the suspect newcomer, both as a secondary school and as a school for girls, created and administered on the fringes of the ramshackle empire of elementary schools upon which the Public Instruction Act of 1880 was expected to impose order. Subject to the centralised control of the minister and his officers from the beginning, its status as a secondary school could not be achieved in the traditional manner through an alliance with the governing classes of Sydney; yet its relationship to the public elementary school was still to emerge.

Sydney Girls' High School was administered by men who inhabited the world of the public elementary school. This administrative reality was encapsulated in the uneasy relationship between Lucy Garvin and Frederick Bridges, whose rise from the ranks of the humble school teacher was contiguous with the early decades of the school's existence. A disciple of William Wilkins, he was reputedly the first male pupil-teacher trained by the Board of National Education in the 1850s and by 1867 he was headmaster of the prestigious Fort Street Public School. A decade later he was appointed inspector and when he and Garvin met professionally he had risen to deputy chief inspector. To Bridges it was an article of faith that 'a spirit of subordination [should] pervade all ranks of the service', and that teachers should set an example of obedience to authority.[117] This mentality ensured that Garvin had to endure endless pinpricks: she was rebuked for appearing in George Street after the time of assembly for afternoon classes; she was rebuked for declaring a half-day holiday at the end of term; she had to submit for approval the names of books for the teachers' library; she must apply for permission to hold a concert; she was refused permission to have the phone connected. Yearly inspection by the primary inspectorate meant that she was obliged to conform to pedagogical practices which had evolved to chasten the working-class children and their teachers in the elementary schools.[118] When Inspector McCredie examined the school for the first time in 1884 he wrote:

> there is no Daily Report Book as in Public Schools, nor any quarterly return kept in progress from week to week. It is desirable that an admission register, a daily report book and quarterly return forms should be furnished to Miss Walker and that she be instructed to keep them for the information of the

Department . . . The teaching is guided by a timetable, but there are no programmes and no record is kept of the work done daily. A register of lessons should be kept and a scheme of lessons programmed for each class in each subject, as in the Public Schools.[119]

Though the Lucy Garvin who emerges from the school's official history is something of a martinet, the officers of the Department often thought otherwise. An inspector who visited in 1901 was shocked by the casual comings and goings of the girls in the classes he inspected. Garvin was asked to 'furnish an explanation in regard to laxity of Discipline'.[120]

Garvin's thirty-five year struggle to shape a secondary school for girls in the looming presence of the primary-trained men was further complicated by the legislative decision to create an alternative form of publicly funded secondary education in New South Wales. The Public Instruction Act of 1880 also provided for the establishment of 'Superior Public Schools in towns and populous districts in which additional lessons in the higher branches of education may be given'.[121] In essence this meant that where sufficient children could be found to form a fifth class on the top of an existing public school, Latin, mathematics, and French would be taught for a small weekly fee. The superior public schools were an immediate success—indeed they were a codification of existing practice rather than a radical new departure—and unlike the high schools they always enjoyed the warm glow of official approval.

By the turn of the century there were 102 superior public schools, and historians agree that they account for the poor performance of the high schools. The *bête noire* of the Sydney high schools was the Fort Street Public School which had in effect turned itself into a high school by the end of the century. In 1894, when his enrolments were declining in the economic recession, Joseph Coates of Sydney Boys' High School protested to the Department:

At Fort St, Crown St, and other leading Public Schools, not only are special classes formed for the 'Junior', but special assistance is given to boys preparing for the 'Senior' and 'Matriculation'. This, of course, is no business of mine, but as long as all this is done for 3d. and our fees are raised in these hard times to 3 guineas, we cannot very well expect a crowded school.[122]

In 1898 Lucy Garvin testified before the Public Service Board that she would not get 'the cream of the Public School girls' as long as they could attend the matriculation classes organised for boys at Fort Street; indeed she feared that her school would soon become a 'feeder' for the Fort Street school. As Garvin understood, the situation was unlikely to change while girls could become public school teachers without attending high school.[123]

Yet Sydney Girls' High School was expected to orient itself towards the public elementary school. The original regulations of 1883 provided for a stiff entrance examination, immortalised by Louise Mack in her autobiographical novel *Teens*. The entrance examination eliminated some of the problems which beset Brisbane Girls' Grammar, although entry requirements were later modified to require only satisfactory completion of the third class at a public school. Scholarships (and later bursaries) were awarded upon the results of entry examinations. Much was made of the first scholarships at the opening ceremony in October 1883—they were awarded 'not as a charity but as a distinction'—and among the recipients who received their honours from Professor Badham was the future novelist, Ethel Turner. For those who passed the entrance examination but were 'duly certified to be unable to pay' there was provision for remission of fees.[124] The examination into the circumstances of the family concerned was always intrusive in the extreme:

> I find that Mrs X is a widow having three children dependent upon her [wrote Inspector Allpass in 1885]. Mrs X is in the employ of Farmer and Co. as a needlewoman. Judging by the . . . scanty manner in which her cottage—a rented one—is furnished, I conclude that Mrs X is a person of straitened means.[125]

The Department gradually backed away from this provision for the remission of fees and its officers took particular exception to girls who entered the school and subsequently asked for fees to be waived. In 1889 Inspector George wrote upon an application: 'were indiscriminate encouragement given to the free education of [enrolled] pupils . . . the School would be swamped'.[126] He recommended strict adherence to the rule of payment in advance. The economic recession of the early 1890s firmed the resolve of Minister F.B. Suttor, who in 1893 replied to a question in parliament on the annual cost of the high schools: 'I have given directions that in future no children, except those receiving bursaries and scholarships, are to be educated in these high schools without paying fees'.[127] In the same year, and in the face of almost universal condemnation, fees rose suddenly from two guineas to three guineas per quarter. Two years later Lucy Garvin was still pleading with the minister for the fees to be restored to their former level.[128] She argued that her enrolments had not initially been affected by the recession but had dropped immediately with the increase in fees. By 1894 enrolments were down to 217. Garvin cited the distress of the girls who were suddenly withdrawn and the disadvantage to those whose stay at school would be shortened. She feared that the excellent results for which the school had become known (detailed in a five-page attachment to her letter) would in future have to be obtained by 'cram'. Frederick Bridges minuted the letter: 'I do not think it would be wise to make any alteration at present'.

Under the circumstances, the occasional outbreaks of official concern about the social origins of the girls have about them a whiff of hypocrisy. Though it did not become the personal fiefdom of an elite, Sydney Girls' High School carried the familiar markings of a middle-class presence. Three lists of parental occupations survive in the Archives of New South Wales—for the years 1884, 1886 and 1899—and it does not require elaborate statistical analysis to reveal that the extremes of Sydney society are under-represented. The aristocrats among the professionals—solicitors, doctors, clergymen, architects, engineers, and politicians—are present, but greatly outnumbered by the lesser professional men in school teaching and the public service. There is a significant presence of the entrepreneurial classes (auctioneer, general agent, manager of boot factory, draper, grocer) but the problems of interpretation are acute; this frustration was apparently shared at the time, as an unknown hand has scribbled in the margin: 'manager of what?' At least as well represented as the entrepreneurial classes are those workers customarily designated as the aristocracy of labour—stonemason, tailor, carpenter, blacksmith, baker, ironmonger. Only three parents are listed as 'labourer'. The category 'widow' is large, though this designation tells us nothing about the social origins of the woman, nor indeed about her livelihood. Only once did the categorisation of 'widow' carry the additional information 'boarding house keeper'. Anecdotal evidence from other sources suggests that the category 'widow' included families on the way up and others on the way down. Fanny Coghlan's mother Dorcas Coghlan is representative of the former group. Her working-class background in Redfern is on the public record because her son, T.A. Coghlan (later Sir Timothy Coghlan), became government statistician and has attracted the attention of historians.[129] Her husband Thomas was a plasterer and after his death she showed great determination and self-sacrifice to ensure that her nine talented children could rise through the public school system into the white-collar professions. It was Mrs Coghlan who complained to Lucy Garvin that Dr Thibault had assaulted her daughter with a book. Ethel Turner's middle-class mother Sarah represents the widow on the way down. She was twice widowed, though she had recently married for the third time when the first list of parental occupations was compiled in 1884. Ethel's stepfather was the model for the irascible Captain Woolcot in *Seven Little Australians*.[130]

Lucy Garvin's own social standing as a member of the upper professional classes of Sydney gave the school a certain social cachet: her close friend Edith Badham was by 1895 headmistress of Sydney Church of England Girls' Grammar School (SCEGGS); Garvin was professionally and socially acceptable to the university professors and their circle. Louisa Macdonald often presented the prizes at speech day, though she noted in a letter to her London friends that she did not much care for Mrs Garvin. From time to time Garvin's own perceptions of her clientele come through the formality of official business:

> I want, urgently, [she wrote in 1900] a cultivated woman, whose pronunciation and voice may be a sort of object lesson and example. The pupils of this school are largely composed of the daughters of poor gentle folk and even the slight errors, made by teachers, in grammar, accent and pronunciation are noted immediately, and lessen the influence and success of the Teacher.[131]

Garvin also experienced the determination of parents to retain the traditional accomplishments in the curriculum. Despite her long-running feud with Etienne Thibault, she was convinced that her school would not thrive if it did not offer music, modern languages and drawing taught by visiting specialist staff. In 1897 she wrote to the Department:

> I beg also respectfully to point out to you that the prestige of this school has considerably suffered in the eyes of the Public by the loss of special teachers such as the French Master, the Drawing Master and the teacher of Cookery. Several parents have given me this as a reason for withdrawing their daughters . . . In French our pupils no longer have the advantage of acquiring a perfectly pure accent by learning from a native.[132]

She requested permission to engage Fraulein Martha Fast, visiting teacher of French and German at SCEGGS and other leading private schools, for six hours per week.[133] Frederick Bridges recommended against the appointment on the grounds of excessive cost and past problems with visiting teachers.

Though there was no public blood-letting comparable with the Fewings affair in Brisbane, there is evidence that Sydney Girls' High School had also reached a premature middle-age by the end of the century. The inspectors' report of 1903, issued in the first month of Frederick Bridges' appointment as acting director general, criticised all aspects of the school's performance. As with Fewings, Garvin's credentials were called into question:

> Mrs Garvin, the Head Mistress is not a scientist, a mathematician, or a classic [sic]. She has, we believe, a good knowledge of French . . . We are of opinion that, if this school is to take its proper place as a High School it should be placed under a Principal, male or female, of wide attainments and scholastic experience. Such a one would be able to shake the spirit of routine that exists, and infuse life and energy into the whole of the school.[134]

Whereas Fewings had been replaced as headmistress because of a perception that she had diluted the academic program of the school, Garvin was criticised on precisely the opposite grounds: '[In the girls' school], as in the boys' High School, the requirements of the University examinations and the desire of the pupils to pass those examinations have converted the school into a coaching institution, and the aim of a wide culture is thereby sacrificed'.[135] There followed a detailed critique of the teaching and organisation of the school, with the work of the women teachers coming in for particular criticism. Hereafter, A.M. Armstrong was to be placed in charge of mathematics 'with authority to classify and arrange courses of study and to examine', and Walter Holmes was to be placed in charge of French and classics, 'with similar authority'. Ironically, a specialist teacher of French, preferably a Frenchman, was to be appointed: there had been 'too much book work and little attempt made to encourage the pupils to use the language as a means of thought and expression'. As a final turn of the knife, Mrs Garvin was advised to visit Fort Street to see what had been accomplished there in the teaching of languages. In pursuit of the 'liberal education' urged by the inspectors, natural science, civics and morals, and physical education were to be introduced into the curriculum.

The report drew attention yet again to the appalling physical conditions in which the school was obliged to operate, hardly a state of affairs which could be sheeted home to Lucy Garvin. The final indignity came in September 1904 when the City of Sydney declared the premises to be 'dangerous to health and therefore a nuisance within the meaning of the . . . Act'.[136] Garvin wrote a pedantic ten-page rebuttal of the report of 1903, choosing not to answer the charges that her school had degenerated into a coaching college and that she was unfit to lead it.[137] Indeed she continued to insist that the academic honours which her girls consistently won vindicated her conduct of the school. Her reply was minuted: 'The Department has every confidence in the correctness of its Officers' reports— . . . she should carry out implicitly the instructions already given—and . . . she be warned that a marked improvement in the general results will be looked for at next Examination.'[138] Both the Fewings affair in 1899 and the attack upon Garvin in 1903 should be seen in the light of considerable disquiet about the influence of university-controlled examinations on the secondary schools of Australia, disquiet which eventually led to an overhaul of the relationship in the twentieth century.[139]

If the report of 1903 was intended as a Fewings-style execution of a woman who no longer served the purposes of those in power, it did not succeed. Garvin remained headmistress until 1918, though on yearly contracts from 1911 when it was revealed that she was five years older than she had claimed. Even then her staff petitioned the Department to retain her services, pleading that at sixty-eight her presence was 'still the source of inspiration that it had so long been to a large number of the most highly educated women of this State'.[140]

The new secondary schools for girls which emerged in the Western nations in the last quarter of the nineteenth century have a special place in the history of women's education, and it was not the intention of this study to dislodge them. They were called into existence by two quintessentially middle-class movements, the emancipation of women and the invention of the meritocracy. If they shared the ambiguities of those potentially emancipatory social movements we should not be surprised. The two Australian schools in this study were established under the rubric of 'the movement for the higher education of women', yet they were established and controlled by men who envisaged no change in the role of women in their society. Ambiguity also accompanied their relentless pursuit of the academic honours which gave entry to the male world of noble deeds when the generality of women still lived their lives within the timeless cycle of child-bearing and family. Did this mean that girls at school experienced a debilitating double load of the masculine and the feminine, as some scholars have suggested, or new and exciting ways of being a woman? Yet the question itself presupposes that monolithic sense of purpose and outcome which this study of two Australian schools brings into question. Proof of intellectual parity with men proved far less elusive than the imagined community of pious young women diligently pursuing the scholarly life. Though they emerged in the same decade from the same broad social movements, by the end of the century Brisbane Grammar and Sydney Girls' were very different schools. Brisbane Grammar had aligned itself with the Queensland governing classes, combining academic honours with the attributes of a high-class Edwardian ladies' college. The respect which Eliza Fewings could still command in the free market of female education was more than a matter of personalities. Sydney Girls' High School had no connection with the ladies' school tradition; it was pushed upwards from the elementary school system. The central administration of the school, its close relationship with the public schools of New South Wales, the physical squalor of the premises in the insalubrious inner city, and its *déclassé* status as a day school ensured that the school could not surround itself with the mystique of the Brisbane Girls' Grammar School. Its shortcomings were tolerated by families on the way up and on the way down whose daughters needed qualifications and a livelihood at least until they married. Yet by the end of the century the two schools faced the same dilemma. The ease with which they had notched up academic honours undermined the very mission to prove the intellectual equality of women which had launched them a quarter of a century before. In the Brisbane school Eliza Fewings had found, in her own words, 'an intellectual workshop', and she had tried to create in its place a school with 'real educational power in the lives of the girls'.[141] One hundred years later that place in the education of women has still to be imagined. Rather than apportion blame, we should read from the troubles of Eliza Fewings and Lucy Garvin the existential dilemma of the academic secondary school for girls at the end of the nineteenth century.

Brisbane Girls' Grammar and Sydney Girls' High came into the twentieth century at odds with the prevailing climate of educational thought. The Edwardian era marked a change in the attitude of the state towards secondary education which at once threatened and reinforced their unique status. In all Australian states governments moved to harness secondary education by the establishment or expansion of their own systems. Their motives were twofold: in a period of rapid industrialisation policy makers perceived a link between secondary education and national prosperity; and a renewed interest in education as handmaiden to the nation hardened the perception that the old pupil-teacher system must be replaced by a system in which the nation's elementary school teachers should attend secondary school. Victoria's first state secondary school, the co-educational Melbourne Continuation School, opened in 1905, and was quickly followed by high schools or agricultural high schools in the major provincial centres. In New South Wales, expansion of the state system began with Newcastle High School in 1906; the Fort Street public schools, which had so discomforted the heads of the Sydney high schools, became high schools in 1911. By 1914, twelve new high schools had been established. In 1912 Queensland began its expansion into state secondary education with high schools in Charters Towers, Gympie, Mt Morgan, Warwick, Bundaberg, and Mackay. The same pattern appeared in South Australia, Western Australia and Tasmania. This decisive intervention of the state into secondary education brought with it a preoccupation with vocationalism which had been muted in the nineteenth-century secondary schools, male and female. Policy makers in all states attempted for the first time to stratify the curriculum of the post-primary school, both within the schools and between schools established for different purposes. Victoria was the most thoroughgoing in its institutional stratification of secondary education, establishing junior technical schools for boys and domestic arts schools for girls which exacerbated differences of class and gender even as they gave working-class children access to schooling beyond the elementary level. This set of ideas, interweaving vocationalism, technical and science education with the national interest, affected the academic girls' schools in complex ways. Wherever the state mandated that the aspiring female teacher proceed through secondary school and into formal teacher training, the academic high schools were the beneficiaries. Yet when the rapidly expanding market-place discovered women as office workers, the free market of education forced into existence the commercial colleges which stole away their senior girls. The same vocational imperative produced an insistent discourse on the need for domestic education for women of all classes which was at odds with the mission of the academic secondary school. The royal commissioners who sat in most states in the early decades of the twentieth interpreted technical education for women as domestic education. To them it was self-evident that women were to serve the national interest as the wives and mothers of the brave new generation of white Australians. They decked the old housewifery out in the language of science, and they turned the prevailing rhetoric decisively from whether women *could* succeed at men's studies (a question settled some decades before) to whether women *should* succeed at men's studies. As 'big' science, the science of national purpose, became the province of the white male elite, the rhetoric of domestic science swelled; its proponents were powerful—Janet Lady Clarke in Melbourne, Rose Scott in Sydney, and as we have seen, Eliza Fewings in Brisbane. Yet in the end it passed lightly over the education of middle-class women. In Victoria the proposed faculty of domestic arts at the University of Melbourne became instead the Emily McPherson College of Domestic Economy. The academic girls' schools colluded with parents to resist the intrusion of domestic education as best they could. The movement pressed itself most successfully upon working-class girls in the mean-spirited domestic arts schools which made their appearance in most states in the Edwardian era. The response of the academic girls' schools to these new circumstances belongs to the history of the twentieth century.

CHAPTER FIVE

The Administration of Gender: The Case of Victoria's 'Lady Teachers', 1850-1900

At mid-century, the calling of the elementary school teacher had still to be invented. By the end of the century, the hundreds of 'lady teachers' who staked a claim to this new professional space had been confined to the lower echelons of a hierarchy dominated by men, a position which they shared with women teaching for the state throughout the Western world. The outcome of this encounter between women and the state was neither natural nor inevitable; their relationship was at once symbiotic and volatile. And it was hugely documented. Thus the lady teacher affords a case study of the public administration of gender which is unique. What follows is a tentative sketch of a vast tract of administrative territory, for even with great diligence and the benefit of hindsight, the historian is often defeated by the labyrinthine ways of the educational state.

The free market and the search for the elementary school teacher, 1850-1872

In the early 1850s, when the rival Denominational and National School Boards began their task of creating public education in the newly created colony of Victoria, the dimensions of the elementary school teacher were uncertain. Yet the ubiquitous maleness of head office, which was to endure for over a century, ensured that the identity of the teacher must emerge through layers of masculine subjectivity which were specific to time and place. The creation of a teaching profession cannot be seen in isolation from the mission of middle-class men to create a bailiwick outside the uncertain pursuit of wealth in the marketplace.[1] The invention of the professions; the expansion of the public service; the bestowal of power and civic subjectivities through democratic institutions; and the invention of quasi-public societies like the Royal Society of Victoria—these were the building blocks of middle-class masculinity in the nineteenth century. Territory had to be marked out and, in its defence, the administration of gender was central.

Yet the creation of a teaching profession centred on the schooling of young children was uniquely burdened with contradictions. The average age of children in publicly funded schools in the 1850s was eight and the battle to retain children over twelve was unrelenting throughout the nineteenth century.[2] Intimacy with small children was stigmatised as the domain of women; as men invaded this traditional world of women its rituals had to be resignified and invested with power. In mirror image, the co-option of women's teaching labour by the educational state constituted an unprecedented female invasion of the public sphere of men. This phenomenon has been enshrined in the literature as the 'feminisation of teaching'.[3] Yet, when the state began to implement its grand design of universal literacy and numeracy, women were already teaching: as mothers in the home; as governesses in the homes of other people; in working-class dame schools; in middle-class female academies; and in Catholic convent schools. Indeed by mid-century insistent voices were already to be heard reminding women of their role as the first teachers of children within the private sphere of home and family. The educational project of the state did not set in train the feminisation of teaching; it set in train the bureaucratisation of women's teaching labour. In the making of pedagogical masculinities, the creation of the lady teacher was a perilous but necessary undertaking.

The comic book feud which the rival school boards sustained, their failure to tempt the generality of children into regular attendance at school, and their inglorious demise in 1862, have deflected attention away from their efforts to craft two parallel teaching forces.[4] Like the Board of Education which replaced them, their faith in the principle of local initiative, enshrined in the legislation until 1872, was to be sorely tested as they attempted to examine, classify and control the polyglot assortment of teachers which local school committees and denominational authorities delivered to their doorsteps.

At mid-century, two conflicting discourses concerning the identity of the elementary school teacher began to emerge. The first derived from the traditional notion of the educated gentleman who could turn his hand to the business of ruling in a multitude of ways. Such men could only be enticed into the new calling of the elementary school teacher by lateral recruitment—that is, by creating the administrative possibility of entry at the top of the profession, privileging literary attainments over what came to be known as the 'art of teaching'. The second discourse positioned the teacher as a secular missionary figure, enculturated as a pupil-teacher within a closed system of teacher training; this notion of the teacher elevated the 'art of teaching' over literary attainments. Its provenance was much more recent and more intimately related to the project of the educational state. This vertical recruitment of children, themselves parsimoniously educated in the state system, was to triumph by the end of the century. These discourses carried with them the differing social purposes which were present in the educational agendas of the 1850s, and both were to have profound implications for the gender of teaching in the colony of Victoria.

Of necessity, lateral recruitment, rather than the pupil-teacher route or the training institution, was the main source of teacher supply in the 1850s.[5] The Board of Education reported that the National School Board had no pupil-teachers at the point of transfer in 1862 and that it inherited only seventy-three from the Denominational School Board.[6] The National School Board was more committed to institutional training than its rival, committing £12,000 to the construction of the National Model School and Training Institution in Spring Street. The Model School section opened in 1854 and it remained Victoria's premier elementary school for many decades. The Normal Institution section was completed in 1856 and by 1859 there were 169 graduates—seventy males and ninety-nine females—of whom only fifty-two were in the employ of the Board.[7] In that year, cutbacks in the budget of the National School Board led to the closure of the Training Institution.

The Denominational School Board spurned an offer of partnership in the venture, pleading its greater commitment to the establishment of new schools and the more generous remuneration of teachers. In reality, the denominational principle was hostile to the establishment of a central training institution where the old spectre of proselytising could once again raise its head. In 1857 the Denominational School Board collaborated with the Church of England to transform the St James' Church of England School in William Street into a training school ostensibly open to all denominations. The St James' and St Paul's Training Institution, as it came to be known, moved to South Yarra in 1867. In 1859, the Board appointed Stephen Chancellor Dixon from England as superintendent at a salary of £500 per annum. Ironically, it was the more modest Denominational School Board Training Institution which survived into the period ushered in by the Common Schools Act of 1862 to embarrass the Board of Education with its cumbersome and costly operations. It was closed in 1869 when the Board of Education opened its own Training Institution, with Dixon as its head, once again crowded into the Model School in Spring Street. This stop-start policy in the institutional training of teachers was to characterise Victoria until well into the twentieth century, effectively preventing an 'end-on' progression of pupil-teachers into a tertiary educational institution. Nor did the generality of pupil-teachers batter upon the doors for admission.

Lateral recruitment of teachers was forced upon the dual boards by the exigencies of crafting a profession out of whatever personnel was to hand. Victoria was an immigrant society; its population trebled in the 1850s with the discovery of the richest gold deposits in the world. The English, Irish and Scottish middle classes were not immune to the temporary insanity brought on by the prospect of instant wealth and Victoria reaped a harvest of well-educated men and women. Few made their fortunes out of gold and many were willing to establish themselves by teaching for the state. It is salutary to realise that, in the first two decades of its existence, the Victorian teaching service had more highly educated, idiosyncratic and self-assured teachers, male and female, than at any other time. The Denominational School Board's report for 1858 commented that:

> Persons of good attainments, both male and female, are frequently induced to emigrate under the hope of finding a field in this country for their talents; a field which is necessarily small, and they are, on this account, glad to avail themselves of the employment to be obtained in the schools. These persons, after being trained, turn out the most efficient class of teachers; and it is to encourage the introduction of such that the Board has adopted its present scheme of classification with its accompanying scale of payments.[8]

In the 1860s and 1870s, inspectors were still remarking upon the leavening presence of these men and women.[9]

There were 'plum recruitments' who combined the virtues of lateral recruitment with the virtues of teacher training—men and women who were already trained and accredited as teachers in the Normal Institutions of England, Scotland and Ireland. Both Boards actively recruited overseas. In 1853, with the Melbourne Model School eight months from completion, secretary to the National School Board, Benjamin Kane, sought the help of the Education Office in Dublin in the selection of Arthur and Ellen Davitt as master and mistress of the new Model and Training Institution at a combined salary of £700. As the sister-in-law of Anthony Trollope, Ellen Davitt enjoyed considerable prestige in Melbourne and became a novelist herself after her colonial teaching career had collapsed.[10] The National School Board also recruited through E.C. Tufnell, Inspector of Schools to the Committee of Council on Education in England, and David Stow, founder of the Glasgow Normal Schools. There are no reliable statistics on these imported teachers but they can be traced through the records of service which survive in the

Directorate of School Education archives, and their welcome was written into the regulations of successive regimes.[11]

Lateral recruitment was not only a pragmatic response to an urgent need for teachers: it was also an outcome of local control and therefore of social purpose. Before 1872, the hiring and firing of teachers was the prerogative of the local governing committees attached to each school, a state of affairs which was condemned by many teachers who replied to the questionnaire from the Higinbotham royal commissioners in 1866.[12] Teachers were in the invidious position of being under contract to a local authority yet paid by a central authority, an anomaly which was to involve the Board of Education in costly litigation in the 1860s.[13] For highly qualified teachers there were considerable rewards in local alliances, as clergy, local committees and parents could and did map their own agendas on to government policy. This close interweaving of state, local and individual strategies had implications for the staffing of schools.

The Catholic clergy, led by Bishop James Goold, were the most interventionist in the day-to-day affairs of their state-assisted denominational schools; their over-riding concern was with the spiritual welfare of their working-class Irish constituency and they did not wish to see the role of the school master disentangled from the role of the clergyman, a decisive factor in their departure from the system after 1872. Regardless of religious affiliation, differing expectations for daughters and sons could also be accommodated more easily with local control. It was sometimes difficult to distinguish the private female academy from the urban denominational girls' school where highly educated women and visiting masters taught modern languages, music and art to the daughters of the middle classes. For the sake of their sons' education, these middle-class parents colluded with local committees to appoint teachers who could offer Latin, mathematics, the modern languages and commercial subjects. Patrick Whyte, the archetypal lateral recruit, argued before the Higinbotham commissioners in 1866 that these alliances frequently undercut denominational affiliations—by which he meant Catholic denominational affiliations.[14] The most conspicuously successful of these *de facto* state grammar schools were Whyte's own Model School and the Geelong National Grammar School, the only government-funded 'elementary' school to exclude girls.[15] The lucrative teaching of these 'higher' subjects was not codified until the Education Act of 1872, when the government sought to discourage the practice. Nevertheless, this flow of students from the state-funded elementary school into the public service, the commercial houses of Melbourne, the university and even the professions, has been largely overlooked in the historiography of Australian education.[16]

A fleeting acquaintance with the policies of the Denominational School Board reveals that, like many parents, it interpreted the meaning of elementary education very liberally indeed. Influential secretary to the Board, Colin Campbell, drew up an ambitious scheme linking its elementary schools to secondary schools and to the university so that the 'humblest pupil, by his own intellect and industry, might obtain the greatest honors and advantages connected with public education'.[17] The Board did indeed make provision for what it termed 'upper departments' in its elementary schools and many schools were eager to participate. But its more ambitious scheme for state-funded grammar schools was thwarted when the funds earmarked for the purpose were diverted into the establishment of the fee-paying church grammar schools, Melbourne and Geelong Grammar Schools, Scotch College, St Patrick's College and later Wesley College.[18] Thus, for a brief moment in 1854, Victoria came within a whisker of establishing state-funded secondary schools for boys, if not for girls, a policy which had to wait for the establishment of the Melbourne Continuation School in 1905. Nevertheless, witnesses before the Higinbotham royal commission of 1866 were agreed that the state was indeed funding secondary education, although they disagreed about whether the practice should continue. Under these circumstances, the identity of the elementary school teacher remained uncertain.

To facilitate the lateral assimilation of suitable candidates of both sexes, the boards instituted yearly literary examinations in Melbourne and the larger centres of population, followed by an 'on the job' examination in the art of teaching. The Denominational School Board, for example, devised an examination and classification system which rested upon two lower levels of a Certificate of Competency, internally controlled by examination and inspection, and four higher classifications in honours, internally controlled and examined until 1870, when it was taken over by the University of Melbourne. Salaries were to be tied to these classifications. In order to give a 'high intellectual impress to elementary education' the Board set out to foster an elite group of teachers through a remarkable alliance with the university professors, who for a short time provided free Saturday lectures. The Denominational School Board's staffing policies were to crash around it in humiliating circumstances: the Board itself was eventually brought to heel by an alliance between its natural allies, the denominational heads, notably Perry and Goold, who required only a rubber stamp upon their activities, and politicians who starved it of funds. The Denominational School Board's policies are nevertheless important, because they were taken over and elaborated by the Board of Education in the Common Schools period.

The differing social purposes which characterised educational provision in the 1850s and 1860s meant that teachers with eminently saleable skills operated within a market-place which made the creation of an orderly teaching profession difficult. The remarkable success of women within this market-place has been discussed in chapter two. Educational boundaries were permeable in ways which became unthinkable later in the century. Professor Martin Howy Irving went from the University of Melbourne to Wesley College as headmaster in 1871 and later became owner-proprietor of Hawthorn Grammar School. He was offered, but declined, the permanent headship of the new Victorian Education Department in 1872.[19] Accustomed as they were to more democratic educational provision, the Scots in early Melbourne were among the most mobile of the school masters. George Morrison went from Scotch College to the headship of Flinders National Grammar School and in 1861 established the Presbyterian Geelong College.[20] As R.J.W. Selleck's study of the Miller teaching family reveals, this game of musical chairs was accessible to less illustrious players, as teachers played the two boards off against each other.[21] 'For sale' notices for schools in receipt of public funding were not unknown and private schools ran through the social structure. Indeed the National School Board, which became increasingly frustrated in its efforts to wean parents away from denominationalism, crossed the border between public and private provision with its policy of non-vested schools instituted in the mid-1850s. It began to take under its wing private schools and teachers, granting aid for salaries and equipment. The Denominational School Board was inclined to take the high moral ground over this issue but the National School Board did tempt into the fold some private entrepreneurs of high repute, including Elizabeth and Albert Mattingley of Errol Street, and Margaret and Hugh Templeton of George Street, Fitzroy.

The state could not remove itself from this market-place until it legislated for compulsory attendance in 1872. In the meantime, its schools were obliged to compete for teachers and clientele; this early pushing and shoving in the market-place is basic to an understanding of the staffing policies which may be traced through the successive regimes. With some perspicacity, the educational state became convinced that attendance depended in large measure upon the quality of the individual school and the exertions of its head teacher. Over the decades successive administrations refined the 'star teacher' system, begun in the 1850s, into a system which was to set rural teacher against urban teacher, assistant teacher against head teacher and female teacher against male teacher for the remainder of the century. The point may be illustrated by reference to the regulations under the Board of Education.[22]

The Common Schools Act of 1862 guaranteed the position of qualified teachers employed by the dual boards.[23] The new Board of Education was terse about the efforts of its predecessors with respect to staffing, although as its top men slid effortlessly from one regime into the next, it was well aware of the difficulties under which its predecessors had laboured. The continuing force of denominationalism was acknowledged in Section XIV which left the appointment of teachers in the hands of the local committees attached to each school, although the Board had power to approve qualifications and 'sanction' dismissals.

The regulations generated by the 1862 Act were published in 1864. They set out a narrow range of base salaries for all teachers, though the Board of Education had resisted giving teachers even this basic entitlement. Masters and mistresses, that is, head teachers, were to receive £100 for men and £80 for women in the first Division of Competency, and £75 and £60 in the second division. Upon this narrow range of base salaries the Board constructed an edifice of additional rewards, most of which benefited head teachers over assistants and men over women. Head teachers classified in honours were to receive 'augmentations' upon their fixed salaries to a ceiling of £60 (less for those classified in second-class honours and for females) calculated on the average attendance. Under clause 13 assistant teachers, to be employed for every fifty children in average attendance, were to be paid at the minimum rates of salary for head teachers, but no augmentations were to be allowed. This was a significant departure from policy under the dual boards and was bitterly resented by assistant teachers who were classified in honours. Rule 13 went straight to the heart of a problem which was to bedevil staffing policy in Victoria—the dispersal of teachers to country areas where conditions were often harsh, the isolation difficult to bear and the teacher's residence execrable. The denial of payment for honours was designed to force highly qualified assistants out of the urban schools into head teacherships in rural areas.

Salaries were also augmented by a percentage of the children's weekly fees which were set (and in theory collected) by the local committees. The division of fees among the staff was a matter for negotiation with the local committee but the potential for injustice did not cease there. The amount of fees which could be charged and collected varied. Poverty affected urban and rural schools alike but small enrolments and erratic attendance fell more heavily upon the rural teacher. Local committees were loath to offend their neighbours by acting as debt collectors and too often the onerous task of collecting fees and arrears fell on the teacher, disrupting relationships with parents who were not yet obligated to send their children to school. Teachers were also entitled to a percentage of fees paid by the state on behalf of 'destitute' children.

Rule 16 of the 1864 regulations ushered in the system of 'payment by results' which is discussed in chapter seven. Though the regulations changed over the years, payment by results was, in essence, a system which made part of the teachers' salaries dependent upon the performance of their pupils at examinations conducted by inspectors. Again, head teachers were more generously rewarded than assistants, an incentive for them to ensure a uniformly high standard of teaching throughout the school. Payment by results was also linked to attendance of individual children, whose results could not be counted if they had attended for less than a certain number of days. Again, this was particularly unfair in country districts and in the poorer suburbs of Melbourne, where attendances fluctuated according to the needs of rural and working-class life. The temptation to falsify the attendance rolls was strong. Other extra sources of income for energetic, and duly qualified, teachers were the preparation of pupil-teachers, and the teaching of drill, gymnastics, drawing and singing, most of which benefited male teachers in urban schools over other groups.

In his evidence before the Higinbotham commission in 1866, Sir James Palmer estimated that an urban headmaster with an average attendance of 200 and a base salary of £100 would earn £634 per annum. Palmer commented approvingly:

> Accomplished masters, like Mr Whyte and Mr Lennon, who, I may remark, are classical scholars, and have a knowledge of French and German, and have received a college education, will always be appreciated, and will derive, and most deservedly so, a high remuneration for their services.[24]

In that year, the highest salary earned by an urban female head teacher was £391 and, though this was considerably less than her male counterparts, it was twice the average earnings of head teachers and four times the average earnings of assistant teachers.[25] Maximum and minimum incomes of teachers in 1866 are shown in Table 1.

Until the mid-1860s, the absent presence in official discourse was the teaching work horse who could be prevailed upon to do the arduous work of elementary school teaching for what the state was prepared to pay its country head teachers and its urban assistants. The Board of Education became more and more terse about the yearly failure rate at its literary examinations, both for lateral entry and for promotion.[26] The Board was constantly embarrassed by the number of unclassified teachers and sub-standard teachers. Palmer himself admitted that only those who 'failed in all subjects or were hopelessly deficient' were actually ejected from the schools, as it was impossible to replace them.[27] Even so, throughout the nineteenth century the situation was always worse than the official version, as pupil-teachers from the age of thirteen and many sewing mistresses were routinely in charge of classes. The Board could appoint staff under the 'temporary permission to act' clause, a provision which went through many

Table 1 Minimum and maximum income of teachers of Common Schools, in the City of Melbourne, suburban and goldfields municipalities, and country districts, for the year ended 30th June 1866

District	Head teachers								Assistant teachers							
	Male				Female				Male				Female			
	Min			Max			Min			Max			Min			Max
	£ s d			£ s d			£ s d			£ s d			£ s d			£ s d
City of Melbourne	170 0 0			533 18 11			137 0 0			391 4 0			81 8 4			413 6 5
Suburban municipalities	116 0 0			656 1 8			126 5 2			316 12 9			76 0 0			189 18 8
Goldfields	111 6 3			414 7 4			142 16 2			175 10 3			82 18 0			162 0 0
Country	114 3 9			369 5 1			116 13 0			116 13 0			nil			nil
For the whole colony	111 6 3			656 1 8			116 13 0			391 4 0			76 0 0			413 6 5

District	Female (Assistant teachers)	
	Min (£ s d)	Max (£ s d)
City of Melbourne	60 0 0	149 0 0
Suburban municipalities	60 0 0	184 4 0
Goldfields	60 0 0	178 5 11
Country	60 0 0	125 10 0
For the whole colony	60 0 0	184 4 0

Source: Royal Commission on Public Education 1867

permutations to ensure that there were unqualified teachers in Victoria's classrooms until the 1970s. The Board also became more and more outspoken about unsuitable teachers who enjoyed local support but failed year after year to pass the qualifying examinations. For remote rural appointments local committees relied heavily upon the Board to find teachers, a reality which it acknowledged in 1866 when it established a central register of candidates for these positions.[28]

In 1866 the Higinbotham royal commissioners called for a return of teachers in the employ of the Board of Education (see Table 2). There were at this time 1,248 teachers (excluding pupil-teachers and sewing mistresses) of whom 728 (or 61 per cent) were head teachers and 520 (or 39 per cent) were assistants, an artefact of the large number of one-teacher schools in the colony. Women constituted 36 per cent of all teachers (48 per cent if pupil-teachers and sewing mistresses are included), 11 per cent of head teachers and 79 per cent of assistant teachers. Thirty-six per cent of teachers were unclassified, in roughly equal numbers of men and women. Women constituted 63 per cent of pupil-teachers. Women were as well qualified as men, in proportion to their numbers.

Table 2   Number of teachers and pupil-teachers employed under the Board of Education, 24 September 1866

Teachers	Head teachers		Assistants		Total
	M	F	M	F	
1st class Honours	6	3	1	-	10
2nd class Honours	66	16	1	15	98
1st division	240	32	24	73	369
2nd division	159	8	46	109	322
Not classified	178	20	38	213	449
Total	649	79	110	410	1248

Pupil-teachers	M	F	Total
First class	65	111	176
Second class	5	12	17
Third class	2	6	8
Fourth class	3	1	4
Total	75	130	205

Source: Royal Commission on Public Education 1867

The married woman teacher

Remarkably, in the same decades there were no regulations excluding women teachers from the rewards of government-subsidised entrepreneurship. The employment of women signalled more than a sullen acceptance of the lady teacher. Victoria's women teachers too were subject to the market forces which shaped the policies of the educational state but they were positioned differently from men. The discourses which surrounded their presence in the schools from the beginning had little to say about their natural endowments as teachers and even less about their manifest availability as cheap labour. The educational state forged its alliance with women on other grounds entirely. The presence of women in Victoria's classrooms was legitimated by a persistent discourse of moral danger, at odds with the official discourse which insisted that the state-funded elementary school was productive of public and private morality. Dissonance between women and the public sphere ensured that, throughout the nineteenth century, there were more boys than girls in the state schools, even after compulsory attendance destroyed parental choice. While sons might be committed to the rough and tumble of the publicly funded school, daughters were a different matter. It was girls who were withdrawn at the slightest hint of moral transgression and moral transgression was routinely detected in the arrival of an unmarried male teacher.

The prototype for the National School Board, the National School Board of New South Wales, had no doubts about the place of married women in its proposed teaching force. In 1850 its first advertisement for teachers read: 'Married couples, and persons who have been regularly trained in the Model School, Ireland, will be preferred.'[29] The New South Wales Board appointed a husband and wife team, William and Ann Wilkins, to head its prestigious Fort Street Model School in the 1850s.[30] Benjamin Kane's letter of recruitment to the Education Office in Dublin also stipulated a married couple, 'if possible, without children', for the Melbourne Model School at a total salary of £800.[31] The National School Board's report for 1857 commented that, while most entrants to the Training Institution were young unmarried men and women,

> in consequence of most of our schools being situated in the country districts, where the schools are small and conducted on the 'mixed' principle, the chief demand is for married teachers: greater confidence being placed in a married person where he has young females in his charge, while the services of the wife, even if she be not specially qualified to act as a literary teacher, are available as a workmistress.[32]

The Board recommended that young married couples be encouraged to enrol but this attempt to institutionalise the husband and wife teaching team was unsuccessful. The special case files of the Education Department and its predecessors are sprinkled with cases of parents, scandalised by some minor transgression, demanding the appointment of a husband and wife.[33] The message was clear enough; the lady teacher too had her market value and the educational state was obliged to purchase respectability through a female presence in its classrooms. This parental preference for the teaching family also explains why marriage, child-bearing and domestic duties were not at first constituted as incompatible with the lot of the elementary school teacher. Indeed the 'periodical requirements attendant on maternity' were never codified in print, although in practice women were given confinement leave of three weeks on condition that they paid a substitute teacher.

It was the lure of the aggregated family income, invisible in the official calculations of teachers' incomes, which made teaching attractive in the nineteenth century. The first report of the new Education Department, published in 1874, contained an appendix which listed staff by individual school.[34] Of the 1,113 schools listed, 275 were small schools staffed by a headmaster and sewing mistress of the same surname. A further 122 schools were staffed by a headmaster and a female first or second assistant of the same surname. And a further eighty-seven schools had pupil-teachers of the same surname as the headmaster or first assistant. This crude head count does not reveal other relationships among the staff, as for example at Walhalla where Henry and Lucy Tisdall were headmaster and first assistant and two of Lucy's sisters, Alice and Clara Weekes, were second assistant and pupil-teacher. The most successful of the family fiefdoms was the Rae family at Ironbark outside Bendigo where John Rae was headmaster, his wife Emily was first assistant, daughter Barbara was second assistant, son William was seventh assistant and three other children, John, Alexander and Helen, were pupil-teachers. Their aggregated family income was over £1,000, more than the sum required to lure the first professors of the University of Melbourne away from the universities of England and Ireland. John Rae also had extensive mining interests in the Bendigo district with his brother William.

This mutual colonisation of the educational state and the teaching family constituted an early manipulation of the teaching labour-market which allowed the authority of the husband over the wife to be translated into the authority of the male teacher over the female teacher. So secure was this common law precedence of the male teacher that it was nowhere codified until the Public Service Act of 1883.[35] Yet from the beginning women were seldom heads of any but the smallest country schools where no man could be found to take the position. This unwritten law excluding women from the manifest rewards of the head teachership was a crucial mechanism in their professional confinement.

The most common teaching family was the head teacher and sewing (or work) mistress in the rural school. Like her social superior in the female academy, the sewing mistress could move with propriety between the public and the private spheres, a daily journey which was greatly facilitated when school and residence were one and the same building. Provision for the teaching of sewing to female pupils appeared in the earliest regulations of the dual boards and these regulations were in due course refined into an edict that *all* female teachers must be qualified in sewing to gain classification. This onerous task was not constituted as a category for extra payment, as were military drill and gymnastics, although it was calculated in the 'results' from the late 1860s, thus bestowing upon the male members of staff a reward for the efforts of the lady teachers. Opinion was polarised between the authorities, who seemed convinced that the sewing lesson underpinned the moral fibre of the nation, and the lady teachers, who bitterly resented this extra burden upon their time, both inside and outside school. So heavily gendered was the humble act of sewing that no male could be asked to teach it and, in small, one-teacher schools staffed by a male, a sewing teacher at £30 per annum could be employed. With the possibility of a pupil-teachership for a son or daughter, a few acres to farm and the post office for good measure, these family fiefdoms were in the nature of a bribe to help in the dispersal of teachers to remote areas where, once ensconced, they defended their territory with great ferocity. Most quarrels which erupted between head teacher and sewing mistress reveal, on closer inspection, a dispossessed wife waiting to dislodge an incumbent woman from a previous regime who had refused to concede the field.[36]

The office of sewing mistress offered rich possibilities for the exploitation of women, and successive regimes were very creative indeed. The National School Board set the pace as early as 1857. It cheerfully suggested to married couples graduating from the Training Institution that the husband would at once receive a handsome salary, while the similarly qualified wife would receive 'a stipend of £30 a year as workmistress, for which she is only required to give up two hours per day'. Only if the school were sufficiently large to warrant the appointment of the wife as a literary teacher would she receive the salary to which her qualifications entitled her.[37] With population movements and school attendance volatile throughout the nineteenth century, fluctuations could and did tip a fully qualified assistant wife over into the category of sewing mistress at a considerable loss of salary. Yet, as her presence as chaperone was required and her assistance with preparation for the onerous 'results' examination was vital, most wives had no choice but to continue their duties as assistant teachers on the pittance of a sewing mistress. The policy was challenged in the early 1860s by Mrs Maria Forster who, with her Cambridge-educated husband George, was typical of the highly educated middle-class teachers in the system at that time.[38] She protested when her salary and status were reduced to that of sewing mistress, taking her case to the Supreme Court (where she lost on the technicality that the new Board of Education was not responsible for the debts of its predecessors), and to a parliamentary select committee which awarded her £150 in unpaid salary. Under the circumstances it is difficult to avoid the suspicion that, when the Forsters were dismissed for falsification of rolls one month later, Benjamin Kane was taking his revenge. In 1868, after the Higinbotham commissioners decreed that the staffing of Common Schools was 'excessive', the Board changed the regulations to allow local committees in smaller schools to employ pupil-teachers and sewing mistresses instead of assistants until attendance reached 100.[39] Some inspectors were forthright about this bureaucratic fiction. In 1870 Inspector Brodribb reported that of the fifty-five sewing mistresses under his jurisdiction most were 'acting as assistants'.[40] A further demotion of female assistants occurred in 1872 when the attendance required before an assistant could be employed was raised from fifty to seventy-five. By the 1880s the Education Department had candidly defined the duties of the sewing mistress as 'needlework and the rudimentary instruction of the younger classes'.[41]

The teaching matriarchs

At the other extreme from the teaching couples in the country schools were the much-envied husbands and wives who held the two top positions in the larger urban schools—among them Patrick and Jane Whyte of the Model School, John and Anne Drake of Collingwood, and Edward and Harriet Rosenblum of Ballarat—urban gentry with fine houses, servants, and children who eschewed the profession of teaching in the next generation. The same moral imperatives which favoured the teaching family in the country led parents to prefer separate departments for their daughters in urban centres. These separate departments were encouraged by the dual boards, especially the Denominational School Board, which allowed some of its girls' schools to become female academies in all but name. Under the patronage of the Board and the Church of England, Mrs Tabitha Pike ran the St James' Girls' School as a *de facto* ladies' academy for nearly twenty years, advertising music, painting and modern languages in her regular press advertisements. One witness before the Higinbotham commission testified that Pike had 'sixty to seventy young ladies who pay highly and provide their own masters, for accomplishments', while the Church of England Dean MacCartney testified that his own daughter attended.[42] Many separate girls' departments fell far short of Tabitha Pike's school. Often the girls were simply taught in a different room, or even divided from the boys by a curtain. Nevertheless, the senior woman in the girls' department was accorded the status of head teacher and paid accordingly. This women's domain has been obliterated by the mistaken assumption that Victoria's publicly funded schools were co-educational from the beginning. Although the 1864 code was silent on the matter, the Board of Education began a covert war of attrition against these separate departments on grounds of economy and 'rational' school organisation.[43] Upon each amalgamation the Board demoted the female head teacher to first assistant with considerable loss of salary and status. The demotion was particularly unjust to those who had been classified in honours for, as assistants, they were also deprived of their payment on that account. Inspector Brodribb shared the Board's opinion that separate departments were an unwarranted expense but he was uneasy about the injustice done to the women and proposed that the first female assistant in larger schools be paid as a head teacher. This concession appeared in the revised regulations of 1869, although without the payment for honours.[44]

Contestation around the issue of co-education underscores the problematical nature of gender for the educational state. While the Board pursued its policy of 'mixed' schooling on the grounds of economy, the women teachers tapped into deeply held beliefs, forming alliances with parents in order to defend their territory. They routinely invoked the threat of mass withdrawal of female pupils if classes were mixed. At Pentridge Common School in 1867 Jane Trotter complained that 'owing to the mixed nature of the public schools five private schools have been opened within a mile of each other'.[45] Isabella Burton of St John's Common School was demoted from head teacher to first assistant when the boys' and girls' departments were amalgamated. The correspondent of the local committee, the Rev. John Barlow, wrote to the Board:

> The mixing of boys and girls has had a very injurious effect on the attendance at the girls' school. I find that Parents have a strong objection to their daughters being taught in class with boys. My own experience of the results of the mixed school system is very unsatisfactory. I consider it to be injurious to both the manners and morals of the girls.[46]

In this case the Board relented but Isabella Burton's struggle for financial compensation was both protracted and unsuccessful. Bessie Stone's Drummond Street Common School survived as a 'select' girls' school until 1874 when the new Department amalgamated it with the nearby St Matthew's school. Stone wrote to the Department:

> With regard to the salary of the first assistant teacher in St Matthews School, I feel assured that from the fact of the boys and girls being taught together in the same classes, a number of girls attending school [my school] will leave, and the average attendance of the combined schools will not exceed by many the numbers now attending St Matthews School, and as this will give a very small salary to the first assistant teacher, I beg most respectfully to decline the offered appointment as I consider my many years of service should entitle me to something better.[47]

As this struggle around the institutional form of female schooling implies, parental preference for women teachers and single-sex schools also ensured that the lady teacher had clout in the free educational market of the 1850s and 60s. It also helps to explain the phenomenon of the private female school in the same decades.

The Higinbotham commissioners certainly did not see the question as settled in 1866. Mrs Mary Jenvey, head teacher of the girls' department of St Mark's, Fitzroy—and the only woman called as a witness—castigated the Board with respect to amalgamations. She was closely questioned on the technicalities of the situation:

> Commissioner: What is the relation that exists between the female teacher and the head teacher of a school?
> Mary Jenvey: I am the head, as far as my school is concerned.
> C: Then is there any relation whatever between the head male teacher and the head female teacher?
> MJ: Not the slightest . . .
> C: What was your net income last year?
> MJ: Three hundred and sixteen pounds, from all sources.
> C: Net?
> MJ: Yes.
> C: That is for yourself?
> MJ: That is for myself; but I derive some part of that from my classification.[48]

The incomprehension of the all-male commission face to face with a female member of the urban head teacher elite prompted Mary Jenvey to elaborate on her situation at St Mark's. It was Jenvey who earned the top female income in the state, and she clearly regarded her fixed salary as small change. Jenvey was at the time under suspension by her local committee over the distribution of the very lucrative fees and her testimony affords an insight into the speculative market which the educational state had created by the mid-1860s. She had taken the school when it was very run down and made it profitable: 'It was a kind of speculation that as soon as I could make it a profitable school the profits should be mine; but as soon as it became profitable, first one per centage was taken off and then a larger one, so that I feel myself very much ill-used indeed.'[49] Jenvey knew how to play the free market forces. She claimed that as a result of her suspension, most of her 130 girls were being kept home in protest by their parents. Not surprisingly, Jenvey regarded the mixing of boys and girls as 'very inexpedient'. She advised that if the sexes were to be mixed, a female teacher should be employed as 'boys suffer less under a mistress than do girls under a master'. The commissioners agreed with the lady teachers:

> We think that the mixing of children of both sexes is objectionable, except in schools where ample accommodation exists, together with such an amount of efficient supervision as can be only rarely provided; and therefore that it is advisable to provide separate schools for boys and girls, at least wherever one hundred and fifty children of each sex are in attendance at the school.[50]

The Board of Education quietly ignored this recommendation, although women demoted from head teacherships were created first assistants above the highest ranking male assistant in recognition of their onerous duties as the senior woman in a mixed school.

Women's participation in the teaching labour-market as moral guardians of female children was shot through with ironies. The free market of education before 1872 shaped an elite of teaching matriarchs, respected by parents and inspectors alike, who were accustomed to wielding power. But it was power embedded in a melodrama of sexual danger. Their accounting of this power, of their efficacy as technicians in the schoolroom, was fatally implicated in this melodrama of sexual danger. In the records of the educational state the lady teacher is often to be found staking a claim to a superior moral authority by virtue of her sex. She became adept at aggregating into moral pollution the small sexual transactions, real or imagined, which she saw around her. Canadian historian Bruce Curtis suggests that the nineteenth-century educational state was in a 'new ... relationship of intellectual, moral and paternal guardianship' with its citizens.[51] If this is so, the lady teacher soon learned to hijack this elaborate technology of moral regulation. Her target was nothing less than the opaque privilege of male sexuality itself. Only the lady teacher stood between the senior girls and the unbridled lust of the male teachers. The lady teacher as

willing agent of moral regulation has proved conceptually uncomfortable for feminist historians, who have preferred to leave the
Mrs Jenveys of the classroom stranded in the shallows of the ridiculous.
In so doing, however, they have missed vital linkages between individual subjectivities, educational system building, and the administration
of gender.

Explanations for the political demise of the Board of Education and
its replacement by the Victorian Education Department have been
thoroughly canvassed, and they are not the main focus of this study.
The Board itself had hoped for a resolution to the constitutional basis
of public education after the royal commission but this was not to be.
Like the dual boards before it, the Board of Education had been obliged
to struggle on in a constant state of uncertainty until the knockout
blow came in 1872. At the end of the Board's regime, the teaching
profession, if such it could be called, was characterised at one extreme
by an urban elite of highly paid and highly respected head teachers
and, at the other, by unqualified and lowly paid teachers, scattered
reluctantly through the rural areas. Pupil-teachers and sewing mistresses
swelled the ranks of the unqualified. Even so, at the point of transfer
from one regime to the other, women were still present in all categories
of the teaching service.

The Education Act of 1872

The Education Act of 1872 left the publicly funded school with modest
pedagogical aims to say the least, hardly a sturdy scaffold for the weight
of masculinities which it was expected to support. The Act reflected a
hardening of social attitudes around state-funded education: on the one
hand it destroyed by default state funding of secondary education; and
on the other, it swept into the schools thousands of children who had
hitherto resisted the blandishments of the state. The Act mandated
attendance between the ages of six and fifteen, and the parliamentary
debates left no doubt as to the humble social origins of the defaulters
who were to be brought into school by the scruff of the neck. At the
Model School, Patrick Whyte had to assure his clientele that they were
still entitled to send their children to the school. This perceptible shift
in the social purpose of the state school (as it was now called) brought
into sharper focus the lineaments of the elementary school teacher.

The Victorian Education Department, which was also created by the
Act of 1872, came into existence burdened with potentially incompatible
staffing imperatives. The need for greater control over recruitment,
training and dispersal of its teachers had crystallised from the Common

Schools experience. The state chose not to regulate the free educational market in which it had been obliged to compete—this did not occur until 1905—but the compulsory attendance of children and the abolition of fees undermined alliances between teachers and parents at the grass roots. The destruction of local control under the 1872 Act also gave the central authority control over its teachers for the first time. Yet at the same time the Education Department was most insistent upon the need to foster a psychology of professionalism among its teachers. Official discourse abruptly abandoned the entrepreneur superstar and began to speak of disinterested public service and professionalism. In the debates surrounding the Act, teachers were promised status as public servants, an orderly system of promotion, and retiring allowances. The humble and obedient servant of the state was also to be 'professional man'.

The instability of these regulatory and professionalising agendas was exacerbated by two further factors. The first was the hypocrisy of the legislature through successive ministries which proclaimed the virtues of mass education yet, even in the boom years of the 1880s, begrudged every penny to a department charged with bringing the blessings of free education to children in every corner of the colony. The second factor was the incompatibility between the masculine project of professionalism and the gender of teaching. The Victorian Education Department was the first administration to know from the outset that, in the buoyant economy of colonial Victoria, the generality of men would not consider elementary school teaching as a calling. This was a pivotal moment in the delineation of the elementary school teacher. The 1872 Act had effectively dismantled the entrepreneurial basis of the teaching industry at precisely the moment when mandatory attendance fuelled a voracious need for teachers. John Rae of Ironbark went before a royal commission in 1883 to complain that the bottom had dropped out of teaching. He was obliged to take in hobble-de-hoys who could not read and write at ten years of age, a fine new state school built in the neighbourhood had stolen his clientele, his income had dropped dramatically, and he had sent his own sons into other occupations. For the last quarter of the nineteenth century the Department's dealings with its female teachers must be read in mirror image, for they reflect the struggle to recruit and reproduce a male teaching elite in the vastly changed circumstances ushered in by the 1872 Act. Women began to mass on the borders of the state teaching service, not as cultured and assured members of the immigrant middle classes, but as colonial-born girls of thirteen.

The Victorian state school system expanded rapidly in the 1870s and 1880s. By the 1880s most children who could get to a school were on the rolls, although they did not attend more regularly than before.

Enrolments rose steeply from 135,962 in 1872 to 224,626 in 1882. Not only did the system expand in absolute numbers after 1872, but the dispersal of the population, always a problem for the educational state in Australia, continued unabated. In its report for 1876 the Department set out the difficulties under which it laboured. The Land Act of 1869 had triggered an exodus from the economically depressed goldfields and from the older agricultural areas where farms were partially exhausted. Dispersal of the population was facilitated by the rapid expansion of the railways both in suburban Melbourne and in country districts. The hard-pressed Education Department found itself providing schools and teachers for the same families two or even three times.[52]

The dislocation experienced by teachers and schools in the 1870s has been largely overshadowed by the constitutional and religious settlements effected by the 1872 Act. The Board of Education handed over to the Department only 453 schools vested in the state (this was a main cause of its downfall) and an astonishing 590 schools 'held in buildings the property of the denominations or of private individuals'.[53] The destruction of the publicly subsidised denominational elementary school system, over which the Common Schools legislation had thrown an administrative cloak, took place in the 1870s, not the 1860s. The Act provided that private or church schools whose property was not vested in the state continue to receive aid until the end of 1873. For five years capitation payments were made for children in these schools where no state school had been established.[54] The Department was gracious enough to admit that this continued support was vital during this turbulent period.[55] The same Department was reticent about which denominational schools it was most eager to destroy but, to its great disappointment, the Catholic system struggled on, recruiting religious orders to replace its lay teachers whose salaries had been paid by the state. The Department's ambitious program of building, amalgamations and closures is closely documented in its annual reports, but the hardships and uncertainties suffered by teachers—including Catholic lay teachers—are acknowledged only in the niggardly provisions for compensation and in the bitter disputes over salaries.[56]

The Department began to implement its professionalising agenda with a revised system of classification which was in fact a modification of the two-tier Certificate of Competency and honours system used by the Board of Education.[57] Teachers were now to be divided into three broad classifications. The lowest class comprised the unclassified teachers, of whom the Department inherited 163. The Department was anxious to rid itself of these unqualified teachers—they were referred to as 'fossils preserved from the old days of denominational schools'—and throughout the 1870s tried to harry them into presenting for the threshold examination for entry to the service. In 1879 they were dismissed *en masse* and the preponderance of males over females (seventy-nine men and fifteen women) lends weight to the Department's constant complaint that the quality of men prepared to take up teaching was lamentably below that of women.[58]

The next category went under the title of 'licence to teach', the new qualification given to those who had passed the very modest threshold literary examination and who had been inspected in the art of teaching and school management. Those with a licence to teach were qualified to be assistants or head teachers in schools where no assistants (other than sewing mistresses) were employed. This category also included the pupil-teachers who had completed their four-year course of training. As anybody who could produce 'satisfactory certificates of moral character and health' could present for the yearly 'licence to teach' examination, the principle of lateral recruitment survived into the new era. The third and highest category, the Certificate of Competency, comprised those who had passed the next highest literary examination and those who had passed the university examinations for first or second class honours. The Certificate of Competency gave the right to fill any teaching position in the Department. All examinations were open to women, although their program in arithmetic was modified and they were required to pass examinations in needlework.

The Department was more forthcoming than its predecessor regarding the position of its teachers, publishing yearly statistics from 1876 onwards. The absolute increase in staff is steady but not spectacular, given the increased numbers of children on the rolls; including sewing mistresses and pupil-teachers, numbers rose from 3,341 in 1876 to 4,184 in 1884. Head teachers continued to outnumber assistants by two to one and men continued to outnumber women as head teachers. The largest group of female heads were now in the 'licence to teach' category—that is, in charge of small country schools. Certificated women were not specifically excluded from any head teachership under the 1872 Act but women as heads of larger schools peaked at seventy-seven in 1884, while in that year there were 683 men in that category. There was a consistently large group of men acting as unclassified heads of small schools until the dismissals of 1879. Women continued to outnumber men as assistants, and the preponderance of females in the 'certificated assistants including honours' category represented the women who had been heads of girls' departments. Thus in the 1870s almost all first assistants in the larger schools were female, the few male first assistants being ex-heads of nearby amalgamated schools. The number of sewing mistresses rose only modestly throughout the period. Pupil-teachers also rose modestly from 951 in 1876 to 1,072 in 1884 but the percentage of females rose from 67.2 to 73.4. This trend was accelerated by the conspicuous success of female candidates in the examinations for pupil-teacher positions mandated by the Public Service Act of 1883.[59] The lot of the pupil-teacher had become a women's issue. The position of women teachers under the revised regulations of 1872 is set out in Tables 3 and 4.

Though the Department and the legislature were nervous about the cost of the new system, in 1873 a decision about the salaries of teachers was a matter of urgency. As the fees abolished by the 1872 Act had been a major component of salaries since the 1850s, the Department was obliged to devise a new basis for the remuneration of its teachers. Official rhetoric turned abruptly from celebration of the high-earning male elite to the need to sacrifice these teachers for the benefit of those at the other extreme.[60] Though teachers had been assured at the passing of the Act that their salaries would not be reduced, many did suffer badly. Chivvied on by George Higinbotham in parliament at the end of 1874, a reluctant Department devised a scheme to compensate teachers for the loss of fees and to broaden the range of basic salaries, but it stood by its controversial decision to link teachers' salaries to the number of children in attendance at individual schools. The range of base salaries for head teachers went from £80 in the smallest country school, with increments for attendance rising to a ceiling of £380 in a school of over 1,000 children.[61] Certificated assistants were to receive a base salary of £80 with increments similarly tagged to attendance up to a ceiling of £240. Before 1872, when the children paid fees, larger schools had meant higher returns for teachers, but their base salaries had been independent of enrolment. Women received salaries at four-fifths the male rate; that is, a salary differential which had become naturalised since the 1850s was now official policy. Certificated first female assistants were the only women to be paid equally with men—unless they were teaching in their husbands' schools—and this was in compensation for the fact that the 1875 regulations delivered the *coup de grâce* against separate female departments. The new scale of salaries under the Education Department addressed only those inequalities between head teachers in schools of comparable enrolments—and between assistants in schools of comparable enrolments—leaving entrenched the inequalities between urban and rural teachers, between head teachers and assistants, and between male and female teachers. Teachers had other reasons to be disillusioned under the new regime: two important promises held out to them—retiring allowances and status as public servants—did not eventuate; the hated policy of payment by results was retained; and payment for honours was discontinued. Bonus payments which survived under the new regime—for 'results', for the training of pupil-teachers,

Table 3 Number and classification of teachers employed in state schools[1], 1876–1879

		1876			1877			1878			1879		
		M	F	T	M	F	T	M	F	T	M	F	T
Head teacher	Certificated[2]	421	14		453	15		474	17		533	27	
	Licensed	408	42		493	86		557	116		617	153	
	Licence pending				247			102	28		74	38	
	Unclassified[3]	227	36	1148		31	1325	124	13	1431	54	6	1502
Assistant	Certificated[2]	61	125		59	177		63	199		77	224	
	Licensed	149	324		156	323		147	339		152	363	
	Licence pending				11			8	35		17	57	
	Unclassified[3]	16	82	757		31	757	3	13	807		6	896
Work mistress	Classified		10			24			10			31	
	Unclassified[3]		475	485		505	529		561	571		492	523
Pupil-teacher		314	637	951	309	656	965	326	725	1051	328	757	1085
Totals		1596	1745	3341	1728	1848	3576	1804	2056	3860	1852	2154	4006

1. Exclusive of capitation schools
2. Including teachers classified in honours
3. And partially classified

Source: Victorian Parliamentary Papers (Legislative Assembly), Reports of the Minister of Public Instruction, for years 1876–1879

Table 4 Number and classification of teachers employed in state schools[1], 1880–1884

		1880			1881			1882			1883			1884		
		M	F	T	M	F	T	M	F	T	M	F	T	M	F	T
Head teacher	Certificated[2]	586	45		597	45		639	61		642	67		683	77	
	Licensed	662	225		674	250		667	302		652	322		623	340	
	Licence pending	25	37		19	39		13	32		15	14		4	7	
				1580			1624			1714			1712			1734
Relieving teacher								15		15	20		20	18		18
Assistant	Certificated[2]	69	269		75	266		78	292		82	304		89	306	
	Licensed	140	370		143	368		118	345		101	327		91	318	
	Licence pending	13	27		19	28		21	20		4	5			3	
				888			899			874			823			807
Work mistress	Certificated		3			1			2			2			5	
	Certificate pending		1			1			2			2			4	
	Licensed		21			15			21			18			25	
	Licence pending		8			5			2			6			2	
	Unclassified		562			558			563			526			517	
				595			580			590			554			553
Pupil-teacher		341	781	1122	330	775	1105	343	778	1121	312	758	1070	285	787	1072
Totals		1836	2349	4185	1857	2351	4208	1894	2420	4314	1828	2351	4179	1793	2391	4184

1. Exclusive of capitation schools
2. Including teachers classified in honours

for drill and gymnastics, for night schools and for heads of schools associated with the Training Institution in Melbourne—continued to reward the urban male teacher, particularly the head teacher. The lady teachers quickly learned their market value under the new regime.

As the 'feminisation' of elementary school teaching had now become lodged in administrative consciousness, the lady teacher was no longer merely a neutral presence in the Department's yearly reports but a phenomenon to be managed to best advantage. The Department had abandoned hope of recruiting suitable male teachers in anything like the numbers required. In 1876 it reported that, though large numbers of candidates continued to present themselves for the yearly examinations, there was still a 'deficiency of duly-qualified male teachers' while qualified females were 'still in excess of demand'. By the late 1870s the Department had articulated a policy to employ women teachers as assistants or as heads of one-teacher schools. Clearly uneasy about the situation, it also began to publish statistics analysed by sex; in the three years from 1877 to 1879 the percentage of female heads rose from 9.9 to 14.9 and the percentage of female assistants rose from 70.1 to 72.5. However, as head teachers still outnumbered assistants in the service, the percentage of women overall had risen only from 31.8 to 36.4. As these statistics exclude pupil-teachers and sewing mistresses they do not give an accurate picture of the number of women teaching children in state schools.[62] Nevertheless, the Department continued to couch its professionalising agenda in admirably gender neutral terms:

> so great has been the extension of the pupil-teacher system under the present regulations, and so many more candidates are now seeking admission to a course of training, that it is likely that, ere long, these two sources of supply will prove sufficient for all our requirements, and that no person will be regarded as eligible for employment as a teacher who has not undergone a previous preparation either as pupil-teacher or in the Training Institution.[63]

In 1877, 39-year-old Englishman, Frederick John Gladman, was appointed to revivify the Training Institution, a vital strategy in the creation of the male teaching elite.[64] For seven years, until his death in 1884, the future leaders of the profession were to cluster devotedly around him: Frank Tate, appointed first director in 1901; Charles Long, official historian of the Education Department; John Betheras, inspector of schools; and John Murphy, a leading teacher unionist in the turbulent 1880s. Undeterred, women continued to outnumber men at the Training College with the result that, by the early 1880s, it was departmental policy to give preference to male candidates. The examination for the 'licence to teach' in December 1878 was the last to be held for lateral entry to the

Students and staff at the Training College, Melbourne, c.1890. Frank Tate, later
Director of Education, is on the left in the back row.
(Directorate of School Education, Victoria)

profession and, in the following year, the unclassified teachers were
dismissed from the service. The Victorian Education Department had
implemented an in-house system of recruiting and training elementary
school teachers which was to endure for over a century.

The Rogers Templeton Commisssion and the Public Service Act, 1883

The first review of the system ushered in by the 1872 Act was the Rogers
Templeton royal commission, appointed in 1881 to 'enquire into and report
upon the administration, organisation, and general condition of the existing
system of public instruction'.[65] The commissioners had other pressing
preoccupations, notably the plight of the state schools as 'godless'
institutions but, with respect to teachers, its main focus was political
patronage in appointments and promotions. The administration of the 1872
Act had failed to deliver an orderly career structure free of the 'great dragon

of patronage'. The right to appoint, transfer and promote lay with the minister and it was not long before the teachers became aware that the patronage of the minister, rather than the qualifications of the candidate, was the determining factor. The Rogers Templeton commissioners themselves alleged that Minister of Public Instruction, William Collard Smith, had required the 'schedule of appointments' to be annotated with the name of the politician soliciting on behalf of a constituent, presumably with an eye to calling in favours at a later date.[66] With remuneration tied to attendance, 'promotion' had come to be defined in practice as employment in a larger school. The impending retirement of the head teacher of a large school could trigger off forty or fifty approaches to the minister, but patronage ran down through the service even to the appointment of pupil-teachers. The reconstitution of the elementary school teacher as a public servant free from political patronage was a major recommendation of the commission.

The minutes of evidence produced by the Rogers Templeton commission are also a digest of prejudices regarding the management of gender at a crucial point in the evolution of the elementary teaching profession. Of the eighty-six witnesses called, thirty-seven were male teachers (mostly heads) and nine were female teachers. Mary Jenvey was one of the few witnesses to give testimony at both the Higinbotham and the Rogers Templeton commissions.[67] She pointed out that after the 1872 Act she had been demoted as head teacher at St Mark's, Fitzroy, and transferred as first assistant to Faraday Street, Carlton. She was still defending single-sex schooling. Her testimony, together with that of Mrs Jane Whyte, now demoted to first assistant at the Model School, revealed that in these two prestigious urban schools powerful teachers had resisted the Department's edict that the sexes should be taught together. Mrs Catherine Streeter, who was shortly to succeed Mary Jenvey at the Faraday Street school, was even more outspoken on the matter; she had been embroiled in a case of sexual misconduct against her head teacher and seemed to believe that wholesale coupling between the sexes was prevented only by her eternal vigilance. She was also the only woman to confront the commissioners on the issue of equal pay.

The male witnesses by no means betrayed their female colleagues; on the contrary, most were generous in their praise and many had teaching wives.[68] But questioners and witnesses alike positioned the lady teacher within certain discourses of gender relations and of the female mind and body. There was agreement that women lacked the physical and psychological stamina ('that robust spirit') needed to teach older boys. Women were especially suited to teach the younger children, an ideological notion which was to be codified by the development of infant departments and specialist qualifications in the next decades. (The argument that older boys taught by women would be rendered effeminate emerged only in the Edwardian era amid the psychology of war.)

The male witnesses were also agreed that women should not be set in authority over men as head teachers. Patrick Whyte of the Model School gave evidence to this effect.[69] The same unease in the presence of female authority underpinned the close questioning concerning the women's monopoly of first assistant positions, a concession which allowed a select group of women to earn salaries in excess of male heads of smaller schools. Head teacher, John Sergeant, had a particular objection to female first assistants who were married to heads of large schools earning £500 a year: 'The lady teacher, his wife, visits the school, that is all it can be called, and draws a salary of £300, I think it is depriving the State of money that is not earned.'[70]

There was a dense interweaving of masculine anxieties around the person of the married female teacher. Ominously, the commissioners called for a list of married women employed, together with the occupations of their husbands.[71] Inspector Ross Cox replied to the question 'Is it desirable that married women should be teachers . . . under fifty years of age?':

> There are some objectionable cases where married ladies have to retire at intervals of twelve or fifteen months constantly, and here their presence in a school is really not nice before mixed classes; but I do not see why a woman should be debarred from a position on account of her being married or why she should be compelled to retire for that reason.[72]

John Spring, headmaster of the huge Gold Street school in Clifton Hill, came prepared with statistics on the absentee rates of men and women on his staff. One married woman had been absent for three weeks 'in consequence of her confinement'. Her children had then contracted scarlet fever and she was instructed by the Department to remain away, 'so that she lost two months out of six'.[73] Yet he did not think it advisable that married women be debarred from employment: 'Every lady considers she is very amiable and beautiful, and counts upon getting a husband, and if she is deprived of her position on getting a husband, she will not come forward, and there will be a dearth of teachers.' John Spring was the only witness to consider the consequences for the married women themselves of the double load which they carried:

> They have to get breakfast before they go in the morning, and when they get home they have to make baby's clothes and so on, so it is a perfect slavery for them . . . It is a difficult matter, but still something requires to be done,

because the strain upon married ladies is more than human nature is able to bear.[74]

Sympathetic though he was, his solution was unworldly; he suggested that married female teachers be required to guarantee that they were 'not engaged in the labour of their household'.

F.A. Nell of Carlton believed that 'a married lady in a school has a very beneficial influence', a reference to the fact that head teachers were loath to ask single women to deal with cases of discipline involving sexual matters.[75] At the other extreme George Oldham, head teacher of Emerald Hill, believed that 'when a female teacher marries she should leave the school'.[76] James Ure of St Kilda thought it was a 'very delicate matter, to have a young married lady [teacher] having a family . . . I have heard of children being nursed [breast fed] in school, and a large family being brought up from the time the teacher was appointed until she left. I think those are things the State ought to avoid.'[77]

The Rogers Templeton commissioners delivered their verdict on the lady teachers in their third report:

> We have taken evidence in reference to the relative advantages of the employment of men and women as teachers. For the younger children we have no doubt that women are more fitted. In the higher classes, if, as the weight of evidence would seem to indicate, girls should be taught in separate classes, we would suggest that women should be employed as their teachers. But in every case where women are employed as teachers some rules should be observed in reference to married women. From the evidence we have taken and the returns obtained, it would appear that wives of men without occupation or of men in various occupations altogether outside the profession of teaching are employed. We think that this is very undesirable, and that, if married women are employed at all, it should be, as far as practicable, only when their husbands are also teachers in the same school, and that even in such cases a declaration should be required that the wife (except in the case of workmistresses) is not engaged in the performance of household duties. Several witnesses gave evidence of the physical incapacity for their school work of women exhausted by the labour of home duties.[78]

As these understandings were absent from the deliberations of the Higinbotham commission sixteen years earlier, it is apparent that the lady teacher had become enmeshed in circumstances specific to the last quarter of the nineteenth century. With James Service as both Premier and Minister of Public Instruction, the recommendation of the commissioners to reconstitute the elementary school teacher as a public servant under the Public Service Board was translated swiftly into action by the Public Service Act of 1883.[79] Though this was a key strategy in the recruitment and retention of men in the service, the state had also constituted 2,351 women as public servants, where they joined a small number of post mistresses, telegraphists, and female turn-keys in gaols and reformatories.

The Education Department greeted the Act in admirably gender neutral terms: 'With little or no increase in expenditure, the office of teacher will be substantially benefited, additional inducements will be given to industry and good conduct, as well as to the acquisition of higher certificates, and the public education of the colony will be materially advanced.'[80] The teachers too were jubilant about their new status, for it was the avowed intention of the Act to create a structure of classification, promotion and transfer based on seniority, literary qualifications and merit. A committee of classifiers was created—John Main, Inspector-General of the Department, W.H. Nicholls, the elected representative of the teachers, and W. Murray Ross, the government nominee—to oversee the creation of five classes of schools with five corresponding classes of teachers placed in order of precedence for promotion on a classified roll. Literary qualifications were once again tied to promotion: the head teacher of a first-class school must be certificated and classified in first honours or hold a degree from the University of Melbourne, and so on down to the head teacher of a fifth-class school who need only be licensed to teach. All appointments, promotions and transfers were under the control of the Public Service Board, and teachers had the right of appeal. Salaries were to be modelled on the salary scales and yearly increments in the other departments of the public service, although they were to be considerably more modest. The four-fifths male/female salary ratio was preserved.

The defeat of the lady teacher

For many teachers the first classified roll, which appeared in 1885, was a disturbing document.[81] The committee of classifiers had proceeded by classifying schools before they classified teachers: that is, first-class schools were constituted as those with an attendance of over 700, while those with less that fifty were fifth-class schools. The classifiers left the teachers in the positions which they held at the passing of the Act, ranking them according to the classification of the school. Only with regard to the teacher's ranking *within* his or her assigned class did the criteria for promotion come into effect. Thus the administration of the Public Service Act confirmed the very injustices which it was designed to overcome, setting in concrete advantages which had been secured by patronage. With classification governed by the size of the school, teachers remained hostage to the attendance of children. The resulting injustices were exacerbated by a provision that teachers were to rise and fall in classification with the fortunes of their school, making a mockery of the promised orderly promotion. Teachers demoted with their school had precedence for promotion back to their former status, while those fortunate enough to rise with their school leap-frogged over those senior to them on the classified roll. The blocks to promotion were quickly apparent. Once again, a virulent form of speculative transfer, that is, an application for transfer to a school which was likely to rise in attendance, replaced orderly promotion. 'Promotion' to a small country school was widely regarded as a sentence of doom. Teachers soon became aware that they could not with diligence rise through the ranks to the top positions within one lifetime, yet the low salaries for fourth- and fifth-class teachers were tailored to beginners who would rise quickly through the system. The public service commissioners had committed 'the fatal error of making one officer's promotion in status and salary dependent upon the death or promotion of another', a pernicious system satirised by Brian James in his novel, *The Advancement of Spencer Button*.[82] The cumulative effect of this parsimony and mismanagement was extremely damaging to the very psychology of professionalism which the system was designed to promote. The Department too had cause for grief, for it had lost the power to transfer its teachers against their will.

Women teachers had special cause to feel betrayed. Everyday understandings that women should not be in authority over men, permeable to negotiation and subversion, passed into legislation with clause 62. This stated that 'every vacancy in the head teachership of a school at which the average attendance exceeds fifty pupils . . . shall be filled by the appointment of a male head teacher'. In the legislature a group of members led by William Hearn and James Mirams tried unsuccessfully to have the threshold raised to 150 on the grounds that 'in the back part of the country girls owed all the culture they acquired to the refining influences of lady teachers'.[83] Women were excluded from the first class of teachers which consisted of thirty-seven men corresponding roughly to the number of large, urban schools in the first class. The most highly qualified women were clustered now in the second class—twenty-eight women, of whom fifteen were married. These were the first assistants, certificated and with first- or second-class honours, whose precedence over the second male assistants had so troubled the royal commissioners in 1882. Among them were women who had been heads of girls' departments before 1872—Anne Drake, Jane Whyte, Catherine Streeter and others. Without explanation, there were only six places allotted for women in the third class, while there were 132 for men. This constituted an almost insuperable block to

Table 5 Number and classification of teachers employed on 31st December 1885

Classification		Males	Females	Total
	First class	36	-	
	Second class	36	-	
Head teachers	Third class	93	-	
	Fourth class	339	5	
	Fifth class	800	383	
		1304	388	1692
	Second class	-	28	
	Third class	37	5	
Assistants	Fourth class	36	73	
	Fifth class	69	240	
	Juniors	27	235	
		169	581	750
Relieving teachers	Fifth class	15	-	15
	First class	72	280	
Pupil-teachers	Second class	62	202	
	Third class	37	163	
	Fourth class	55	201	
		226	846	1072
Sewing mistresses			521	521
Grand totals		1714	2336	4050

Source: Victorian Parliamentary Papers (Legislative Assembly), Report of the Minister of Public Instruction, 1885–86.

promotion for the eighty-two women in the fourth class. By far the largest group of female teachers—780—were classified in the lowest, or fifth, class and their chances of promotion were remote. This was not the final indignity. Again without explanation, a further group of 240 women and thirty-six men were placed on a newly created division at the bottom the fifth class and designated 'junior assistants'. In this group were many who had been classified teachers before the Public Service Act of 1883, and these were the only teachers who were to receive no increments. The longest serving among them was Mrs Kate Bell, a licensed teacher of the La Trobe Street school, who had been appointed on 1 July 1856. The position of women teachers after the implementation of the Public Service Act of 1883 is shown in Table 5.

In this manner the construction of a male elite in the profession of elementary teaching passed into legislative possibility. It would be convenient to conclude that the defeat of Victoria's lady teachers was forced upon an unwilling educational bureaucracy by public service men intolerant of women in their midst. In fact, the schema which underpinned the first classified roll of 1885 bears an uncanny resemblance to a previous document drawn up within the Department in 1880 by Frederick Gladman and Inspectors Main, Brodribb, Topp and Wilson Brown.[84] The two-tiered collectivity of masculine self-interest which produced this male elite—the Victorian Education Department and the Public Service—was soon to be overlaid by a third collectivity, as teachers began to organise effectively for the first time.

The Victorian Lady Teachers' Association

If the officers of the Victorian Education Department had hoped for a quiet life after the passing of the Public Service Act they must have been downcast. After 1883, alterations to salaries, promotions and classification could only be achieved by amendment to the legislation, and the Department's dealings with its teachers came under far greater public scrutiny than before. Whereas the entire legislative base of Victorian public education to 1883 had been achieved by three major Acts and one minor amending Act, by 1905 there had been twenty major and minor Acts. The inevitable result was to generate the public perception of a wholesale attack on that icon of nineteenth-century social legislation, the Education Act of 1872.

To add to the discomfort of the Department and the legislature, the teachers began to organise effectively for the first time. As Andrew Spaull makes clear, the rise of teacher unionism in Victoria should not be seen in isolation from similar developments in the other states and in other Western nations in the same decades.[85] Nevertheless, the immediate catalyst in Victoria was the injustices suffered by Victorian teachers under the administration of the Public Service Act. They began as they were to go on, organising factionally around specific grievances. Regional groups were also quick to form, the most radical groups centred in Ballarat and Sandhurst. In December 1885 the factions came together to form the State Schools Teachers' Union of Victoria (SSTUV) which held its first annual conference at Sandhurst the following Easter. In the 1880s and 1890s the SSTUV was in many ways more outspoken and politically astute than in any decade until the 1940s, when the teachers mounted a political campaign around the issue of the salaries' tribunal.

The most successful lobby group in the 1880s was the Male Assistant Teachers' Association who were able to threaten mass resignations if the lot of the fourth- and fifth-class men was not improved. Their demands were accommodated in the first of the amending Acts, the Education (Teachers) Act of 1888, although the salary increases were paid from July 1886. These increases were not granted to women, thus destroying the four-fifths ratio to which they were legally entitled under the 1883 Act. They were to spend the next two decades attempting to restore that ratio. Two minor concessions were granted to women under the 1888 Act: the first eased the block to promotion in the third class; the second granted a special allowance of £12 per annum to female teachers 'when in charge of certain schools which from their remoteness or surroundings are considered undesirable appointments'.

The Victorian Lady Teachers' Association (VLTA) was formed in 1885, one of the first female trade unions in Australia. It was a roll-call of the teaching matriarchs who had experienced their oppression as contingent, humiliating, and grounded in the day-to-day politics of the school. The rapidity with which the lady teachers embraced collective action should also be seen against the wider political movements of the 1880s. Farley Kelly dates the women's movement in Victoria from the 1880s, a movement which she suggests emerged from an eclectic background of 'political radicalism . . . religious scepticism [and] well-organised temperance women'.[86] The Victorian Women's Suffrage Society was formed in 1884, and Judith Biddington suggests that the teachers' experiences with the suffrage movement were 'if not the starting point of the significant campaigns they waged on equal pay and superannuation, so inextricably interwoven with these campaigns that it is difficult to separate them'.[87] Clare Brennan, Clara and Alice Weekes, Jane Davison and Helen Gibbs were all office-bearers in the VLTA and active suffragists. Biddington also suggests that the link between the VLTA and the suffrage movement ensured that the association did not succeed in attracting the majority of women teachers. Certainly, the grasp of the VLTA on gender politics was firm:

As a sex we are labouring under many and unreasonable handicaps. Men's interests are not women's interests, therefore there is a great need for solidarity amongst women. There are no prizes allowed us in the Education Department, we are excluded from all the higher positions. As there is no valid reason why this inequality and discrimination should continue to exist, women teachers should demand, with one voice, that they be wiped away.[88]

In common with the suffragists, they were inclined to regard the vote as a universal panacea, urging upon their membership the hope that 'when the suffrage is granted to women the claims of the female teachers will receive greater consideration'.[89] The challenge which the women teachers mounted to their dispossession in the 1880s should be read within the context of women's broader demands for access to the political state.

The first separate deputation of the VLTA to the Minister of Public Instruction, Charles Pearson, took place in May 1886, as a direct response to the concessions won by the assistant masters in that year.[90] The women argued their case on grounds which were to become familiar over the next decades. Women teachers were qualified equally with men and performed the same work, often in one-teacher schools. In mixed schools the services of women teachers were indispensable. Women had the additional burden of sewing for which men had the services of a sewing mistress. Single women often supported relatives and in remote country schools were obliged to keep a relative living with them. Their chances of promotion were much less than those of their male colleagues: indeed they had every reason to believe that 'the act was passed with a view of crushing them out of the service'. The VLTA identified the position of the pupil-teacher as a women's issue from the outset. In that year there were 831 female pupil-teachers and only 245 males. In the same year there were 262 qualified females on the employment register waiting for appointments.

Charles Pearson, who received the VLTA deputation, was in an unenviable position. The liberality of the views he had expressed in the Pearson commission report of 1878 ensured that he received a warm welcome from the teachers when he became Minister of Public Instruction in the Gillies-Deakin Ministry in 1886. As founding headmaster of Presbyterian Ladies' College, as a campaigner for women's entry to the university and as a supporter of women's suffrage he was seen as a champion of women's rights. He had even espoused the women teachers' cause in the debates on the Public Service Bill in 1883.[91] Yet in his dealings with the lady teachers he was to prove less than generous. On this occasion he went to the heart of his dilemma. He expressed sympathy with the petitioners but reminded them that, as a minister, he had to consider the question of finance 'more rigidly' than when he was an independent member. Reminded that he had recently found money to placate the powerful Melbourne male assistants, he had little choice but to invoke the iron law of supply and demand. He pointed out that, while the supply of male teachers fell short of the Department's requirements, women continued to seek employment regardless of the injustices which the VLTA had so eloquently represented. He reminded them that, while male teachers must go wherever they were sent, female teachers could refuse to go.

The case of Mary Helena Stark

Pearson's oblique reference to this enduring female horror of the bush school went to the heart of departmental authority over its teachers. The right of the female teacher to refuse a remote country appointment was indeed enshrined in the legislation of 1883.[92] It was soon clear that the newly created 'junior assistant' category was intended to force female teachers out of the cities and towns into the one-teacher schools, and behind this policy lay the enduring power of the rural politicians. The Department found itself in an untenable position. For the very notion of a young, unmarried woman, unchaperoned and in pursuit of a livelihood, violated understandings of womanhood at the deepest level. Needless to say, many city bred women were happy to invoke the protection of clause 63; Pearson claimed that 250 had done so in 1885-6.[93] They did not wish to leave their families and the society of people their own age; they did not earn enough money to live independently; the conditions in which they were expected to live were frequently appalling; and they were often not welcome when they arrived. The issue of control over the lady teacher came to a head in the case of Mary Helena Stark.

Mary Stark was an unlikely subject for a *cause célèbre*. Irish-born and Catholic, she was a member of the genteel poor who taught, reluctantly and in poor health, because she had a mother and a sister partially dependent upon her.[94] In 1885, aged thirty-five and after twenty-one years in the service, she was designated a junior assistant on the first classified roll. Stark's appeal was among the hundreds which flooded in to the Public Service Board and, like most, it was disallowed. In October 1886 the VLTA resolved to meet the expenses of obtaining a legal opinion on the position of the junior assistants prior to the Act.[95] When this proved encouraging, Stark, who was a prominent member of the association, mounted a legal challenge to her classification. In March 1888, Chief Justice Higinbotham, presiding in the Supreme Court, decided in her favour, directing the classifiers to 'classify the applicant in some one or other of the sub-classes' set out in the Act. To those at the time who did not fully understand the issues at stake, it appeared that the Premier, Duncan Gillies, the Attorney-General, H. J. Wrixon, and the Minister, Charles Pearson, had indeed gone 'Stark mad', for they announced that there would be an appeal to the Privy Council in England. Meanwhile, though Stark had been classified in the fifth class, she was not to be paid the increments or the arrears due to her. Neither did the Department intend either to classify or to compensate any of the other 'junior assistants' in Stark's position. Moreover, when the Stark case was before the court, the Department had harassed many of these teachers into signing a waiver to any claim for arrears. In May 1890 the Privy Council also decided in Mary Stark's favour but in the intervening years her health had deteriorated. Her reluctant letter of resignation to the Department arrived only days before the Public Service Board recommended that her services be dispensed with. On 15 December 1891, the day on which she wrote her letter, she died. Stark's legal victory over the combined forces of premier, attorney general and minister of public instruction, tinged as it was with the poignancy of her death, is a timely reminder that women too could invoke the processes of the state on their own behalf. Yet Stark's victory achieved little in the long run; it necessitated a change of departmental tactics but the change did not even wait upon a final resolution of her case.

In December 1888, with the appeal to the Privy Council pending, the Gillies ministry passed an Act 'to make better provision for the employment, transfer and promotion of teachers . . . and for other purposes'.[96] Among the 'other purposes' were two which had a direct bearing on the Stark case. The Department regained certain powers to transfer teachers against their will without reference to the Public Service Board if the transfer was 'required in the public interest'. It also gained the power to establish 'temporary unclassified schools . . . in thinly-peopled districts' and to staff them with unqualified teachers. The minister, not the Public Service commissioner, had the right to appoint and dismiss such teachers and, if the school became classified, to replace the temporary teacher with a classified teacher. The regulations set down an impressive array of qualifications which the temporary teacher *might* possess but, in essence, young people of seventeen could be appointed with only a 'full course of free instruction in State schools' as a guarantee of their suitability. The unclassified teacher had entered again through the back door.[97] Pearson guided the bill through parliament by appealing to rural members, and twelve months later there were 230 temporary unclassified schools staffed by ninety-eight men and 132 women. Pearson had reasons other than his defeat at the hands of Mary Stark for assembling this ramshackle labour force less than a decade after his Department had declared a closed shop against the unqualified teacher. In November 1889, the Gillies government legislated to remove married women from the Public Service and therefore from the teaching profession.[98]

The revolving door

The mass dismissal of married women teachers from the Victorian Education Department five years later in 1894 has been portrayed in the literature as a retrenchment measure, and so in one sense it was. Yet this reading of events does not account for the timing of the enabling legislation, well before the economic recession had begun to influence either the government or the Education Department. The clause in the 1889 Public Service Act relating to married women provided that 'no married woman shall be eligible for appointment to any office in the public service ... [and] ... every woman employed in the public service who marries after the passing of the Act shall immediately upon her marriage retire'.[99] The clause safeguarded any retiring allowances to which women were entitled. It also exempted sewing mistresses in state schools, and matrons and female warders in gaols, asylums or reformatory institutions run by the state.

This peremptory expulsion of married women has drawn the attention of historians away from the preceding clause 13 in the Act. This gave the Public Service Board the power to 'make regulations for facilitating the employment of women in those departments ... in which it may seem desirable to employ them ... [and to] determine the salary or wages to be paid to women'. No such clause appeared in the Public Service Act of 1883 or the original legislation in 1862, and it gave the Board potentially draconian powers to regulate women's access to the public service labour-market on terms different from those enjoyed by men.[100] The two clauses must therefore be read together, for the one relates to the future of single women in the Public Service and the other to married women who were no longer eligible for employment. In the debates on the bill, Gillies himself encapsulated this 'facilitation' of women's public service employment: 'When [a married woman] left the service, she created a vacancy for another young lady, who, if she got a good opportunity of being married, would be very glad, in turn, to leave the service, and make way for somebody else'.[101]

By 1889, the right of single women to economic independence before marriage was beyond dispute; a consensus on the issue underpinned the reform of middle-class female education and it proved to be far less contentious than the campaign for female suffrage. Again Gillies put the situation succinctly:

> Young ladies entered the public service because it was a means of obtaining an honest and proper livelihood. Many of them had been left under circumstances which rendered it necessary that they should earn their own living, and there was no better place, as a rule, for a young lady to do that

than in the public service. It was an honorable service, and a great many young ladies were extremely anxious to be in it.[102]

Yet the right of the single woman to work for a living had to be reconciled with the masculine project of professionalisation encapsulated in the reform of the Public Service in the 1880s. Herein lies the significance of the clauses relating to women. The politicians also concentrated on the clause concerning married women and there was general agreement that their employment would be subversive of the institution of marriage. A few disputed the wisdom of the measure, though on widely different grounds: radical reformer and suffragist, Dr William Maloney, defended on principle all women's right to work; James Munro feared that public service women would refuse to marry and instead stay in the service 'leading immoral lives'.[103] The Education Department made no public attempt to have its teachers exempted from the provisions of the Act, though the exemption of sewing mistresses means that there had been discussion behind the scenes. In any case, the Department immediately began to implement the policy, although women who were already married in 1889 were not obliged to resign. The expulsion of the married female teacher was not initially a desperation measure of the economic depression, but part of an earlier agenda to limit women's access to the professionalising white-collar labour market.

As Victoria slid into the worst economic depression in its history, the Public Service was severely pruned and salaries cut across the board.[104] There was wide agreement at the time that education was singled out for savage treatment, and the Education Department had no choice but to implement a wide range of cost-cutting measures which were to cripple the schools for many years. Even within those parameters, women were harshly treated. The Teachers Act of 1893 drastically reduced the number of assistants, of whom the majority were women, and replaced them with pupil-teachers and monitors, the latter a category newly created for the purpose.[105] By the mid-1890s, the term 'pupil-teacher' had effectively lost its meaning, and many women were to teach for up to ten years on a pupil-teacher's salary with no right to increments or 'results'. Salaries were further reduced by the Teachers' Salaries Act, also passed in 1893.[106] In 1895 the notorious 'regrading Act' abolished the classification of schools and teachers established by the Public Service Act of 1883.[107] In effect, it further reduced the teacher-pupil ratio and teachers' salaries by adding a further two classes of schools and teachers.

In 1894, the Minister of Public Instruction, Richard Baker, announced a savage round of retrenchments: all women over fifty (they had gained the right to retire at fifty in 1888); all male teachers over fifty with twenty-five years service; all male teachers over sixty; and all married women.[108] In numerical terms, the group of married women whom the Department now proposed to dismiss was not large, but their experience and qualifications made their loss far more significant than any numerical calculation, a point which the VLTA underscored in its annual report for that year:

> A most valuable section of our teachers has been compelled to retire, the majority of the married ladies and those ladies who had served for thirty years, most of them being in the prime of their life and powers. It has been a sad blow to our association, as many of them have been members of it from its foundation, and several were among the promoters. The sudden removal of these experienced teachers cannot fail to have a most detrimental effect on our schools.[109]

The document was signed by the VLTA president, Lucy Tisdall, who was among the married women to be dismissed. The importance of these teaching matriarchs is also underscored by the fact that, by the mid-1890s, one-third of all women were unqualified—the recently appointed unclassified teachers, the pupil-teachers, the monitors and the sewing mistresses. The position of women teachers by 1896 is shown in Table 6.

In the circumstances of the 1890s, when the possession of one income in a family was a great good fortune, the dismissal of the married women in itself roused no great passions. Indeed the response of the male-dominated SSTUV was lukewarm to say the least.[110] There the matter may have rested had it not been for the action of the Patterson government in denying to these women the pension rights preserved for married women obliged to retire under the 1889 Act, rights which were to be allowed to other retrenched teachers in 1894. The *Australasian Schoolmaster* attributed the defeat of Minister of Education Baker at the subsequent election to the antagonism roused by this discriminatory measure. The new Minister of Education in the incoming Turner government, Alexander Peacock, attempted a compromise by allowing the married women who were fifty years of age and those with over thirty years of service to retire on pensions, and offering the others a lump sum compensation payment. About half took the compensation, while the remainder decided upon a legal challenge. The unpleasant duty of testing the decision in court fell to 47-year-old Mrs Jane Mattingley.[111] She claimed wrongful dismissal on very technical grounds and was ultimately unsuccessful, a judgement which allowed the government to extricate itself from what had become an embarrassing situation with the payment of £17,250 in

Table 6   Number and classification of teachers employed on 31st December 1896

	Classification	Males	Females	Total
	First class	37	-	
	Second class	32	-	
Head teachers	Third class	60	-	
	Fourth class	229	-	
	Fifth class	638	274	
	Sixth class	59	84	
	Seventh class	61	79	
		1116	437	1553
	Second class	-	30	
	Third class	36	31	
Assistants	Fourth class	39	58	
	Fifth class	66	184	
	Sixth class	2	132	
	Eighth class	8	90	
		151	525	676
Relieving teachers	Fifth class	17	24	41
Unclassified head teachers		73	81	154
Totals classified and unclassified		1357	1067	2424
	First class	223	765	
Pupil-teachers	Second class	47	176	
	Third class	23	65	
	Fourth class	55	111	
		348	1117	1465
Monitors		55	168	223
Sewing mistresses			385	385
Grand totals		1760	2737	4497

Source: Victorian Parliamentary Papers (Legislative Assembly), Report of the Minister of Public Instruction, 1896-97.

compensation, as against the £3,500 per annum in pensions payable had it lost the case. With the inevitable hardening of attitudes to women as breadwinners in the economic circumstances of the 1890s, the Mattingley case did not arouse anything like the public sympathy generated by the case of Mary Stark. But the treatment of the married women was every bit as small-minded and devious.

For women like Lucy Tisdall and Jane Mattingley, the events of 1894 brought an unhappy end to their professional careers as state school teachers, although the resourceful Tisdall family established the private girls' school, Rosbercon, and Lucy lived to draw her pension until her eighty-seventh year. The Department did not dispense with the services of married women entirely. It played a cat and mouse game, using their services as a reserve pool of cheap labour where nobody else could be found to staff the schools. Donna Dwyer's moving study of Grace Neven and her 'lonely, itinerant career ... through thirty-seven years and forty-eight schools', captures the human cost to women desperate for a livelihood but denied the right to tenure.[112] As with the Stark case, the injustices done to individual married women should not be allowed to overshadow the real significance of the expulsion of married women from the teaching service. They were not again allowed equal access to the teaching labour-market until the Teaching Service (Married Women's) Act in 1956. For the majority of young women who entered teaching in the first half of the twentieth century, the Department had installed a revolving door. In the calling of the elementary school teacher the construction of a male teaching elite was a *fait accompli*. It is the finest irony of the administration of gender that it created the aging spinster in the infant room, paid to be exemplar of the ever-present mother with children who were not her own. I salute the peculiar talent of the educational state for managing gender by reconstituting relationships in the deceptive guise of rationality and objectivity.

CHAPTER SIX

The 'Everyday World' of Women Who Taught: Some Theoretical Considerations

Theory and historical narrative

This chapter has its origins in an initial attempt to write about what I had tentatively entitled 'The everyday world of women who taught'. For some years, I had been painstakingly indexing references to this 'everyday world'; by this I mean details about life outside school hours—courtship, marriage, childbirth and childcare, household duties, leisure activities, church-going, relationships with the community—those aspects of daily life which are not, strictly speaking, part of the duties of a teacher. I had been recovering this material from the records of the colonial education departments and their predecessors, roughly for the period 1850 to 1880, those decades of relative fluidity when ordinary people had more chance of influencing the course of events. I also wanted to give a human face to the women who made a fleeting appearance in the previous chapter.

Despite the opacity of everyday life in the texts of the public world, I learned a surprising amount about the private lives of nineteenth-century women teaching for the state. In the case of Mrs Jane Dempster, sewing mistress at the Avoca State School in 1881, this 'everyday' information came to light because the servant girl brought a paternity suit against Dempster's husband, also a teacher at the school.[1] This alerted me to the fact that households of teachers, even in the most fragile of circumstances, often included servants. In court it was suggested that the father of the child may have been a young male assistant teacher who lived with the Dempsters, so I know that Jane Dempster took in boarders to supplement the family income. I also know something of Jane's religious affiliation and leisure-time activities, because she was a member of the sewing circle at the Avoca Wesleyan schoolroom. At least, that is where she was during the alleged seduction. Though the Dempster case made distressing reading—he was, of course, dismissed from the Department—it yielded up incidental details about the lives of ordinary teachers.

The household of Joseph Derrick, headmaster of the Richmond State School, included two servants.[2] This information comes from the correspondence he held with the Victorian Education Department in an attempt to save his position during the amalgamations after the 1872 Education Act. The letters also reveal that his wife, Brunette, who taught throughout their married life, bore ten children, four of whom died—the last birth a few days before they lost their case and were transferred to the less lucrative Yarraville school on the windswept plains to the west of Melbourne. Mrs Rosa Magill, deserted by her 'dissipated and unprincipled' husband and supporting her three children by teaching, arrived late one morning at the Mount Pleasant State School 'in consequence of having to give over a dishonest domestic to the authorities'.[3] Magill was ultimately defeated by her circumstances and declared insolvent, owing tradesmen £123 10s 9d. I have a complete list of her personal possessions at this low point in her life. Her case prompted a terse departmental memo:

> Her schedule is of so disgraceful a character that Mrs Magill cannot be retained longer in the Dept. Teachers with fixed salaries and pensions should understand that they must live within their income and not prey as in this case on the tradespeople of the district.[4]

As these vignettes suggest, the material circumstances of teachers' lives may sometimes be sketched in from the correspondence files of the educational state. In the 1860s, fifteen-year-old Agnes Grant, pupil-teacher and later assistant at the Rose Street Common School, Fitzroy, returned home each day to a rented, two-roomed weatherboard cottage which she shared with her widowed mother and four younger brothers and sisters.[5] Her circumstances became public knowledge when she charged the headmaster with breach of promise and attempted seduction, precipitating two internal inquiries, two court cases and a parliamentary select committee. From these riches we learn that her mother took in sewing, though her main source of income was her son's wage of 17s 6d as a civil servant and Agnes's meagre salary as a pupil-teacher. Something of the everyday life of their small community comes through the evidence of school committee member, Edwin Wilson:

> The neighbourhood of Rose-street is remarkable. You could not go outside to do anything but it would be talked about all over the neighbourhood . . . It is like a country place there. There is a half dozen of small streets which are a place to themselves.[6]

In contrast, Mrs Jane Whyte, whom we have already met as first assistant of the Model School and wife of its headmaster, Patrick Whyte, lived in a nine-roomed 'gentleman's establishment' in Victoria Parade, East Melbourne. As first assistant in charge of the girls' section, Jane's salary was £350 a year earned, as her biographers suggest, at considerable cost: 'She bore eight children in nine years, working each time until the eve of her confinement and generally—and with increasing difficulty—returning to work three weeks later.'[7]

Complaints from young women teaching in the country are legion and these too reveal much about the material conditions of their lives. On the goldfields of central Victoria, the Scottish sisters, Margaret and Catherine Miller, lived in their tent school, 'their privacy protected by a curtain'.[8] Mrs Mary Catford (née Corr), 26-year-old widow of a Wesleyan minister, left with two infants to support, was appointed in 1878 to a school at Girgarre East in the north of Victoria. Her living quarters were 'very small . . . [and] built facing the afternoon sun so that in summer it is impossible to live in them'.[9] The remote and lonely residence was burgled; it had no adequate fencing to keep out the stray cattle and horses; and there were snakes in the brush fence between school and residence.

That such intimate details of the daily lives of teachers survive at all is a miracle, and cataloguing detail after detail is a harmless enough pastime; historians should take an interest in the minutiae of private lives. The question is: what can we usefully do with this information when we find it? What kind of history of the everyday life of women teachers might we write? In the 1970s, it would still have been possible to craft a variant of the 'women's culture' genre, an ethnographic account of the lady teacher off duty, so to speak. More recently, voices have been raised warning of the pitfalls of this kind of endeavour. It is no longer possible to embark upon an unproblematical search for the real woman (or the real teacher) beneath the detritus layered down by centuries of asymmetrical power relationships between men and women.

Canadian sociologist, Dorothy Smith, is concerned that feminist scholars break out of the busywork of ethnography which circles round to confirm the very categories which have both constituted and confined women. In *The Everyday World as Problematic*, Smith's project is the demystification of women's estate. She begins from the premise that women have not known how to make themselves the subject of sociological inquiry—I would add historical inquiry.[10] She proposes an organisation of inquiry which 'begins with where women *actually* are and addresses the problem of how our everyday worlds are put together in relations that are not wholly discoverable within the everyday world'.[11] In Smith's view, it should not be our intention to valorise the everyday world of women, as it was constituted in the past or as it is constituted now. To adapt E.P. Thompson's felicitous phrase, such an existential state could be 'otiose, intellectually vacant, devoid of quickening, and plain bloody poor'.[12] It is remarkable how often women's activities, especially working-class women's activities, deconstruct into what nobody else wants to do. Adrienne Rich also had in mind the danger inherent in valorising the cultural world of women when she drew a distinction between 'the *potential* relationship of any woman to her powers of reproduction and to children; and the *institution* [of motherhood] which aims at ensuring that potential—and all women—shall remain under male control'.[13] These voices amount to a serious assault upon the pioneering work on women's sphere by Carroll Smith-Rosenberg, Nancy Cott and others, not because the world of women, as they depicted it, did not in some sense exist but because they paid too little heed to the extent to which 'women's culture' was an artefact of the dominant culture within which it existed.[14] The demise of the public and private spheres as substantive, discrete categories of human existence is a major achievement of feminist theory. It is essential now to begin from an awareness of the interdependence of the public and the private, and to pursue the everyday world of women on to the infinitely more difficult terrain of power, ideologies and subjectivities.

Although it is fifty years since Anna Freud suggested that it was dangerous for women to take into the classroom structures of maternal thinking and behaving, few historians of women teachers have chosen to enter this difficult area.[15] Geraldine Clifford's conceptualisation of teaching as a seed bed of feminism is one exception; another is Sari Knopp Biklen's use of the heroism/domestication dichotomy in relation to women teachers.[16] Of particular importance is the work of Carolyn Steedman. She chides historians of education for their institutional focus and suggests that:

> To write any history of women in classrooms means an encounter with [institutional] . . . history, an encounter in which the first priority must be to shift the perspective, to see the prisonhouse in the light of history and politics, infinitely connected with the world outside, whose artefact it is.[17]

Steedman's innovative work addresses directly the link between everyday life and life within the classroom, interrogating the existential meaning of women's teaching work, historically and in the present. Steedman suggests that the women who flooded into the state-funded classrooms of the Western nations in the nineteenth century were the architects of, not the imitators of, the 'good mother' ideal. This ideal, she suggests, rests on belief in the importance of attention to the child and responsiveness to its needs, in the prime responsibility of the natural mother as a consistent presence, and in the psychological effectiveness of love.[18] Earlier in the nineteenth century, Steedman suggests, the 'good mother' was exemplar and guide to her children but not omnipresent and always loving; the forerunner of the lady teacher was not the mother but the nursery maid, incarcerated on the fourth floor with the children, paid to be ever vigilant. To this working-class figure we might add the middle-class governess. Steedman asks us to consider that 'the lineaments of modern good mothering' may have been developed by women who were not the natural mothers of the children in their care but were paid for their services. Steedman notes the roots of these ideas (the 'mother made conscious') in the work of German educationist and philosopher of the kindergarten movement, Friedrich Froebel, and Swiss philosopher and pioneer educator of the poor, Johann Pestalozzi.[19] She also canvasses the difficulties for middle-class women teachers in making the 'prescribed act of identification and empathy with working-class children', a theme which she develops in her biography of British socialist and child-saver, Margaret McMillan.[20] Steedman's provocative— and disturbing—thesis places squarely on the agenda the inter-dependence of the two worlds of the woman teacher.

In my own work I have suggested that the everyday world of the woman teaching for the state encompassed a daily journey out of her physical and moral enclosure within domestic space (notionally female space) and into the public domain (notionally male space).[21] The masculine privilege of moving freely between domestic and public space was bestowed upon the female teacher by bureaucratic edict. Unlike the generality of women, she was not culturally invisible. Colonial Australia was not yet the gregarious village society of a pre-industrial world through which women could pass unremarked about their appointed tasks; the geography of womanly propriety had to be redrawn imperceptibly by countless daily journeys, as women followed their traditional childwork out from the home and into the publicly provided elementary school.

With Carolyn Steedman, I have argued that the lady teacher journeyed daily between two workplaces, each of which was profoundly shaped by the other. Her traditional responsibilities within the home were reshaped in ways which are now extremely difficult to recover. In the thousands of documents I have read I have found only a couple of references to the breast-feeding of infants by married women teachers, many of whom gave birth to children every two years throughout their employment by the state. Yet everyday life also dogged the footsteps of the woman teacher; as Steedman suggests, married or unmarried, she arrived at her second place of work only to resume her relationship with children. This is precisely why she was tolerated as a paid employee of the state. There her childwork was transformed; it was subjected to work discipline—bought, timed and reconstituted within the masculine paradigm of military discipline and emotional distance. The educational state never ceased to speak of a pedagogy of pleasure derived from the idyll of the mother and her children; but women were co-opted by the state into a different reality. The crude technology of the public elementary school was the means by which women's work with children was repositioned in time and space in order to prosecute the grand nineteenth-century design of universal literacy and numeracy. In the same decades that Steedman's idyll of the middle-class mother was being assembled, thousands of young women teachers were brutalised in the elementary schools of Australia. Their daily journey between two workplaces was then, as it is now, more than just a matter of hard work.

As the work of Smith and Steedman indicates, postmodernist scepticism about the credentials of the essential self did not appear on the borders of feminist history without warning. Nevertheless, it presently looms large behind any project of biography and subjectivity— such as the everyday world of women who taught. To paraphrase Denise Riley, Sojourner Truth's famous refrain, 'Ain't I a woman?', should now be rendered as 'Ain't I a fluctuating identity?'—if with 'catastrophic loss of grace' in the new version.[22] In common with Smith, Riley argues for the 'inherent shakiness of the designation "women" which exists prior to both its revolutionary and conservative deployments'.[23] Her purpose is to 'pin down this instability as the lot of feminism, which resolves certain perplexities in the history of feminism and its vacillations, but also points to its potentially inexhaustible flexibility in pursuing its aims'. This position enables Riley to embrace a 'lively and indeed revivifying irony about this "woman" who is the subject of all tongues'.

Riley's marriage of postmodernism and feminism need not in itself discomfort the biographer/historian; indeed the notion of 'instability' in the category of woman is an insight which has underpinned the feminist history project for some time now. Yet something is amiss between feminist historians and postmodernists. When text and discourse are presented as the primary sites of struggle, when history becomes simply another fiction to be deconstructed, historians shift uneasily in their seats. This unease is illustrated by the spirited exchange between Marian Aveling and Kay Schaffer over the status of Schaffer's text, *Women and the Bush*, as history.[24] Aveling baulks at Schaffer's privileging of the literary and historical texts of a masculinist Australian cultural tradition over the materials (texts) with which historians more commonly engage:

To characterise history as produced by discourse is at once self-evident and inadequate. Certainly the past can only be imagined . . . but the historian does that imagining by engaging with texts of a different kind from those that Schaffer allows into her story. The 'real' ('actual') texts of history are not the history books written by historians but the letters, the diaries, the parliamentary debates, the police reports, the laundry bills within whose particular discourses women and men now dead have inscribed meaning. To assume that you can read the meaning as they inscribed it is of course an illusion, but there is still a great actuality about such documents. They don't carry the conviction of a friend talking to you over a cup of coffee, but they sometimes come close.[25]

Aveling finds much to praise in Schaffer's study—and reading Schaffer's analysis of Lawson and Baynton is indeed 'like reading Millett on Lawrence and Mailer' twenty years ago—but she still wants to argue that historical/material reality is out there somewhere and that 'maybe it makes things happen'.

As if this is not enough for the would-be feminist biographer, the postmodernist critique of 'telling women's lives' (to use the current terminology) also raises the related issue of the narrative and its part in the writing of history. American historian Joan Scott, for example, would argue that 'the story is no longer about the things that have happened to women and men and how they have related to them' but about 'how subjective and collective meanings of women and men as categories of identity have been constructed'.[26] For Joan Burstyn, the 'something' which is amiss between feminist historians and postmodernists springs from an older dilemma for historians, feminist and otherwise, who feel themselves obliged to choose between a theoretical and a narrative approach to the writing of history.[27] Burstyn argues that while this dilemma is not new, it is sharpened for feminist historians by two circumstances: the interdisciplinary nature of women's studies, which encourages scholars to borrow freely from more theoretically based disciplines; and, more controversially, the status anxiety of feminist faculty who, as relatively new and suspect arrivals on campus, feel an urgent need to clothe their work in the respectable garb of theory. Burstyn is typical of one feminist reaction to the challenge of postmodernism. She comes down on the side of narrative, arguing that women, especially, experienced their lives as narrative and to abandon the story for the theory does violence to their experience in the past. She is also concerned that, in a field as new as women's history where empirical work is still in its infancy, 'the drum beat of other people's theories' is both perilous and misleading. In any case, she argues, theories go quickly out of fashion.

Yet feminist historians with a commitment to narrative history need
not embrace, as does Burstyn (following Lawrence Stone), a return to
traditional narrative history, long since suspect as the meta-narrative of
the masculine world.[28] There is, for example, the kind of ethnographic
historical narrative which Rhys Isaac employed in his study, *The
Transformation of Virginia*. Isaac asserts that: 'the storyteller's art,
informed by ethnographic perspectives, must be developed as a vital part
of social history'.[29] Writing in the 1970s, Isaac did not feel the need to
argue his credentials in postmodernist, or indeed feminist, terms. The
stuff of Isaac's work, what might be termed 'narrative vignettes', are
often all we can retrieve of women's lives, lived as they were in
obscurity. Foucault's fine-textured analysis of power, of 'capillary power',
alerts us to the possible rewards of paying close attention to these
glimpses of lives being lived. Where the female subjects are also teachers,
uniquely interactive with the state, their stories have even greater
potential.

Is there still a voice in which the feminist historian may speak about
the 'everyday world' of women who taught? In the final section of
this chapter I will look at the lives of two women who taught for the
state in the nineteenth century. It is not my intention to place the
theoretical writings of others like a grid over the lives of these two
women. I want to proceed on the assumption that theory and
historical narrative may inform each other—that the writing of
women's lives may be enhanced by, rather than paralysed by,
postmodernist insights into the act of 'knowing' and the status of text,
historian and subjectivity. Elizabeth O'Connor and Eliza Fletcher
were two of the many nineteenth-century women who taught for the
state.[30] The lives of both women were obscure and ultimately tragic,
atypical even among the women who earned their living as teachers.
Why then invoke these particular stories in this context? I could simply
say that because the experiences of both women have haunted me
since I first read the documents in the Public Record Office, I wanted
to know what happened to them and to inscribe on the record a
gesture of compassion—both respectable reasons for telling the
stories of women's lives in the past. In Marian Aveling's terms, this
would be a 'necessarily intersubjective' relationship to the historical
records; in Kay Schaffer's terms, a 'fundamentally intertextual'
encounter.[31] The stories of Elizabeth O'Connor and Eliza Fletcher also
signal to the feminist historian in the present an anomaly, a disruption
which may constitute the starting point to challenge the naturalised
categories which constitute the humble and obedient servant of the
state.

Elizabeth O'Connor

Elizabeth Mary O'Connor was born Elizabeth Boyle in 1838 in County Tipperary, Ireland.[32] Twenty-six years later, in Geelong, she married James O'Connor, school teacher, eight years her senior and also from County Tipperary. He had been a teacher with the National Board in Ireland, holding a rank which entitled him to be highly classified by the Board of Education in Victoria; she also held an Irish National Certificate, dated 25 November 1861. Thus the O'Connors brought with them from Ireland the lowly cultural capital which should have given them an entree to the lesser professional classes as they emerged in Australia at mid-century.

After their marriage, the O'Connors taught together at Duneed Common School near Geelong, a state-assisted Catholic school opened in July 1853 under the auspices of the Denominational School Board, he as head teacher and she as sewing mistress—a classification which, as we have seen, reflected the numbers enrolled rather than her qualifications or daily duties in the school.[33] In 1866, their fortunes took a turn for the better when they were promoted, as head teacher and first assistant, to a larger Catholic denominational school, St Augustine's Common School, in Bourke Street, Melbourne. As with many city schools sponsored jointly by church and state under the Denominational School Board, St Augustine's was divided into boys' and girls' sections; as first assistant, Elizabeth could claim the position of head teacher of the girls' school on a substantially higher salary than an assistant. On their joint income the O'Connors could have lived in modest comfort had their resources not been taxed by the arrival of five children between 1864 and 1871—all but the first-born survived—and Elizabeth would have had little choice but to go on teaching throughout these years, as indeed she was legally entitled to do. In the early 1870s, circumstances began to conspire against the O'Connors. The Education Act of 1872 was in large part an anti-Catholic measure and aid to St Augustine's school ceased as from the end of 1873. The newly created Victorian Education Department set in train a massive reorganisation of its schools, and the fate of Catholic lay teachers, whom the church could no longer afford to pay, is a story still to be told. Elizabeth and James O'Connor were lucky enough to be transferred together to the newly established and much larger state school in La Trobe Street West, he demoted to third assistant and she demoted to fifth assistant.[34] The loss of salary and status would have been considerable.

At this point, the narrative of events in the everyday world of the O'Connors becomes crucial. In 1874, James was found to be suffering from tuberculosis and was diagnosed as unlikely to recover.[35] He struggled on throughout 1875, first on leave with full pay, then on half pay and finally on leave without salary. By July of that year Elizabeth was again pregnant. She was granted the automatic three weeks leave of absence from 28 February 1876 but her last child, a son named James for his father, did not arrive until 18 March after a protracted confinement which left her in poor health.[36] She was obliged to seek a further six weeks leave during which time her husband died, aged forty-seven years.[37] As Elizabeth was now reduced to a single salary which presupposed her status as a dependent woman without family responsibilities, it became increasingly difficult for her to negotiate the rules and regulations which assumed her total availability as an employee of the state. The Department minuted her letter requiring further leave: 'In accordance with the Ministerial Order on this subject, Mrs O'Connor cannot be paid for any period subsequent to the expiration of the three weeks leave granted in [letter no.] 76/7769.'[38] As O'Connor had resumed duty on 11 April, a few days after her husband's funeral, she had exceeded her leave entitlement by three weeks and deductions had been made from her salary. On 25 May, O'Connor protested, pointing out that her husband had died during her confinement and subsequent illness, whereupon the Department decided that: 'Her case appears ... special.'[39] In early July, the head teacher of the La Trobe Street school was again reporting her absence, invoking her as 'woman' with the explanatory note: 'in consequence of the illness of her infant'. Indeed his disapproval was palpable: he requested 'a male [substitute] if possible as nearly all my teachers are female'. The men at head office would not be chivvied off the terrain of the public: the letter is minuted that such leave is not allowed and that payment must be deducted unless she could provide a substitute—'Under recent Ministerial Order'.[40] The baby James died on 31 July 1876.[41] It is by now apparent that a separate account of Elizabeth O'Connor's private life would have little explanatory power.

The historian does not need the imprimatur of any theory to confess to anger and concern at what happened to Elizabeth O'Connor in those years. Nevertheless, the dialectic between narrative and theory, between the events of Elizabeth's life and postmodernist insistence upon multiple readings of the category 'woman', allows us to consider that the category 'woman' was further destabilised by Elizabeth's status as an employee of the state. The brutality of those texts produced by the educational state, or their reading as brutal by one feminist historian in the present, subverts the naturalising category of 'wife and mother'. The unspoken oppression of women within nineteenth-century marriage—sexual availability in the absence of contraception—is made manifest when the woman has cultural visibility as a servant of the state.

In early 1877, Elizabeth O'Connor was absent for a few days when she and her children contracted the eye disease which periodically swept through the colony's elementary schools.[42] She was still fighting on, for in the same year she was censured and fined when she accompanied her local parliamentarian to the offices of the Education Department 'with a view to bringing her application for promotion before the Department'— a common form of patronage before teachers became public servants under the Public Service Act of 1883.[43] Despite the displeasure of her employers at her personal appearance before them in school time, the intercession of the politician was successful, for her record notes that in March 1877 she was transferred as first female assistant to Taradale State School in central Victoria.[44] At the time of her transfer, the Taradale school had an average attendance of 205 and, as Elizabeth was now a first female assistant paid equally with men, her salary was £100 per annum with a possible 50 per cent bonus for 'results'.

O'Connor's extreme vulnerability as a widowed teacher with a family of four to support again becomes painfully apparent. It is here that the narrative of Elizabeth's life which can be assembled from the sparse records of the Education Department yields some insight into her subjectivity. On 26 May 1877, less than three months after her arrival in Taradale, the hard-pressed and seemingly reluctant head teacher, John Burston, wrote to the Department enclosing a cutting from the *Mount Alexander Mail*. It contained the information that Elizabeth O'Connor had been brought before a local J.P. under the Lunacy Act and incarcerated in the 'lunacy ward' of the Castlemaine Hospital.[45]

It is necessary to take a moment here to note the processes at work assembling the records on women teachers housed in the Victorian Public Record Office. Cuttings from newspapers are a common strategy. They subvert the impersonal script of the bureaucratic texts, allowing the personal and the particular to intrude upon the official business of the school in a carefully orchestrated revelation of the misdeeds of one of the parties to the local dispute. The discourses of law and medicine are also frequently pressed into service, as are voices assembled under the rubric of 'the common talk of the town'. These documents constitute a proto-historical narrative assembled by those who precede historians—the invisible servants of archival material already invested with what Carolyn Steedman has termed, 'the massive authority of the storyteller'.[46]

The reticence of the middle-class ascendancy of Castlemaine when one of its own fell from grace is apparent in the newspaper clipping concerning Elizabeth O'Connor which head teacher Burston appended to his letter:

Some time since a person named O'Connor died in Melbourne, and his widow has since been appointed as assistant teacher in the State school No.614, Taradale. Grief caused by her bereavement, and the care and anxiety of bringing up a large family, have, however, so unsettled her reason that steps had to be taken by her friends in her behalf. Yesterday she was brought by the police to the Hospital, and placed in the lunacy ward, whence, it is anticipated, care and attention will in a few weeks effect a complete recovery.[47]

This text is of more than antiquarian interest. In common with the other texts which carry the stories of Elizabeth O'Connor and Eliza Fletcher, the lady teacher is an object of solicitude; she is positioned as both teacher and mother but she is not *censured* for being both teacher and mother. The unseen hand of the bureaucrat-as-storyteller is revealed by the fact that Burston did not take the trouble to send the notice which appeared in the *Mount Alexander Mail* nine days later, advising that Mrs O'Connor had indeed been restored in health and was able to rejoin her family and resume her duties in the school.[48]

To be fair to Burston, it is apparent from subsequent events, if not from the *Mount Alexander Mail*'s sanitised version of the affair, that Elizabeth O'Connor was drinking heavily. She had come as a woman alone with four children to support, as a stranger and as a Catholic, into a *de facto* Protestant school which masqueraded as neutral territory under the benign patronage of the state. She was an anomaly, outside the discourses which constituted and reconstituted the 'good woman' in the nineteenth century; she had been gathered in by the processes of law and medicine which existed for the containment of disorderly women. Yet she was still a servant of the state: the Education Department in Melbourne minuted Burston's letter: 'Ask Superintendent of Castlemaine Hospital for a report re the likelihood of her being fit for duty', inquiring earnestly of itself in the process whether the fee for Dr McGrath's report should be deducted from her salary.

Perhaps out of respect for Elizabeth O'Connor as mother and as teacher, Dr McGrath's report is not the damning document which it might have been. It stated that she was suffering from 'acute mania' and passed on the evidence of the sergeant who had arrested her that she had been 'desponding and suffering from diarrhoea'. McGrath advised the Department that he had heard the rumours of drinking but that her delirium was not *delirium tremens*.[49] He recommended her removal to some 'more cheerful' locality.[50] Mrs O'Connor was discharged on 3 June when she returned to Taradale. In the meantime, news had travelled fast, for another teacher had applied for the first female assistantship at Taradale on the assumption that it was vacant.

Upon Dr McGrath's suggestion that O'Connor could return to duty, the Department minuted his report: 'Give one more trial.' By the end of June, O'Connor was again drinking heavily but was granted a reprieve on the grounds that she had not been aware that she was already on her last trial.[51] By early October she had again drunk herself into oblivion and the head teacher reported obliquely to the Department:

> I thought it advisable to visit Mrs O'Connor personally to advise and admonish her as requested by you on a previous occasion—I found her in a state which renders it very improbable that she will be able to conduct her duties for some time, and I very much regret to add that the nature of her illness is such as to render it very dubious as to the cause from which it has arisen—and I therefore deem it my unpleasant duty to call your attention to the matter, thinking I have already, perhaps, kept silent too long.[52]

The letter is minuted: 'Request him to state distinctly if he means that he found her in a state of intoxication.' Burston concurred that he had indeed found her in a state of intoxication, adding: 'I earnestly trust for Mrs O'Connor's sake that you will think it advisable to remove her to another school.'[53] It was this letter which prompted the Education Department to begin an inquiry into the affair.

The finality of an official inquiry shocked Elizabeth O'Connor into writing the only letter of hers which I have in my possession. She chose not to mention the charge of alcoholism; she claimed instead that she had suffered from ill health and overwork throughout August and September, and hinted that the headmaster wanted her position for a relative waiting in the wings:

> I most humbly hope and pray that the Hon. the Minister, will consider my extremely painful case, as an old servant who has been in the service of this colony nearly thirteen years, and that of my deceased husband who served sixteen years and lost his health in the state school La Trobe St W.N.1278. I am a widow with four orphans to support, three girls and a boy, between the ages of six and eleven years with no means to bring them up but what I earn by my profession as teacher, which duties I have performed zealously from a very early age . . . If the Hon. the Minister do me the great favour of deciding favorably my hard case, I most earnestly wish for a removal where I might enjoy peace at last.[54]

In her attempt to avoid the charge of disorderly woman, O'Connor stakes her claim in both the public and the private spheres: she is 'an old servant of the state'; she has ownership of a profession which she has pursued from an early age; *and* she is 'a widow with four orphans to support'. The seeds of her destruction lay not in some official conspiracy to deny her claim to either but in the seductive assumption that she could be both. Inspector Charles Fynan's report of the case is dated 22 October 1877.[55] He took evidence from Eliza Bartlett, pupil-teacher, who testified that she had seen O'Connor drunk in her home and at school; from John Burston who said that on the same day she had been dead drunk on a sofa, unable to understand anything or speak coherently; from a Mrs Sutherland who had seen her fall over on the way to school; and from the police sergeant who had taken her to the Castlemaine Hospital. While Inspector Fynan was not a heartless or vindictive man, he entertained 'not the slightest doubt' that O'Connor's absences were due to alcohol and that she frequently came to school intoxicated.

> From what I have heard of the state of her house and the manner in which her children are neglected it appears clear to me that she spends her whole income in purchasing drink ... Her extreme misery and her mentioning about her four orphans induced me to state that I would deal as lightly as I could with her. But I can only say that I am certain the charges made against her have been fully proved and hope that the Dept may take a lenient view of the subject and not cast her and her helpless children on the world by dismissing her from the service.

Fynan's remark about the interior of O'Connor's house and the condition of her children is the only official recognition of what must have been the common talk of the town in Taradale. His superior in Melbourne marked the report: 'I cannot recommend that any further indulgence be shown to Mrs O'Connor. She should, in my opinion, be removed from the service.' On 19 November 1877 an order-in-council dispensed with her services 'in consequence of intemperance'.[56]

There was a postscript to the O'Connor affair. In July 1881, she applied, from an address in Hotham Street, North Melbourne, for compensation for her husband's death in the service of the Education Department. She pleaded that: 'I was ignorant of the rules of the Civil Service entitling me to compensation.' This letter was minuted: 'not *entitled* to any compensation whatsoever for her late husband, but the question of recommending Parliament to vote a gratuity (which could not exceed nine months pay) will be submitted to the Minister'.[57] In December 1881, Elizabeth O'Connor was awarded £139 16s 9d.[58]

Eliza Fletcher

Eliza Fletcher (née Olsen) was born in Braidwood, New South Wales, in 1854. By the time she entered training as a teacher with the Victorian

Education Department in January 1873 her parents, Thomas and Catherine Olsen, were farmers outside Ararat in north western Victoria. Eliza's stint at the Training Institution, at eighteen years of age and without any record as a pupil-teacher, sets her apart from the generality of teachers at the time.[59] As board and clothing in Melbourne were costly, the episode has about it an air of purposeful investment in a daughter's future. In August 1875, she was appointed as temporary fifth assistant to Stawell State School and on 1 January 1876 to Ararat.[60] Here she met thirty-year-old Irish-born Joseph Fletcher, also teaching in the school, and they were married in the following September at St Mary's Catholic Church in Ararat.[61] Five months later, in February of 1877, Eliza miscarried (the term abortion was used on one occasion) and on 14 May 1877 she died.

The hazards of childbirth in nineteenth-century Australia do not need further elaboration. Eliza suffered more than most. The autopsy revealed that:

> there were no external marks of violence. The body was somewhat emaciated; the lungs were pale and bloodless; there were numerous recent tubercles; there were about five ounces of fluid about the heart, and about twenty ounces on the right side of the chest; in the abdomen there were also numerous recent tubercles, and the intestines were completely matted together from the effects of old peritonitis which might be of three months' or of five years' standing. She has also polyps of the womb, which could not be discovered during her life; this would tend to cause frequent loss of blood and miscarriages; there was effusion on the brain; the deceased died of general tuberculosis.[62]

Here is the category 'woman' at its most elemental; I am at a loss to know how one would further deconstruct such a text. With Linda Gordon, I would wish to claim a voice for the historian which intervenes somewhere between Eliza's suffering and an infinite regress of understandings of what happened.[63] From this report it is apparent that Eliza Fletcher was doomed before the miscarriage occurred but she took three months to die and she died in great agony.

As with the O'Connor case, the public records constitute a volatile mix of bureaucratic storytelling with the testimony of doctors, lawyers and townsfolk.[64] There are about a dozen letters which passed between the Ararat school and the Victorian Education Department; a medical certificate describing Eliza Fletcher's condition; a newspaper clipping from the *Ararat Advertiser* with its account of the coroner's inquest into her death; and three statutory declarations sworn after the event by her father, her eldest sister and another teacher from the school, Eliza Munro.

Again, the documents were carefully assembled at the time, in a specific context—this time, in order to restore to equilibrium a town which had been deeply disturbed by the death of its young teacher. Was the anomaly fundamentally Eliza's presence, as a woman, in the public sphere—her cultural visibility as a 'lady teacher'? Would she have otherwise died discreetly in the privacy of her home?

Those present at the time displaced the locus of disruption on to her husband, Joseph Fletcher, and in a sense they were right. Once again, theory cannot stand without the scaffold of the narrative. To paraphrase Marian Aveling, women's bodies were out there somewhere and perhaps they made things happen.[65] Well before Eliza's death, the wrath of her own family, the staff of the school and the community of Ararat, had fallen upon the husband for his treatment of his ailing wife. Two weeks before her death, the head teacher, Robert Welsh, wrote to the Department:

> The case, to my mind, is a most painful one, and has become the common talk of the town, and I have reluctantly, come to the conclusion that his [Joseph Fletcher's] stay here will be most prejudicial to the best interests of the school.[66]

Welsh appended to this letter a damning medical report on Eliza Fletcher's condition from Dr James Galbraith:

> I find her suffering from debility after miscarriage, she is totally unfit for the work of teaching, and I have no hope of her being fit in less than three months. I have reason to think that she has been treated cruelly by her husband who has failed to provide medical attendance for her and who has allowed or compelled her to teach in the school and to cook and do other housekeeping duties, when she was barely fit to stand, and ought to have been in bed. Should this illness end in death I believe a charge of manslaughter will lie against her husband.

We know that all of Taradale knew their teacher was a drinker but we know it only through the smallest scraps of evidence. In the case of Eliza Fletcher, the coroner's inquest, held before a jury of twelve men and reported extensively by the *Ararat Advertiser*, is rich in ethnographic detail which takes us on to the difficult terrain of subjectivity. Eliza miscarried on 21 February 1877. Her husband neither called a doctor nor informed her family, living on their farm outside the town. Her father discovered that she had suffered a miscarriage only when he called at her home five days later. A hint of pre-existing tension between the household of the father and the household of the husband comes through Olsen's telling of this encounter: 'I saw my daughter on the 26th

February; she was then very ill; I inquired what was the matter, but she made no reply; Mr Fletcher came to the door and told me what was the matter.' The next day Eliza was seen for the first time by a doctor, Caleb Law, who testified at the inquest that he had found her 'suffering from haemorrhage to a greater extent than she could bear; I came to the conclusion that she had an abortion'. He agreed that medicine and foods which he had prescribed were procured for her by Joseph Fletcher.

On 3 March, her mother, Catherine Olsen, first visited Eliza and on the advice of Dr Law took her home to the farm for ten days. When Eliza returned to Ararat she was accompanied by her eldest sister, Sarah Olsen, who stayed for just over four weeks. During this time Eliza returned to her teaching duties at the Ararat school. Surprisingly, since the main purpose of the inquest was to determine whether Joseph Fletcher should be charged with manslaughter, Sarah Olsen was not called as a witness. She did swear a statutory declaration which was among the documents subsequently assembled by the head teacher to procure Joseph Fletcher's removal from Ararat. She stated that she went, at her brother-in-law's request, to nurse her sister and to take care of the house. From Sarah Olsen's evidence, which is amply corroborated by other sources, it becomes clear that Joseph Fletcher had grossly underestimated the gravity of his wife's condition and was stubbornly convinced that she would recover if she left her bed, took regular and brisk exercise in the fresh air, and resumed her housekeeping and teaching duties. Sarah witnessed many distressing scenes as Fletcher imposed this regime upon his wife; she claimed that he locked his wife in the house to prevent her going back to her parents' home when Sarah's visit came to an end. According to her testimony, two women brought food to the house but 'Mr Fletcher said he did not like it as it looked as if he could not afford to get it'.[67]

Eliza Fletcher's arrival back at school after Easter precipitated the affair irrevocably into the public record. The head teacher and two assistants later testified that she was in a weakened condition and totally unfit for duty.[68] That she was dragging herself to school at her husband's behest was by now, in the head teacher's words, 'the common talk of the town'.[69] Since the odium of family, colleagues and townspeople had failed to shake the authority of the husband over the wife, the head teacher chose at last to invoke Eliza as a servant of the state and to demand the intervention of her employer. On 9 April, Robert Welsh informed the Department in writing of the circumstances under which Eliza Fletcher had returned to duty: '[she] is so weak that she can scarcely walk across the schoolroom floor and should not, in my opinion, have returned to duty yet, but Mr Fletcher will have her work'.[70] The letter is minuted: 'She should see M.O.[medical officer].' It was this instruction which Welsh showed to Joseph Fletcher but again he refused to allow her to see a doctor. Shortly afterwards, the battle between the father and the husband over Eliza's welfare tipped towards the father. Welsh's next letter to the Department stated that: 'I have learned since that Mrs Fletcher's father has interfered and called in Dr Galbraith to examine his daughter.' It was Dr Galbraith's report, portending a charge of manslaughter against Fletcher, which later precipitated the coroner's inquest. Incredibly, Joseph Fletcher remained obdurate.[71]

Eliza Fletcher died at her parents' home eighteen days later. At the inquest the jury found that she died from tuberculosis, a verdict delivered with the comment that 'this jury are of opinion that Mr Fletcher did not show that kindly feeling towards his wife that might have been expected of him'.[72] This indictment the Department duly inscribed on his record, although there is nothing on Eliza's record but the fact of her death.[73] Joseph Fletcher was transferred to Mt Jeffcott State School, also in the north west of Victoria, but resigned in January 1878. When in 1882 he attempted to re-enter the service, his file was marked: 'Informed that as he voluntarily severed his connection with the Department he cannot be employed while there are so many other applicants who have hitherto had no offer.'

Being a woman/being a teacher

A commitment to the historian's craft predisposes us to follow up every last clue in the surviving documents: in O'Connor's case, when did she arrive in Victoria from Ireland and with whom?; was Thomas Boyle, the previous head teacher at St Augustine's, her father or brother?; who owned the house in Dudley Street where her infant died?; have the rate books for Taradale survived?; the police records?; the records of the Castlemaine Hospital? A similar set of questions arises from the Fletcher case in Ararat. While the historian properly sets off in search of further evidence, the processes of nineteenth-century bureaucracy have constructed their own brutal truth about two women teachers which speaks with astonishing immediacy to the feminist historian in the 1990s. It is the lifeblood of bureaucracy that it seeks to obliterate the personal and the private, privileging the public and the universal; yet these documents carve out of the totality of the women's lives the vignettes of their destruction. In the process they invoke just those material conditions of women's lives which have been rendered problematical by postmodernist interventions in feminist history. Neither woman is ever censured for being a married woman and a teacher; they are deemed equally able to be present in the public sphere. This constituted a denial of the specificity of female bodies, of their confinement within domestic space and within the emerging mystique of motherhood. It is an assumption which is exposed as fraudulent when the personal and the particular haemorrhage through the texts, precisely because of the presence of women, because of the specificity of their women's bodies. The personal and the particular are in dialectical relationship with the public and the universal within the texts which recreate the lives of teaching women; they insist upon being heard.

The women were destroyed by the very possibility that they could be both women and teachers in the particular circumstances of their times. O'Connor was obliged to support a family of four on the wages of an assistant mistress which assumed that she was a dependent woman. At the risk of present-centred arrogance, in the case of Eliza Fletcher we should interrogate further the meaning of 'need'; she had a husband who was employed as a teacher; her family were manifestly anxious to come to her assistance. Joseph Fletcher's actions were grotesque, as everybody at the time agreed. Certainly, he stands starkly for the ancient domination of men over women, for the authority of the husband over the wife. His authority over Eliza helps us to understand that, when the state colonised the family as teaching labour, it also colonised the subjectivity of the family, a crucial mechanism which allowed it in subsequent decades to translate the patriarchal authority of the father into the patriarchal authority of the state, constructing a teaching force which placed men in authority over women.

But Eliza-as-victim will no longer do, nor will any other essential Eliza. Her unhappy death illuminates, if nothing else, a woman caught in the quicksands of conflicting subjectivities—wife, daughter, sister, teacher and servant of the state. The instability of the category 'woman' was indeed at the centre of Eliza's existential nightmare, as it was for all women teachers who tried to be equally present with men in the public sphere. Women colonised the nineteenth-century elementary school before the efflorescence of female subjectivities which we now recognise as first-wave feminism. They were without the words to name their existential dilemma. Was this a pivotal moment in the history of that category 'woman'? It was, after all, the next generation of women who began to limit their fertility and to demand civil equality with men. There is indeed a voice in which the feminist historian may speak about the everyday world of women who taught but that world is infinitely more complex than we might have imagined.

CHAPTER SEVEN

Daughters of the State: Theoretical Reflections on the First Compulsory Generations, 1870–1890

In the last quarter of the nineteenth century, all Australian colonies legislated for centralised state systems of elementary education, beginning with Victoria in 1872 and ending with Western Australia in 1893.[1] Though they are sometimes known as the 'free, secular and compulsory' Acts, there was sufficient variation in the fine print to defeat this categorisation. The intention, however, was clear enough. All colonies eventually created departments of education under a minister of the crown, withdrew effective power from local authorities and parents, withdrew state aid from church schools, separated secular instruction from religious instruction, abolished fees and mandated attendance at school. Though historians have differed over the meanings of this remarkable phenomenon, they would agree that the Acts are the most important and controversial legislation in the history of Australian education, giving to state elementary schooling its essential characteristics for over one hundred years.

It is salutary to realise that a society which invested so much in sexual difference created for those below the benchmark of gentility a common system of schooling for both their daughters and sons. Gendered subjectivities were to be schooled under the one roof. There was no heroic battle to admit girls to the state elementary school; there was never the slightest suggestion that they should be kept out. Yet in the last two decades the history of women's education has thrived upon the politics of exclusion. Faced with a *fait accompli*, we have been robbed of the narrative. We have responded by pushing aside the commonality of experience between girls and boys to peer anxiously at the differences; a little less arithmetic, a great deal of sewing, and the pervasive masculinity of the *Royal Readers*—hardly solid bluestone foundations on which to build the edifice of separate spheres and the sexual division of labour.[2] The possibility that the masculinist state may have created the conditions for women to imagine their lives differently has not informed the questions which we ask.

This ungenerous historiography of state elementary education is symptomatic of a wider malaise. The first decades of mass state education in Australia, from the Victorian Education Act of 1872 to the economic depression of the 1890s, are little understood in Australian social history. Those who venture beyond the constitutional and religious turmoil which accompanied the Acts will find that, on the basis of surprisingly little research, the schools themselves have been condemned rather than understood. In historiographical terms, this narrative of hope deferred was the necessary precondition for the valorisation of a new breed of educational administrators in the Edwardian era—Frank Tate in Victoria, Peter Board in New South Wales, and Alfred Williams in South Australia. In this heavy bill of indictment the curriculum was narrowly focused on the three Rs and unrelated to the real world; it was taught in a mechanistic fashion by teachers ill-prepared in the pupil-teacher system and over inclined to use the cane; elementary education was not articulated with secondary education, a serious block to the development of technical education in the national interest; educational administration was outmoded and repressive; the system of inspection was inquisitorial rather than helpful; buildings and equipment had been allowed to deteriorate. This chapter does not make good these shortcomings in the historiography of women's education or in the historiography of state schooling generally; instead it clears some theoretical ground upon which a new agenda for research might be built.

Gender contradictions: the Model Schools and child-centred pedagogy

We could begin with the commonplace observation that the institution of the state school was created and governed by men; it was routinely conceptualised and spoken about as a male collectivity. The large urban schools built in red brick and Gothic to house the first compulsory generations were public icons, an architectural expression of the state's triumph over denominationalism, over local interests and over families. The schools marked out public space within which the state could oversee the remaking of childhood in the new circumstances of the emerging urban, industrial society. In this new domain relationships between adult and child could be abstracted from everyday life, where the proprieties of class, gender and age were deemed to be under siege. In the mass school systems which developed, adult authority over children became theatre, re-enacted every day through a common set of practices which over the years took on a patina of inevitability.

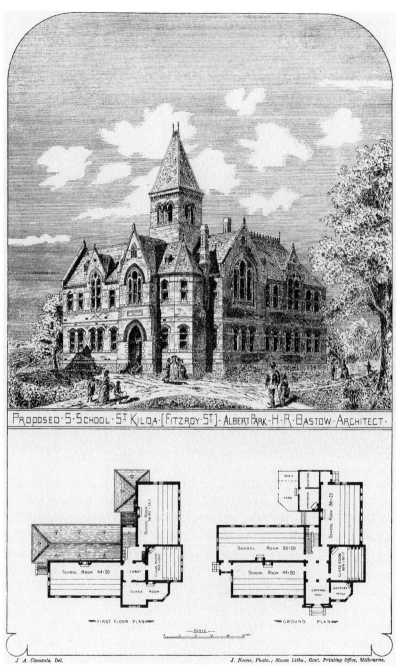

Architect H.R. Bastow's drawings of proposed state school, Fitzroy Street, St Kilda, 1878.
(Directorate of School Education, Victoria)

The most striking features of this new technology of the school were rationality, order, military precision, and emotional distance, characteristics which placed it within the domain of the masculine. Its institutional exemplar was the city Model School; its defining innovations were the classification of children by age and attainment, the set timetable and the set program of work, and the quasi-mystical figure of the trained teacher. As R.J.W. Selleck has noted, certain architectural innovations flowed from these practices.[3] The stepped gallery made its appearance, a tiered arrangement of benches which placed the children under the gaze of the teacher. In due course, the huge monitorial school room was partially subdivided to provide separate spaces which came to be known as classrooms where children could be withdrawn for 'simultaneous' oral instruction. Proponents of the new pedagogy placed great store by the enclosure and surveillance of the school playground, 'the uncovered schoolroom' as it came to be known, in the development of moral habits. The despised 'other' to the Model School was the rural school, attended by thousands of Australian children, where the intimate pedagogy of the familial and the feminine entered again by the back door.

The genealogy of the Australian Model School reveals the contradictions which gave to nineteenth-century mass schooling the poignancy of pre-ordained failure. In the 1830s British architects of the Model School, among them David Stow of the Glasgow Normal School and James Kay-Shuttleworth of the Battersea Training Institution, co-opted the child-centred pedagogy developed by the Continental philosopher/pedagogues Johann Pestalozzi (1746–1827) and Friedrich Froebel (1782–1852). This pedagogy rested upon a benign view of the child as fundamentally good, and childhood itself as a discrete stage of human existence in which the child was peculiarly susceptible to education. Though they employed different metaphors and different practices, they believed that the child was potentially a rational being, that its natural impulses should be the centre of the educative process, and that education should simultaneously address the child's intellectual, moral and physical development. Underpinning this pedagogy was the notion that society itself was susceptible to improvement through education. It was this last proposition which ensured that the ideas of the Continental thinkers had a hearing in Britain, where the conviction had gained ground that the children of the urban poor should be educated if the social order were to be defended. The essential contradiction in these two agendas—the child-centred pedagogy of pleasure and the technology of the Model School—has been noted often enough; the tensions between the pedagogy of the feminine—Froebel's teacher as the 'mother made conscious'—and the technology of the masculine has gone unremarked.

Interior of Chewton State School, central Victoria, in the Edwardian era, showing the uneasy marriage of the 'New Education' and the old ways. The author's father is in the second row on the left.

The traffic in this new educational know-how was international well before the Australian colonies legislated into existence the cumbersome machinery to carry it into the schools. In the manner of all educational innovations, these ideas rippled away from the source of inspiration into the Normal Schools and training institutions of Australia where they held out the seductive promise of taming the children of convicts and gold seekers. In the hands of Australia's first generation of educational administrators, men like William Wilkins of New South Wales and John Hartley of South Australia, the technology of the Model School soon overwhelmed the Pestalozzian pedagogy of the child. So pervasive did this technology of the Model School become that it cast all other forms of organisation as 'alternative', a nomenclature which to this day marks them as suspect in the shaping of masculinities.

Historiography of compulsory education

Feminist historians working in the field of education have had to confront two conflicting paradigms which sought to explain the rise of mass compulsory schooling, paradigms which exerted a powerful influence in Britain, North America and Australia in the 1960s and 1970s.[4] The earlier, so-called Liberal/Whig explanation, interpreted the rise of mass schooling as a benign project of the state to educate the people in their own interests and for the common good. Adherents of this paradigm focused on conflict between (Catholic) church and state, conceptualising the latter as either a neutral arbiter between conflicting groups or as a defender of the common good against warring and divisive religious bodies. The dissenting or 'revisionist' explanation, developed by a younger generation of historians in the 1970s, saw mass state schooling as imposed upon working-class children with the aim of instilling discipline in the developing capitalist workplace and docility in the face of new, democratic forms of government which emerged in the Australian colonies in the 1850s. Revisionist historians utilised a broadly Marxist concept of the state as the embodiment of bourgeois power and economic self interest. It is not contended here that either school of historians was 'wrong' in any substantive sense of the word; each was a product of its time and each highlighted certain aspects of a particular historical phenomenon while obscuring others. Both attributed to 'great men' a monolithic sense of purpose which gave little credence to the agency of ordinary people who were at the receiving end of education. As both conceptualised the school child as the future citizen/worker, and therefore male, neither could adequately explain the inclusion of females in elementary school systems, let alone shed any light on how girls may have experienced the nineteenth-century schoolroom.

The treatment of women's experience by the younger revisionist historians was the more problematical, dedicated as they were to the exposure and dismantling of asymmetries of power. As Madeleine Grumet has argued in the United States context, revisionism was 'myopic in its preoccupation with those processes of schooling that support class structure and the relationships of the workplace'.[5] She argued that the revisionists ignored the gender order, recapitulating instead the hegemony of masculine work and experience, and overlooking the reproductive experience of mothers, daughters and teachers.

To be fair, Grumet's reaction was provoked by an earlier, somewhat simplistic version of the revisionist thesis which emphasised the links between mass state schooling on the one hand and urbanisation and industrial capitalism on the other. This thesis has itself been reworked in recent years, not the least because it failed to explain why state schooling emerged in rural, as well as in urban, areas. Australian revisionists such as Ian Davey and Pavla Miller began to theorise gender sooner and in a more systematic way than their colleagues in Britain or North America. Through their research into working-class family life, children's economic activity and school attendance they documented and sought to explain gender differences in schooling and family life. In a series of influential articles, Miller and Davey have since refined their earlier work to account for the 'well-known but awkward fact that the model for nineteenth-century school systems was not generated in the most advanced capitalist and democratic states [England and the United States] but in the relatively "backward" absolutist state of eighteenth-century Prussia'.[6] In a complex argument which cannot be fully explicated here, Miller and Davey now suggest that the central dynamic in the development of mass state schooling was 'the transformation of patriarchal forms rather than the transition to capitalism'. In this way, gender and age relations become central to the reworked revisionist project and we begin to understand why female subjectivities should also be in need of schooling. Though Miller and Davey do not call on the work of Michel Foucault, they would agree with his thesis of a paradigm shift in forms of governance which saw the emergence of the prison, the reformatory, the asylum for the insane and the state school in the nineteenth century. It nevertheless requires a leap of faith to move from early Prussia back to nineteenth-century Australia. Nor do Miller and Davey suggest how, in a society bent on polarising masculinity and femininity, female and male subjectivities might be schooled in the one system. And, like the earlier simplistic strands of revisionism, their conceptualisation of female schooling in the nineteenth century remains relentlessly negative.

Nor does the determination of the state to include girls in its grand design for universal literacy sit easily with feminist theorising on women and the state. Carole Pateman's analysis of the gendered political ideology of the Enlightenment was discussed in chapter one. Her argument regarding women's differential treatment within a political-ideological regime which purported to be universalistic is cogent, yet it cannot explain why girls and boys sat together in nineteenth-century classrooms. Feminist theorists have exposed the extent to which the state has been underpinned by the taken-for-granted orthodoxy that the public and the private spheres are substantive, discrete categories of human existence, the former constituting the natural domain of men and the latter constituting the natural domain of women. In similar vein, Marxist-feminist thinkers such as Mary McIntosh and Michele Barrett argue that the state within capitalist societies does not directly oppress women, but contributes to their oppression through its support of a specific form of household which controls both their reproductive and productive labour.[7] However, as feminist theorists of the state agree that an essential condition for the subordination of women within any patriarchal system is control of women's access to the means of livelihood, we are left with the intriguing question: why did the nineteenth-century state insist that girls go to school?

Compulsory schooling and secular morality

If it was the intention of the nineteenth-century state to withhold from women the outward trappings and the inner subjectivity of the citizen/ worker, we must look elsewhere to explain the presence of girls in state schools. We could consider the state school as an arena for the delineation of the 'good woman'. The mission of the state school to render children moral was compromised by the religious settlement achieved in the centralising legislation. We cannot understand the anxious moral vigil which our forbears mounted over the institution of the state school unless we understand that the children of the first compulsory generations tested the waters for the momentous proposition that secular knowledge and secular rituals could render society moral. The secular solution to the endless denominational bickering over education was a political *coup de grâce*, not a religious settlement. Even then, politicians lost their nerve and Victoria was the only colony to be thoroughgoing in ejecting religious teaching from the schools.[8] The irony of this segregation of secular from religious knowledge in the very institutions which were charged with the moral welfare of the young was not lost on the enemies of public education. The spectre of the 'godless institution' was raised by Catholics who never forgave the 'great betrayal' of their own schools, and by non-Conformists who fought a rear-guard action to reinstate religious education in the curriculum of the state school. The humble Sunday school took on a new lease of life in the special circumstances of the Australian colonies; generations of state school children were bribed into attendance with prizes and picnics, scrubbed up by mothers who welcomed a brief respite in the cramped cottages of the inner cities.

The South Australian and Victorian royal commissioners of the 1880s, charged with the first accounting of mass compulsory schooling, elicited hundreds of pages of testimony concerning the moral outcome of the secular state school. At a moment's notice, Secretary to the Victorian Education Department, Gilbert Wilson Brown, was obliged to send his clerks scrambling through files in search of 'immorality and indecency' in the public schools of Victoria. 'I shall be very glad', he pleaded, 'if the Commission will accept the return without the names being given, as in many cases the charges were not sustained, and it would be a very cruel thing if the names were published'.[9] What he found did not amount to much, though it may alert us to the semiotics of the sexual in the world of the state school: the scribblings of child pornographers on lavatory walls; obscene notes passed in school; the occasional sexual fumblings of precocious children; 'night cans' overturned in playgrounds. Ministers of religion outnumbered school teachers before the South Australian Commission but few would be pressed into agreeing that the moral character of youth had deteriorated since the bible had ceased to be read in school.[10] In the end, the commissioners could do little else but reflect the diversity of opinions which they had heard upon the subject of religious teaching in South Australian schools.[11] Inevitably, the collective gaze fell upon the hapless teachers. Though they could not be trusted with a bible in their hands, they were to become, in the words of one Victorian inspector, 'ministers of culture and social order'; it was their duty to

> stem the rising tide of larrikinism and lawlessness, to purify the vernacular language from its foulness, obscenity, and blasphemy, to foster in young people habits of order, industry, and honesty, to give a higher tone to society, and to promote the general weal of the community.[12]

It was this anxious moral vigil, this perception that an entire generation of Australian school children was in peril, which imprisoned teachers and children alike in a system which creaked and groaned under its own internal contradictions.

Schooling good women

The state school had a moral mission specific to the female child. Indisputably, the ritual battle over working-class masculinities in the classroom was the more spectacular, if only because it was unwinnable. Australian manliness was incompatible with submission to the will of others; it had to encompass a brotherhood across the social rankings in the market-place of labour and in defence of Empire. The dimensions of the good woman were, however, not negotiable.

The secular moral world which state schoolgirls were invited to enter was profoundly gendered. It was predicated on a view of history which celebrated the progress of the white, Protestant races, elevated the British Empire to the pinnacle of human progress, and placed men in authority over women. This moral world was encapsulated in the prescribed readers and school papers which constituted the only reading matter in the lives of many nineteenth-century children. The London-based Nelson *Royal Readers* provided generations of Protestant children with a common cultural experience. By the late 1870s, the *Royal*

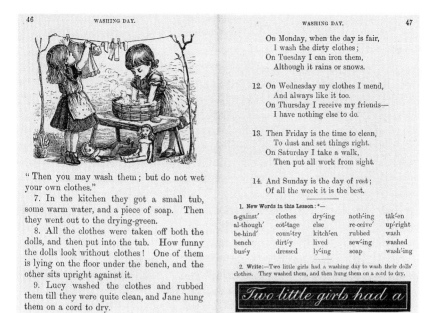

46   WASHING DAY.   WASHING DAY.   47

" Then you may wash them; but do not wet your own clothes."

7. In the kitchen they got a small tub, some warm water, and a piece of soap. Then they went out to the drying-green.

8. All the clothes were taken off both the dolls, and then put into the tub. How funny the dolls look without clothes! One of them is lying on the floor under the bench, and the other sits upright against it.

9. Lucy washed the clothes and rubbed them till they were quite clean, and Jane hung them on a cord to dry.

10. When the dolls were dressed again in their clean clothes, they looked like two little queens.

11. Here is a week's work for a little girl:—

On Monday, when the day is fair,
I wash the dirty clothes;
On Tuesday I can iron them,
Although it rains or snows.

12. On Wednesday my clothes I mend,
And always like it too.
On Thursday I receive my friends—
I have nothing else to do.

13. Then Friday is the time to clean,
To dust and set things right.
On Saturday I take a walk,
Then put all work from sight.

14. And Sunday is the day of rest;
Of all the week it is the best.

1. **New Words in this Lesson:** *—

a-gainst'	clothes	dry'ing	noth'ing	täk'en
al-though'	cot'tage	else	re-ceive'	up'right
be-hind'	coun'try	kitch'en	rubbed	wash
bench	dirt'y	lived	sew'ing	washed
bus'y	dressed	ly'ing	soap	wash'ing

2. **Write:**—Two little girls had a washing day to wash their dolls' clothes. They washed them, and then hung them on a cord to dry.

Two little girls had a

3. **Learn** *(the days of the week are new words in this lesson):*—

Sun'day	Tues'day	Thurs'day	Sat'ur-day
Mon'day	Wed'nes-day	Fri'day	Christ'mas

(700)   4

Royal Reader, number one, 1891, 'Washing Day'.

Readers, elegantly produced, hard bound, and prodigally illustrated with lithographs, had replaced the antiquated and religiously tainted *Irish National Readers*. The *Royal Readers* assumed without question the superiority of the white races and the pre-eminence of men. The north temperate zone was the work-shop of the world where civilisation was most highly developed and the great events of history had been enacted.[13] The excessive heat of the Tropics enfeebled man, allowing passion to dominate over intellect and reason. Britain was the epicentre of civilisation, diffusing 'the influence of her spirit and the energy of her sons' throughout the world. Nor were the *Royal Readers* mealy-mouthed about the connection between war and trade. So thickly were British colonies and naval stations scattered over the face of the earth that her warships could speedily reach every commercial centre on the globe. Children were exhorted to admire the dignity of labour which carried to every doorstep the products of British industry and British skill. Though Catholic children in Catholic schools were taught a different history, a different literature and a different patriotism, both Catholic and

No stop, no stay. She knew not that she drew her breath. Beneath her feet Providence fastened every loose stone, and to her hands strengthened every root. How was she ever to descend? That fear but once crossed her heart, as she went up— up—up—to the little image of her own flesh and blood. "The God who holds me now from perish-

Royal Reader, number four, 1880. 'The Frantic Mother' is an illustration of the story 'The Golden Eagle's Nest'.

Protestant schoolgirls alike were exhorted to be good wives and mothers in the private sphere of home and family.

Female transgression of this gendered moral world was commonly rendered as sexual transgression. When the state created this new arena for the schooling of female sexual subjectivities it also created the state schoolgirl—in company with the black girl and servant girl—as a metaphor for sexuality out of control. The manuscript evidence housed in the archives of education departments captures the sexual anxieties of Australia's administrating classes. One such case occurred in the Victorian country town of Kyneton in 1880.[14] There is ample evidence that the senior girls at the Kyneton State School, led by fourteen-year-old Euphemia R., had colonised the school with a robust female culture reminiscent of the factory girls who so troubled middle-class men in the nineteenth century. Presented with a young male teacher, the Kyneton girls had quickly grasped that the balance of sexual power could be tipped in their favour. Matters came to a head when a mother complained to the first assistant teacher, Mrs Elizabeth Hall, about indecent language among the senior girls. Mrs Hall reported this to the headmaster, John Storie, who asked her to caution the girls. Storie later wrote that he passed this duty over to Mrs Hall because 'a caution on such a delicate subject would come with more propriety from a lady'. Here is our female teacher as moral guardian of the female scholars. As the girls left the room, Mrs Hall found on the floor a crudely suggestive note written to the young male teacher, William Littlejohn, in disguised handwriting, but apparently signed by Euphemia R. The note implicated two other girls in the class. The absurdity of signing a note written in disguised handwriting apparently did not suggest itself to Euphemia's accusers. A stalemate ensued, with the teachers sticking to their story (that Euphemia denied writing the note *before* she was accused of writing it) and the girls to theirs (that somebody else had written the note). Euphemia R. fled home, without permission, to seek the protection of her parents.

This trivial incident and its attendant flurry of record keeping testifies to the burgeoning capacities of the educational state to contest the meanings of female sexuality. The headmaster acted immediately, 'in order to avoid a public scandal', and suggested by letter to Euphemia's parents that she be sent to a private school where she would have the 'strict and constant supervision of a female teacher that her case seems to . . . urgently require'. He suggested to the other two families that they keep their daughters home for one month 'subject to proper supervision and control'. Elizabeth Hall visited the families to urge this course of action. In the 1880s, however, the authority of the state school over families was fragile. All three families demanded an inquiry by the local

Board of Advice, a watered-down form of local school governance which replaced powerful local committees after the 1872 Act. In this manner discourses concerning the dimensions of the 'good woman' passed into legalistic mode with evidence, cross-examination and witnesses—the paraphernalia of an obsessive search for truth. The network widened again with an inquiry at departmental level by Inspector Thomas Brodribb at which counsel for both teachers and parents were present. Brodribb, manifestly suspicious of Euphemia, decided upon a verdict of 'not sufficiently proven'. The enormity of naming her as the author of the note was clearly understood by all parties—hence the obsessive and legalistic search for truth and the reluctance to find her guilty. But guilty of what?

The key to the child's guilt or innocence was her possession of the explicit sexual knowledge needed to write the note to William Littlejohn. The note proposed *inter alia* that 'you must keep me in and I will give you a fuck . . . I want someone to put their big cock in me', ending with a comical blend of courtesy and crudity: 'I remain, Phemy R. to Mr Littlejohn and Kate wants one too.' Nineteenth-century discourse concerning children and sexual knowledge swung between a conviction that working-class children living in cramped conditions could hardly fail to learn the facts of reproduction—and were therefore in need of redemption—and an urgent need to believe that the very essence of childhood was innocence/ignorance of sexuality. Two people commented on the *manner* of Euphemia's possessing this knowledge. John Storie wrote in his report that 'the letter seemed to point to something worse than mere words picked up and used without meaning or understanding'. William Fisher, counsel for the teachers at the Brodribb inquiry, argued that 'the indecent letter showed knowledge beyond which a mere child could possibly be possessed of'. Inspector Brodribb commented that, while she was by no means womanly in aspect, Euphemia had 'a very sensual mouth'. This pursuit of Euphemia R. through the discursive categories of child, non-child, schoolgirl and woman would be amusing if the consequences had not been so serious. In Bruce Curtis's terms, it is here that we find 'regimes of gender relations' intersecting with 'regimes of knowledge/power' in social practice which both defines and contests the dimensions of the 'good woman'.[15]

The school and the family

To claim on such evidence, as some historians have, that Australian parents were at war with the educational state is dubious to say the least.

In the last quarter of the nineteenth century, education departments could not cope with parental demands for schools. In 1880 alone, Victoria had 350 applications for new schools, only twenty-five of which were refused.[16] Literacy had become an issue of respectability and marriageability well before the intervention of the state into popular education in the Western nations. Once established, however, the state school was obsessive in its demands, and family responses were as various as the circumstances of the families themselves.

There were always those who saw the state school as a low tide of gentility which they were determined to avoid. And to the surprise of the triumphant secularists, many Catholic families refused to send their children to state schools after the abolition of state aid to Catholic schools. The state schools were, however, supported by the beneficiaries of the buoyant Australian economy which transformed the major cities in the first decades of compulsory education. In Graeme Davison's words, 'Marvellous Melbourne' was a city 'intoxicated with the idea of growth for growth's sake'.[17] White-collar employment exploded in both the private and public sectors. Many shop keepers, small builders, and other family businesses shared in the general prosperity, as did the aristocracy of blue-collar workers, particularly in the building and engineering trades. In the 1880s, thousands of Australian families, many of them the first generation of suburban dwellers, could contemplate forgoing the labour of their sons and daughters in order to send them to the new state schools. These were the families whose material conditions allowed them to embrace the ideal of the male breadwinner and the mother at home with the children, a social form of mothering which remained dominant until the second women's movement in the 1970s. The state schools did not sit like a neutral grid over the economic and social landscape of the towns and cities; like the high schools in the twentieth century, they took on the characteristics of the clientele they served.

By the 1880s the right of women to a respectable occupation, at least before marriage, was no longer in dispute, and staying on at state school also became an investment in a daughter's future. In most colonies, pupil-teacherships were reserved for state school pupils. Margaret Berry, for forty-seven years headmistress of the Brisbane Model School, testified before a Queensland royal commission in 1875 that most of the girls in her senior classes wanted to be teachers. Important in securing middle-class loyalty was the close link which developed between the Public Service and the state school. In Victoria, the wide-ranging Public Service Act of 1883 established an internally controlled competitive examination.[18] Thereafter, ambitious headmasters were only too happy to promote the idea that boys, and increasingly girls, educated in the free program of the state schools could pass the entry examination. In the 1880s, paid employment for young women began to diversify. Just as an earlier generation of women had deserted domestic service for factory work, the first compulsory generations of girls educated in the state schools began to enter nursing, telegraphy, office work, and sales assistantships in the glamorous new department stores. These female white-collar jobs required skills, not only in literacy and numeracy, but in the conscious manipulation of appearance, manner and voice. The role of the state schools and the women teachers in nurturing this new generation of young women has never been considered, let alone systematically investigated.

The relationship between the marginal working-class family and the state school was always more troubled. Many families faced a grim struggle which put beyond their reach the stable family life which the institution of the state school took for granted. Urban economies demanded that the waged labourer be geographically mobile and dependent on casual work. Even in the 1880s workplaces tended to be ephemeral, under-capitalised and make-shift, often little more than craft or family-based businesses, subject to erratic and seasonal supplies of raw materials.[19] In the boom of the 1880s the building industry provided employment but demanded mobility. The numbers seeking work in urban areas swelled when seasonal work in rural areas came to an end, and with the successive waves of immigration which characterised Australia throughout the nineteenth century.

Women were even more vulnerable, as their participation in waged labour had to be reconciled with the care of children and the household. They were often 'outworkers', especially in the clothing industry, a virulent form of exploitation which had become a *cause célèbre* by the end of the century. Middle-class understandings of the 'good' domestic servant, the celibate woman who lived in the household of her employer, were incompatible with working-class family life, forcing married women into the most menial and casual of domestic work—washing clothes and charring on a daily basis. For the desperate, there was street selling, rag picking, petty crime and prostitution. In this precarious urban economy children's labour was essential and parents fought to maintain some control over their time.

Teachers whose salaries depended in part upon the attendance of children knew the patterns of working-class life. Attendance was thin on market days; children were kept at home on Fridays to scavenge for fuel; they fetched and delivered the piece work from sweat shops in inner city lanes; when parents were out of work or ill, children searched for work; boys disappeared from school by mid-afternoon to sell the first edition of the afternoon papers or to deliver grocery orders; children of

Sydney Punch, 23 February 1878, on the issue of compulsory education.

both sexes sold fruit, flowers and matches on the streets. The sexual division of labour within the home meant that girls were absent on washing days; they were absent when a new baby was born; they were absent minding younger children when the mother obtained work outside the home.

To the dismay of the authorities, some urban working-class families used the clauses which were intended to shelter middle-class children from the horrors of the state school. Private schools catering for working-class children continued to flourish in the 1880s, particularly in states like South Australia which legislated for compulsion but not for free education. Official statistics on private schools are not helpful, as they do not discriminate between schools attended by children of different social classes. The Hindmarsh Public School in working-class Adelaide was one of the largest in South Australia. It was built in 1876 to accommodate 1,000 children but when head teacher, William Young, a graduate of Dublin University, gave his evidence before the royal commission in 1881 there were only 700 on the rolls. As to why the splendid Hindmarsh school was neither full nor well attended, Young was in no doubt. He estimated that there were eight or nine working-class private schools in the vicinity, with a spasmodic attendance of 400 to 500 children.[20] He was highly critical of these schools which, he believed, did a positive injury to the children. They were allowed to attend school as they pleased and 'no habits of cleanliness, neatness, or propriety of conduct [were] inculcated'.

Ian Davey's study of the 8,000 entries in the Hindmarsh Public School admission register in the last quarter of the century gives a unique insight into the relationship between social class, gender and schooling in a working-class district.[21] William Young's fears about the resilience of the working-class private school are confirmed—25 per cent of girls and 18 per cent of boys admitted in the years 1884 to 1899 came from private schools; the children came and went at an alarming rate, they failed to meet attendance requirements, and a large proportion of both sexes finished their formal schooling before eleven years of age. The majority of the Hindmarsh children experienced failure at school. Davey calculates that only 41 per cent of middle-class daughters, 31 per cent of the daughters of skilled workers, and 11 per cent of the daughters of unskilled workers who attended school for three years or more were promoted annually. The percentage of boys in each category was slightly higher. Davey concludes that most of these working-class children left school without regret to enter the casual, unskilled labour market. As Pavla Miller has argued, the 'failure' of the poorest children at school was built into the system.[22]

Family and school were also difficult to reconcile in rural Australia. As the economy continued to rely heavily upon primary production and mining, education departments were obliged to follow a moving frontier of settlement which was scarcely less volatile in 1900 than it had been at mid-century. The gold rushes went in an anti-clockwise direction

Mt Morgan State School, Queensland (Queensland State Archives)

around the Australian continent, starting in central Victoria in the early 1850s and ending at Coolgardie and Kalgoorlie in the 1890s. The hard-pressed Western Australian Education Department found itself building schools for Victorian children, which it staffed with Victorian-trained teachers, refugees alike from the economic depression in the East. By the 1870s, the children of the Cornish copper miners were scattered through south-eastern South Australia. In the next decade, schools were built in mining townships as far apart as Broken Hill, Mt Morgan and Mt Lyell.

The small, under-capitalised family farm which resulted from the Australian selection and closer settlement legislation was uniquely greedy for the labour of children. Generations of children in rural Australia regarded the school as a haven from the relentless round of milking, fencing, ploughing, harvesting and housework. Demands on children's labour were often seasonal, a state of affairs accepted sullenly by education authorities who were more inclined to tolerate child labour in the rural family than in the urban family. Attendance of children at school in the Mt Gambier district of South Australia was regulated by the planting and harvesting of potato crops; as late as 1909 Mildura children had an official dispensation during the fruit picking season.[23] As Australians learned the painful lesson that the land would not support a race of yeoman farmers, fathers were obliged to leave at intervals to earn cash as contractors and casual labourers. Children of both sexes shared with their mothers the double burden of responsibility which Henry Lawson depicted in 'The Drover's Wife'. Girls rode on horseback or walked for miles through the bush, taking mid-week supplies to fathers and brothers as railway construction through the district provided casual labouring work. The marginal farming family shaded off into the itinerant labouring family for whom the educational state reserved a special contempt. The generality of families did not reject state schooling; they learned to reconcile compulsory school attendance with the needs of family life. No state achieved the regular attendance at school of every child until well into the twentieth century. It was the misfortune of the nineteenth-century departments to carry out their duties in a society which had not yet made up its mind to forgo the labour of children, let alone assume the burden of social welfare which would eventually free children from hard labour. Politicians, both urban and rural, were also employers of labour, and factory legislation regulating the employment of children was ineffective or non-existent until the end of the century.

In the 1970s, when feminist historians set out to write the history of women's education, they began with two legitimate but conflicting

Timmering East State School (and Post Office), central Victoria. The head-master, Joseph Dare, and the children won many prizes for their school garden. (Directorate of School Education, Victoria)

agendas, one concerned with critique and the other with celebration. These historians were themselves part of the second women's movement and the inequalities of the 1970s were part of their 'lived experience': the dearth of women in leadership positions in educational institutions; the gendered nature of the curriculum; the hidden agendas of co-educational schools, text books and teacher education programs. It was a legitimate question to ask, with Jill Kerr Conway, why educational reforms in the past had apparently conservative outcomes in the present. At the same time, women's history itself began as a political act to restore to women their own past; no matter how disturbing that past might be, women's history was quintessentially an act of celebration.

The historiography of women's education has been fundamentally shaped by this uneasy marriage of celebration and critique. For this reason, Sara Delamont's notion of 'double conformity' has been particularly influential.[24] Writing in the 1970s, Delamont was concerned to understand how girls' schools which had espoused intellectual equality with men continued to reproduce traditional gender characteristics and relationships. She coined the term 'double conformity' to describe a process of strict adherence on the part of both educators and educated to two sets of rigid standards: 'those of ladylike behaviour at all times *and* those of the dominant male cultural and educational system'. Two decades later it is apparent that there are problems with the notion of double conformity. To begin with, it is present-centred; concern with present shortcomings locks the historian into a perception of failure in the past. The notion of double conformity is also overly dependent upon prescription, that is, upon what was supposed to happen rather than what did happen. Henry Handel Richardson's novel, *The Getting of Wisdom*, which depicted life at the Presbyterian Ladies' College in the 1880s, was shocking to the school community in the twentieth century precisely because it dealt with the oppositional discourses which the girls wove in and around the official life of the school. Writing in the 1970s, Delamont also accepted as given the gendered categories of human behaviour central to her thesis; she is in danger of circling round to imprison women in the very categories which attempted to define and confine them in the nineteenth century. Neither can Delamont's thesis tolerate the possibility that women's response to conflicting norms of behaviour may be anything other than disappointing. Most importantly in the present context, the notion of double conformity as it has been employed in the historiography of women's education is class bound; these are middle-class prescriptions for behaviour. We have only to shift the focus to the girls at the Kyneton State School in the 1880s to understand that not all women were receptive to the injunction to be modest and chaste at all times. A theoretical construct which was, in the 1970s, a new and stimulating way of accounting for the 'failure' of women's education now stands squarely in the path of conceptual advance.

It is now time for a new generation to call into question the assumptions of an older generation of historians. To begin with, they must recast the notion of double conformity and prise it away from its middle-class origins. They must invest it with the possibility that the injunction to conform to two apparently incompatible sets of behaviour may lead to just that 'potentially inexhaustive flexibility' which Denise Riley proposes as the historical lot of feminism.[25] What kind of history might emerge if we began with women's own experience of mass schooling and worked outwards from that point? We might begin with the humble sewing lesson. The sewing lesson entered the curriculum of the state school as a symbolic marker of the 'domestic', abstracted from its cultural meanings in women's lives. In the masculinist frame of reference, a sewing woman was a chaste woman, a woman in her place. Yet outside the classroom women did not experience sewing in this way. Like baking bread and shelling peas, sewing was integrated into their particularistic relationships with other women—in the words of Dorothy Smith, 'a moment in the moving skein of family and tradition'.[26] Sewing was also a saleable skill. The purchase of a treadle sewing machine was an important event in women's lives, a hedge against destitution and a milestone in the matrilineal descent of self. Some women refused to marry until they owned a sewing machine.

Yet upon the ubiquitous sewing lesson rested the agenda of the educational state to deliver the female child safely back to the world of home and family. It would be a new and interesting question to ask whether the act of sewing, embedded within the social relations of the classroom, led not to the subjectivity of the dutiful wife but to the tailoresses' strike of 1882. We could ask a similar set of questions concerning other shifts in female subjectivity which were coterminous with the first generations of compulsory schooling: the inexorable decline of the birth-rate; and the mass refusal of Australian women to be servants in other women's homes.

What sort of history would emerge if we began with a class of girls in the Redfern Public School in 1880 and traced them outwards, as we have done with university graduates and the alumni of the more prestigious girls' secondary schools? Would we arrive at the doors of the Women's Christian Temperance Union and the Newtown Branch of the Womanhood Suffrage League of New South Wales? Women began to organise across a wide range of issues from the 1880s onwards, yet our perceptions of this social movement have been 'top down'. We have not asked whether the experience of the nineteenth-century state school gave to women the preconditions for action in the public sphere, the means to act in concert for a cause beyond the personal and the particular. Were these the preconditions for new and powerful ways of being a woman to emerge?

CHAPTER EIGHT

The Schooling of Outcast Girls, 1860–1900

Riot at the Biloela Reformatory

On Tuesday 25 November 1873 four members of the New South Wales Public Charities Royal Commission paid a visit to the Biloela Reformatory for Girls on Cockatoo Island in Sydney Harbour. Headed by William Charles Windeyer, the committee arrived on the forbidding ex-convict island to find the hard-pressed superintendent, George Lucas, in a state of siege. The timing of a riot among the female inmates was perhaps not coincidental, nor could the commissioners overlook the evidence of the rebellion. On the previous Friday morning six of the girls, led by seventeen-year-old Mary W., began systematically to smash the windows, a strategy which they had convinced themselves would lead to the dismissal of the hated George Lucas and his wife, Mary Ann. The six offenders were captured and incarcerated in dormitory three, their bedding removed, their diet reduced to bread and water, and the windows boarded up from the outside. Punishment of this kind was customarily referred to by the girls as 'doing fourteen days'. On the Sunday evening the girls managed to set fire to the floor matting which they had heaped against the door in the hope of burning it down. For much of Sunday night the girls in dormitory four supported the incarcerated girls with a cacophony of shrieking, singing, laughing and sexual banter with the sailors whose ship was docked within earshot on the beach. On Monday morning Lucas retaliated by refusing to unlock their door. This precipitated a riot in dormitory four in which the girls destroyed water buckets, slop buckets and bedsteads. When Lucas finally ventured in (accompanied by three policemen) he found that a caricature of himself with his genitalia exposed had been drawn on the wall, and labelled accordingly. All parties to the dispute, including Lucas, subsequently agreed that he lost control of himself. He beat and kicked several of the girls severely; he hit fifteen-year-old Annie S. across her breasts with a cane and, in a bizarre attempt to wipe the graffiti from the wall with her hair, knocked her to the ground and stood upon her.

214

Eventually the beds were removed from dormitory four and the girls incarcerated in the same manner as the girls in dormitory three. Twenty-four hours later the royal commissioners began their tour of inspection.

Sometime on Tuesday 25 November, seventeen-year-old Sarah B., by common consent the leader of the girls in the reformatory, gained access to the royal commissioners, though there is no evidence as to how she did so. Shortly thereafter William Windeyer, Samuel Goold, Charles Cowper and Joseph Wearne found their way to dormitory three, and they included in the minutes of the days' proceedings a description of what they saw:

> On opening the door of this dormitory, eight girls, from fourteen to seventeen years of age, were found in a half-naked condition, and all without shoes or stockings. The room had a stone floor, was without a chimney, had every window closely boarded up, was without an article of furniture, and had a foul and sickly smell, every call of nature being there answered by its inmates ... Into this room, when still damp from recent scrubbing, it appeared that eight girls had been put, and kept in the dark from Friday morning till the visit of the Commission on Tuesday night, in the semi-nude condition in which they were found. Fed on bread and water, they drank, as they said, like dogs, from a bucket placed in the room, no utensils being allowed. Three were so hoarse from the effects of their confinement in the closed up room and sleeping on the flags, no bedding having been allowed them but blankets, that they were almost unable to speak.[1]

The commissioners ordered their immediate release and suggested to the Lucases that they should devise some 'more judicious' method of dealing with the girls in future. The following day, ten girls were called as official witnesses before the commission, many of them with severe bruising on their bodies. Their remarkable testimony, which did indeed lead to the dismissal of George and Mary Lucas, provides a point of departure for a study of outcast girls in the years 1860 to 1900.

The state school and the exclusion of 'outcast' children

When Henry Parkes rose in the parliament to defend his Public Instruction Bill in late 1879 he proposed to establish:

> a splendid system of instruction for the young; ... splendid in throwing open the door of our schools to all children of all sects, making no distinction in faith, asking no question where the child had been born, what may be his condition of life, or what the position of his parents, but inviting all to sit side

by side in receiving that primary instruction which must be the foundation of all further education.[2]

Historians have unwittingly colluded with politicians like Parkes to conceal a falsehood at the heart of the ambitious education Acts of the nineteenth century. While the legislation purported to embrace all colonial children, in practice it did no such thing, nor was it ever intended to. One unfortunate consequence of this collusion is that the history of the schooling of outcast children has been written as if it had a life of its own, aligned perhaps with the history of charity and criminality, but unconnected to the mainstream agendas of the educational state. In the interstices, the covert exclusionary practices of the educational state have gone largely unremarked.

Yet as late as 1884, journalist and historian, Alexander Sutherland, could write unselfconsciously in the Melbourne *Argus*:

> The ordinary state school is no place for children who are neglected by their parents, and never receive that fundamental home education which the state school teacher is bound to assume in the case of the great bulk of his pupils . . . he cannot but feel coldly disposed to pupils of this class. It may be illegal, but it is natural . . . Nor is the community at large any better disposed to the admission of these social waifs. Those mothers, who take an honest pride in the smartness and cleanliness of their families, naturally—and very properly too—give strict injunctions to their families to keep as far off as possible from that dirty creature, who, they are told, has intruded his rags and his vermin among clean, tidy, respectable children . . . Lastly, the neglected child himself is equally opposed to our present system, or want of a system.[3]

Those responsible for the administration of the education Acts were seldom as outspoken as Sutherland, but the exclusionary practices which he described had been honed over the decades by teachers, parents, children and inspectors—even by truant officers themselves.

James Ellis, truant officer and sometime school teacher to the outcast children of Little Bourke Street, gave evidence before the Rogers Templeton Royal Commission in 1882.[4] Ellis' turf was that imagined heartland of depravity which Graeme Davison suggests was as necessary to the self-image of 'marvellous Melbourne' as its civic buildings, its mansions and its boulevards.[5] By the time he gave his evidence, Ellis was a disillusioned man. In 1875, the Department had appointed him headmaster of the Bourke Street school which he had commenced with four children. When, however, the school was in a flourishing state, it had been taken away from him and in a flagrant act of political patronage given to another headmaster. Ellis' evidence has the recklessness of a man with nothing to lose. He had, he said, endeavoured to alert departmental officers to the plight of the 'ragged' children, but his superiors had done all they could to thwart his work. He calculated that in his truancy district there were 400 to 500 of these children. Pressed by the commissioners to define the line between children of the 'ragged classes' and children of the 'respectable classes', Ellis did not hesitate: unrespectable children were to be seen running about the streets at night; boys and girls mixed promiscuously together; they were disrespectful; they were filthy and unkempt; they used bad language; they scavenged on the streets; and they were thieves.

Though he shared the prejudices of his class and his time, James Ellis was a kindly man who had evidently won respect among the community into which his work had plunged him. The journalist of low life John Stanley James, alias the 'Vagabond', paid Ellis' Bourke Street school a visit unannounced in the late 1870s and spoke warmly of what he found.[6] He rated the state-supported school far above the philanthropic ragged schools which were becoming increasingly anachronistic as the state intervened in the schooling of children. Much of his report was concerned with the exotic even within the exotic; William Ah Sing was the five-year-old son of a Chinese father and an Irish mother whom Ellis claimed to have found in a pitiable condition in Little Bourke Street. He was one of sixteen Eurasian children in attendance, whom the 'Vagabond' reckoned to be 'the best dressed and cared for, and ... decidedly the smartest'. There were also children who had been 'begged off' by Ellis, when before the magistrate for stealing. Many were dressed in clothes and shoes he had collected on their behalf. Nearly 60 per cent of the children were Catholic and, though they were periodically removed by their priests, they usually drifted back when the routine of the denominational schools proved too exacting. On the day of the journalist's visit, lessons from the ordinary curriculum of the state school were in progress and discipline, in his view, was not unduly harsh. After school he accompanied James Ellis through the 'byways, brothels, and opium dens' of the neighbourhood and visited the homes of some of the children. He confirmed that Ellis was indeed on friendly terms with the neighbourhood, especially the Chinese parents of Little Bourke Street, and he pronounced himself satisfied that the children 'were rendered morally better' by attendance at James Ellis' school. In the 1870s and 1880s, there were those who believed that state schools of this kind, set aside for the 'gutter children', would emerge as a matter of course.

The ambivalence of the educational state towards children of doubtful morality crystallised around the institution of the state-supported night school after attendance at school became compulsory. Some believed that night schools should provide for children above the statutory age who were already in day-time employment at the passing of the compulsory provisions; Inspector Charles Topp of the Victorian Education Department understood that the night school was meant as a safety-valve because 'it was not known whether the [compulsory] clause would be popular or not, and it was intended to give parents an escape';[7] others more candidly suggested that they should sweep in the 'gutter' children who would not be tolerated in the state schools.

Whatever the original intention, the night schools fell quickly into disrepute, magnifying the anxieties surrounding the state schools themselves. Inspectors and truant officers agreed that school-age children in day-time employment attended the night school intermittently to escape prosecution. In 1879 Inspector Robert Craig surveyed the occupations of two hundred school-age children attending night schools in Fitzroy and Collingwood.[8] Of the hundred girls, fifty-three were in domestic service, thirty-five were in factories (boot, hat, glue and washing blue), and twelve were in clothing factories or dressmaking. Of the hundred boys, twenty-eight were assistants in shops or offices, or employed as messengers and paper boys, eight were in factories (biscuit, cigar and ginger beer), three were in clothing factories or tailoring, twenty-four were in the boot trade, ten were with printers, four with carpenters or cabinet makers, seventeen were at other trades and six were at home. The authorities were by no means always unsympathetic to the plight of the very poor who made use of the night schools; in 1882 Stephen Uridge, truant officer in the Fitzroy area of Melbourne, tracked down a boy of ten who was not attending any school.[9] He learned that the boy was earning four shillings a week to support his mother who otherwise would have had to go to a Benevolent Asylum. Uridge appealed to the Board of Advice to permit the child to attend night school but was refused. Inspectors, truant officers and teachers, disillusioned with the night schools, were happy to oblige with evidence of the juvenile class warfare which came to be known as 'larrikinism'. Worse, these schools were 'open to the objection of causing young people of both sexes to be about the streets after nine o'clock at night'.[10] Children of the 'unrespectable poor' maintained an unrelenting battle for the right to be present in the streets at night, and in the institution of the night school the authorities had inadvertently given them a legitimate excuse for being out after dark. The presence of girls at the night schools intensified middle-class fears of sexual transgression.

Aboriginal children

The covert technology of exclusion was at its most efficient in the case of Aboriginal children. They were not 'outcast' in the same sense as the children of white society; nor indeed were they deprived of education. The Aboriginal people had their own systems of education based on a way of life philosophically and culturally at odds with white society. Aboriginal people did acquire strategic literacy in an alien culture for their own purposes, in the same way that people in the Western nations had earlier acquired literacy outside the structures of formal education. One of the many political campaigns against the Board for the Protection of Aborigines which used the 'white' weapons of petitions to parliament and letters to newspapers was mounted by the Aborigines at Coranderrk in the years 1875 to 1883.[11] By and large the Aboriginal people did not beat on the doors of white schools for admission but, when they did, the documentary evidence recaptures in microcosm a frontier which has been largely ignored by historians of black/white relations in Australia.

One of the few systematic explorations of race relations in the state schools of nineteenth-century Australia is James Fletcher's study of New South Wales.[12] Fletcher argues that while the educational state enunciated a policy of 'clean, clad and courteous'—that is, that Aboriginal children were free to attend state schools if they met certain standards of behaviour and appearance—in reality, white parents and children colluded with teachers and inspectors to drive them out. They did not always succeed, but Fletcher presents overwhelming evidence that the schools were inhospitable to the black children.

A typical skirmish which escalated through the hierarchy of authority took place at Rollands Plains in the mid-1880s when white parents petitioned Minister of Education William Trickett to exclude black children on the grounds that 'they are immoral and use bad language, and live in the usual blacks' camp'.[13] Inspector Willis on the spot reported that the teacher had no fault to find with the Aboriginal children, though he segregated them strictly 'in order to render their presence as little offensive as possible'. Nevertheless, Willis recommended that 'the Aboriginal children enrolled at this school be expelled therefrom'. His superior, District Inspector McCredie, disagreed and recommended that in this case the 'clean, clad and courteous' policy be adhered to. His immediate superior again reversed the decision in a judgement which inadvertently revealed the reality behind official policy: 'In theory this seems an improper thing to do, but white people will not allow their children to associate with the blacks and it is useless to compel them.' In this case, Minister Trickett had the last word, annotating the correspondence 'I cannot agree—so long as these children are properly dressed, clean and healthy and nothing [sic] against their moral character, I do not think they should be excluded.' The white parents had no choice but sullenly to accept the decision. A census in 1882 estimated that there were about 9,000 Aboriginal people living in New South Wales. Of the 1,500 school-aged children, one out of eight was at school compared to five out of six white children. As a result of incidents like that at Rollands Plains, New South Wales, in the 1880s, began to develop a separate system of publicly funded schools for Aboriginal children, typically provisional or half-time schools staffed by untrained teachers.[14] By the late 1930s there were about forty such schools in operation.

Black children were also exposed to white schooling in mission schools on the reserves which emerged as the solution to the Aboriginal 'problem' in the nineteenth century. As Henry Reynolds has argued, 'the missionaries mounted an intellectual challenge to Aboriginal society and culture far more deliberate, and consistent, than any other group of Europeans in colonial society'.[15] The mission school was central to this agenda to destroy the belief systems of the black people. In Victoria there were mission schools at six Aboriginal stations administered by the Board for the Protection of Aborigines: Ebenezer (Lake Hindmarsh), Lake Condah, Framlingham, Coranderrk, Ramahyuck and Lake Tyers. Taking evidence on white schooling in the mid-1860s, the Higinbotham commissioners were in ignorance of these schools and were disinclined to regard them as educational institutions.[16] Their attention was drawn to the schools by the Rev. Donald McDonald. He argued that the Moravian missionaries at Ebenezer and Ramahyuck, whose work 'among the remains of the Aboriginal tribes' he had observed at first hand, should be salaried as they were doing important educational work largely unsupported by the Board.[17] The Rev. Patrick Simpson also urged upon the commissioners that the educational work of the Moravian missionaries be supported by the state.[18] He testified that their 'peculiar talent for managing the natives' was akin to an hereditary art passed on from father to son. The Higinbotham commissioners recommended that a separate grant be made for instruction in 'missionary educational settlements for the Aborigines and the instruction of the Chinese [many of whom, the commissioners were astounded to hear, were literate in their own language], and for the purpose of aiding ragged schools'.[19] This did not translate easily into policy and for many years the mission schools remained in limbo between the Board for the Protection of Aborigines and the Education Department.[20] Thus the mission schools developed as a separate system of schooling for Aboriginal children which was impoverished even by the standards of bush schooling for white children.

Poonindie Lutheran Mission School, South Australia, c.1885.
(La Trobe Library, Melbourne, photographer Samuel White Sweet)

An understanding of the world of dependence which the Moravian missionaries sought to create comes through the life story of Bessy Cameron (née Flower, 1851–1895), a black woman of the Nyungar people whose tribal lands were in Western Australia near Albany.[21] She had been taken from her parents by a white woman, Anne Camfield, in one of the numberless casual 'adoptions' which preceded the mass official abduction of Aboriginal children in the twentieth century. Bessy Cameron was raised and educated at the Annesfield Native Institution at Albany. Camfield's practice was apparently underpinned by a cultural definition of Aboriginality, as she assumed that the differences between the two races would disappear if black children received the same education as white children. Bessy received a middle-class education in the female accomplishments and emerged from Annesfield a cultured, well-read and articulate young woman. Remarkably for a woman of her time and race, she spent some time in 'a Sydney model school' preparing herself to teach with Camfield at the Native Institution in Albany. There is evidence that the Camfields also contemplated Bessy's marriage to a European man.

Sometime in the mid-1860s Bessy Cameron came to the notice of the increasingly powerful and autocratic Moravian missionary, Brother Friedrich August Hagenauer, who had arrived in Melbourne from Saxony with his co-worker F.W. Spieseke in 1858 and established the Ebenezer Mission in north western Victoria. In 1862 Hagenauer and his wife Christina, also a missionary from Saxony, established the Ramahyuck Mission in Gippsland in partnership with the Presbyterian Church. With the blessing of the Camfields, he took Bessy to Ramahyuck, where he confidently expected her to act as what we would now call a role model for his reluctant *protégés*, the Kurnai of Gippsland, who, a generation earlier, had fought a bitter frontier battle for the possession of their land. Her role as cultural mediator was underscored by her geographical location within the mission, between the Hagenauers' residence and the fenced-off weatherboard cottages and mia-mias in the Aboriginal village. Always short of money, Hagenauer was an astute publicist who stage-managed many visits by important white people, and Bessy was briefly a celebrity as an exemplar of black Christian womanhood.

Bessy Cameron was the teacher at the mission school at Ramahyuck until 1869, and many letters from Hagenauer to the Board for the Protection of Aborigines testify to her success. In that year the Board of Education took it over as a half-time rural school, whereupon she was demoted to the status of matron of the children's boarding house and the Rev. Karl Kramer was appointed in her place. In 1871 local guardian of the Aborigines, Alfred Howitt, described this boarding house which was crucial to Hagenauer's plans to separate the children from their parents even within the precincts of the mission:

> On each side of the school room are dormitories—one for the boys and one for the girls, and at the end two neat little rooms—a sitting room and bedroom where the 'mother and father' live, *Mr and Mrs Cameron.* Two Blacks—the wife educated at a Mission in Western Australia—she plays the harmonium. Their little rooms are very neat and just as whites might occupy, a few books and some [needle] work and some nicknacks were lying about.[22]

These quasi-boarding schools were eventually established on all the Victorian Aboriginal stations.[23] The Mr Cameron mentioned in Howitt's account was Donald Cameron, a young man of mixed descent whom Hagenauer had obtained with all speed from the Ebenezer Mission when Bessy wanted to marry a local white man. Though it was blessed by the church, the marriage to Cameron was the beginning of Bessy's fall from grace with the Hagenauers and she ended her life in abject poverty, a wandering mendicant upon the Board, accepted by neither culture. As the mission school depended crucially upon the ability of the missionaries to confine Aboriginal parents to the reserves, it was no accident that Hagenauer was the chief architect of the infamous 'Half-caste' Act of 1886. Until draconian state control over the black people was achieved by legislation, the mission schools were frequently seen as a 'failure', not because Aboriginal children failed to learn as well as white children the basic skills on offer, but because they refused to reject their families and their own way of life. This frustration is encapsulated in the report of Commissioner of Police, W.E. Parry-Okeden, from the mission station in the Bloomfield River district of Queensland in 1898:

> the young children, girls and boys, are taught English, writing, and elementary arithmetic—but they come and go as they please . . . the mission people have no control over them, and therein lies the secret of what I would call their non-success . . . [while] the children learn Christianity and its doctrines by day they can learn every conceivable vice by night.[24]

Social theory and the reformation of children

The duplicitous relationship of the educational state with colonial children on the edge of 'respectable society' was sorely tested by four groups of children: those who were 'outcast' by virtue of their race; those who were in a state of destitution, a social category which could still hold out the possibility of respectability; those who came to public notice as 'neglected' and were sometimes assumed to have a guilty knowledge of vice and corruption; and those who had placed themselves beyond the pale by committing misdemeanours or crimes which brought them before the courts. The policies and practices of the state towards these children should be examined in the light of social theory which argues that behaviours included under the rubric of 'delinquency' are not inherently deviant but are rendered so by the laws and mores of a particular society at a particular time. In this view, outbursts of moral panic about the behaviour of children can point to significant shifts in the social order and therefore in techniques of race, class and gender domination. Historians like Michelle Cale and Kerry Wimshurst have argued that the social construction of delinquency has particular consequences for female children, as control of reproduction, and therefore of sexuality, is customarily achieved through the control of women's bodies rather than men's bodies.[25] Across cultures and across time, female sexual behaviour tolerated in one society may, in another, lead to the incarceration of the child in a reformatory or even in an asylum for the insane. Gender differences in the understandings of delinquency in late nineteenth-century Australia are encapsulated in the customary description of street youth as 'larrikins and prostitutes', a description which deplores the *loutish* behaviour of the boys but the *sexual* behaviour of girls.

Scholars in the field agree that there have been three major stages in the history of child welfare and that these have been linked to prevailing views of childhood and the family.[26] The first stage is characterised as a revulsion against the 1834 Poor Law Amendment Act in England, which had abolished outdoor relief for the able-bodied and incarcerated children with the aged, the infirm and the 'simple minded' within the forbidding confines of the poor house. Child criminals were also incarcerated with adults in prisons. In the 1840s English reformers, Mary Carpenter and Matthew Davenport Hill prominent among them, began to argue that reformation of the young among the 'perishing classes' was impossible without separate institutions, and this social movement culminated in the establishment of industrial schools for the neglected and reformatory schools for the criminal.[27] Though Australian society did not produce the extremes of poverty suffered in the slums of Manchester and Liverpool, its convict origins made legislators receptive to the idea that certain groups of children should be separated for their own good from their parents. This official predisposition to interfere in families was strengthened by the social dislocation and hardship caused by the gold rushes in the 1850s. Industrial and reformatory schools were legislated into existence in Australia in the 1860s. The second phase of child welfare is characterised as the 'boarding-out' system which took off in Australia in the 1870s. 'Boarding-out' was in essence an early attempt to foster children in respectable homes of their own social class, for the payment of a sum of money for the child's upkeep. The third phase in the history of child welfare was precipitated by a change of heart about direct financial support to the family itself in the early decades of the twentieth century: this support took the form of maternity allowances, widows' pensions and the like. The same decades also saw the creation of children's courts and of the probationary system, which returned erring youngsters to their families rather than incarcerating them in institutions. This third phase lies outside the scope of this study.

It is immediately apparent that this three-stage schema does not account for the experiences of Aboriginal children. Though there is evidence that there were occasional black children in industrial schools as early as the 1860s, usually noted in reception documents as 'half-caste', the mass official incarceration of Aboriginal children in institutions was triggered by the Victorian 'Half-caste' Act of 1886 and the Queensland 'Black Act' of 1897 and its imitators in the other states. These Acts bore an uncanny resemblance to the industrial and reformatory school legislation of the 1860s, but extended their draconian powers to cover all Aboriginal people, adults and children alike. The Acts were neurotically concerned to define Aboriginality itself in order to force those of mixed descent out of the reserves and into the white community, and it was these so-called 'half-caste' children who were commonly taken from their parents and placed in institutions. Thus the trajectory of events was quite different for Aboriginal children. They were not 'boarded-out' in any great numbers in the last quarter of the nineteenth century and the mass capture of children of Aboriginal descent began in the twentieth century.

The problem of definitions

The technology for the official abduction of white children was put in place by the 'neglected and criminal children' legislation passed by most colonies in the 1860s. This was by no means the first attempt to regulate the lives of children in Australia, but it marked a watershed between charitable endeavour propped up by piecemeal government support and the dominance of the state in the treatment of children perceived to be at risk.[28] Victoria's Neglected and Criminal Children's Act of 1864 set the pattern.[29] It provided for the establishment of industrial and reformatory schools wholly maintained by the state, and for private institutions—in effect, Catholic institutions—subsidised at the rate of five shillings per week for each child. The legal definition of a neglected child, which was draconian to say the least, underscores the elision between immorality and poverty central to the mind-set of the Victorian era: any child found begging or being in a public place for the purpose of begging; any child found wandering about the streets or sleeping in the open air; any child not having a home or any visible means of subsistence; any child living in a brothel or with a person known or reputed to be a thief, a prostitute or a drunkard, or with any person convicted of vagrancy; and any child whose parents claimed that she or he was uncontrollable. Only the Queensland legislation made specific mention of Aboriginal children and they were included by virtue of their race rather than by virtue of their failure to measure up to the expectations of the dominant middle-class culture. Children designated 'neglected' under the Victorian Act could be apprehended by a constable without a warrant and taken before two justices who could commit the child to an industrial school for up to seven years. Children convicted of criminal offences could be sent by the courts to a reformatory school for a similar period. Other clauses provided for the separation of incarcerated children by sex (a practice which further destroyed families by separating brothers and sisters), for parental contribution to the upkeep of the children, and for licensing children out to service.

Any analysis of the treatment of institutionalised children in nineteenth-century Australia quickly becomes entangled in definitions. The Victorian legislation purported to be clear cut; it consigned proto-criminal children to industrial schools and convicted children to reformatories. The legislation which created industrial and reformatory schools in South Australia was the Destitute Persons Relief Act and the schools were under the control of the Destitute Board. Though the legal definition of a neglected child was almost identical with the proto-criminal definition in Victoria, the South Australian regulations generated by the Act immediately shifted ground by declaring as the object of the industrial school 'the maintenance, clothing, and education of *destitute* children [my italics]'.[30] The first South Australian industrial school to be established was known as the Brighton Industrial School, yet its notorious successor was frequently referred to as the Magill Asylum. Queensland's Industrial and Reformatory Schools Act was passed in 1865 but the state did not establish new schools, continuing to rely upon on the Diamantina and St Vincent's Orphanages established as Protestant and Catholic institutions in the early 1860s. The term 'orphanage' persisted into the period when Queensland's institutions came more securely under state control with the appointment of a Minister and a Board of General Education in January 1876. Four years later the Orphanages Act 1879 further tightened the control of the state over institutions for the reception of outcast children as well as providing for the licensing of private (again Catholic) orphanages.

Though reformatory schools for the 'incorrigibles' and those convicted of crimes persisted throughout the period, they were sometimes little more than separate enclaves within industrial schools and their internal practices were frequently indistinguishable from those of the industrial schools. This was the case with the Biloela Reformatory School on Cockatoo Island. A generic term such as 'reforming institutions' is a useful way through these complexities. Matters are further complicated by the speed with which institutions opened and closed, amalgamated, separated and changed places, especially as the boarding-out of children began to empty the industrial schools in the 1870s. The determined researcher may track the institutions through government gazettes and annual reports of the relevant departments.

The 'barracks' era in the reformation of children

The industrial school movement in any sense of a social movement based on a coherent set of principles and practices collapsed in upon itself virtually from the beginning. A mere eight years after the passing of the Victorian Act, J.T. Harcourt, who established the first industrial school at Princes Bridge, testified before the Royal Commission on Penal and Prison Discipline: 'We missed the mark to start with, and we have never been able to overtake the work or to get the schools into proper form, and at this day we still miss the mark for which Industrial Schools were intended.'[31] The huge, barracks-like industrial schools typified by Princes Bridge and Sunbury in Victoria, Magill in South Australia and Randwick in New South Wales fell quickly into disrepute. The middle classes were prone to conflate poverty with immorality, but they were not immune to the suffering of children, and they were soon faced with incontrovertible evidence that the inmates of the new industrial schools sickened and died at an alarming rate. Many children were in a weakened condition when they were admitted and diseases spread rapidly in the cramped and unsanitary conditions of the institutions. South Australia's first industrial school was already the subject of a select parliamentary committee by mid-1867. The committee which visited the Brighton Industrial School concluded that 'the statements publicly circulated some months ago, as to the filthy and diseased state of the children . . . were fully borne out by the facts of the case'.[32] Even before the children arrived at Brighton from temporary barracks accommodation they presented a 'squalid and emaciated appearance'; their health had declined rapidly, and ophthalmia (often resulting in blindness), skin diseases and other illnesses were endemic. They were then moved precipitously to Brighton, where little provision had been made for their reception, to a house 'miserably out of repair' and hardly big enough to house one-third of their number. The committee was in no doubt that 'the overcrowding, filth, and noisome effluvia of the place' were responsible for the sickness and death among the children. They were also terse about the 'many ladies and gentlemen' who had visited the school and recorded in the visitor's book comments certifying to the healthy condition of the children. They recommended that the new asylum building at Magill be completed with all speed. Of the 103 children resident in the Brighton Industrial School in mid-1867 forty-six had skin diseases and ophthalmia. Twelve children had already died.[33]

Though the South Australian parliamentarians expressed the hope that the tragedy of the Brighton school was but a temporary setback, the parsimony of successive colonial legislatures ensured that industrial schools continued to be established in unsuitable premises. The Victorian royal commissioners of 1872 described the Immigrants' Home which became the Princes Bridge Industrial School for Girls as:

> In all respects unsuitable for the purpose . . . The buildings form a portion of the military barrack, and the local military force occupies the other portion. Such a situation for a school of several hundred girls is so obviously unsuitable that it needs not to be enlarged upon. There are, besides, grave objections to the site. It lies on the edge of a swamp, and has an exceedingly cheerless aspect. There is no land around it for recreation; the only playground the children have being a bare yard, destitute of grass. The ventilation is defective, even to the extent of being prejudicial to health; and the appliances for physical comfort, although they may be suitable for a body of soldiers, are not adapted to the requirements of girls and infants.[34]

Member of the Board of Visitors to industrial schools, Police Magistrate Evelyn Sturt, testified that even with 'every possible precaution consistent with cleanliness, with ventilation, and extreme attention on the part of the attendants' disease spread rapidly among the inmates. He urged that the Princes Bridge school be closed. Melbourne Coroner Richard Youl, also an official visitor, testified that the Geelong Industrial School for girls was 'one of those painful shameful things that is too cruel to be believed'. The girls slept in the gaol corridor or in airless cells without light and they had only the gaol yard for recreation. In his opinion, the girls were no better off than if they had been in gaol. Worse, he thought that he detected in the girls 'a most painful appearance of precocity and solicitation . . . making it to a great extent a place from which you may expect a very large number of prostitutes to be eventually drafted'.

The failure of industrial school administrators adequately to categorise the children in their care ran like a litany through the testimony of royal commissioners, investigative journalists and private do-gooders in the nineteenth century. English philanthropists Rosamund and Florence Hill who visited Cockatoo Island in 1873 were critical of the manner in which 'little children whose sole qualification for admission consisted of their destitution' were intermingled with 'young women whose loose conduct has led to their committal'.[35] This negligence was more than a failure of internal administration. In their report of 1873 on public charities in New South Wales, William Windeyer and his fellow commissioners drew attention to the 'ignorance of the law existing amongst those whose duty it is to enforce the provisions of the Industrial Schools and Reformatory Acts'. It had come to light that the police magistrate of Sydney was unaware of the course to be followed with convicted children, while many justices of the peace were ignorant of the difference between the industrial and the reformatory school as set out in the Act.

Nor was official incompetence the only problem confronting the administrators of industrial and reformatory schools. As the desperately poor children of Australia's principal cities flooded into the industrial schools the very categories of respectable and unrespectable upon which stern Victorian morality rested collapsed. The industrial schools quickly became refuges for the children of the destitute for whom no organised system of relief existed. As Donella Jaggs has argued, this *de facto* system of poor relief came within the purview of those dealing with crime and potential crime, a source of ambiguity which was to bedevil child welfare for the next century. William Templeton, police magistrate and member of the Victorian Royal Commission on Penal and Prison Discipline, condemned the system on precisely these grounds. Magistrates, he believed, had virtually no alternative but to commit innocent children inappropriately because there was no other system of relief available:

> I very much doubt if it be possible to stop the present practice until some adequate provision be made for such cases, for, bad as the present system is, and demoralizing as I consider it to be, it saves the Government from the absolute necessity of introducing some measure to provide for the relief of such cases, it exempts the local bodies from the expense which such a measure would certainly impose upon them and it saves the pockets of private individuals from giving subscriptions to the families deserted or left destitute by their parents. I may say that the practice of sending children to the industrial schools is one which is very popular.[36]

To the incomprehension of men like Templeton, colonial families were desperate enough to use the reforming institutions as a means of temporary relief, reclaiming their children when their fortunes took a turn for the better. It is hardly a matter for celebration that parents were sufficiently desperate to commit their children to these dismal institutions, but it is clear that even the poorest families were not supine before the governing classes who were bent on remaking their children. The evidence of Matron Martha Pears of the Diamantina Orphanage before the Queensland royal commission of 1875 throws some light on the uses which the parents made of such institutions—and upon the ignorance of the middle-class commissioners, some of whom lived within walking distance of the orphanage in Wickham Terrace. Martha Pears testified that most of her children were not orphaned, but destitute or deserted.

Martha Pears: There are deserted children, some who have lost their mother, and those whose father is perhaps a shepherd on a station, and has no means of looking after them.

Commissioner: And he is at liberty to send his children to the Orphanage?

MP: Yes; he sends, perhaps, three children, but he has to contribute towards their support. Then there are some, the children . . . of a widow, perhaps, who goes to service, and sends her one child to the Orphanage, . . .

C: Do all that class of persons contribute?

MP: Yes . . .

C: And how do they get on with their education?

MP: . . . As soon as a child is getting on with its lessons, it is taken away from the school . . .

C: In point of fact, your Orphanage is a place of refuge for destitute children rather than for education?

MP: Yes.[37]

The annual report of Inspector of Orphanages Charles Horrocks regularly commented upon parents attempting to have their children admitted to Queensland's orphanages. 'The Diamantina Orphanage is not a boarding-house [he wrote in 1885] . . . [These] parents are able-bodied people, and it is wrong that they should attempt to turn over their infant to the State. Not recommended.'[38] Those who were admitted under the stern gaze of Inspector Horrocks included children who were illegitimate, those deserted by both parents, those whose fathers had deserted, and those whose mothers were destitute, ill, drunken, insane, or in gaol.

While parents might use the reforming institutions as temporary shelter, the educational aims of the industrial and reformatory schools were far more ambitious. The schools were to be total institutions in the sense intended by Erving Goffman and Michel Foucault: that is, they were to be institutions in which surveillance, example, routine, cleanliness, Godliness and corporal punishment would effect the transformation of one class by another; they were also to train the children in skills which would enable them to earn a living when they were discharged; and they were obliged to provide schooling commensurate with that in state elementary schools. There is ample testimony from critics at the time that the reforming institutions failed on all counts.

Sexuality and the female offender

While disillusionment with the industrial schools comes down to us largely through middle-class testimony, the regular riots in the female institutions such as Biloela give some insight into the reformatory regime from the perspective of the girls themselves. It quickly became orthodoxy that female offenders were more recalcitrant and more degraded than their male counterparts, a discovery which was puzzling to a society bent on believing that women were by nature more virtuous than men. The most notorious of the riots occurred at the Newcastle Industrial School in the late 1860s and at its successor, the Biloela Industrial School, in the early 1870s. The Newcastle school was established in ex-military barracks in 1868 under the Industrial Schools Act of 1866 and, in accordance with contemporary practice in England, its original regulations placed the institution under the control of a 'matron-superintendent'. Mrs Agnes King was the first appointment and, though she was to have a long and distinguished career as a female administrator in child welfare, she was replaced in 1868 by Lieutenant Joseph Clarke as superintendent and his wife Marion as matron.[39] The customary unruly behaviour of the girls appears to have escalated into violence soon afterwards. In March 1871 Senior Sergeant John Lane described the moral economy of a classical female riot in his report from Newcastle to his superiors in Sydney:

> No 1. Ward commenced such a scene of riot and disorder I never witnessed before or during my ten years on Cockatoo Island with the worst of Criminals. Some of these young children employed themselves in singing obscene songs others cursing swearing, others cutting up their Beds and Bedding and throwing it out of the windows, others were breaking the Iron bedsteads and with the end torn off forcing out the window sashes that were already broken and throwing them on the ground, and they also destroyed the chamber utensils scattering the contents on the floor, this conduct was carried on until 9.30 p.m. when they seemed fairly hoarse and exhausted and they went to sleep—in another Ward No.3 some girls stripped naked and danced in the middle of the room the Gas burning at the windows being broken and blinds torn down they were in view of persons passing in the Street but being immediately reported by the Constable on duty the Superintendent turned the Gas off.[40]

Despite mounting evidence of the Clarkes' brutal administration at Newcastle, Sergeant Lane added: 'The Supt. has at all times acted in the most kind and indulgent manner towards these girls'. If the girls had intended to bring their protest to the notice of the outside world they were successful. The press coverage was both sensational and titillating and the citizens of Newcastle were soon petitioning to have the school removed from the town. When it became apparent that Clarke had lost control he was dismissed and the institution transferred to Biloela on Cockatoo Island where the royal commissioners paid their visit in 1873.

We cannot understand this savage treatment of female children, or indeed the robust moral economy of resistance, unless we understand that the captive girls of the industrial and reformatory schools bore the full force of an assault on female sexuality which was all-embracing in its ambition to render women asexual, chaste and submissive. Outcast girls intuitively understood what was at stake, for their apparently random protests systematically subverted the ideal of the modest and submissive female who was the central icon in the regulatory regime surrounding female sexuality. Their protests were structured round an overt display of forbidden sexual knowledge—bad language, bawdy songs, public displays of nudity, 'boldness' of facial expression, and explicit sexual invitations to the men in authority over them and those who were sent to subdue them. The Biloela riot which emerges from the testimony of the girls to the royal commissioners follows the same pattern of violence, destruction and sexual challenge. The girls who were rescued from dormitory three were 'in a half naked condition' not because Lucas ordered their clothes to be confiscated, but because they had taken them off at the beginning of the riot. Possession of sexual knowledge was central to this ritual battle over female subjectivities; this is the significance of the caricature of Lucas with his genitals exposed. 'The mere presence of a girl who has mysterious and forbidden knowledge [warned English reformer, Mary Carpenter], is a most dangerous stimulant to evil, and excites in the other girls their latent passions.'[41] Reformers clung to the notion that the innocent child could be remade from the sexually contaminated non-child, that it was possible to 'erase from the tablets of the memory' episodes from her unreclaimed days.[42]

The technology for the remaking of the female self can be reconstructed from the regime of the Magill Reformatory in South Australia.[43] Typically, girls were admitted to the reformatory as 'uncontrollable', sometimes at the request of a parent. A South Australian police report on seventeen-year-old Charlotte B., instigated by her mother, described her as 'undoubtedly uncontrollable'.[44] The evidence against her was that she stayed away from home for weeks at a time and that the neighbours gave her 'a bad character'. Charlotte was arrested, brought before the Police Court as an uncontrollable girl and sentenced to the reformatory school. The mother of thirteen-year-old Theresa M. had spent a long period of time in gaol for murder.[45] Upon her release she found that Theresa would not submit to her authority and she reported her as 'uncontrollable'. The police again made inquiries of the neighbours; they described Theresa as a 'bold and impudent' girl who was often out late at night. Theresa M. was also sent to the Magill Reformatory. Here the girls were, in theory, subjected to the following

The Magill Reformatory, South Australia, completed in 1867. (La Trobe Library, Melbourne)

regime. Strict silence was to be kept at school, at work, at meals and in the dormitories; 'lewd, profane, or immodest talk or gestures' were forbidden. The reformatory was arranged in three classes, 'in accordance with the character and general deportment of the inmates'. In class one were the girls who were obedient, respectful in deportment, hard working and who abstained from bad language. They were exempted from 'specific or uniform dress' and from the 'hardest work in scrubbing'. Their other privileges included a singing class, books of an 'entertaining and instructive kind', outside recreation and an occasional walk outside the institution. They could receive visits from relatives once a month with the permission of the State Children's Council and in the presence of the matron. The reward for three months' good behaviour was to be sent out to service. The regime for the second class of girls was a stricter version of that enjoyed by the most privileged class. Class three was made up of all newcomers and those who showed 'little or no desire to improve'. They were to be kept at constant work, consisting of the hardest scrubbing and washing, with no recreation; they were to be dressed in dark blue; and they were to be allowed visitors only in the case of serious illness. Somewhere between the chilling intentions of this reforming regime and the riot on Cockatoo Island lay the reality of daily life in the nineteenth-century female reformatory.

Sexuality, class and gender were at the heart of the Brookside Reformatory scandal which embarrassed the Victorian Department for Neglected Children and Reformatories in 1899. As Margaret Pawsey has argued in her study of the Brookside affair, in the 1880s legislation regulating the reformation of juvenile offenders became more overtly discriminatory against females on the grounds of sexual behaviour.[46] The Juvenile Offenders Act of 1887 mandated the further separation of any girls committed to institutions on the grounds that they had been living an immoral or depraved life; indeed the matron was instructed to further separate those whom she 'had reason to believe' had been living an immoral or depraved life. There was no similar categorisation of boys and the regulations in effect criminalised any expression of female sexuality, real or originating in the preconceptions of the beholder. Kerry Wimshurst's study of South Australian girls in reformatories endorses Pawsey's thesis that admissions for anticipated sexual delinquency were far more common in the last quarter of the nineteenth century.[47] What this intra-mural separation of the sexually contaminated child might mean in practice was solemnly debated by the politicians considering the Victorian legislation in 1887. Alfred Deakin was inclined to the view that at meal times a curtain might prevent contamination, as long as strict separation was enforced in the sleeping quarters and at play.

Margaret Pawsey's research brings to life the girls who were briefly at the centre of the Brookside affair and the manner in which children were entrapped by nineteenth-century child-saving legislation. Only one girl, thirteen-year-old Mabel M., was convicted of an offence other than the nebulous charges of being neglected, vagrant or uncontrollable. Described in the press as a 'flashily dressed girl of thirteen years', she had stolen money while employed at the Hunt Club Hotel in North Melbourne. Sixteen-year-old Daisy S. admitted to 'leading an immoral life with Chinamen', a fall from grace which needed no further comment in the nineteenth century. Letitia M., fourteen and apparently an orphan who had been living with an aunt, simply came under the category of 'neglected'; at her mandatory medical examination she was wrongly suspected of being pregnant. It was noted that she was very untruthful and had at some time brought a charge against a man. Eleven-year-old Selina W. had been apprehended for 'behaving in an insulting manner in a public street' and committed before the South Melbourne Bench as 'neglected'. Her female companion in crime unwisely admitted to behaving improperly with boys and turning somersaults in front of them. As a Catholic she was sent to the female reformatory at Abbotsford. Harriet W. was committed by her father as 'uncontrollable' at twelve years of age, apparently after an unsuccessful attempt to send her out to service in the previous year. At nine years of age she had been sexually assaulted and her medical examination duly noted that she had been 'tampered with'. Rosina M., orphaned and seventeen years of age, had been in and out of privately run orphanages and done battle with at least three employers as a domestic servant. The circumstances of the seventh girl, Jessie N., are unknown, although both her parents were still living. In every case the families were noted as poor *but* respectable. The fortunes of these girls came together when, on the basis of their own testimony, the officer at the receiving depot of the Coburg Reformatory drafted them to the Brookside Reformatory rather than to an industrial school.

The quasi-private Brookside Reformatory was established in 1887 by Mrs Elizabeth Rowe, daughter of the Archdeacon of Melbourne and Geelong, Theodore Stretch. It was of particular importance to the Protestant ascendancy of Melbourne, as the Catholic Sisters at the Abbotsford Reformatory, spruiked as an exemplar of the work of reclamation, had been a silent reproach to the Protestant community for over two decades. The royal commissioners of 1872 had urged that the reclamation of Protestant girls should also be in private hands. The catalyst for Elizabeth Rowe's decision to enter the lists was a similar call by her close friend and Secretary of the Department for Neglected Children and Reformatory Schools, George Guillaume, in his annual report of 1886. The Brookside Reformatory figured prominently in the papers which Guillaume sent to the Fourth International Reformatory Congress in St Petersburg in 1890, papers which were published and widely circulated in Australia.[48] The reputation of Brookside as a new departure in the reclamation of hardened cases travelled widely and it travelled well.

In 1891 Queensland Inspector of Orphanages, Charles Horrocks, visited Brookside and published a glowing account in his annual report.[49] The reformatory was not part of the Rowes' sheep station, Glenfine, but on another property an hour's buggy ride away, a journey designed to defeat the most determined relatives of the inmates. Horrocks interviewed Elizabeth Rowe, who lived at Glenfine and visited from time to time, and her staff, Miss King, the matron, and her assistant Miss Hamilton, whose task it was to watch over the girls day and night. He inspected the two cottages, one for the younger girls and one for those 'older in years and more deeply learned in the ways of vice'. A married bailiff lived on the farm but no servants were kept. Horrocks reported that the girls were required to 'do farm work, learn how to plant a garden . . . milk, herd cattle, ride, [and] split firewood'. They had sewing lessons every afternoon and did all the 'cooking, baking, scrubbing, and cleaning'. According to Horrocks, Elizabeth Rowe showed him documentary evidence that most of the girls had 'fallen' and were 'most depraved' when they arrived. It was by now orthodoxy that, under the brisk but kindly regime at Brookside, her success at reclamation was near universal. Though Horrocks makes no mention of speaking to the girls, he concluded that they were 'very fond of their country home', that they quickly repudiated their former ways and that they made accomplished farm servants when their terms expired.

In July 1899 the seven inmates of Brookside whom we have already met absconded, a time-honoured form of resistance to incarceration, and not in the normal course of events the stuff of headlines. Two circumstances were to transform this commonplace incident into a *cause célèbre*: that the girls, 'hatless and very poorly clothed', were missing for two nights in cold weather; and that, some time after their apprehension by the Ballarat police, their story of a brutal regime at Brookside was leaked to the *Ballarat Courier*. Several aspects of the case caused considerable public disquiet. The girls claimed that they were forced to do the rough outdoor work of the farm—they had to fell, split and cart the firewood, sink wells, dig post holes and erect fencing, as well as plough, harrow and bring in the harvest. If they were returned to Brookside they claimed that they would be beaten with a 'discarded belly band' (part of the harness of a horse), their hair would be cut off, they would be placed on a diet of bread and water and made to do farm work without shoes or stockings. On the day they had absconded they claimed to have left behind a girl bruised from a whipping and tied to her bed for tearing her clothes.

In their attempts to reclaim control of the public discourse on the Brookside affair, Melbourne's administrating classes were prepared to distort the truth. Between them they claimed variously that the girls did not carry out the rough, 'unsexing' work of the farm; that such work was necessary to dampen down the passions of the girls; and that, in any case, such work was commonplace for the wives and daughters of struggling selectors. They denied that punishments such as those described by the girls were meted out but claimed that they were necessary in cases of this kind. They were quite prepared to attribute to the absconders a record of unspeakable depravity and to characterise their families as vicious and criminal when their own records showed that this was not the case. When the Brookside affair refused to disappear from the newspapers, the Brookside medical officer—also Mrs Rowe's family doctor—took the unusual step of committing to paper allegations of masturbation among the girls:

> One of the greatest troubles we have to deal with is the extremely hurtful habit of masturbation. We have constantly to be on the lookout for it both for the individual's sake as well as for the danger of her teaching the habit to a young member. It is my opinion that plenty of exercise is one of our most powerful means of treating this erotism [sic].[50]

In his eagerness to exonerate Mrs Rowe and her staff he undercut their own evidence that the girls had lied about the physical chastisement they had endured. He did occasionally have to order the tying of a girl's hands to cure the habit of masturbation. Corporal punishment was applied, but sparingly, and only to check persistent vicious habits. Isolation on a diet of bread and water was used as a last resort and the cutting of hair was reserved for absconders.

Thomas Millar, who had by now succeeded the more enlightened George Guillaume as head of the Department, made the tactical error of inviting any remaining doubters to visit Brookside, and the *Argus* sent a journalist, Alice Henry, to report on the institution at first hand. Her report made a mockery of the official inquiry held by Millar and Inspector Young of the Ballarat police, at which the girls had retracted their allegations without reservation. Henry had no trouble in confirming that the girls did in fact provide the regular labour force on the farm; indeed it would have been difficult to explain how else the farm work was done. She also corroborated the girls' original claims about punishment by the simple expedient of inspecting the punishment book, a strategy which had apparently not occurred to Millar and Young. It was, she told her readers, a sickening record: whipping so frequent as to suggest its futility to all but the most obtuse; for absconding, hair cut off, boots and stockings taken away, isolation and whipping; for other offences, walking around the interior of the buildings for three hours wearing a strait-jacket. Alice Henry pronounced the much-vaunted Brookside Reformatory outmoded and ineffective, its staff ignorant and untrained and its management of public money unsatisfactory. Though Alice Henry's report caused a further flurry of official denials, the Brookside affair subsided in due course. Elizabeth Rowe died in the following year and her work at Brookside was carried on by Matron King until 1903 when Millar's successor closed the institution on the grounds made public by Alice Henry five years before.

The making of servants

While the protagonists in the Brookside affair might rule out of court the rough 'unsexing' labour of farm work, they were in agreement that domestic labour was somehow productive of the 'good woman'. They were also in agreement that the girls in reforming institutions should be the next generation of domestic servants. The architects and administrators of the neglected and criminal children's legislation defined industrial skills for boys as a variety of occupations commensurate with their station in life. In the case of girls, industrial skills were narrowly defined as domestic skills. Gender differences in the industrial training of boys and girls are clear in the regulations governing the Magill Industrial School: 'The boys of the school shall be carefully educated, and also taught and employed at useful work; and the girls in needlework, cooking, and other household employments, so as to fit them respectively for service or for trade in after life.'[51] The 'needlemistress' was to teach the girls 'the various branches of sewing, including the use of the sewing machine', and the cook was to teach them 'the art of cooking'. The duties of the nurse included instructing the girls in 'any industrial work to which they may be allotted, in order to qualify them as useful servants'.

The system implicit in the Magill regulations—that the industrial training of girls could be carried out by the general staff as they went about their daily work—foundered upon the reality that the mass catering, sewing, laundering and cleaning necessary to the economical running of a large institution did not lend itself to the intimacies of the mother inducting her daughter into the household arts. The New South Wales commissioners of 1873 condemned the regime on Cockatoo Island on precisely these grounds. They recommended that:

> in this and all other institutions for the training of children it is highly important that their domestic work should, as far as possible, be performed by the children themselves; the substitution for their labour of elaborate machinery in kitchens and laundries being . . . calculated to unfit the children for employment in homes unprovided with steam machinery and mechanical contrivances for saving labour.[52]

In reality, girls as young as five or six, often frail and in poor health, either had to endure the drudgery of the mass laundries, kitchens and bakeries where scalds and burns were commonplace or receive no instruction at all. The inventories of articles washed and garments sewn which appeared year after year in annual reports are eloquent testimony to the fact that generations of girls were exploited in commercial enterprises centred in state-supported, including Catholic, institutions.

The strongest evidence for the failure of the reforming institutions to instruct the girls in the household arts, let alone in the *mentalité* of the servant girl, comes down to us through the never-ending battle waged between the girls sent out into service and the women to whom they were assigned. Under the legislation children in state care could be hired out, as distinct from formally apprenticed out, at the age of twelve and there was never any lack of applicants for their services. This official traffic in female children as domestic labour was legitimated by the payment of a few shillings a week into a bank account in the child's name, a nest egg which allegedly brought relatives hovering like vultures when she was discharged from the care of the state. By the mid-1880s the same Charles Horrocks who found the Brookside Reformatory so much to his liking was eager to expand his empire by the establishment of a domestic arts school for girls 'in connection with the Diamantina and St Vincent's Orphanages' where girls could learn domestic skills before going out into service. He was therefore only too happy to publish evidence of the ineptitude of the girls he hired out as domestics. In 1889, 46 per cent of girls were returned as unsuitable: 'There is a very general complaint amongst mistresses [he wrote in that year] that orphan girls . . . are completely ignorant of the most ordinary household work.' The girls returned to his care were variously described as unmanageable, immoral, disobedient, impertinent, lazy, untruthful and slovenly. These unwilling recruits to household labour often took refuge in 'passive resistance'. In his report for 1890 Horrocks returned warmly to the subject:

> It cannot truthfully be said that the girls have given equal satisfaction with the boys; far from it. They have caused a great deal of trouble and some

disappointment to those in charge of them. Some are perfectly incorrigible and have had no less than four situations in the year; some seem to be full of pride of the wrong sort, and look on work of any kind with contempt—a ridiculous thing indeed for a girl who has to earn her own living.[53]

The boarding-out era

In 1874, the Victorian royal commissioners inquiring into the condition of industrial schools wrote an epitaph for a system which was already discredited.

Schools of this class are proved, by the universal testimony of all competent witnesses in countries where they have been tried, to be alike prejudicial to the moral and industrial training of the children brought up in them, and at the same time extremely expensive to the State. This holds especially true as regards girls.[54]

Borrowing freely from the testimony of the English philanthropists Florence and Rosamund Hill, the commissioners urged that 'self-reliance, mutual helpfulness, and knowledge of common things, which are inseparable from family life' could not be developed in institutions where regimentation and loss of individuality were inevitable. They concluded that the short history of the industrial schools in Australia confirmed the evidence accumulating from overseas. As the commissioners reminded their readers, the industrial schools were also expensive. The boarding-out system not only promised to return the outcast children of the colonies to the sanctuary of the family; it held out the seductive promise of saving money.

In the light of this testimony, the claim by Kerry Wimshurst and others that domestic ideology began to shape the lives of Australia's outcast children only in the 1890s is in need of revision. The idea that a family milieu was crucial in the work of reclamation goes back to the most famous of all the nineteenth-century reforming institutions, the Agricultural Colony and Prison of Mettray, established in France in 1840. From the 1870s, Australian parliamentary reports and royal commissions routinely carried accounts of Mettray and its imitators in England and the United States.[55] Characterised by Michel Foucault as the first correctional institution in France to combine what he termed the coercive technologies of behaviour—cloister, prison, school and regiment— Mettray's ideological underpinnings were the moral superiority of the family group over any other form of social organisation and the regenerative powers of country life and labour. As with James Kay-Shuttleworth's Battersea Training College, Mettray was a family without women but its message was unmistakable. Grotesque as it may appear in hindsight, there were initially hopes that the industrial schools themselves could be run on the principle of the family. When Australia's industrial schools foundered, the ideology of the family in the moral regeneration of children was already in place and it was but a short step to the new orthodoxy of 'boarding out' as a solution to a problem which refused to go away.

The constitutional authority to board out children in the care of the state was achieved by and large through amendments to existing legislation.[56] There were regional differences in administration: in Victoria the system was administered directly by the relevant department, while in New South Wales and South Australia departments were headed by boards of commissioners. South Australia established its powerful State Children's Council in 1887. The social cachet of the boarding-out movement is apparent in the membership of the council; its founding president was Sir Edward Stirling and its most active members were the philanthropist reformers Catherine Helen Spence and Caroline Emily Clark. There was a direct link with the English child-saving movement as Emily Clark was the niece of Matthew Davenport Hill and the cousin of Florence and Rosamund Hill. Throughout the initial, unhappy years of the industrial school experiment, Spence, Clark and their circle pushed for the introduction of boarding-out, a system which they juxtaposed with 'fostering [children] in the hotbed of their own moral disease'.[57] The State Children's Council was virtually a continuation of the Boarding-Out Society established by Emily Clark as an unofficial boarding-out agency to the Destitute Board in 1872. The minute books for this body are extant and they reveal problems which committee members apparently thought it politic not to reveal in their public campaign for the boarding-out system.[58] Indeed the final report of the South Australian Destitute Act Royal Commission, issued in 1885, was critical of many aspects of the boarding-out system.[59] Nevertheless, Catherine Helen Spence could still write many years later that at its last meeting in 1886 the Boarding-Out Society did not anticipate extinction but 'a resurgence, with fuller powers, with wider scope, and with a great future before it'.[60]

State control of boarded-out children was more voracious of administrative time than the aggregation of children in reforming institutions. In South Australia 'head office' grew from an initial complement of six in 1887—the secretary, one inspector, three clerks and a medical officer—to twenty paid employees by 1910. Catherine Helen Spence recalled that the first recording clerk, Mrs Lucy Duval Hood, could 'tell you where [each child] was, and if it was doing well or ill, without looking at the books'.[61] The practice of boarding out state children depended upon three administrative 'layers': the men and women at the centre (the South Australian State Council was innovative in its promotion of women in paid employment); the committees of 'lady visitors' on the spot; and the head teachers of the state schools in which the boarded-out children were now to be educated.

To begin with, the moral character and circumstances of prospective foster parents had to be established and a similar set of regulations developed in each colony to govern who could take in the children and under what circumstances.[62] In Queensland, where the smaller population and scattered settlement impeded the policy of boarding-out for many years, reasons for refusing applications were listed in annual reports: the dwelling was too far from a state school; it was in a 'slum' locality; sleeping arrangements were unsuitable—girls in particular were not to be placed on verandahs or in out-buildings, and no children were to sleep in a marital bedroom; the house was dirty and untidy; there were paying boarders or grown-up sons present; there were too many children in the prospective host family; the husband was 'addicted to drink and . . . bad language'; the family had insufficient means of support; the inspector detected the 'evident intention of making it pay'; or the household was not of the appropriate religious persuasion.[63]

Regular visitation of the children was mandatory in all colonies, a task shared between increasingly hard-pressed inspectorates and the network of unpaid 'lady visitors' committees' in each locality. In South Australia, the form to be filled in by the visitor asked if the child was clean, healthy, well clothed and well behaved, what sleeping accommodation was provided, whether any complaints were made by or about the child (the child must be interviewed apart from the foster parent), whether the child regularly attended school, Sunday school and church, whether the child was receiving 'training likely to fit him for useful work', whether the child's official issue of clothing was complete, and whether anything in the house might be improved.[64] Selections from the lady visitors' reports published annually in the reports of the relevant departments were part of the relentless official propaganda for the boarding-out system. Mrs Tuck, correspondent for the Queensland district of Red Hill, wrote in 1888:

> We are of opinion that the boarded-out system is a grand improvement upon institutional training, and earnestly recommend that it be extended. In this district all the children are well cared for and trained into home life by their foster-mothers who become quite attached to them. The homes were well chosen and all the children are happy, united, and without an exception obedient.[65]

Having scattered the children under its protection far and wide, the state needed people on the spot to rescue them in emergencies and the regulations made provision for this: 'The children . . . who were placed with Mrs. S. [wrote Mrs Harrington from the Maryborough district in 1889] have hitherto been reported upon favourably, as regards cleanliness; however, her neighbours complained that the children were frequently too severely chastised.'[66] With the sanction of Charles Horrocks, Mrs Harrington had found them another home. Visits by the lady visitors were also intrusive and unfavourable reports were often based on their own assumptions about good mothering. Mrs Kerr, also of the Maryborough district, reported on the situation of Mary T.: 'The accommodation is not desirable, and the cleanliness which should be observed is not. Mrs L. is a kind foster parent, and the child seems very happy. I intend to caution Mrs L. that if she does not manifest a desire to be more cleanly I shall have to remove the child.' The activities of the visiting committees, which included well-meaning picnics and Christmas 'treats', gave the boarded-out children little hope of blending in with the community and avoiding the stigma of the destitute or orphaned child.

The indefatigable journalist 'Vagabond' took it upon himself to investigate the boarding-out system in Victoria in 1874. By December of that year 648 children had been boarded out, and eighty-five ladies' committees in fifty-two districts presided over their welfare. Two years later, over one thousand children had been placed out and the number of committees had grown to 113.[67] The 'Vagabond' attended the monthly muster of boarded-out children at the Richmond Town Hall where foster mothers were obliged to present them for inspection in order to receive from the ladies' committee their maintenance payments. The Richmond committee was presided over by the women of the wealthy and powerful Henty family. Written with the jocular condescension which he deemed appropriate for his vignettes of low life, the 'Vagabond's report captures the unedifying spectacle of one group of women exercising power over another:

As the foster-parents and their charges trooped in, they were recognized by Miss Henty and the ladies under whose special care the children might be. The little ones generally seemed delighted with the attention they received. 'Ah! those are my boys,' a lady would say, and, after a little laugh at the joke, the children would be passed round and inspected, and their personal appearance, points, and improvement canvassed with all that loving zest and attention to detail which a man only lavishes on a horse . . . the maternal instinct strong within them, the ladies crowed and delighted over these orphans . . . until I began to wish I was a 'neglected child' boarded out in the Richmond district.[68]

The 'Vagabond' was not yet convinced that this monthly ritual was proof of the superiority of the boarding-out system. Unannounced and masquerading as a figure of authority, he dropped in at six homes in the Richmond district where children had been boarded out. He was greatly entertained by the agitation caused by his visits; one foster mother mistook him for the natural father come to reclaim his child; another woman of 'careless and slatternly appearance [and] catholic views on the subject of dirt' was very much frightened at his sudden appearance and tried to hide the children from him. In general though, he found 'nothing to cavil at'; the children, he concluded, were far healthier and happier than if they had been 'mewed up in some great school or reformatory'.

As a further safeguard against ill-treatment or exploitation, administrators encouraged the boarded-out children to write to them for help and advice. Charles Horrocks encouraged the practice, 'to make them feel they have a protector in the State, which is ever watchful for their interests and willing and able to shield them from ill-treatment or oppression'. This correspondence, he believed, would not only 'promote feelings of respect and gratitude in the children towards the State', but act as a check on the foster parents.[69] The only systematic study of girls boarded out in the nineteenth century, Margaret Barbelet's *Far From a Low Gutter Girl*, is based on the manuscript correspondence which survives in the State Archives of South Australia.[70] The letters written by girls and their working-class foster parents are, in Barbelet's own words, 'despatches from the domestic front', a unique record of those who seldom contribute to the written records of the past. The following account of life as a boarded-out girl is based on Barbelet's study.

Despite official certainties that the boarded-out child had regained the sanctuary of family life, there was one circumstance which marked out her life from the natural children in the household. Boarded-out girls lived with the knowledge that they could be returned or sent to another household at any time. Some unfortunate children moved through six or seven foster homes. Those who remembered their natural parents or longed to know about them, suffered a double burden of uncertainty; indeed the boarding-out system was in some ways more brutal than the industrial school system in its determination to obliterate all traces of the child's former life. Children were returned to the state for any number of reasons, mostly beyond their control. A farmer from Strathalbyn, South Australia, wrote pragmatically to the secretary of the State Children's Department:

> [I am] unable to continue operations on the farm . . . on account of the want
> of sufficient capital I am obliged to abandon the lease and sell off the stock
> etc. As it will cause some considerable monetary loss I am desirous of

economising expenditure in the future and am writing this to ask if your Council will permit me [to] return the child . . . to the care of the state.[71]

Administrators and even foster parents had little compunction in using the threat of removal as a weapon to control the girls, a form of blackmail which often elicited frantic letters to head office in Adelaide. In 1903 a child pleaded with the secretary: 'I will try to please in future please don't take me away, I will keep the room and my box tidy and I promise you won't hear any more complaints'.[72] Children were returned for misconduct, for absconding, because they were 'unsuitable', because the home was unsatisfactory, because of the ill health or financial reverses of the guardian, or because the home was breaking up. Amorphous terms such as 'misconduct' and 'mutual dissatisfaction' covered a multitude of woes—pilfering, slovenliness, laziness, bed wetting, masturbation, running away, sulking and even 'acting like a lady'. One exasperated foster mother wrote in 1901: 'The State girls want to be kept as ladies and not do any work.'[73]

A constant source of friction in the three-way transactions between the state, the guardian and the child was the nature and amount of work which could be extracted from the boarded-out child.[74] Alerted by an anonymous letter concerning the exploitation of an eleven-year-old girl, the inspector who visited the home reported:

[the child] rises at 5.15 am goes for the cows, milks 2 cows, sets the breakfast, washes up, goes to school. She returns to her dinner in the middle of the day and washes up before going back to school. When school is over she gets morning wood and feeds two pigs goes again for the cows milks two of them, sets the tea and takes the cows back to the paddock. After tea, she cleans her boots, washes up the tea things darns her own stockings Mrs Hartmann's and a child's socks does her homework and goes to bed at 9.30 pm.[75]

In this case the inspector agreed with the anonymous neighbour that the demands on the child were unreasonable. 'Mutual dissatisfaction' also revolved around the foster parent's right to inflict corporal punishment. Administrators and lady visitors were often called upon to differentiate between acceptable parental discipline and outright brutality. One foster mother accused of the latter wrote in her own defence: 'Did whip her with a willow stick for telling lies and being disobedient but never did so severely.'[76]

The last line of defence between boarded-out children and unsuitable foster parents was the head teacher of the local school. The South Australian code of 1887 is typical in that it required every boarded-out child to attend school daily between the ages of seven and thirteen unless he or she had earlier passed the standard required by the Education Act. The school teacher was required to report every three months on the child's attendance, progress and appearance. As with the reports of the lady visitors, these reports were stage-managed by administrators with a vested interest in proving that the boarding-out system was a panacea in the care of state children. An unnamed Queensland teacher wrote in 1891:

> I may say they have much better homes, and are better clothed and fed, than many children in the neighbourhood whose parents are living. I have observed that many people who board State children take as much interest in their welfare as they do in that of their own children. In the case of many State children . . . it is very evident that in the loss of their parents they have perhaps gained considerably. Most of those children with whom I have come in contact are free from that cringing, 'pity me', dependent look so characteristic of workhouse children in the British Islands.[77]

If their printed reports can be taken at face value, teachers showed admirable forbearance with children who were troublesome at first but responded to the wise and kindly regime of the state school. These printed reports are also admirably free from the tendency to stigmatise state children as intellectually inferior by virtue of their doubtful origins. On the contrary, the letters chosen for publication constructed an official orthodoxy that, though the children were behind in their work when they arrived, the regular attendance demanded by the state ensured that they quickly caught up with and sometimes overtook their classmates. Margaret Barbelet's work on the manuscript records in South Australia is a useful antidote to this official consensus.

In 1889 the headmaster of Unley Park public school in South Australia wrote to the State Children's Department to report upon Dolly X. She was, in his view, 'a most rebellious and troublesome girl; . . . untruthful and untrustworthy; she is constantly stealing . . . and she is, to put it mildly, very immodest'. He considered her presence a great danger to the other girls and inferred that she should be placed in a reformatory.[78] Not all teachers wrote to complain of the boarded-out children, but their reports nevertheless were at variance with the party line propagated by the guardian state. In 1907 a school teacher wrote anxiously to the inspector:

> [the child] is often late and sometimes kept home for trivial excuses. The child says that she rises at 6 o'clock and works till school time and when she returns in the afternoon . . . She is a very thin child and painfully shy, in fact rather dull mentally and I find difficulty in ascertaining whether she is happy here. She says she often gets the strap on the hands and shoulders. She has

her meals in the kitchen with the servant. . . . I am sure she is taken for the sole purpose of helping with the work and that there is no home atmosphere and little if any love to help in a child's development.[79]

Barbelet presents convincing evidence that boarded-out children did indeed bear a stigma in the ordinary state school. She suggests that many teachers, like the headmaster quoted above, mistook the reticence of the mistreated child for mental retardation. A country headmaster inadvertently betrayed his prejudices when he wrote to the department concerning a bright and intelligent boarded-out girl who was popular with the other girls. She was, in his opinion, 'rather above the usual run of State Children it has been my lot to encounter'.[80] More typical was the report which read: [She is] dull, timid and unresponsive. She keeps aloof from other children and does not join in their play. In appearance she lacks care in details, her bloomers being too long and made like a boy's knickers. She also wears the same frock every day and her hair is not arranged nicely.'[81] Boarded-out children were sometimes victimised by sadistic teachers. One report read: 'It is alleged that [Miss Y] frequently slaps her on the bare legs, and makes fun of her before the classes and is most impatient with her dullness . . . she seems to dread going to school and worries about her lessons.'[82] The child had been happy with her previous teacher who was kindly and brought her on in her work. Boarded-out children were required to leave school at thirteen and pleas from parents and teachers for special consideration fell on deaf ears. Like most children of their time and social class, few state children went on to secondary school.

The uncertainty of life as a boarded-out child was exacerbated by the knowledge that at thirteen childhood came to an abrupt end and life began as a domestic servant. Girls who had been happy or even tolerably content in their foster homes now faced another parting of the ways, unless the foster family could afford to pay the wages due for the domestic labour of the state ward. The overwhelming majority of female state wards became domestic servants, as did the Aboriginal girls whose lives were controlled by the state protection boards; indeed successive administrators frowned on the effort of the girls to rise out of this despised occupation into the ranks of the shop girl, the office girl or the dressmaker. Most had little choice but to make the best of a life of drudgery until they were free from the control of the state. As Ada W. wrote secretly to her sister: 'In this hole of a place I see the same thing day after day and nothen to look forward to I must wait pashintly and the time will come some time [sic].'[83] Life was hard and rebellion meant return to the industrial school or even the reformatory, not reunion with the foster parents. By common consent, state wards who had been boarded out made better servants than girls straight from the industrial and reformatory schools, but the domestic warfare which Charles Horrocks chronicled also broke out from time to time. In the case of the boarded-out girls we have their own testimony.

As Margaret Barbelet suggests, any number of factors could make the difference between routine drudgery and an intolerable situation: whether the home was in the country or the city; the temper of the mistress of the house; the number of other servants kept; whether a washerwoman came in to do the laundry; the attitude of the daughters to the servant girl; or the presence of men who regarded her as sexual prey. Mabel E. complained in 1901:

> I have all the work to do and no one to help me there is nine cows to milk night and morning . . . you can think how miserable it must be to have no one to speak to only the daughter and mistress growling at me all the time.[84]

Rose R. considered that she should not have to clean the boots of several adult men and, when she declined to do so, '[Mrs Edwards] called me several nasty names and I said that I would write to Mr. Gray . . . I went to pass her at the door when she lifted her hand and struck me on the face.'[85] Margaret K. wrote to the department that she had tried to do her best but 'there are 5 young children; the eldest being 8 years old and the youngest only 8 months. I have to do for them and the housework as well as I am but 14 years old I find I cannot manage it.'[86] Once the girls had left the home of their foster parents to make their way as domestic servants, their right to a social life also became contested territory, with the department and the 'mistress' conspiring to enforce a regime which was restrictive even by the standards of the day. As Barbelet comments, '[foster parents] frequently wrote to the Department seeking guidance on the "fine print" of their mandate'.

> I have tried to get Florrie girls for companions that are respectable and older than she, not girls who giggle if they see a boy in the street . . . I think it would be a revelation to even you . . . if you could hear her conversation when she is speaking with any one she is familiar with . . . If she goes out it takes her 15 minutes to dress . . . all these things speak for themselves.[87]

It was assumed that state wards were by nature more uninhibited sexually than middle-class women. This assumption of sexual availability fell with particular force upon Aboriginal girls placed out to service. Bessy Cameron's daughters were sent out into service against her wishes and Maggie became pregnant while working as a servant girl at a Lake Tyers boarding house.[88] The mere possibility that sexual intimacy could occur was enough to damn the servant girl. One woman wrote to the Department about 'her' girl who stayed out until ten o'clock with a man under a tree opposite the house: 'I cannot be burdened with the responsibility of a girl who is simply determined to go wrong and about whose future I regret to say . . . I know will be a very sad and hopeless one.' Proof that sexual intercourse had occurred resulted in immediate incarceration in a reformatory. It is a sad irony that most sexual assaults on wards of the state took place in the homes where they had been placed to protect them from the depredations of the outside world. The testimony of the girls usually reveals something less than a lascivious intent to seduce the unsuspecting men of the household; many victims of sexual assault were ignorant even of the anatomical facts of the act which had been perpetrated upon them. ('Mr B. pulled my clothes and did something else . . . [he] put his hands between my legs and he put something that was between his own legs into me.')[89] When a ward of the state became pregnant she faced an impossible situation. Typically, she would give birth in a charitable lying-in home, her board paid by the state, giving the child up immediately to be boarded out while she returned to make a meagre living as a servant in another household. Though Charles Horrocks' reports regularly listed reasons for the return of the servant girls, pregnancy was never mentioned. Horrocks himself was prepared to admit that 'most' of the unmarried mothers who applied to place their children in the care of the state were servant girls, but the idea that the men of the households in which girls worked might be the fathers seems never to have occurred to him. There was, he reported, a 'great reluctance on the part of the [servant girls] to give the father's name, and when they do it is sometimes a fictitious one'.[90] Occasionally the Secretary of the State Children's Board would consent to the marriage of one of its wards but more typically there was no escape until the official age of release which rose steadily until in some states it reached twenty-one years of age.

No doubt there were children who fared better as foster children in private homes than they would have done in large impersonal institutions. Nevertheless it is an unpalatable fact that 'boarding-out' was a system which placed the children of the destitute in the homes of the almost destitute, where the meagre allowance for the upkeep of the children made the difference between stable and unstable poverty. It was also a system which consigned the daughters of the poor to a period of virtual slavery as domestic servants. It would be comforting to think that, with the development of family support systems in the twentieth century, the role of the state was confined to the genuinely orphaned or abandoned. This was not the case. In the very decades when finer sensibilities reoriented welfare policies towards family support, the state turned with greater ferocity than ever before upon Aboriginal families. In New South Wales alone between 1883 and 1969, 5,625 children were taken from their families and placed under the 'protection' of the state. In church and government institutions, Aboriginal girls in their turn were shaped into a proletariat of female labour, sent at thirteen years of age to work as servants in the homes of white Australian women under conditions far more exploitative than anything experienced by white girls in the nineteenth century. The story of these girls is now emerging from a tradition of oral history which should not be colonised by white historians, no matter how good their intentions. It is also an unpalatable fact that in the twentieth century Australia received thousands of destitute children from the United Kingdom, some of whom where brutalised in Australian institutions run by religious organisations. We should also remember that, in the late twentieth century, homeless children are once more a 'social problem' on the streets of Australia's capital cities.

Epilogue

With a baroque revisionist flourish Virginia Woolf declared that the appearance of the female novel at the end of the eighteenth century was 'of greater importance than the crusades or the Wars of the Roses'.[1] The writing of a novel, she argued, was a symbolic act which set many women on the path to intellectual and financial independence. Woolf's thesis is intriguing, framed as it is by her essay on the education of women, *A Room of One's Own*. As a historian of education I want to argue that the 'lady novelist' did not emerge in a vacuum. She was the product of an exponential growth in women's literacy in the same decades; before women could write novels—or shopping lists—they had to learn to read and write. Woolf's thesis is nevertheless apposite; literacy brings with it the potential for women to imagine their lives differently. For this reason the education of all women has been contested territory.

Though I have made many shopping lists, my novels have remained unwritten; instead, I became a historian, occupying that contested territory of women's education which never ceases to intrigue and infuriate me. With Jill Kerr Conway I concur that it was not my education in a co-educational high school, nor my experiences as an undergraduate at a co-educational university which caused me to imagine my life differently.[2] The emancipatory promise of literacy is potential. For many women of my generation the catalyst was the second women's movement of the 1970s which pitched us into an abrupt and painful remaking of self. My new life as a historian and an academic is lived in the company of another self who might have lived my mother's life. The legacy of this personal history is clear enough; I am fascinated by the narratives of women's lives interacting with structures of power not of their own making. In my search for understanding of these dynamics I have borrowed other women's lives already lived, endowing them with meanings idiosyncratically my own. I have made space for the failed lady-principal, the disorderly schoolgirl and the lady teacher who drank, as well as those who flourished in the new educational institutions for women. In the gender politics of women's education saints and sinners

251

share a commonality of subversion. A multiplicity of small subversions mined from women's lives in the past has flowed into my own experiences as a reluctant (and sometimes disorderly) school girl and a lady teacher by default. Other women's lives and my own in turn have flowed into my reading, thinking and talking about history, women and education in the last two decades. I make no spurious claims of sisterhood between the women whose lives I have appropriated, nor do I assume that they would wish to know themselves as I have depicted them. The knowing woman is truculent, enigmatic and elusive.

ABBREVIATIONS

ADB	*Australian Dictionary of Biography*
AS	*Australasian Schoolmaster*
BC	*Brisbane Courier*
BGGS	Brisbane Girls' Grammar School
BGS	Brisbane Grammar School
DSE	Directorate of School Education (Victoria)
Hig.Comm.	Higinbotham Royal Commission
JCH	Janet Clarke Hall
Leg.Ass.	Legislative Assembly
MLA	Member of the Legislative Assembly
NSWPD	*New South Wales Parliamentary Debates*
NSWPP	*New South Wales Parliamentary Papers*
NSWSA	New South Wales State Archives
PROSA	Public Record Office of South Australia
QPD	*Queensland Parliamentary Debates*
QPP	*Queensland Parliamentary Papers*
Reg.BDM	Registry of Births, Deaths and Marriages
Rep.Bd.Ed.	Report of the Board of Education
Rep.DSB	Report of the Denominational School Board
Rep.Min.Ed.	Report of the Minister of Education
Rep.Min.PI	Report of the Minister of Public Instruction
Rep.NSB	Report of the National School Board
Rog.Temp.	Rogers Templeton Royal Commission
SAGG	*South Australian Government Gazette*
SAPP	*South Australian Parliamentary Papers*
SARC	South Australian Royal Commission
SGHS	Sydney Girls' High School
SLV	State Library of Victoria
SMH	*Sydney Morning Herald*
SSTUV	State Schools Teachers' Union of Victoria
SWC	Sydney Women's College
UCWS	United Council of Woman Suffrage
UMA	University of Melbourne Archives
VGG	*Victorian Government Gazette*
VLTA	Victorian Lady Teachers' Association
VPD	*Victorian Parliamentary Debates*
VPP	*Victorian Parliamentary Papers*
VPRO	Victorian Public Record Office
VPRS	Victorian Public Record Series
VWSS	Victorian Women's Suffrage Society
V&R	*Vision and Realisation*

253

Notes

INTRODUCTION

1 Mackinnon, *The New Women*, ch. 2.
2 Jones, *Nothing Seemed Impossible*, p. 89.
3 Pawsey, 'Annie Wilkins'.
4 Dinnerstein, *The Mermaid and the Minotaur*, p. ix.
5 Grimshaw et al, *Creating a Nation*, p. 4.
6 Lake and Kelly, *Double Time*, p. vii.
7 Riley, *Am I That Name?*
8 For example, Morgan, *My Place*.
9 Prentice and Theobald, *Women Who Taught*.

1 THE WOMAN AT THE PIANO

1 My ideas concerning the 'woman at the piano' were developed before the appearance of Jane Campion's film, *The Piano*, but I am gratified by her support of my thesis.
2 Richardson, *The Getting of Wisdom*, pp. 82-3.
3 University of Melbourne, mins of Senate, vol. 1, p. 61, 7 May 1872, UMA.
4 For funding of denominational schools see Austin, *Australian Education*; for denominational secondary schools see Sherington et al, *Learning to Lead*.
5 Smith, *Essays*, p. 187.
6 Darwin, *A Plan for the Conduct of Female Education*.
7 Barbauld, *The Female Speaker*; Hamilton, *Letters*; Hester Chapone, *Letters*.
8 Montagu's words are from Hopkins, *Hannah More*, p. 24; the quotations from Hannah More which follow are from *Strictures*.
9 This analysis of the accomplishments curriculum is based on newspaper advertisements and prospectuses from the period. For a different interpretation see Windschuttle, 'Educating the daughters of the ruling class', pp. 105-33.
10 Windschuttle, 'Educating the daughters of the ruling class'.
11 For the ladies' academy tradition in Canada see Gidney and Millar, *Inventing Secondary Education*, and Houston and Prentice, *Schooling and Scholars*.
12 For literacy in the West, see *History of Education Quarterly*, vol. 30, no. 4, 1990.

13 Pateman, *The Sexual Contract*.
14 With particular reference to education see Miller and Davey, 'Family formation', in Theobald and Selleck, *Family, School and State*, pp. 1-24.
15 Davidoff and Hall, *Family Fortunes*.
16 More, *Strictures*, p. 20.
17 *British Parliamentary Papers 1864*, Schools Inquiry Commission Report. Education General. Irish University Press Series (hereafter Taunton Commission) vol. 1, ch. 6, pp. 553-4.
18 Ellis, *The Women of England*, pp. 194-5.
19 For modern versions of 'women's ways of knowing' see Gilligan, *In a Different Voice* and Belenky et al, *Women's Ways of Knowing*.
20 Sandford, *Woman*, p. 68.
21 Sinclair, *Modern Accomplishments*, p. 294.
22 Grosz, 'Notes', p. 3.
23 Ortner, 'Is female to male?' in Rosaldo and Lamphere, *Women, Culture and Society*; for a more recent overview of the literature see Ralston, 'Deceptive dichotomies', pp. 65-82.
24 Tomaselli, 'The Enlightenment debate on women', pp. 101-24.
25 Burstyn, *Victorian Education*.
26 Williams, *Culture and Society*, chs 3-4.
27 Wollstonecraft, *A Vindication*, p. 68.

2 THE LOST LADIES' SCHOOLS OF COLONIAL AUSTRALIA

1 Lindsay, *Picnic At Hanging Rock*; ch. 2 is based on my doctoral thesis, Theobald, 'Women and schools'.
2 Lindsay, *Picnic at Hanging Rock*, p. 9.
3 For example, Fitzpatrick, *PLC Melbourne*, ch. 2.
4 Rivett, 'Deakin's confidante', p. 49; Catherine Deakin was Rivett's great aunt.
5 Harley, 'Alfred Deakin at home', pp. 30-37.
6 Rivett, 'Deakin's confidante', p. 45.
7 Fitzpatrick, *PLC Melbourne*, pp. 53-4, 66, 104.
8 Frazer and Palmer, *Records of the Pioneer Women*, p. 136.
9 *Kyneton Observer*, 29 September 1857, p. 1.
10 *Kyneton Observer*, 16 October 1857, p. 3.
11 *Kyneton Guardian*, 3 January 1863, p. 3.
12 For example, *Argus*, 2 January 1864, p. 8.
13 For the details see *Argus*, 10 August 1870, p. 8 and 23 November 1872, p. 7.
14 Deakin papers, MS 4913, box 2, folder 9, diary of Catherine Deakin, National Library, Canberra.
15 Details from G.T. Stilwell, 'Mr and Mrs George Carr Clark', pp. 72-109 unless otherwise stated.
16 Stilwell, 'Mr and Mrs George Carr Clark', p. 78.
17 *Hobart Town Gazette*, 2 July 1825.
18 Mackaness, *Some Private Correspondence*, pp. 93-8.

19 Backhouse and Tyler, *The Life and Labours*, p. 157.
20 Robinson, *The Echoes Fade Not*, ch. 2. Details are from this source unless otherwise noted.
21 *Argus*, 25 August 1859, p. 8.
22 *Argus*, 21 October 1861, p. 8.
23 Mackinnon papers, MS 9470, letters of Elizabeth Tripp to John Hastie, La Trobe Library collection, SLV.
24 Margaret Tripp's letters to her mother, undated but mid-1872. Copies in possession of author.
25 For the Trinity Hostel affair, see ch. 3 below.
26 Brown family papers, Australian Copying Project microfiche, SLV. All letters, testimonials and prospectuses quoted are from this collection.
27 Marriage certificate of Jane Hay Brown and Andrew Hamilton, 12 June 1860.
28 Letter, Jane Hamilton to her family, 26 April 1867.
29 The Vieusseux papers, in private hands, were tracked down by Ken Clements, who generously shared all of his research with me; see also Theobald, 'Julie Vieusseux' in Lake and Kelly, *Double Time*.
30 *Argus*, 4 November 1853, p. 9.
31 *Argus*, 4 November 1853, p. 9.
32 *Prospectus*, 1863.
33 *Prospectus*, 1863.
34 *Southern Sphere*, 1 December 1911, p. 11.
35 J.E. Bromby Papers, MS 8847, Diary of J.E. Bromby, 15 July 1869, p. 32, La Trobe Collection, SLV.
36 Williamson (Kyle), 'What do you do with herstory?'.
37 Windschuttle, 'Educating the daughters'; Gerald Noble, 'Secondary education in VDL'; Williamson, 'What do you do with herstory?'; Jones, *Nothing Seemed Impossible*; Riordan, 'Private venture schools'.
38 Statistics on children in the public and private systems were published in annual reports of the ministers. In Victoria, 1878–1893, a 'return of private schools' listed non-government schools by name and gave the number of pupils, male and female, at each school.
39 See Hammerton, *Emigrant Gentlewomen*.
40 Theobald, 'Women and schools', ch. 3.
41 Registration of Teachers and Schools Act 1905, no. 2013.
42 Zainu'ddin, 'The poor widow', pp. 29–42.
43 VPRS 10061, numbers 748, 749, 751, VPRO.
44 VPRS 10061, numbers 6093, 6095, VPRO.
45 VPRS 10061, numbers 1312, 754, 3156, 3937, 6195, 6397, 6398, VPRO.
46 *Argus*, 26 January 1870, p. 7.
47 Leigh House *Prospectus*, 1873.
48 See Foucault, *The History of Sexuality*; for the incidents mentioned, see Theobald, 'Women and schools', ch. 3.
49 For purpose-built schools see Theobald, 'Women and schools', ch. 3.
50 *Kyneton Observer*, 20 December 1863, n.p.

51 *Argus*, 14 January 1864, p. 3.
52 For example, Adams, 'Picnic at Hanging Rock', p. 91.
53 Frith, 'Fact and fiction'.
54 Hay, *Chronicles of Clyde*, pp. 1–2.
55 *ADB*, vol. 9, pp. 255–6.

3   THE KEYSTONE OF THE ARCH?

1 Kelly, *Degrees of Liberation*, ch. 1; *ADB*, vol. 9, p. 136. Lydia Harris, who completed with Guerin, missed her place in history by choosing a later graduation ceremony.
2 Bygott and Cable, *Pioneer Women Graduates*, p. 9.
3 *Argus*, 18 April 1891, p. 5.
4 The Oxford and Cambridge locals were public examinations for schools, as distinct from the matriculation, or entrance, examination; the University of Sydney followed the Oxbridge model, with public examinations separate from its matriculation examination, while at the University of Melbourne the matriculation examination served both purposes.
5 See Hone, 'The movement for the higher education of women'; Zainu'ddin, 'The admission of women'; matriculation entries and results in UMA.
6 *Argus*, editorials and letters in June and July 1871.
7 *ADB*, vol. 3, pp. 108–11.
8 University of Melbourne Council minutes, 30 October 1871, UMA.
9 Details of campaign from Zainu'ddin, 'The admission of women', unless otherwise noted.
10 J.E. Bromby Papers, MS 8847, Diary of J.E. Bromby, p. 45, La Trobe Collection, SLV.
11 *Age*, 24 June 1874.
12 Pearson, *Public Education*, p. 111 (Pearson Commission, *VPP*).
13 Pearson Commission, Appendix A, clause 12, p. 166.
14 Letter, Andrew Harper to University council, 15 October 1879, UMA.
15 Bygott and Cable, *Pioneer Women Graduates*; Turney et al, *Australia's First*, ch. 6.
16 For the Sydney university men and the women's movement see Roberts, *Maybanke Anderson*.
17 *SMH*, 28 July 1879.
18 Quoted in Turney et al, *Australia's First*, p. 185.
19 University of Sydney, mins of Senate, 4 May 1881; 47 Vic. no. 17, cl. 3.
20 Quoted in Turney et al, *Australia's First*, p. 174.
21 Quoted in Turney et al, *Australia's First*, p. 173.
22 See Mackinnon, 'Awakening Women'; Mackinnon, *The New Women*; Jones, *Nothing Seemed Impossible*.
23 Mackinnon, *The New Women*, p. 21.
24 Quoted in Mackinnon, *The New Women*, p. 23.
25 For example, Bryant, *The Unexpected Revolution*.
26 Pedersen, 'The reform of women's secondary and higher education'.

27 Macintyre, *A Colonial Liberalism.*
28 Mackinnon, 'Awakening women', ch. 3.
29 Sidgwick, *Health Statistics.*
30 Solomon, *In the Company of Educated Women*, ch. 8.
31 Kelly, *Degrees of Liberation*, p. 57.
32 For marriage rates, see MacDonald, *Marriage in Australia.*
33 Conway, 'Perspectives'.
34 Smith, *The Everyday World*; Gilligan, *In a Different Voice*; Belenky et al, *Women's Ways of Knowing.*
35 Kelly, *Degrees of Liberation*, ch. 2.
36 Kelly, *On the Edge of Discovery*, ch. 2.
37 Dow and Scholes, 'Christina Montgomery' in Selleck and Sullivan, *Not So Eminent Victorians.*
38 Biddington, 'Julia Flynn' in Lake and Kelly, *Double Time.*
39 Quoted in Mackinnon, *The New Women*, p. 44.
40 Kelly, *Degrees of Liberation*, p. 14.
41 Quoted in Zainu'ddin, 'The admission of women', p. 77.
42 Reports and letters concerning the admission of women to the medical school, Allen to Council, 12 March 1887, UMA.
43 Reports and letters, Girdlestone to Council, 10 March 1887, UMA.
44 Reports and letters, Allen to Council, 22 April 1885, UMA.
45 Quoted in Bygott and Cable, *Pioneer Women Graduates*, p. 37.
46 Mackinnon, *The New Women*, pp. 44-95.
47 Bygott and Cable, *Pioneer Women Graduates*, p. 21; Helen Phillips was appointed tutor to the women students in 1891.
48 Delamont, 'The contradictions' in Delamont and Duffin, *The Nineteenth-Century Woman.*
49 Tisdall, *Forerunners*, p. 168.
50 Kelly, *Degrees of Liberation*, p. 37.
51 Bygott and Cable, *Pioneer Women Graduates*, p. 22.
52 Mackinnon, *The New Women*, p. 220.
53 Kelly, *Degrees of Liberation*, p. 35.
54 Jones, *Nothing Seemed Impossible*, ch. 5 and appendix A.
55 Gardiner, *Janet Clarke Hall*, ch. 1; Queen's College had a small number of resident women in its early years.
56 Maddern, *St Hilda's College.*
57 *ADB*, vol. 10, pp. 54-7; the quotation is from Gardiner, *Janet Clarke Hall*, p. 1.
58 Alexander to Leeper, 31 July and 23 August 1888, Leeper to Alexander, 4, 30 August 1888, JCH archives.
59 Testimonials of E.M. Hensley, JCH archives.
60 Correspondence between Hensley and Leeper, October 1889 to September 1890, JCH archives.
61 *Argus*, 18 April 1891, p. 5.
62 Grimwade and a'Beckett to Goe, 6 July 1892, JCH archives.
63 McCarthy and Theobald, *Melbourne Girls' Grammar School*, chs 1 and 2.

64 *ADB*, vol. 10, pp. 253-4; Hole and Treweeke, *The History of the Women's College*, chs 1-3.
65 Austin, *The Webbs' Australian Diary*, p. 49.
66 Papers relating to the appointment of Louisa Macdonald, SWC archives.
67 Macdonald, *Letters of Application and Testimonials*, 1891, SWC archives.
68 Quoted in Allen, *Rose Scott*, p. 105.
69 Macdonald's letters to 'Pixie', SWC archives.
70 Macdonald to Grove, 29 June 1895, SWC archives.
71 Allen, *Rose Scott*, pp. 108, 139.
72 Macdonald to Grove, 2 August 1896, SWC archives.
73 Allen, *Rose Scott*, p. 164.
74 Macdonald to Grove, 23 September 1894.
75 Macdonald to Grove, 20 October 1893, SWC archives.
76 Vicinus, *Independent Women*, ch. 5; Palmieri, 'Here was fellowship' in Prentice and Theobald, *Women Who Taught*; Edwards, 'Educational institutions or extended families?'.
77 Jeffreys, *The Spinster and her Enemies*.
78 Macdonald to Grove, 25 July 1896, SWC archives.
79 Vicinus, 'One life to stand beside me', p. 605.
80 Macdonald to Grove, 25 May 1895, SWC archives.
81 Macdonald to Grove, 16 December 1894, SWC archives.
82 Macdonald to Grove, 13 October 1894, SWC archives.
83 Zainu'ddin, 'The admission of women'.
84 Quoted in Vicinus, *Independent Women*, p. 122; 'the keystone of the arch' is from Zimmern, *The Renaissance of Girls' Education*.

4 INVENTING THE SECONDARY SCHOOL FOR GIRLS

1 *Journal of the Women's Education Union*, vol. 3, no. 29, 1875, pp. 78-9.
2 Fitzpatrick, *PLC Melbourne*.
3 *QPD*, vol. 15, 1873, p. 223; Lawry, 'Charles Lilley' in Turney, *Pioneers*, vol. 2.
4 *NSWPD*, 1880, vol. 2, pp. 1190-91.
5 Prideaux, *Brisbane Girls' Grammar School*; Mackinnon, *One Foot on the Ladder*; Norman, *The Brown and the Yellow*.
6 Norman, *The Brown and the Yellow*, p. 21.
7 Fogarty, *Catholic Education*, vol. 2, pp. 332 and 342.
8 O'Donoghue, 'The Sisters of Mercy' in Logan and Watson, *Soldiers of the Service*; Allen, *The Labourers' Friend*.
9 Kyle, *Her Natural Destiny*, pp. 103-110.
10 Theobald, 'Women and schools', ch. 6.
11 Jones, *Nothing Seemed Impossible*, pp. 68-86.
12 *BC*, 15 November 1875.
13 Tyack and Hansot, *Learning Together*, p. 117.
14 Sherington et al, *Learning to Lead*, chs 1 and 6.
15 French, 'Secondary education'.

16 Grammar Schools Act 1860 (24 Vic. no. 7).
17 An Act to Provide for Primary Education in Queensland 1860 (24 Vic. no. 6).
18 State Education Act 1875 (39 Vic. no. 11); Sullivan, 'Fifty years of opposition'.
19 Goodman, *Secondary Education*, p. 34; the girls' grammar schools differed in their establishment and relationship to boys' grammar schools. Townsville Grammar School went co-educational in the 1890s during a time of financial crisis.
20 Pedersen, 'Schoolmistresses and headmistresses'; see also Gouldner, *The Future of Intellectuals*.
21 Lawry, 'Charles Lilley'.
22 *BC*, 15 November 1875.
23 Reprinted in Prideaux, *Brisbane Girls' Grammar School*, pp. 29-30.
24 Hornibrook, *Bibliography*, p. 57. The present principal of the school, Judith Hancock, has been unable to find any record of this school in Bath.
25 *Ballarat Courier*, 14-20 January 1869.
26 Hornibrook, *Bibliography*, p. 57.
27 Letter book 1 (1872-76), letter 141 gives Mrs O'Connor's address as Leigh House, Richmond, BGS archives; for Leigh House, see Theobald, 'Women and schools', ch. 2.
28 Trustees minutes, 14 December 1874, BGS archives.
29 Trustees, incoming letters, T.B. Stephens to trustees, 25 November 1875; this was Thomas Blacket Stephens, MLA, chairman of trustees 1869-1871.
30 The relevant documents are reprinted in Prideaux, *Brisbane Girls' Grammar School*, ch. 5.
31 Trustees, incoming letters, Weigall to Harlin, 1 July 1875, BGS archives.
32 *BC*, 20 November 1875.
33 *BC*, 15 November 1875.
34 Prideaux, *Brisbane Girls' Grammar School*, p. 46.
35 *BC*, 20 November 1875.
36 *BC*, 12, 20 and 27 January 1877.
37 Prideaux, *Brisbane Girls' Grammar School*, ch. 5.
38 Prideaux, *Brisbane Girls' Grammar School*, p. 47, letter dated 14 December 1876.
39 *Queensland Government Gazette*, vol. 19, 16 December 1876, no. 76, pp. 1345-6.
40 *BC*, 1 March 1876.
41 Trustees, incoming letters, R.H. Roe, 'The girls' school', 30 November 1877, BGS Archives.
42 Prideaux, *Brisbane Girls' Grammar School*, ch. 6.
43 Trustees, outgoing letters, Lilley to Bernard, 8 February 1878, BGS archives.
44 Prideaux, *Brisbane Girls' Grammar School*, ch. 7.
45 Prideaux, *Brisbane Girls' Grammar School*, ch. 8.
46 Fitzpatrick, *PLC Melbourne*, p. 104; Prideaux, *Brisbane Girls' Grammar School*, ch. 9.

47 For two accounts of the 'Fewings affair', see Watson, 'Miss Fewings'; and Clarke, 'The formidable Miss Fewings' in Logan and Watson, *Soldiers of the Service.*

48 *ADB*, vol. 8, p. 490; documents relating to Fewings' appointment, BGS archives.

49 Evans, *Education and Female Emancipation.*

50 List of applicants, founding principal of SWC, SWC archives.

51 Trustees, incoming letters, Downs to trustees, 21 October 1895, BGS archives.

52 Trustees' report on BGGS, written by Woolcock and Griffith, 24 July 1899, BGS archives.

53 *ADB*, 'Samuel Griffith', vol. 9, pp. 112-19; 'John Woolcock', vol. 12, pp. 570-71; 'John Gibson', vol. 8, pp. 652-3; 'Lewis Bernays', vol. 3, p. 149; 'Edwyn Lilley', vol. 5, pp. 87-8.

54 *BC*, 13, 14, and 16 December 1897.

55 *Queenslander*, 29 February 1896, p. 413.

56 *Newnham College Register*, vol. 1, p. 33.

57 *Newnham College Register; Girton College Register.*

58 For example, Amy Barrington, 'Queensland schools', *Girton Review*, August 1894.

59 Austin, *The Webbs' Australian Diary*, p. 43.

60 Sellers, *The Brisbane Girls' Grammar School*, copy in BGS archives.

61 Trustees, incoming letters, Sellers to trustees, 25 May 1899, BGS archives.

62 Trustees, incoming letters, Fewings to trustees, 27 May and 18 August 1899, BGS archives.

63 *BC*, September to December, 1899; *Journal of Education*, October 1900, p. 612; the story was almost certainly supplied by Sellers.

64 *BC*, 18 September 1899.

65 *BC*, 19 September 1899, Leontine Cooper had been on the staff of BGGS.

66 *BC*, 18 September 1899.

67 *BC*, 26 September 1899.

68 Watson, 'Miss Fewings', p. 668.

69 *BC*, 21 September 1899.

70 *BC*, 26 September 1899.

71 *BC*, 5 January 1877.

72 Prideaux, *Brisbane Girls' Grammar School*, p. 54.

73 For Fairfax Prize winners, see Prideaux, *Brisbane Girls' Grammar School*, p. 7; for scholarships generally, see McKenzie-Smith and Watson, 'Labour [sic] omnia vincit' in Logan and Watson, *Soldiers of the Service.*

74 *BC*, 2 October 1899.

75 See succeeding BGGS annual reports, copies in BGGS archives.

76 *Girton Review*, August 1894, p. 7.

77 Theobald, 'The PLC mystique'.

78 Quoted in Goodman, *Secondary Education*, p. 91.

79 Calculated from statistics given in Prideaux, *Brisbane Girls' Grammar School*, pp. 6 and 19.

80 Freeman, *History of Somerville House.*
81 Obituary of Maud Sellers, *Newnham College Roll Letter*, 1940, pp. 58-62.
82 Public Instruction Act, 1880 (Vic. 43 no. 23), cl. 6, (1) and (11).
83 SGHS corres., 5/17733.3, G. Reid, ministerial order, 13 January 1883, NSWSA.
84 *ADB*, vol. 11, pp. 347-54.
85 *SMH*, 30 June 1883.
86 *SMH*, 22 August 1883; *NSW Government Gazette*, vol. 314, 27 July 1883, p.4000.
87 *SMH*, 8 October 1883.
88 Both speeches reported in *SMH*, 9 October 1883.
89 *NSWPP 1889*, vols 5-6, Rep.Min.PI, 1888, p. 20.
90 *ADB*, vol. 8, pp. 628-29; Norman, *The Brown and the Yellow*, chs 3 and 15.
91 See Reid's speech, *SMH*, 9 October 1883.
92 For the NSW Public Service Act of 1895 and its attack on married women, see Deacon, *Managing Gender*, pp. 144-50.
93 For example, SGHS corres., 5/17743, Garvin to Dept, 95/63809, 2 November 1895, NSWSA.
94 SGHS corres., 5/17733.3, SGHS prospectus, December 1883, NSWSA.
95 *SMH*, 15 December 1889.
96 *NSWPP 1889*, vols 7-8, Rep.Min.PI, 1889, Appendix XIV, p. 163.
97 *SMH*, 17 December 1907.
98 SGHS corres., 5/17733.3, Thibault to Dept, 86/7070, 11 March 1886, NSWSA.
99 SGHS corres., 5/17733.3, McCredie to chief inspector, 84/27292, 7 October 1884, NSWSA.
100 SGHS corres., 5/17733.3, Garvin to Dept, 87/23469, 4 October 1887, NSWSA.
101 Norman, *The Brown and the Yellow*, p. 222.
102 SGHS corres., 5/17744, Thompson to Dept, 03/07052, 2 February 1903, NSWSA.
103 SGHS corres., 5/17733.3, Bowmaker to Dept, 92/17630, 2 April 1892, NSWSA.
104 SGHS corres., 5/17733.3, Watson to Dept, 85/20805, 24 July 1885, NSWSA.
105 SGHS corres., 5/17733.3, Grossman to Dept, 89/22614, 22 May 1889, NSWSA.
106 Lauchland, 'The Maitland Girls' High School', pp. 376-89.
107 SGHS corres., 5/17733.3, Whitfeld to Dept, 85/24046, 24 August 1885, NSWSA.
108 Letters incoming, Caroline Whitfeld to trustees, 23 March 1889, BGS archives.
109 SGHS corres., 5/17743, Whitfeld to Dept, 96/72465, 8 Dec. 1896, NSWSA; the *Sydney Women's College Calendar* for 1907 lists her as teaching at Ascham.

110 SGHS corres., 5/17744, Barnes to Dept., 05/63039, 21 November 1905, NSWSA.
111 *Girton College Register*, p. 12.
112 Calculated from the *New South Wales Government Gazette*, vol. 434, 27 June 1896, p. 3864.
113 SGHS corres., 5/17733.3, Thompson to Dept, 87/15728, 16 May 1887; Garvin to Dept, 87/17410, 2 June 1887, NSWSA.
114 SGHS corres., 5/17743, Bowmaker to Dept, 01/05797, 9 February 1901, NSWSA.
115 SGHS corres., 5/17733.3, Grossman to Dept, 90/27494, 13 June 1890, NSWSA.
116 SGHS corres., 5/17744, Whitfeld to Dept, 05/38944, 19 July 1905, NSWSA.
117 *ADB*, vol. 3, pp. 229-30.
118 For a discussion of these practices see ch. 7 below.
119 SGHS corres., 5/17733.3, McCredie to Dept., 84/23056, 17 July 1884, NSWSA.
120 SGHS corres., McCredie to Dept, 01/5928, 13 September 1901, NSWSA.
121 Public Instruction Act 1880 (43 Vic. no. 23).
122 SGHS corres., 5/17743, Coates to Dept., 94/41938, 27 July 1894, NSWSA.
123 SGHS corres., 5/17743, 'Public Service Board Interview: Mrs Garvin, teacher, Girls' High School', 13 June 1898, NSWSA.
124 *SMH*, 9 October 1883.
125 SGHS corres., 5/17733.3, Allpass to Dept, 85/31912, 16 November 1885, NSWSA.
126 SGHS corres., Inspector George to Dept, 23 February 1889, NSWSA.
127 *NSWPD, 1892-3*, vol. LXIV, 22 March 1893, p. 5383.
128 SGHS corres., 5/17743, Garvin to Dept, 95/62452, 24 October 1895 and 95/68395, 28 November 1895, NSWSA.
129 *ADB*, vol. 8, pp. 48-51; for the Coghlan family see Deacon, *Managing Gender*, ch. 4.
130 *ADB*, vol. 12, pp. 290-92.
131 SGHS corres., 5/17743, Garvin to Dept, 8 November 1900, 1900/73873, NSWSA.
132 SGHS corres., 5/17743, Garvin to Dept, 97/7570, 9 February 1897, NSWSA.
133 SGHS corres., 5/17743, Garvin to Dept, 99/8127, 9 February 1899, NSWSA.
134 SGHS corres., 5/17744, inspection of girls' high school 1903, 03/09987, 16 February 1904.
135 Inspection of girls' high school, 1903.
136 SGHS corres., 5/17744, City of Sydney to Minister of Public Instruction, 30 September 1904, NSWSA.
137 SGHS corres., 5/17744, Garvin to chief inspector, 04/35748, 7 June 1904, NSWSA.
138 SGHS corres., 5/17744, Garvin to Dept, 04/35748, 10 May 1904, NSWSA.
139 Turney et al, *Australia's First*, ch. 9.
140 Norman, *The Brown and the Yellow*, p. 63.
141 Trustees, incoming letters, Fewings to trustees, 27 May 1899, BGS archives.

5   THE ADMINISTRATION OF GENDER

1 See for example, Deacon, *Managing Gender.*
2 Detailed statistics on enrolments, average attendance, age etc. are included in annual reports to parliament in each colony throughout the century.
3 For the feminisation debate, see Prentice and Theobald, 'The historiography of women teachers' in Prentice and Theobald, *Women Who Taught.*
4 Denis Grundy's work on the history of teachers has been very helpful; see, for example, Grundy, 'The political economy' in Murray-Smith, *Melbourne Studies.*
5 Garden, *The Melbourne Teacher Training Colleges*, ch. 1.
6 *VPP 1864-5*, Rep.Bd.Ed., 1864, p. 13.
7 *VPP 1859-69*, Rep.NSB, 1859, p. 11.
8 *VPP 1859-60*, Rep.DSB, 1858-9, pp. 11-12.
9 *VPP 1864-5*, Rep.Bd.Ed., 1864, p. 45.
10 *VPP 1854-5*, Rep.NSB, 1854, p. 47; for Ellen Davitt's life in Victoria, see Sussex, 'Introduction' in Davitt, *Force and Fraud: a tale of the bush.*
11 The DSE holds the personal records of all teachers employed in Victoria from the 1850s onwards.
12 *VPP 1867*, Hig.Comm., 1867, mins, Appendix C.
13 For example, Theobald, 'Agnes Grant' in Selleck and Sullivan, *Not So Eminent Victorians.*
14 Hig.Comm., mins, Patrick Whyte, pp. 254-68.
15 Hooper, 'The tale of two schools'.
16 See below, ch. 7.
17 *VPP 1856-7*, Rep.DSB, 1856, p. 9.
18 For this incident, see Hooper, 'Vision unrealised'.
19 *ADB*, vol. 4, pp. 462-4.
20 *ADB*, vol. 5, p. 298.
21 Selleck, 'A goldfields family' in Theobald and Selleck, *Family, School and State.*
22 *VGG*, no. 13, 1864, pp. 257-78.
23 Common Schools Act, 1862 (25 Vic. no. 149).
24 *VPP*, Hig.Comm., mins, p. 37.
25 Hig.Comm., mins, Appendix L.; the woman was almost certainly Mary Jenvey.
26 For example, *VPP 1867*, Rep.Bd.Ed., 1866, p. 17.
27 Hig.Comm., mins, p. 36.
28 *VPP 1867*, Rep.Bd.Ed., 1866, p. 19.
29 Quoted in Burnswoods and Fletcher, *Sydney and the Bush*, p. 52.
30 Turney, 'William Wilkins' in Turney, *Pioneers*, vol. 1. Ann Wilkins died in childbirth on the voyage out.
31 *VPP 1854-5*, Rep.NSB, 1853, p. 47.
32 *VPP 1858*, Rep.NSB, 1857, p. 10.
33 VPRS 892, VPRO.

34 *VPP 1874*, Rep.Min.Ed., 1873-4, Appendix 1, pp. 1-89.
35 Public Service Act, 1883 (46 Vic. no. 773).
36 See Theobald, 'Women's teaching labour' in Theobald and Selleck, *Family, School and State.*
37 *VPP 1858*, Rep.NSB, 1857, p. 11.
38 *VPP 1867*, 'Report . . . on Mr G.M. Forster's Case'; VPRS 892, no. 14, VPRO; teacher record of Maria Forster, DSE archives.
39 *VPP 1868*, Rep.Bd.Ed., 1867, p. 17; under the 1864 regulations an assistant teacher was allowed for every 50 pupils in average attendance (Reg.14), a sewing mistress was allowed for every 36-50 children if the head teacher was not a female (Reg.15), and a pupil-teacher was allowed for every 35 in average attendance (Appendix B, Reg.7).
40 *VPP 1868*, Rep.Bd.Ed., 1867, p. 53.
41 *VPP 1886*, Rep.Min.Ed., 1885, p. xv.
42 *VPP*, Hig.Comm., mins, pp. 112 and 212; teacher record of Tabitha Pike, DSE archives.
43 For example, *VPP 1865*, Rep.Bd.Ed., 1864, p. 11.
44 *VPP 1871*, Rep.Bd.Ed., 1870, 'General regulations', p. 12.
45 VPRS 892, no. 113, 67/4981, VPRO.
46 VPRS 892, no. 117, 69/7632, VPRO; teacher record of Isabella Burton, DSE archives.
47 VPRS 892, no. 417, 74/7481; teacher records of Helen Thompson and Bessie Stone, DSE archives.
48 Hig.Comm., mins, pp. 285-6.
49 Hig.Comm., mins, p. 286.
50 Hig.Comm., p. 25.
51 Curtis, *True Government*, p. 8.
52 *VPP 1877*, Rep.Min.Ed., 1876, pp. 6-7.
53 *VPP 1874*, Rep.Min.Ed., 1873-4, p. iii.
54 Education Act, 1872 (36 Vic. no. 447), cl. 10; for denominational schools which closed after 1872, see Blake, *Vision and Realisation*, vols 2 and 3.
55 *VPP 1874*, Rep.Min.Ed., 1873, p. iii.
56 *VPP 1876*, Rep.Min.Ed., 1875-6, Appendix E, p. 32, has a list of people compensated for losses caused by the 1872 Act.
57 *VPP 1875*, Regulations Under the Education Act 1872 . . . 13 July 1875 (1875 Regs); there is a helpful explanation of these regulations in Sweetman et al, *A History of State Education*, chs 9-11.
58 *VPP 1880*, Rep.Min.Ed., 1879-80, Inspector Cox's remark about 'fossils' is on p. 204.
59 For Inspector Holland on this, see *VPP 1888*, Rep.Min.Ed., 1887-8, p. 142.
60 *VPP 1874*, Rep.Min.Ed., 1873, pp. vii.
61 1875 Regs, p. 2.
62 *VPP 1879*, Rep.Min.Ed., 1878-9, p. 10.
63 *VPP 1876*, Rep.Min.Ed., 1875-6, p. x.
64 For Gladman, see Selleck, *Frank Tate*.
65 *VPP 1884*, Rog.Temp.Comm.

66 Rog.Temp., 2nd report, p. iv.
67 Rog.Temp., mins, pp. 316-17.
68 Rog.Temp., for a digest of their views, see mins, p. lxii; the witnesses with teaching wives were Patrick Whyte, Julius Stach, T.H. Templeton, A.G. Connell and J.A. Ure.
69 Rog.Temp., mins, p. 107.
70 Rog.Temp., mins, p. 182.
71 Rog.Temp., 2nd Rep., Appendix E (m).
72 Rog.Temp., mins, p. 289.
73 Rog.Temp., mins, p. 225.
74 Rog.Temp., mins, p. 226.
75 Rog.Temp., mins, p. 157.
76 Rog.Temp., mins, p. 187.
77 Rog.Temp., mins, p. 218.
78 *VPP 1884*, Rog.Temp. 3rd rep., 1884, vol. 3, p. 26.
79 Rog.Temp., 2nd rep., 1883, pp. iii-vii.
80 *VPP 1883*, Rep.Min.Ed., 1882-3, p. xx.
81 *VGG*, no. 1, 1 January 1885, pp. 1-98, first classified roll, 1885.
82 *AS*, vol. 6, no. 68, 1885, p. 118; James, *The Advancement of Spencer Button*.
83 *AS*, vol. 6, no. 75, 1885, p. 57.
84 *AS*, vol. 2, no. 21, 1881, pp. 136-8.
85 Spaull, 'Fields of disappointment'.
86 Kelly, 'The "Woman Question"', ch. 1 and Appendix A.
87 Biddington, 'The role of women teachers', pp. 145-6.
88 Quoted in Biddington, 'The role of women teachers', p. 147.
89 *VLTA Fourteenth Annual Report*, Melbourne, 1898, p. 4. Julia Davison, president, and Alice Weekes, secretary, were both members of the VWSS and its successors, the UCWS and the Women's Political Association.
90 Full reports in *Argus*, 9 May 1886 and *AS*, vol. 7, no. 83, 1886, pp. 355-6.
91 Biddington, 'The role of women teachers', p. 59.
92 Public Service Act, 1883 (46 Vic. no. 773), cl. 63, p. 15.
93 *AS*, vol. 8, no. 90, 1886, p. 84.
94 Selleck, 'Mary Helena Stark' in Prentice and Theobald, *Women Who Taught*.
95 *AS*, vol. 8, no. 90, p. 86.
96 Education (Teachers) Act, 1888 (52 Vic. no. 1001).
97 *VPP 1889*, vol. 3, 'Regulations under the Education (Teachers) Act 1888'.
98 Public Service Act, 1889 (53 Vic. no. 1024), clauses 13-15.
99 Public Service Act, 1889, cl. 12; for a comparison with NSW, see Deacon, *Managing Gender*, ch. 5.
100 An Act to Regulate the Civil Service, 1862 (25 Vic. no. 160).
101 *VPD 1889*, Leg.Ass., vol. 60, 3 July 1889, p. 430.
102 *VPD 1889*, vol. 60, 1889, p. 430.
103 *VPD 1889*, vol. 60, 1889, pp. 429-30.
104 For Education Department retrenchment measures, see *AS*, vol. 14, no. 175, 1893, p. 163.

105 Teachers Act, 1893 (56 Vic. no. 1302).
106 Teachers Salaries Act, 1892 (56 Vic. no. 1334).
107 Teachers Act, 1895 (57 Vic. no. 1382).
108 See Scholes, 'Education and the women's movement', ch. 5.
109 VLTA 10th report, p. 1.
110 Quoted in Ashford, 'The status of women teachers', p. 173.
111 This account of the Mattingley case is from Scholes, 'Education and the women's movement', pp. 207-210.
112 Dwyer, 'Good and mad women teachers', p. 1.

6   THE 'EVERYDAY WORLD' OF WOMEN WHO TAUGHT

1   VPRS 892, no.764, VPRO.
2   VPRS 892, no.419, VPRO.
3   VPRS 892, no.705, VPRO.
4   VPRS 892, no.705, 1880/3518, VPRO.
5   VPRS 892, no.35, VPRO; Theobald, 'Agnes Grant' in Selleck and Sullivan, *Not So Eminent Victorians.*
6   Theobald, 'Agnes Grant', pp. 81-2.
7   Pawsey and Elliott, 'Patrick Whyte' in Selleck and Sullivan, *Not so Eminent Victorians*, p. 73.
8   Selleck, 'A goldfields family' in Theobald and Selleck, *Family, School and State.*
9   Zainu'ddin, 'The Corr family' in Selleck and Sullivan, *Not So Eminent Victorians*, pp. 162-3.
10 Smith, *The Everyday World*, ch. 1.
11 Smith, *The Everyday World*, ch. 1.
12 Thompson, 'Time, work-discipline, and industrial capitalism', p. 93.
13 Rich, *Of Woman Born*, p. 13.
14 Smith-Rosenberg, 'The female world'; Cott, *The Bonds of Womanhood.*
15 Freud, 'The role of the teacher'.
16 Clifford, 'Lady Teachers' in Lawn and Grace, *Teachers*; Biklen, 'Feminism, methodology and point of view' in Yates, *Feminism and Education.*
17 Steedman, 'Prisonhouses' in Grace and Lawn, *Teachers*, p. 120.
18 Steedman, 'Prisonhouses' in Lawn and Grace, *Teachers*, p. 121; see also Steedman, 'The mother made conscious'; and Steedman, *The Tidy House.*
19 See ch. 7 below.
20 Steedman, *Childhood, Culture and Class.*
21 Theobald, 'The "everyday world" '.
22 Riley, *Am I That Name?*, p. 1.
23 Riley, *Am I That Name?*, p. 98.
24 Rowley and Aveling, 'Two views'; Schaffer, 'Postmodernism and history'. The book is Schaffer, *Women and the Bush.*
25 Aveling, 'Two views', pp. 128-9.
26 Scott, *Gender and the Politics of History*, p. 6.

27 Burstyn, 'Narrative'; see also *Gender and History*, vol. 2, no. 1, 1990, special edition on auto/biography; and Magarey et al, *Writing Lives*.
28 Stone, 'The revival of the narrative'.
29 Isaac, *The Transformation of Virginia*.
30 The surnames of the two women have been changed.
31 Schaffer, 'Postmodernism and history', p. 93.
32 Careers of the O'Connors from VPRS 892, numbers 596 and 772, VPRO; and teacher records numbers 1600 and 1601, DSE archives.
33 Blake, *Vision and Realisation*, vol. 2, p. 1007.
34 Blake, *Vision and Realisation*, vol. 3, p. 62.
35 VPRS 892, no. 772, 75/985, VPRO.
36 Birth Certificate no. 2305, James O'Connor, 18 March 1876, Reg.BDM.
37 VPRS 892, no. 596, 76/7962, VPRO.
38 VPRS 892, no. 596, 76/12104, VPRO.
39 VPRS 892, no. 596, 76/18288, VPRO.
40 VPRS 892, no. 596, 76/24162, VPRO.
41 Death Certificate no. 1436, James O'Connor, 31 July 1876, Reg.BDM.
42 VPRS 892, no. 596, 77/8915, 77/9070, VPRO.
43 VPRS 892, no. 596, 77/2706, VPRO.
44 Teacher record no. 1601, Elizabeth O'Connor.
45 VPRS 892, no. 596, 77/18432, VPRO.
46 Steedman, *Childhood, Culture and Class*, p. 245.
47 *Mount Alexander Mail*, 26 May 1877.
48 *Mount Alexander Mail*, 4 June 1877.
49 VPRS 892, no. 596, 77/20208, VPRO.
50 VPRS 892, no. 596, 77/19541, VPRO.
51 VPRS 892, no. 596, 77/22428 and 23276, VPRO.
52 VPRS 892, no. 596, 77/38106, VPRO.
53 VPRS 892, no. 596, 77/39209, VPRO.
54 VPRS 892, no. 596, 77/39677, VPRO.
55 VPRS 892, no. 596, 77/40554, VPRO.
56 VPRS 892, no. 596, 77/45075, VPRO.
57 VPRS 892, no. 772, 81/32042, VPRO.
58 VPRS 892, no. 772, 81/51392, VPRO.
59 Blake, *Vision and Realisation*, vol. 3, pp.307-8.
60 Teacher record no. 7178, Eliza Fletcher.
61 Marriage Certificate no. 2878, Eliza and Joseph Fletcher, 23 September 1876, Reg.BDM.
62 *Ararat Advertiser*, 18 May 1877.
63 Gordon, 'Response to Joan Scott'.
64 VPRS 892, no. 765, VPRO.
65 Aveling, 'Two views', p. 128.
66 VPRS 892, no. 765, 77/15235, VPRO.
67 VPRS 892, no. 765, Sarah Olsen's statutory declaration is appended to 77/18270, VPRO.

68 VPRS 892, no. 765, Eliza Munro's statutory declaration is attached to 77/18270, VPRO.
69 VPRS 892, no. 765, 77/15235, VPRO.
70 VPRS 892, no. 765, 77/12753, VPRO.
71 VPRS 892, no. 765, Thomas Owen's statutory declaration is attached to 77/18270, VPRO.
72 *Ararat Advertiser*, 18 May 1877.
73 Teacher record no. 4394, Joseph Fletcher.

7   DAUGHTERS OF THE STATE

1 Education Act, 1872 (36 Vic. no. 447), *Victorian Statutes*; Education Act 1875 (39 Vic. no. 11), *South Australian Statutes*; State Education Act, 1875 (39 Vic. no. 11), *Queensland Statutes*; Public Instruction Act, 1880 (43 Vic. no. 23), *New South Wales Statutes*; Education Act, 1885 (49 Vic. no. 15), *Tasmanian Statutes*; Elementary Act 1871, Amendment Act, 1894 (58 Vic. no. 30), *Statutes of Western Australia*.
2 For girls at state schools, see Kyle, *Her Natural Destiny*, chs 2-4; Jones, *Nothing Seemed Impossible*, ch. 1.
3 Selleck, *James Kay-Shuttleworth*.
4 For an overview, see Kaestle, 'Historical methods' in Jaeger, *Complementary Methods*.
5 Grumet, *Bitter Milk*, p. 34.
6 Miller and Davey, 'Patriarchal governance', p. 339.
7 For an overview, see Knuttila, *State Theories*.
8 SARC, 1883, pp. xiii-xxxv for legislation governing elementary education in England, Australia and New Zealand.
9 *VPP*, Rog.Temp., first report, 1882, mins, p. 24.
10 SARC, 1883 report, pp. 77-8.
11 SARC, 1883 report, pp. vi-vii.
12 *VPP 1876*, Rep.Min.PI, 1875, pp. 47-8.
13 *Royal Readers No. VI*, Nelson, London, 1885, book 6, p. 122.
14 VPRS 892, no. 736 for the Kyneton case.
15 Curtis, ' "Illicit" sexuality'.
16 *VPP 1881*, Rep.Min.PI, 1880, Appendix F(2), pp. 125-32.
17 Davison, *Marvellous Melbourne*, p. 72.
18 Public Service Act, 1883 (46 Vic. no. 773), cl. 38, p. 242.
19 See Fisher, 'The family and the Sydney economy' in Grimshaw et al, *Families*.
20 SARC, 1881 report, p. 98.
21 Davey, 'Growing up' in Grimshaw et al, *Families*.
22 Miller, *Long Division*.
23 *Education Gazette and Teachers' Aid*, 20 March 1909, p. 131.
24 Delamont, 'Contradictions' in Delamont and Duffin, *The Nineteenth-Century Woman*.
25 Riley, *Am I That Name?*.

26 Smith, *The Everyday World*, p. 23.

8   THE SCHOOLING OF OUTCAST GIRLS

1 *NSWPP 1873-4*, Royal Commission on Public Charities, vol. 2, p. 27; for the girls' evidence, pp. 295-308; for NSW, see Ramsland, *Children of the Back Lanes*; for Victoria, see Jaggs, *Neglected and Criminal*; for SA, see Barbelet, *Far From a Low Gutter Girl.*
2 Quoted in Fletcher, *Documents*, pp. 73-4.
3 *Argus*, 21 June 1884.
4 *VPP 1884*, Rog.Temp. 1884, mins, pp. 72-6.
5 Davison et al, *Outcasts*, ch. 1.
6 James, *The Vagabond Papers*, ch. 19.
7 Rog.Temp., 1884 report, p. 265, cl. 9022.
8 *VPP 1880*, Rep.Min.PI, 1879-80, p. 192.
9 Rog.Temp., 1884 report, p. 71.
10 *VPP 1879*, Rep.Min.PI, 1878-9, p. 195.
11 For the politics of Aboriginal literacy, see Christie, *Aborigines*, ch. 8.
12 Fletcher, *Clean, Clad and Courteous*; and Fletcher, *Documents.*
13 Fletcher, *Documents*, pp. 77-8.
14 *Government Schools of NSW*, p. 10.
15 Reynolds, *The Other Side*, p. 191.
16 *VPP 1867*, Hig.Comm., 1867, p. 14.
17 Hig.Comm., mins, p. 70.
18 Hig.Comm. mins, pp. 230-2.
19 Hig.Comm., p. 44; for literacy rates among the Chinese, see evidence of Ah Mouy, mins, p. 275.
20 See Blake, *Vision and Realisation*, vol. 2, p. 90 (Lake Condah), p. 205 (Ebenezer) and vol. 3, p. 410 (Coranderrk), p. 1073 (Ramahyuck), p. 1080 (Lake Tyers); there is no mention of Framlingham becoming a state school.
21 This account of Cameron's life is based on Attwood, 'Bessy Cameron'.
22 Quoted in Attwood, 'Bessy Cameron', p. 29.
23 Christie, *Aborigines*, p. 171.
24 *QPP 1898*, Condition of the Aborigines, Report of the Commissioner of Police on the Working of the 'Aboriginals Protection and Restriction of the Sale of Opium Act, 1897', 1898, p. 3.
25 Cale, 'Girls and the perception of sexual danger'; Wimshurst, 'Child-saving'.
26 Barbelet, *Far From a Low Gutter Girl*, ch. 8.
27 For the English background, see Silver, *The Education of the Poor.*
28 For previous state regulation, see Kyle, *Her Natural Destiny*, ch. 1.
29 The Neglected and Criminal Children's Act, 1864 (27 Vic. no. 216).
30 *SAPP 1867*, vol. 2, no. 27, Destitute Board Regulations, section XII, p. 8.
31 *VPP 1872*, Royal Commission on Penal and Prison Discipline, 1872, third report, Industrial and Reformatory Schools, mins, p. 1.

32 *SAPP 1867*, vol 3, no. 91, Report of the Select Committee . . . on the Destitute Poor, Progress Report, pp. 3-4.
33 *SAPP 1867*, vol. 2, no. 50, Brighton Industrial School, p. 1.
34 *VPP 1872*, no. 55, Third Report of the Royal Commission on Penal and Prison Discipline, Industrial and Reformatory Schools, p. vi.
35 Davenport-Hill, *Children of the State*, ch. 8.
36 *VPP 1872*, Royal Commission on Penal and Prison Discipline, p. 17.
37 *QPP 1875*, Report of the Royal Commission into Educational Institutions, 1875, mins, pp. 122-3.
38 *QPP 1886*, Report of the Inspector of Orphanages, 1885, p. 12.
39 For Agnes King, see Kyle, 'Agnes King Inter Alios'; for regulations, see *NSW Government Gazette*, no. 201, 18 August 1868, Industrial School for Girls at Newcastle, Regulations, pp. 2606-09.
40 Quoted in Daniels and Murnane, *Uphill All the Way*, pp. 29-30.
41 Quoted in Cale, 'Girls and the perception of sexual danger', p. 206.
42 *Age*, 25 January 1890.
43 *SAGG*, 6 January 1887, pp. 2-3.
44 State Children's Department, 1890, case no. 845, PROSA.
45 State Children's Department, 1895, case no. 108, PROSA.
46 This account of the Brookside affair is based on Pawsey, 'Outcast girls', unless otherwise mentioned.
47 Wimshurst, 'Child-saving'.
48 Guillaume and Connor, *Reformatory and Preventative Systems*, pp. 22-3.
49 *QPP 1892*, Report of the Inspector of Orphanages, 1891, pp. 10-11.
50 Quoted in Pawsey, 'Outcast girls', p. 12.
51 *SAPP 1873*, vol. 3, no. 41, Destitute Poor Board Regulations, p. 6.
52 *NSWPP 1873*, Royal Commission on Public Charities, vol. 2, p. 29.
53 *QPP 1891*, Report of the Inspector of Orphanages, 1890, p. 4.
54 *VPP 1874*, no. 44, 'Second report of the Royal Commission on Industrial and Reformatory Schools and the Sanatory Station', p. 4.
55 Ramsland, 'The agricultural colony at Mettray'.
56 See Jaggs, *Neglected and Criminal*; Ramsland, *Children of the Back Lanes*; Barbelet, *Far From a Low Gutter Girl*.
57 Spence, *State Children*, p. 15.
58 Boarding Out Society Minute Book, GRG 27/33, PROSA.
59 *SAPP 1885*, vol. 4, no. 228, Second Report of the Commission . . . on the Destitute Act, 1881, The Boarding-Out System, p. xlv ff.
60 Spence, *State Children*, p. 25.
61 Spence, *State Children*, p. 28.
62 For example, *VGG*, no. 14, 5 March 1875, pp. 406-7, and *SAGG*, 9 June 1887, pp. 1136-7.
63 *QPP 1891*, Report of the Inspector of Orphanages, 1890, p. 3.
64 Spence, *State Children*, p. 146.
65 *QPP 1889*, Report of the Inspector of Orphanages, 1888, p. 7.
66 *QPP 1890*, Report of the Inspector of Orphanages, 1889, p. 8.

67 *VPP 1875*, Report of the Inspector of Industrial and Reformatory Schools, 1874, p. 4, and *VPP 1877*, 1876, p. 4.
68 James, *The Vagabond Papers*, p. 197.
69 *QPP 1886*, Report of the Inspector of Orphanages, 1885, p. 2.
70 Barbelet, *Far From a Low Gutter Girl*.
71 Barbelet, *Far From a Low Gutter Girl*, p. 12.
72 Barbelet, *Far From a Low Gutter Girl*, p. 15.
73 Barbelet, *Far From a Low Gutter Girl*, p. 40.
74 For the debate on children's labour, see ch. 7 above.
75 Barbelet, *Far From a Low Gutter Girl*, p. 17.
76 Barbelet, *Far From a Low Gutter Girl*, pp. 3-4.
77 *QPP 1892*, Report of the Inspector of Orphanages, 1891, p. 11.
78 State Children's Council Correspondence, GRG 27/1, letter dated 17 December 1889, PROSA.
79 Barbelet, *Far From a Low Gutter Girl*, pp. 18-19.
80 Barbelet, *Far From a Low Gutter Girl*, p. 163.
81 Barbelet, *Far From a Low Gutter Girl*, p. 162.
82 Barbelet, *Far From a Low Gutter Girl*, p. 163.
83 Barbelet, *Far From a Low Gutter Girl*, p. 27.
84 Barbelet, *Far From a Low Gutter Girl*, p. 30.
85 Barbelet, *Far From a Low Gutter Girl*, p. 33.
86 Barbelet, *Far From a Low Gutter Girl*, p. 34.
87 Barbelet, *Far From a Low Gutter Girl*, p. 77.
88 Attwood, 'Bessy Cameron', p. 43.
89 Barbelet, *Far From a Low Gutter Girl*, p. 91.
90 *QPP 1892*, Report of the Inspector of Orphanages, 1891, p. 2.

EPILOGUE

1 Woolf, *A Room of One's Own*, p. 97.
2 See above, ch. 3.

Select Bibliography

1. OFFICIAL PAPERS

(a) Published

British Parliamentary Papers 1864:
Schools Inquiry Commission Report (Taunton Commission).
Education Gazette and Teachers' Aid.
New South Wales Government Gazette.
New South Wales Parliamentary Debates (NSWPD).
New South Wales Parliamentary Papers (NSWPP):
Reports of the Minister of Public Instruction (and predecessors) (Rep.Min.PI);
Reports of the State Children's Relief Department (and predecessors); Royal
Commission on Public Charities, 1873-4; Royal Commission on Primary,
Secondary, Technical and Other Branches of Education, 1903-5.
New South Wales Statutes.
Queensland Parliamentary Debates (QPD).
Queensland Parliamentary Papers (QPP):
Reports of the Secretary of Public Instruction (and predecessors); Reports
of the Inspector of Orphanages; Royal Commission of Enquiry into
Educational Institutions, 1875; Report on the Working of the 'Aboriginals
Protection and Restriction of the Sale of Opium Act, 1897', 1898;
Commission of Inquiry into the General Working of the Civil Service, 1889.
Queensland Statutes.
Registry of Births, Deaths and Marriages (Reg.BDM), (Victoria).
South Australian Government Gazette (SAGG).
South Australian Parliamentary Papers (SAPP):
Reports to the Minister of Public Instruction (and predecessors); Reports of
the State Children's Council; Select Committee of the Legislative Council on
the Destitute Poor, 1867; Select Committee of the House of Assembly on the
Working of the Education Act, 1868; Royal Commission on the Workings of
the Education Acts, 1881-3; Royal Commission on the Destitute Act 1881,
1883-4; Royal Commission on Education, 1910-13.
South Australian Statutes.
Statutes of Western Australia.
Tasmanian Statutes.
Victorian Government Gazette (VGG).
Victorian Parliamentary Debates (VPD).
Victorian Parliamentary Papers (VPP):

Reports of the Minister of Public Instruction (and predecessors); Reports of the Department for Industrial and Reformatory Schools (later Department for Neglected Children and Reformatory Schools); Royal Commission Appointed to Enquire into Public Education, 1867 (Higinbotham Commission (Hig.Comm.)); Royal Commission into Charitable Institutions, 1871; Royal Commission on Industrial and Reformatory Schools and the Sanatory Station, 1872-4; Royal Commission on Penal and Prison Discipline, 1872; Royal Commission of Enquiry on the State of Public Education in Victoria, 1877 (Pearson Commission); Royal Commission Appointed to Enquire into and Report Upon the . . . System of Public Instruction, 1882-4 (Rogers Templeton Commission (Rog.Temp.Comm.)); Royal Commission on Technical Education, 1899-1901 (Fink Commission).
Victorian Statutes.

(b) Manuscript

Brisbane Grammar School (BGS) Archives (holds most of the records of Brisbane Girls' Grammar School for the nineteenth century):
   Trustees' letter books, 1872-1876; Incoming letters, 1875-1900 (includes papers relating to the appointment and dismissal of Eliza Fewings); Trustees' minute books (those for the girls' school are separate after 1882).
Directorate of School Education (DSE) (Victoria) Archives:
   Teachers' register.
Janet Clarke Hall (JCH) Archives:
   Trinity College Hostel Ladies' Council minutes, 1888-1892; Correspondence files, 1886-1900; List of students, 1886+.
New South Wales State Archives (NSWSA):
   Sydney Girls' High School (SGHS) correspondence.
Public Record Office of South Australia (PROSA):
   State Children's Council correspondence, 1887+; Boarding-Out Society minutes books, 1879-85; Inspectresses' reports on licensed foster-mothers and wet-nurses, 1880-91; Daily report book of the Industrial School, Brighton, 1867-82; Register of admissions of the Industrial School, Boys' Reformatory School and Girls' Reformatory School, 1865-82.
Queensland State Archives:
   Brisbane Girls' Grammar School Prospectuses, containing details of biannual examinations, regulations governing the school, staff, and head mistresses' reports, 1884-1900; Head mistresses' reports on scholarship holders at the Brisbane Girls' Grammar School; Official documents concerning the dismissal of Eliza Fewings.
Sydney Women's College (SWC) Archives:
   Minutes of the Council; General correspondence; Collection of printed circulars relating to the establishment of the college; Ladies' Committee minutes books, circulars and correspondence, principally relating to raising funds for the establishment of the college; Register of students; Papers relating to the appointment of Louisa Macdonald; Letters of Louisa Macdonald to 'Pixie Grove'; Newspaper clippings collection.

Trinity College Archives (houses early records of Janet Clarke Hall):
Minutes of the Council, 1883-1900; Annual reports; Trinity College Calendars, 1883-8; Letter books, 1885-1900.
University of Melbourne Archives (UMA):
Correspondence file, admission of women, 1869-87; Minutes of the Senate; Minutes of the Council; Matriculation entries and results; Princess Ida Club records; Women Medical Students' Society records.
University of Sydney Archives:
Minutes of the Senate.
Victorian Public Record Office (VPRO), Series (VPRS):
640 Education Department, schools correspondence files, 1878-1962; 795 School buildings files; 892 Special case files; 903 Board of Education, inward correspondence files, 1862-72; 10300 Council of Public Education, closed schools files; 10061 Council of Public Education, teacher registration files.

2. MANUSCRIPTS AND UNPUBLISHED RECORDS

Bromby, J.E., papers, MS 8847, La Trobe collection, State Library of Victoria.
Brown family papers, Australian Copying microfiche, State Library of Victoria.
Deakin papers, MS 4913, National Library, Canberra.
Mackinnon papers, MS 9470, La Trobe Library collection, State Library of Victoria.
Tisdall papers, MS 8592, La Trobe Library collection, State Library of Victoria.
Tripp, Margaret, letters to her mother. Copies in possession of author.
Vieusseux family papers, private collection.

3. NEWSPAPERS AND PERIODICALS

Advertiser, 1875-1900.
Age, 1850-1900.
Ararat Advertiser, 1877.
Argus, 1853-1891.
Australasian Schoolmaster and Literary Review, 1881-1893.
Ballarat Courier, 1869.
Brisbane Courier, 1875-1900.
Hobart Town Gazette, 1825.
Kyneton Guardian, 1863.
Kyneton Observer, 1857-1863.
Mount Alexander Mail, 1877.
Queenslander, 1896.
Southern Sphere, 1911.
Sydney Morning Herald, 1879-1907.

4. SECONDARY SOURCES

Adams, P. 'Picnic at Hanging Rock' in *Higher School Certificate English Resource Book 1977*. Dove Communications, Melbourne, 1976.

276   *Knowing Women*

Allen, J. *Rose Scott: vision and revision in feminism*. Oxford University Press, Melbourne, 1994.

Allen, M. *The Labourer's Friend: Sisters of Mercy in Victoria and Tasmania*. Hargreen Publishing, Melbourne, 1989.

Anchen, J., *Frank Tate and His Work for Education*. Australian Council for Education Research, Melbourne, 1956.

Attwood, B. ' "In the name of all my coloured brethren and sisters": a biography of Bessy Cameron'. *Hecate*, vol. 12, nos 1 and 2, 1986.

Austin, A. *Australian Education 1788-1900: church, state and public education in colonial Australia*. Pitman, Melbourne, 1961.

Austin, A. *The Webbs' Australian Diary 1898*. Pitman, Melbourne, 1965.

Australian Dictionary of Biography, vols 1-12, 1788-1939 (various eds). Melbourne University Press, Melbourne, 1966-1990.

Bacchi, C. *Same Difference: feminism and sexual difference*. Allen and Unwin, Sydney, 1990.

Backhouse, J. and Tyler, C. *The Life and Labours of George Washington Walker*. Bennett, London, 1862.

Barbauld, A. *The Female Speaker*. Johnson, London, 1811.

Barbelet, M. *Far From a Low Gutter Girl: the forgotten world of state wards: South Australia 1887-1940*. Oxford University Press, Melbourne, 1983.

Barcan, A. *A History of Australian Education*. Oxford University Press, Melbourne, 1980.

Barrington, A. 'Queensland schools'. *Girton Review*, August 1894.

Belenky, M., Clinchy, B., Goldberger, N., and Tarule, J. *Women's Ways of Knowing: the development of self, voice, and mind*. Basic Books, New York, 1986.

Blackmore, J. *Making Educational History: a feminist perspective*. Deakin University, Geelong, 1992.

Blainey, G. *A Centenary History of the University of Melbourne*. Melbourne University Press, Melbourne, 1957.

Blake, L. (ed.) *Vision and Realisation: a centenary history of state education in Victoria*, (3 vols). Education Department of Victoria, Melbourne, 1973.

Bryant, M. *The Unexpected Revolution: a study in the history of the education of women and girls in the nineteenth century*. University of London, London, 1979.

Burchell, L. *Victorian Schools: a study in colonial government architecture 1837-1900*. Melbourne University Press, Melbourne, 1980.

Burnswoods, J. and Fletcher, J. *Sydney and the Bush: a pictorial history of education in New South Wales*. NSW Department of Education, Sydney, 1980.

Burstyn, J. *Victorian Education and the Ideal of Womanhood*. Croom Helm, London, 1980.

Burstyn, J. 'Narrative versus theoretical approaches: a dilemma for historians of women'. *History of Education Review*, vol. 19, no. 2, 1990.

Bygott, U. and Cable, K. *Pioneer Women Graduates of the University of Sydney 1881-1921*. University of Sydney, Sydney, 1985.

Cale, M. 'Girls and the perception of sexual danger in the Victorian reformatory system'. *History*, vol. 78, no. 253, 1993.

Calendar of the Women's College Within the University of Sydney. 1893-1900.

Carter, J. *Nothing to Spare: recollections of Australian pioneering women.* Penguin, Melbourne, 1985.

Chambers, C. *Lessons For Ladies: a social history of girls' education in Australasia 1870-1900.* Hale and Iremonger, Sydney, 1986.

Chapone, H. *Letters on the Improvement of the Mind.* Sharpe, London, 1822.

Christie, M. *Aborigines in Colonial Victoria 1835-86.* Sydney University Press, Sydney, 1979.

Clarke, E. *Female Teachers in Queensland State Schools: a history 1860-1983.* Queensland Department of Education, Brisbane, 1985.

Clarke, P. *The Governesses: letters from the colonies, 1862-1882.* Allen and Unwin, Sydney, 1985.

Clifford, G. (ed.) *Lone Voyagers: academic women in coeducational institutions, 1870-1937.* Feminist Press, New York, 1989.

Conway, J. 'Perspectives on the history of women's education in the United States'. *History of Education Quarterly*, Spring 1974.

Cott, F. *The Bonds of Womanhood: 'Woman's Sphere' in New England, 1780-1835.* Yale University Press, New Haven, 1977.

Curtis, B. *Building the Educational State: Canada West, 1836-1871.* Falmer Press, London (Ont.), 1988.

Curtis, B. ' "Illicit" sexuality and public education in Ontario, 1840-1907'. *Historical Studies in Education*, vol. 1, no. 1, 1989.

Curtis, B. *True Government by Choice Men?: inspection, education, and state formation in Canada West.* University of Toronto Press, Toronto, 1992.

Daniels, K. and Murnane, M. (eds) *Uphill All the Way: a documentary history of women in Australia.* Queensland University Press, St Lucia, 1980.

Darwin, E. *A Plan for the Conduct of Female Education in Boarding Schools.* Johnson, Derby, 1797.

Davenport-Hill, F. *Children of the State.* Macmillan, London, 1889.

Davey, I. 'Capitalism, patriarchy and the origins of mass schooling'. *History of Education Review*, vol. 16, no. 2, 1987.

Davidoff, L. and Hall, C. *Family Fortunes: men and women of the English middle class 1780-1850.* Hutchinson, London, 1987.

Davison, G. *The Rise and Fall of Marvellous Melbourne.* Melbourne University Press, Melbourne, 1979.

Davison, G., Dunstan, D. and McConville, C. (eds) *The Outcasts of Melbourne.* Allen and Unwin, Sydney, 1985.

Davitt, E. *Force and Fraud: a tale of the bush.* Mulini Press, Canberra, 1993. First published 1856.

Deacon, D. *Managing Gender: the state, the new middle class and women workers 1830-1930.* Oxford University Press, Melbourne, 1989.

Delamont, S. and Duffin, L. (eds) *The Nineteenth-Century Woman: her cultural and physical world.* Croom Helm, London, 1978.

Dinnerstein, D. *The Mermaid and the Minotaur: sexual arrangements and human malaise*. Harper and Row, New York, 1977.

Docherty, J. *'The Emily Mac': the Emily MacPherson College 1906-1979*. Ormond, Melbourne, 1981.

Dow, G. *George Higinbotham: church and state*. Pitman, Melbourne, 1964.

Dyhouse, C. *Girls Growing Up in Late Victorian and Edwardian England*. Routledge and Kegan Paul, London, 1981.

Edwards, E. 'Educational institutions or extended families?: the reconstruction of gender in women's colleges'. *Gender and Education*, vol. 2, no. 1, 1990.

Ellis, S. *The Women of England: moral, political and domestic habits*. Griffin, London, 1839.

Evans, W.G. *Education and Female Emancipation: the Welsh experience, 1847-1914*. University of Wales Press, Cardiff, 1990.

Fitzpatrick, K. *PLC Melbourne: the first century, 1875-1975*. Presbyterian Ladies College, Melbourne, 1975.

Fletcher, J. *Clean, Clad and Courteous: a history of Aboriginal education in New South Wales*. J.J. Fletcher, Sydney, 1989.

Fletcher, J. *Documents in the History of Aboriginal Education in New South Wales*. Fletcher, Sydney, 1989.

Fogarty, R. *Catholic Education in Australia 1806-1950*, (2 vols). Melbourne University Press, Melbourne, 1959.

Foucault, M. *The History of Sexuality: volume one, an introduction*. Penguin, Harmondsworth, 1981.

Frances, R. *The Politics of Work: gender and labour in Victoria, 1880-1939*. Cambridge University Press, Cambridge, 1993.

Frazer, F. and Palmer, N. (eds) *Records of the Pioneer Women of Victoria 1835-60*. Osboldstone, Melbourne, 1937.

Freeman, P. *History of Somerville House, 1899-1949*. Smith and Paterson, Brisbane, 1949.

Freud, A. 'The role of the teacher'. *Harvard Education Review*, vol. 22, no. 4, 1952.

Garden, D. *The Melbourne Teacher Training Colleges: from training institution to Melbourne State College 1870-1982*. Heinemann, Melbourne, 1982.

Gardiner, L. *Tintern School and Anglican Girls' Education 1877-1977*. Tintern, Ringwood, 1977.

Gardiner, L. *Janet Clarke Hall 1886-1986*. Hyland House, Melbourne, 1986.

Gardner, W. *Colonial Cap and Gown: studies in the mid-Victorian universities of Australasia*. University of Canterbury, Canterbury, 1979.

Gidney, R. and Millar, W. *Inventing Secondary Education: the rise of the high school in nineteenth-century Ontario*. McGill Queen's University Press, Montreal, 1990.

Gilligan, C. *In a Different Voice: psychological theory and women's development*. Harvard University Press, Cambridge (Mass.), 1982.

Girton College Register 1869-1946. Girton College, Cambridge, 1948.

Gladman, F. *School Work*. Jarrold, London, 1885.

Gladman, F. *School Method*, (rev. edn). Jarrold, London, 1897.

Goodman, R. *Secondary Education in Queensland, 1860-1960*. Australian National University Press, Canberra, 1968.

Gordon, L. 'Response to Joan Scott'. *Signs*, vol. 15, no. 4, 1990.

Gouldner, A. *The Future of Intellectuals and the Rise of the New Class*. Seabury Press, New York, 1979.

Government Schools of New South Wales, 1848 to 1993. New South Wales Department of School Education, Sydney, 1993.

Green, A. *Education and State Formation: the rise of education systems in England, France and the USA*. Macmillan, London, 1990.

Grimshaw, P., McConville, C. and McEwen, E. (eds) *Families in Colonial Australia*. Allen and Unwin, Sydney, 1985.

Grimshaw, P., Lake, M., McGrath, A. and Quartly, M. *Creating a Nation*. McPhee Gribble, Melbourne, 1994.

Grosz, E. 'Notes towards a corporeal feminism'. *Australian Feminist Studies*, no. 5, 1987.

Grumet, M. *Bitter Milk: women and teaching*. University of Massachusetts Press, Amherst, 1988.

Grundy, D. *'Secular, Compulsory and Free': the Education Act of 1872*. Melbourne University Press, Melbourne, 1972.

Grundy, D. 'The political economy of the denominational system of schools in Victoria', in S. Murray-Smith (ed.) *Melbourne Studies in Education 1981*. Melbourne University Press, Melbourne, 1981.

Grundy, D. 'The formation of a disordered teaching service in Victoria, 1851- 1871'. *History of Education Review*, vol. 18, no. 2, 1989.

Guillaume G. and Connor, E. (eds) *The Development and Working of the Reformatory and Preventative Systems in the Colony of Victoria, Australia, 1864-1890*. Government of Victoria, Melbourne, 1891.

Hamilton, E. *Letters Addressed to the Daughters of a Nobleman on the Formation of Religious and Moral Principle*. Cadell and Davies, London, 1806.

Hammerton, J. *Emigrant Gentlewomen: genteel poverty and female emigration 1830-1914*. Australian National University Press, Canberra, 1979.

Harley, J. 'Alfred Deakin at home'. *Victorian Historical Journal*, vol. 59, no. 1, 1988.

Hay, O. *Chronicles of Clyde*. Brown Prior Anderson, Melbourne, 1964.

Hicks, N. *'This Sin and Scandal': Australia's population debate 1891-1911*. Australian National University Press, Canberra, 1978.

Hill, F. *Children of the State*. Macmillan, London, 1889.

Hill, F. and Hill, R. *What We Saw in Australia*. Macmillan, London, 1875.

Hole, W. and Treweeke, A. *The History of the Women's College Within the University of Sydney*. Angus and Robertson, Sydney, 1953.

Hooper, C. 'Vision unrealised: state secondary education in Victoria, 1850-1872'. *History of Education Review*, vol. 19, no. 1, 1990.

Hooper, C. 'The tale of two schools: the Geelong Grammar School and the Geelong National Grammar School'. Australian and New Zealand History of Education Society conference papers, Adelaide, 1992.

Hopkins, M. *Hannah More and her Circle*. Longman, New York, 1947.

Hornibrook, J. *Bibliography of Queensland Verse with Biographical Notes.* Government Printer, Brisbane, 1953.

Houston, S. and Prentice, A. *Schooling and Scholars in Nineteenth-Century Ontario.* University of Toronto Press, Toronto, 1988.

Hyams, B. *From Compliance to Confrontation: 140 years of teachers' unions in South Australia 1851-1991.* Auslib Press, Adelaide, 1992.

Hyams, B., Trethewey, L., Condon, B., Vick, M. and Grundy, D. (eds) *Learning and Other Things: sources for a social history of education in South Australia.* South Australian Government Printer, Adelaide, 1988.

Isaac, R. *The Transformation of Virginia 1740-1790.* University of North Carolina Press, Chapel Hill, 1982.

Jaeger, R. (ed.) *Complementary Methods for Research in Education.* American Educational Research Association, Washington, 1988.

Jaggs, D. *Neglected and Criminal: foundations of child welfare legislation in Victoria.* Phillip Institute of Technology, Melbourne, 1986.

James, B. *The Advancement of Spencer Button.* Angus and Robertson, Sydney, 1967.

James, J. *The Vagabond Papers,* ed. Michael Canon. Melbourne University Press, Melbourne, 1969.

Jeffreys, S. *The Spinster and her Enemies: feminism and sexuality 1880-1930.* Pandora, London, 1985.

Jones, H. *Nothing Seemed Impossible: women's education and social change in South Australia 1875-1915.* University of Queensland Press, St Lucia, 1985.

Jones, H. *In Her Own Name: women in South Australian history.* Wakefield Press, Adelaide, 1986.

Journal of the Women's Education Union, vol. 3, no. 29, 1875.

Kelly, F. *Degrees of Liberation: a short history of women in the University of Melbourne.* The Women Graduates Centenary Committee, Melbourne, 1985.

Kelly, F. (ed.) *On the Edge of Discovery; Australian women in science.* Text Publishing Company, Melbourne, 1993.

Knuttila, M. *State Theories: from liberalism to the challenge of feminism.* Fernwood, Halifax, 1992.

Kyle, N. 'Agnes King Inter Alios: reformatory school administrators in New South Wales, 1869-1904'. *Journal of Australian Studies,* no. 15, 1984.

——. *Her Natural Destiny: the education of women in New South Wales.* New South Wales University Press, Sydney, 1986.

Lake, M. and Kelly, F. (eds) *Double Time: women in Victoria—150 years.* Penguin, Melbourne, 1985.

Lauchland, E. 'The Maitland Girls' High School'. *Journal of the Royal Australian Historical Society,* vol. 31, 1945.

Lawn, M. and Grace, G. (eds) *Teachers: the culture and politics of work.* Falmer Press, London, 1987.

Lindsay, J. *Picnic at Hanging Rock.* Penguin, Harmondsworth, 1967.

Logan, G. and Clarke, E. *State Education in Queensland: a brief history.* Queensland Department of Education, Brisbane, 1984.

Logan, G. and Watson, T. (eds) *Soldiers of the Service: some early Queensland educators and their schools*. History of Queensland Education Society, Brisbane, 1992.

Macdonald, L. *The Women's College Within the University of Sydney*. Sydney Women's College, Sydney, 1949.

Macdonald, L. 'The economic position of women'. *Australian Economist*, vol. 3, no. 2, 1893.

MacDonald, P. *Marriage in Australia: age at first marriage and proportions marrying, 1860-1971*. Australian National University, Canberra, 1974.

Macintyre, S. *A Colonial Liberalism: the lost world of three Victorian visionaries*. Oxford University Press, Melbourne, 1991.

Mackaness, G. (ed.) *Some Private Correspondence of Sir John and Lady Jane Franklin*. Ford, Sydney, 1947.

Mackinnon, A. *One Foot on the Ladder: origins and outcomes of girls' secondary schooling in South Australia*. University of Queensland Press, St Lucia, 1984.

Mackinnon, A. *The New Women: Adelaide's early women graduates*. Wakefield Press, Adelaide, 1986.

McCarthy, R. and Theobald, M. (eds) *Melbourne Girls' Grammar School: centenary essays, 1893-1993*. Hyland House, Melbourne, 1993.

Maddern, P. *St Hilda's College: forerunners and foundations*. St Hilda's College, Melbourne, 1989.

Magarey, S. *Unbridling the Tongues of Women: a biography of Catherine Helen Spence*. Hale and Iremonger, Sydney, 1985.

Magarey, S., Guerin, C. and Hamilton, P. (eds) *Writing Lives: feminist biography and autobiography*. Australian Feminist Studies Publications, Adelaide, 1992.

Magarey, S., Rowley, S. and Sheridan, S. (eds) *Debutante Nation: feminism contests the 1890s*. Allen and Unwin, Sydney, 1993.

Martin, A. *Henry Parkes: a biography*. Melbourne University Press, Melbourne, 1980.

Miller, P. *Long Division: state schooling in South Australian society*. Wakefield Press, Adelaide, 1986.

Miller, P. and Davey, I. 'Patriarchal governance, schooling and the state'. Australian and New Zealand History of Education Society conference papers, Adelaide, 1992.

More, H. *Strictures on the Modern System of Education*. Cadell and Davies, London, 1801.

Morgan, S. *My Place*. Fremantle Arts Centre Press, Fremantle, 1987.

Newnham College Register 1871-1923. Newnham College, Cambridge, 1979.

Norman, L. *The Brown and the Yellow: Sydney Girls' High School 1883-1983*. Oxford University Press, Melbourne, 1983.

O'Connor, C. *The Sisters, Faithful Companions of Jesus, in Australia*. FCJ Sisters, Melbourne, 1982.

O'Donoghue, M. *Mother Vincent Whitty: woman and educator in a masculine society*. Melbourne University Press, Melbourne, 1972.

Oldfield, A. *Woman Suffrage in Australia: a gift or a struggle?*. Cambridge University Press, Cambridge, 1992.

Pateman, C. *The Sexual Contract*. Polity Press, Cambridge, 1988.

Pawsey, M. 'Annie Wilkins: life on the margins of nineteenth-century Collingwood'. Faculty of Education, University of Melbourne, 1992.

Pawsey, M. 'Outcast girls: the Brookside Reformatory affair, 1899'. Australian and New Zealand History of Education Society Conference papers, Adelaide, 1993.

Pearson, C. *The Higher Culture of Women*. Mullen, Melbourne, 1875.

Pedersen, J. 'Schoolmistresses and headmistresses: elites and education in nineteenth-century England'. *Journal of British Studies*, vol. 15, no. 1, 1975.

Pedersen, J. 'The reform of women's secondary and higher education: institutional change and social values in mid and late Victorian England'. *History of Education Quarterly*, Spring 1979.

Prentice A. and Theobald, M. (eds) *Women who Taught: perspectives on the history of women and teaching*. University of Toronto Press, Toronto, 1991.

Prideaux, P. *Brisbane Girls' Grammar School: the first sixty years 1875-1935*. Boolarong Publications, Brisbane, 1985.

Ralston, C. 'Deceptive dichotomies: private/public and nature/culture, gender relations in Tonga in the early contact period'. *Australian Feminist Studies*, no. 12, 1990.

Ramsland, J. *Children of the Back Lanes: destitute and neglected children in colonial New South Wales*. New South Wales University Press, Sydney, 1986.

Ramsland, J. 'The agricultural colony at Mettray: a nineteenth-century approach to the institutionalisation of delinquent boys', in D. Stockley (ed.) *Melbourne Studies in Education 1987-88*. La Trobe University Press, Melbourne, 1989.

Reiger, M. *The Disenchantment of the Home: modernizing the Australian family 1880-1940*. Oxford, Melbourne, 1985.

Reynolds, H. *The Other Side of the Frontier: Aboriginal resistance to the European invasion of Australia*. Penguin, Melbourne, 1981.

Rich, A. *Of Woman Born: motherhood as experience and institution*. Virago, London, 1986.

Richardson, H.H. *The Getting of Wisdom*. Heinemann, London, 1970. First published 1910.

Riley, D. *Am I That Name? feminism and the category of 'woman' in history*. University of Minnesota Press, Minneapolis, 1988.

Rivett, R. 'Deakin's confidante'. *Overland*, no. 69, 1978.

Roberts, J. *Maybanke Anderson: sex, suffrage and social reform*. Hale and Iremonger, Sydney, 1993.

Robinson, J. *The Echoes Fade Not: a history of Toorak College*. Toorak College, Melbourne, 1987.

Rosaldo, M. and Lamphere, L. (eds) *Women, Culture and Society*. Stanford University Press, Stanford, 1974.

Rowley, S. and Aveling, M. 'Two views of *Women and the Bush*'. *Australian Feminist Studies*, no. 10, 1989.

Royal Readers Nos 1-6. Nelson, London, various editions.

Sandford, E. *Woman, in her Social and Domestic Character*. Longman, London, 1831.

Schaffer, K. *Women and the Bush: forces of desire in the Australian cultural tradition*. Cambridge University Press, Cambridge, 1988.

Schaffer, K. 'Postmodernism and history: a reply to Marian Aveling'. *Australian Feminist Studies*, no. 11, 1990.

Scott, E. *A History of the University of Melbourne*. Melbourne University Press, Melbourne, 1936.

Scott, J. *Gender and the Politics of History*. Columbia University Press, New York, 1988.

Selleck, R. *The New Education: the English background 1870-1914*. Pitman, Melbourne, 1968.

Selleck, R. *Frank Tate: a biography*. Melbourne University Press, Melbourne, 1982.

Selleck, R. *Sir James Kay-Shuttleworth: journey of an outsider*. Woburn Press, London, 1994.

Selleck, R. and Sullivan, M. (eds) *Not So Eminent Victorians*. Melbourne University Press, Melbourne, 1984.

Sellers, M. *The Brisbane Girls' Grammar School*. Sellers, Brisbane, 1900.

Sherington, G., Petersen, R. and Brice, I. *Learning to Lead: a history of girls' and boys' corporate secondary schools in Australia*. Allen and Unwin, Sydney, 1987.

Sidgwick, E. *Health Statistics of Women Students of Cambridge and Oxford and Their Sisters*. Cambridge University Press, Cambridge, 1912.

Silver, H. and Silver, P. *The Education of the Poor*. Routledge and Kegan Paul, London, 1974.

Sinclair, E. *Modern Accomplishments*. Nisbet, London, 1836.

Smith, D. *The Everyday World as Problematic: a feminist sociology*. University of Toronto Press, Toronto, 1987.

Smith, S. *Essays, by Sydney Smith, Reprinted from the Edinburgh Review 1802-1818*. Routledge, London, 1874.

Smith-Rosenberg, C. 'The female world of love and ritual: relations between women in nineteenth-century America'. *Signs*, vol. 1, no. 1, 1975.

Solomon, B. *In the Company of Educated Women*. Yale University Press, New Haven, 1985.

Spaull, A. 'Fields of disappointment: the writing of teacher union history in Canada'. *Historical Studies in Education*, vol. 3, no. 1, 1991.

Spence, C. *State Children in Australia: a history of boarding out and its developments*. Vardon, Adelaide, 1907.

Steedman, C. ' "The mother made conscious": the historical development of a primary school pedagogy'. *History Workshop Journal*, no. 20, 1985.

Steedman, C. *The Tidy House*. Virago, London, 1982.

Steedman, C. *Childhood, Culture and Class in Britain: Margaret McMillan, 1860-1931*. Virago, London, 1990.

Stilwell, G. 'Mr and Mrs George Carr of "Ellinthorp hall" '. *Tasmanian Historical Research Association: papers and proceedings*, vol. 11, no. 4, 1964.

Stone, L. 'The revival of the narrative: reflections on a new old history'. *Past and Present*, vol. 58, 1979.

Sullivan, M. 'Fifty years of opposition to Queensland's grammar schools', in S. Murray-Smith (ed.) *Melbourne Studies in Education 1974*. Melbourne University Press, Melbourne, 1974.

Swanwick, F. *Our Girls and Their Secondary Education: dedicated to Charles Lilley and the other trustees of the Brisbane Grammar School.* Swanwick, Brisbane, 1874.

Sweetman, E., Long, C. and Smyth, J. *A History of State Education in Victoria*. Education Department of Victoria, Melbourne, 1922.

Taylor, S. and Henry, M. (eds) *Battlers and Bluestockings: women's place in Australian education*. Australian College of Education, Canberra, 1988.

Theobald, M. *Ruyton Remembers 1878-1978*. Hawthorn Press, Melbourne, 1978.

Theobald, M. 'The PLC mystique: reflections on the reform of female education in nineteenth-century Australia'. *Australian Historical Studies*, vol. 23, no. 92, 1989.

Theobald, M. 'The "everyday world" of women who taught'. *History of Education Review*, vol. 19, no. 2, 1990.

Theobald, M. and Selleck, R. (eds) *Family, School and State in Australian History*. Allen and Unwin, Sydney, 1990.

Thompson, E. 'Time, work-discipline, and industrial capitalism'. *Past and Present*, no. 38, 1967.

Tisdall, C. *Forerunners: the saga of a family of teachers*. Graham Publications, Walhalla, 1979.

Tomaselli, S. 'The Enlightenment debate on women'. *History Workshop Journal*, no. 20, 1985.

Tregenza, J. *Professor of Democracy: the life of Charles Henry Pearson, 1830-1894, Oxford don and Australian radical*. Melbourne University Press, Melbourne, 1968.

Turney, C. (ed.) *Pioneers of Australian Education: a study of the development of education in New South Wales in the nineteenth century*, (vol. 1). Sydney University Press, Sydney, 1969.

Turney, C. (ed.) *Pioneers of Australian Education: studies of the development of education in the Australian colonies 1850-1900*, (vol. 2). Sydney University Press, Sydney, 1972.

Turney, C. *Sources in the History of Australian Education: a book of readings*. Angus and Robertson, Sydney, 1975.

Turney, C., Bygott, U. and Chippendale, P. *Australia's First: a history of the University of Sydney, Volume 1 1850-1939*. Hale and Iremonger, Sydney, 1991.

Tyack, D. and Hansot, E. *Learning Together; a history of coeducation in American public schools*. Yale University Press, New Haven, 1990.

Vicinus, M. ' "One life to stand beside me": emotional conflicts in first-generation college women in England'. *Feminist Studies*, vol. 8, no. 3, 1982.

Vicinus, M. *Independent Women: work and community for single women 1850-1920*. Virago, London, 1985.

Warren, D. *American Teachers: histories of a profession at work*. Macmillan, New York, 1989.

Watson, T. 'Miss Fewings versus Mr Griffith: a matter of honour'. Australian and New Zealand History of Education Society Conference paper, Auckland, 1990.

Williams, R. *Culture and Society 1870-1950*. Pelican, Harmondsworth, 1982.

Williamson, N. 'What do you do with herstory when you find it? A look at Mary Ann Flower's Sydney Ladies' College, 1854-1888'. Australian and New Zealand History of Education Society Conference papers, Melbourne, 1984.

Wimshurst, K. 'Child-saving and urban school reform in South Australia at the turn of the century', in I. Palmer (ed.) *Melbourne Studies in Education 1983*. Melbourne University Press, Melbourne, 1983.

Windschuttle, E. 'Educating the daughters of the ruling class in colonial New South Wales', in S. Murray-Smith (ed.) *Melbourne Studies in Education 1980*. Melbourne University Press, Melbourne, 1980.

Wollstonecraft, M. *A Vindication of the Rights of Woman*. Norton, New York, 1967. First published 1792.

Woolf, V. *A Room of One's Own*. Grafton Books, London, 1978. First published 1929.

Wyeth, E. *Education in Queensland: a history of education in Queensland and in the Moreton Bay District of New South Wales*. Australian Council for Educational Research, Melbourne, 1953.

Yates, L. (ed.) *Feminism and Education*. La Trobe University Press, Melbourne, 1993.

Zainu'ddin, A. 'The admission of women to the University of Melbourne 1869-1903', in S. Murray-Smith (ed.) *Melbourne Studies in Education 1973*. Melbourne University Press, Melbourne, 1973.

Zainu'ddin, A. *They Dreamt of a School: a centenary history of Methodist Ladies' College Kew, 1882-1982*. Hyland House, Melbourne, 1982.

Zainu'ddin, A. ' "The poor widow, the ignoramus and the humbug": an examination of rhetoric and reality in Victoria's 1905 Act for the Registration of Teachers and Schools'. *History of Education Review*, vol. 13, no. 2, 1984.

Zimmern, A. *The Renaissance of Girls' Education*. Croom Helm, London, 1898.

5. UNPUBLISHED DISSERTATIONS

Amies, M. 'Home education and colonial ideals of womanhood', Ph.D. thesis, Monash University, 1986.

Ashford, K. 'The status of women teachers in the Victorian Education Department at the turn of the century 1888-1914', M.Ed. thesis, Monash University, 1981.

Biddington, J. 'The role of women teachers in the Victorian Education Department 1872-1925', M.Ed. thesis, University of Melbourne, 1977.

Biddington, J. ' "Something to Fall Back On": women, work and education in seven Victorian high schools, 1905-1945', Ph.D. thesis, University of Melbourne, 1994.

Biddington, R. 'Policies in primary teacher training in Victoria 1850-1950', Ph.D. thesis, University of Melbourne, 1978.

Burley, S. 'None more anonymous? Catholic teaching nuns, their secondary schools and students in South Australia, 1880-1925', M.Ed. thesis, University of Adelaide, 1992.

Dwyer, D. 'Good and mad women teachers: the case of Grace Neven', M.Ed. thesis, University of Melbourne, 1993.

Ford, O. 'Voices from below: family, school and community on the Braybrook plains, 1854-1892', M.Ed. thesis, University of Melbourne, 1993.

French, E. 'Secondary education and the Australian social order', Ph.D. thesis, University of Melbourne, 1958.

Frith, S. 'Fact and fiction in Joan Lindsay's *Picnic at Hanging Rock*', M.Ed. thesis, University of Melbourne, 1990.

Hone, J. 'The movement for the higher education of women in the later nineteenth century', M.A. thesis, Monash University, 1965.

Jones, G. 'A lady in every sense of the word', M.A. thesis, University of Melbourne, 1982.

Kelly, F. 'The "Woman Question" in Melbourne, 1880-1914', Ph.D. thesis, Monash University, 1982.

McGrath, A. 'Some convent traditions in Victoria, 1860-1910: a study of the background and development of the traditions of the convent school in Victoria, from 1860-1910', M.Ed. thesis, University of Melbourne, 1964.

Mackinnon, A. 'Awakening Women: women, higher education and family formation in South Australia 1880-1920', Ph.D. thesis, University of Adelaide, 1989.

Milburn, J. 'Girls' secondary education in New South Wales', M.Ed. thesis, University of Sydney, 1965.

Noble, G. 'Secondary education in Van Diemen's Land 1820-1857', M.Ed. thesis, University of Melbourne, 1972.

Riordan, N. 'Private venture schools in Western Australia between 1829 and 1914: an analysis of their contribution to education', M.Ed. thesis, University of Western Australia, 1990.

Scholes, L. 'Education and the women's movement in Victoria, 1875-1914', Ph.D. thesis, University of Melbourne, 1984.

Theobald, M. 'Women and schools in colonial Victoria, 1840-1910', Ph.D. thesis, Monash University, 1985.

Thomas, S. 'Learning to be a Good Woman; post primary education for girls in Victorian state schools, 1900-1939', M.Ed. thesis, University of Melbourne, 1987.

Vick, M. 'Schools, school communities and the state in mid nineteenth century NSW, SA and Victoria', Ph.D. thesis, University of Adelaide, 1991.

Index

Melbourne Church of England Girls'
Grammar School, 10, 30, 33, 79-80
Melbourne Continuation School (later
Melbourne Boys' High School),
127, 135
Melbourne Grammar School, 10, 31-2,
33, 46, 135
Merton Hall, *see* Melbourne Church of
England Girls' Grammar School
Methodist Ladies' College, Kew, 1, 3, 98,
118
Millar, Thomas, 237-8
Miller family, Catherine and Margaret,
136, 175
Montgomery, Christina, 68
Moore, Professor Harrison, 72, 73
Moravian missionaries, 220-23
More, Hannah, 13-14, 20, 21-2
Morris family, Edith, Mary, 68, 74, 79
Mt Morgan State School, 209
Munro, James, 169

National Model School and Training
(Normal) Institution, Melbourne
132-3, 134, 141, 148, 157, *see also*
Training Institution
National School Board, New South
Wales, 141
National School Board, Victoria, 130-36,
141-2, 143
Newcastle High School, 127
Newcastle Industrial School (became
Biloela Industrial School), 231
Newman College, University of
Melbourne, 74
Newnham College, Cambridge, 39-40,
60, 72, 76-7, 80, 82, 103, 105-6
Normanhurst, 93
North London Collegiate School, 64, 93,
see also Buss, Frances
North Sydney Girls' High School, 118
Nyungar people, 221

Oberwyl, 53, 93
O'Brien, Marion, 117
O'Connor family, Alice, Daniel, Janet,
Janet (née Dods), Kate, 97-101,
102, 110, 112, 115, 117
O'Connor family, Elizabeth (née Boyle),
James, 180-86, 187
O'Hara family, Dr Annie, Dr Elizabeth,
Patrick, 1, 66
Olsen family, Catherine, Eliza (later Mrs
Fletcher), Sarah, Thomas, 186-91
O'Reilly, Dr Susie, 70
Ormiston Ladies' College, 50, 51
Ormond College, University of
Melbourne, 74-5, 78

Ormond, Francis, 74
outcast girls, (*see also* Aboriginal girls)
boarding-out of, 224, 225, 240-50
child welfare legislation concerning, 2,
223, 224-7, 234, 241
church involvement with, 220-23, 250
deviance/sexuality of, 216, 217, 223-4,
225-6, 230-40, 248-9
experiences of incarceration, 214-15,
227-30, 230-40
families of, 229-30
hired out as servants, 239-40, 247-50
historical phases in child welfare
concerning, 224-5
reforming institutions for, 2, 214, 225-40
schooling of, 2, 230, 234-5, 238-9,
245-7
sexual abuse of, 248-9
Oxford University, 59, 64, 71, 76-7,
82-3, 92

Palmer, Sir James, 138
Parkes family, Sir Henry, Menie, 82, 92,
215
Pears, Martha, 229-30
Pearson, Charles, 31, 59-60, 64, 98, 165-7
Pearson Royal Commission, 60
Pells, Charlotte, 103, 105, 119
Perry, Bishop Charles, 10-12, 17, 19, 57,
59, 135
Pestalozzi, Johann, 177, 195
Picnic at Hanging Rock, see Lindsay, Joan
Pike, Tabitha, 144
Poonindie Lutheran Mission School, 221
postmodernism and history, 178-80,
182-3, 187, 190-91
Presbyterian Ladies' College, Melbourne, 6,
9, 27, 30, 31, 33, 34, 47, 56, 59-60,
91-2, 93, 97-8, 103, 165, 212
Princes Bridge Industrial School, 2, 227,
228
Princess Ida Club, University of
Melbourne, 72-4
protestantism and women's education, 16
Public Charities Royal Commission, New
South Wales, 214, 228, 238-9
Purbrick, Susannah Darke, *see* Ellinthorp
Hall
Pye, Ellen, 40

Queen's College, London, 59-60
Queen's College, University of
Melbourne, 74-5, 78
Queensland grammar schools, 55, 92,
95-113
Queensland Royal Commission of
Enquiry into Educational
Institutions, 1875, 205, 229-30